AF861277

solutions@syngress.com

With more than 1,500,000 copies of our MCSE, MCSD, CompTIA, and Cisco study guides in print, we continue to look for ways we can better serve the information needs of our readers. One way we do that is by listening.

Readers like yourself have been telling us they want an Internet-based service that would extend and enhance the value of our books. Based on reader feedback and our own strategic plan, we have created a Web site that we hope will exceed your expectations.

Solutions@syngress.com is an interactive treasure trove of useful information focusing on our book topics and related technologies. The site offers the following features:

- One-year warranty against content obsolescence due to vendor product upgrades. You can access online updates for any affected chapters.
- "Ask the Author"™ customer query forms that enable you to post questions to our authors and editors.
- Exclusive monthly mailings in which our experts provide answers to reader queries and clear explanations of complex material.
- Regularly updated links to sites specially selected by our editors for readers desiring additional reliable information on key topics.

Best of all, the book you're now holding is your key to this amazing site. Just go to **www.syngress.com/solutions**, and keep this book handy when you register to verify your purchase.

Thank you for giving us the opportunity to serve your needs. And be sure to let us know if there's anything else we can do to help you get the maximum value from your investment. We're listening.

www.syngress.com/solutions

SYNGRESS®

SYNGRESS®

1 YEAR UPGRADE
BUYER PROTECTION PLAN

SYNGRESS.COM 1 YEAR UPGRADE BUYER PROTECTION PLAN

Palm OS Web Application

Developer's Guide

Developing and Delivering PQAs with Web Clipping

Ben Combee
R. Eric Lyons
David C. Matthews
Rory Lysaght

KEY	SERIAL NUMBER
001	DJG4T945T5
002	AKLRT4MLE4
003	VMERL3N54N
004	SGD34B39UN
005	8LU8MU6N7H
006	NFG4RNTEM4
007	BWBVHTR46T
008	QPB9R565MR
009	83N5M4BKAS
010	GT6YH22WFC

PUBLISHED BY
Syngress Publishing, Inc.
800 Hingham Street
Rockland, MA 02370

Palm OS Web Application Developer's Guide: Including PQA and Web Clipping

Printed in the United States of America

1 2 3 4 5 6 7 8 9 0

ISBN: 1-928994-32-6

Technical Editor: Ben Combee
Technical Reviewer: Calvin Swart
Co-Publisher: Richard Kristof
Acquisitions Editor: Catherine B. Nolan
Developmental Editor: Kate Glennon
CD Production: Michael Donovan

Freelance Editorial Manager: Maribeth Corona-Evans
Cover Designer: Michael Kavish
Page Layout and Art by: Shannon Tozier
Copy Editor: Darren Meiss
Indexer: Robert Saigh

Distributed by Publishers Group West in the United States and by Jaguar Book Group in Canada

Acknowledgments

We would like to acknowledge the following people for their kindness and support in making this book possible.

Richard Kristof and Duncan Anderson of Global Knowledge, for their generous access to the IT industry's best courses, instructors, and training facilities.

Ralph Troupe, Rhonda St. John, and the team at Callisma for their invaluable insight into the challenges of designing, deploying and supporting world-class enterprise networks.

Karen Cross, Lance Tilford, Meaghan Cunningham, Kim Wylie, Harry Kirchner, Bill Richter, Kevin Votel, Brittin Clark, and Kent Anderson of Publishers Group West for sharing their incredible marketing experience and expertise.

Mary Ging, Caroline Hird, Simon Beale, Caroline Wheeler, Victoria Fuller, Jonathan Bunkell, and Klaus Beran of Harcourt International for making certain that our vision remains worldwide in scope.

Anneke Baeten, Annabel Dent, and Laurie Giles of Harcourt Australia for all their help.

David Buckland, Wendi Wong, Daniel Loh, Marie Chieng, Lucy Chong, Leslie Lim, Audrey Gan, and Joseph Chan of Transquest Publishers for the enthusiasm with which they receive our books.

Kwon Sung June at Acorn Publishing for his support.

Ethan Atkin at Cranbury International for his help in expanding the Syngress program.

Joe Pisco, Helen Moyer, and the great folks at InterCity Press for all their help.

Acknowledgments

Ben Combee would like to thank the following people for their support and contributions to the book:

Thank you to Charles Wilson, John Wirth, and Anil Patel. To David Fedor, Danny Epstein, Peter Epstein, Ken Krugler, Keith Rollin, and the other helpful Palm employees that contribute to the online forums. To Neil Rhodes, Aaron Ardiri, and John Marshall for their work on free development tools for the Palm. To Vernard and Kim Martin, Charles and Heather Patisaul, and finally to Lamar, Rose, Cyndi, and Kaye Combee.

Contributors

David C. Matthews is an Independent Consultant located in Huntsville, AL. He has over 20 years of full life cycle software development experience and currently specializes in wireless Web technologies. He has contributed to several books on developing PalmOS Web clipping applications, DHTML, and JavaScript. David has also overseen several development projects, including a voice-activated wireless Web interface for wearable computer control of an aviation maintenance management system, a Web-centric wireless GPS-based golfer PDA, and a Web-centric inventory management system with barcode support. An Instrument Rated Private Pilot, David is also an IEEE member and holds a bachelor's degree in Electrical Engineering from Auburn University. He has completed post-graduate work in Electrical Engineering at The University of Alabama in Huntsville.

Rory Lysaght is a Mobile Device Specialist at Ripcord Systems, a wireless startup based in Seattle and London. At Ripcord, Rory put together one of the first wireless GSM iPAQs in Europe. He has worked in Web and wireless development in the US, Europe, and Japan. He has contributed articles to several online and paper publications, including *Web Review* and the *EE Times*. Prior to this, Rory worked as a photojournalist, publishing numerous documentary stories in magazines in the same three continents. He is a member of the WAP forum and the Palm developer network. He lives in Seattle, WA.

R. Eric Lyons is a Palm OS Application Developer who designs and develops wireless stock trading and wireless e-mail applications. In addition to these applications, he assisted with the design of the client toolkit for the Touchpoint 4.0 mobile enterprise platform. Eric's background includes positions as Software Engineer for EASE CT Solutions and Application Developer at Syntellect. Eric holds a bachelor's degree from

Clemson University and is a member of the Atlanta Palm OS Developer's Group. In his spare time, Eric is a musician in the Atlanta Freedom Marching Band.

Hari Bhaskaran is the Principal Software Architect for JP Mobile where he builds client-server solutions that connect wireless handhelds with JP Mobile's server products. His Palm development work includes the award-winning OneTouch Mail (recipient of the 1998 Best Handheld Software award, *Mobile Computing Magazine*) and OmniSky products, as well as BeamLink. Hari has a bachelor's degree in Computer Science from R.E.C Calicut, India. He currently resides in Richardson, TX. Hari would like to thank his wife, Suma, for her love and support. Hari would also like to thank his collegues Alex Farcasiu, Joan Garcia, and all his friends at JP Mobile for their help.

Foreword by

Adam Tow has been passionate about the handheld industry ever since he purchased his first handheld, the Apple Newton MessagePad, in September, 1993. Adam is currently the Manager of Technology at Palm, Inc., the worldwide leader of mobile computing, where he is actively involved in the company's wireless initiatives. Prior to joining Palm, Adam founded and directed Foundation Systems, a mobile computing solutions firm, where he consulted with Palm and OmniSky on the release of two critically acclaimed consumer wireless devices, the Palm VII organizer and the OmniSky Palm V handheld. Adam has presented on Web clipping development at PalmSource and the Palm Developer's Conference. In addition, his company's software for the Newton and Palm OS platforms has been sold in over 22 countries and has been featured in publications such as *Pen Computing Magazine*, *Mobile Computing*, and the *San Francisco Chronicle*. He has been interviewed in *Interface Magazine* and on C|Net and ZDNN. He is the founding member of the Stanford Palm User Group.

Adam received his bachelor's degree from Stanford University in Symbolic Systems, with a focus in Human-Computer Interaction. His other passions include photography, digital multimedia, and online journalism. Adam can be reached on the Web at www.tow.com/ or via e-mail at adam@tow.com.

Technical Editor and Contributor

Ben Combee is a Lead Software Developer at Metrowerks where he is responsible for the future direction of the CodeWarrior for Palm OS tools, the leading C and C++ development toolset used in the Palm community. Ben is also working on future wireless strategy for Metrowerks and its parent company, Motorola. In the past, he was the lead architect for wireless devices with Veriprise Wireless where he developed custom applications and libraries for the Palm VII/VIIx, Omnisky Minstrel, and Glenarye @ctiveLink wireless systems. His application, VChat, won "Best INetLib Application" in the PalmHack contest at the 2000 PalmSource show. Ben has also been the lead developer for the CodeWarrior C/C++ compiler for Intel and AMD microprocessors, and he presented a talk about Linux compiler technology at the 1999 Annual Linux Showcase. Before this, he helped design microcontrollers and operating systems for Motorola's advanced pager products. Ben has a bachelor's degree in Computer Science from the Georgia Institute of Technology. While at Georgia Tech, Ben served as the president of the Association for Computing Machinery (ACM) chapter for two years. Ben is an active participant in Palm's online developer forums, having answered over 600 questions posted by fellow Palm developers. Ben lives in Austin, TX.

Technical Reviewer

Calvin Swart joined the Computer Science research staff at IBM's Thomas J. Watson Research Center in 1985. He has served in research and programming roles in numerous graphics, networking, and interpersonal communications projects. Most recently, he participated in the design and programming of solutions in several areas including K-12 Internet access and wireless e-business, one example being a Palm shopping application for Safeway UK. He is interested in embedded programming on small devices and their use in e-business. Calvin resides in Poughkeepsie, NY.

About the CD

This CD-ROM contains the code files that are used in each chapter of this book. The code files for each chapter are located in a "chXX" directory. For example, the files for Chapter 8 are in ch08. The organizational structure of these directories varies. For some chapters, the files are named by the figure number. In other chapters, the files are organized by the projects that are presented within the chapter.

Files ending with .htm and .html are HTML files. Usually, these are inputs to the Web Clipping Application Builder program that is used to make Web clippings. These may have associated graphic files. Some chapters have files with a .pl extension. These are Perl source files and are designed to be installed as CGI scripts on your Web server. Chapter 8 contains files with .php extensions; these are Web pages with embedded scripts that get executed by the PHP interpreter on a Web server.

Chapters 10 and 11 each contain programs written in C for Palm OS. The examples in Chapter 10 were all produced with CodeWarrior for Palm OS, Release 7. These are small enough to work with the demo version of CodeWarrior for Palm OS that is included on this CD-ROM. The programs in Chapter 11 were written using PRC Tools, the port of the GNU C compiler to Palm OS. These also come with CodeWarrior projects. Most of the programs in Chapter 11 can be built with the demo edition of CodeWarrior, but the final program is too large to work with the included demo.

Also contained on this CD-ROM are full versions of several useful Web server programs, all built for Microsoft Windows. Included are the latest versions (at the time of publication) of PHP, Apache Server, and ActivePerl. To install the ZIP files, you need some sort of unzip utility, such as WinZip (www.winzip.com). To install the .msi files, you need the Windows Installer. This package is built into Windows 2000, Windows XP, and Windows Me. For older OS releases, you can download Windows Installer from www.microsoft.com/msdownload/platformsdk/instmsi.htm. If you want to check for newer versions of the software, see the following Web sites: Apache Server (http://httpd.apache.org), ActivePerl (http://aspn.activestate.com/ASPN/Perl), and PHP (http://php.apache.org).

Look for this CD icon to obtain files used in the book demonstrations.

Contents

Load Web Clipping Applications on Your Device

New Web clipping applications can be added to Palm VII devices in the same fashion that Palm OS applications are installed. Web clipping applications can be added to a Palm VII by using the Install Tool application on a desktop computer and performing a HotSync operation with the device.

Learn How to Install Icons in the Application Launcher

Learn What HTML Tags Are Available and How to Use Them

The most common body tags available in the HTML 3.2 specification are available in the Web clipping HTML definition. Content with these tags applied may render differently to fit the small Palm OS device screen.

Learn the Four Colors Available for Most Devices and How to Use Them Most Effectively

Color Name	Hex
Black	#000000
Silver	#C0C0C0
Gray	#808080
White	#FFFFFF

Why Doesn't Password Obscure My Input?

When you enter your password, rather than echoing asterisks like desktop Web browsers do, Clipper pops up a dialog box in which you enter the password in the clear. This is done to address the problem of using the Palm OS graffiti input scheme. Showing the characters is necessary for the user to know what they are actually scribbling. Without that feedback, you could easily enter wrong data. Palm's compromise is to show this password input for only the brief time that the user is entering the text.

Use Date and Time Variables with the History Text

HistoryListText Displayed

Find Answers to Your Questions About the Palm.Net Proxy

Q: Where should proxy server problems be reported?

A: Visit the Proxy Server Feedback page at http://oasis.palm.com/dev/support/ask.cfm?page=38 and include pertinent information, such as the steps required to produce the problem, date and time of the first occurrence (including time zone), and so on.

Q: What can I do to stay abreast of the latest developments in WCA debugging technology?

A: A good first step is to join the Web Clipping Announcement list and Web Clipping Forum using the forms at www.palmos.com/dev/tech/support/forums.

Identify Sessions Using Cookies

- Cookies let you store data on the device that can be retrieved at a later time.
- Cookies are supported only in Web clipping on Palm OS 4.0 and later devices.
- Although cookies can be used to make the user's life much easier, by storing preferences or login information, they can also be used to secretly track which sites a user visits.

Use Enhanced %LOCATION

Because position-aware WCAs often need to convert %ZIPCODE to other position qualifiers (State and County, for example), a new Palm-specific variable has been created within Palm OS 4.0. Named %LOCATION, it provides a robust mechanism for obtaining additional qualifiers for the current base station.

Learn the Type Parameters for the Add Palm Data Plug-In

Type Number	Description
1	Add date book entry
2	Add address book entry
3	Add to-do list entry
4	Add memo pad entry
5	Add expense record

WARNING

If you forget to include "https://" as part of the *resNameP*, you may find that your HTTPS transaction was degraded to HTTP even if you specified the *inetSchemeHTTPS* argument to **INetLibSockOpen()**. Unfortunately, INetLib does not warn you about this mistake.

Foreword

In looking back upon my years in the handheld industry, I keep reminding myself of how far we've come. I fondly recall purchasing my first handheld in September, 1993. A marvel to carry and use, the device unchained me from my bulky laptop and quickly became my primary mobile companion, holding vast amounts of personal information that I referred to daily.

At a local user group meeting in 1996, I used for the first time the Pilot 1000, a new pocket-sized handheld from Palm Computing. This product struck a resonant chord in me for its usefulness and portability. It made its mark in the marketplace too, reaching one million units sold faster than any prior computer hardware product. Five years later, over 13 million people worldwide have adopted Palm organizers as indispensable tools for organizing and managing their lives. Palm handhelds owe their success to a refined focus on simplicity, ease of use, portability, and the user. Often referred to as the Zen of Palm, this overarching design philosophy is what distinguishes Palm from many of its competitors.

Initially, Palm handhelds functioned admirably as satellites to a user's desktop computer. These devices were able to connect to the Internet through external modems, but the resulting solution, unfortunately, was often too bulky and inconvenient for long-term use. In 1999, Palm signaled the intersection of handhelds and the wireless Web in releasing the Palm VII organizer to the U.S. market. What started out as a device to organize one's life had now become something that could access the larger world of information on the Internet while still remaining eminently pocketable.

Many of us were introduced to the Internet in the early 1990s. During those years, the most common form of connecting to the Net was through modems, which typically ran at speeds ranging from 9.6 to 28.8 kilobits per second (kbps). Information was conveyed primarily through text, with a few images sprinkled throughout to add some color to the Web pages. Today the Internet has become ubiquitous, and we continually access complex, image-laden pages at speeds many times faster than previously possible. The voracious bandwidth appetites of Flash multimedia presentations, QuickTime movies, and streaming MP3s would choke yesterday's Net connections.

The past is present, however, with the wireless Web. Internet-enabled mobile devices, such as the Palm VII, connect at speeds closer to the 9.6 kbps modem we have long since retired, a far cry from the LAN or DSL connections we use in our workplaces and homes. It is also clear that much of the content on the Internet today has not been designed for this segment of Net devices. A typical wireless handheld does not have a speedy data connection with which to download hundreds of kilobytes of data in seconds, nor does it have a high-resolution screen capable of adequately rendering such information. As a result, developing applications for the wireless Web demands a different attitude and approach than developing for the traditional Web; it requires careful thought, planning, and new models for data visualization. After all, no one wants to look at a small display that is littered with advertisements in place of actual information! The wireless Web also forces developers to optimize their content so that it takes up the least amount of bandwidth.

Lest we become disenchanted with the prospect of wireless development with such restrictions, remember that a new class of functionality is enabled by mobile Internet devices. Unlike desktop or even laptop computers, wireless handhelds can be carried by their owners for 10 to 12 hours a day. Exciting opportunities, such as location-based services and messaging are only possible when the Internet is truly everywhere you go.

Much like the handheld industry was in 1993, the wireless Internet still in its infancy. As handhelds had before them, wireless devices will continue to gain in functionality and popularity over time. More powerful handhelds with high-resolution screens and fast Net connections loom on the industry's horizon. At first glance, it might be easy to dismiss the importance of a mobile Web design philosophy in light of such upcoming products. The dynamics of mobile computing, however, are very different from those of desktop computing, and they call for such a philosophy to stay at the forefront of the developer's mind. In a mobile environment, speed and access to relevant information will always be more important than fancy, time-consuming presentation. The design philosophy behind Palm handhelds—a strong focus on the user, ease of use and relevance—serve as excellent guiding principles for developing wireless, mobile applications. It is on this note that we visit the subject of this book. The ability to harness the power of the Internet with the simplicity of the Palm is a key skill you will learn from reading *Palm OS Web Application Developers Guide: Including PQA and Web Clipping*.

Our Audience

There is a wealth of resources for learning Web development in print and online. There is a dearth, however, of quality guides detailing the extension of the Web to mobile devices. This book fills that gap and has been written for anybody who is interested in developing Web applications for the Palm OS. For newcomers, welcome to the exciting world of mobile Web development! With clear and concise examples, you will develop a great design foundation for your future Web development projects. If you are a professional Web developer whose company wants to extend its Web presence to the wireless community, get ready to learn how to translate and optimize your Web sites for viewing on Palm devices. Finally, if you are a developer within the Palm Economy, you will learn how to transform your device-centric Palm apps into Web-enabled and Web-centric apps. This book is unique in its detailed coverage of Palm's Internet Library (INetLib), which is used to develop native C/C++ Palm OS applications that access the Internet. Whatever your reason, *Palm OS Web Application Developers Guide: Including PQA and Web Clipping* will serve as your guide in demystifying the Web design process on the Palm.

The Contents

In short, this book details how to create Web applications for the Palm OS using the Web clipping technology that is found on many Palm Powered products, such as the Palm VIIx wireless handheld, the Palm m100 with the Mobile Internet Kit, and the Kyocera QCP 6035 Smartphone. The book can be separated into three sections. The first two chapters are introductory and provide a glimpse into the philosophy and technology behind Web clipping:

- Chapter 1, *Introducing Web Clipping*, introduces you to the concept of Web clipping and the thinking behind its development.
- Chapter 2, *Building a Simple Web Clipping Application*, takes you step-by-step in creating your first Web clipping application.

Chapters 3 through 9 form the foundation for learning how to develop efficient and compelling Palm-optimized Web applications. These chapters delve deeply into the development process on both the device and server.

- Chapter 3, *Building WCAs Using HTML*, outlines the HTML 3.2 subset that Web clipping supports, with detailed information and diagrams on how such content is rendered on Palm devices.
- Chapter 4, *Using Images in Web Clipping*, shows you how to make maximum use of images to enhance your Web clipping applications.
- Chapter 5, *Interacting with Forms*, describes how to capture user input on the device for delivery to and processing by your server-based scripts.
- Chapter 6, *Optimizing WCAs for the Palm*, introduces key techniques for making your Web content look great on Palm handhelds.
- Chapter 7, *Debugging Web Clipping Applications*, teaches you important skills for ensuring your Web clipping applications are ready for prime time.
- Chapter 8, *Identifying Users and Sessions*, explains how you can maintain state within your applications.
- Chapter 9, *Locating Mobile Users*, shows you how to use the unique features of Web clipping to create location-based services for your handheld Web applications.

Developers looking to better integrate their Web applications with the built-in and third-party applications on the Palm handheld should be excited to read the final two chapters, which cover the following advanced topics:

- Chapter 10, *Integrating Web Clipping with Palm OS Applications*, outlines how your Web clipping applications can integrate and interact with other Palm OS applications on your device.
- Chapter 11, *Using the Internet Library with Palm OS Applications*, details how to add Internet capabilities to your existing C/C++ based Palm OS applications.

And lastly, the Fast Track Appendix which summarizes the key facts and concepts for optimizing your Web applications.

It is important to stress here that the techniques and skills that you will gain from this guide will prove useful to your development efforts for mobile devices beyond those powered by the Palm OS and Web clipping. The future paints a landscape of a handheld and wireless marketplace where Palm is an important player among many others who are delivering mobile Internet solutions. The design issues that you will face while developing applications for the Palm, such as display size, low available memory, and bandwidth constraints, are the same as those faced by all other mobile, connected devices. The knowledge, skill, and ability to address these issues will prove invaluable in your future mobile projects.

We have certainly come a long way since the first consumer handhelds rolled off the manufacturing line in the early 1990s. We are just at the beginning, however, of leveraging the power of the Internet with the simplicity and portability of mobile devices. It's up to us to define and create the wireless Web. Let's get to work!

—*Adam Tow,*
adam@tow.com

Chapter 1

Introducing Web Clipping

Solutions in this chapter:

- What Is Web Clipping?
- Loading Web Clipping Applications on Your Device
- Loading Web Clipping Applications on the Palm OS Emulator
- Using Clipper
- Using Clipper on Palm OS Devices
- Using Clipper to Get Access to Web Information

☑ Summary

☑ Solutions Fast Track

☑ Frequently Asked Questions

Introduction

In October 1999, Palm, Inc. entered the wireless Internet market with the introduction of the Palm VII organizer. Although the Palm VII wasn't the first portable device to feature built-in wireless networking, it was the first based on the successful Palm OS operating system, and it had an irresistible combination of size, battery life, throughput, and coverage area.

In designing the Palm VII, Palm, Inc. had several advantages over its competitors. First, it was based on an established operating system with a variety of applications already available. The Palm VII would be useful beyond its wireless capabilities. Second, it leveraged an existing wireless network in BellSouth Wireless Data's Mobitex system. Because of its wide deployment, users discovered that they could use it all across the nation. Finally, Palm, Inc. created a Web content delivery technology called Web clipping. Based on Hypertext Markup Language (HTML), Web clipping content is optimized for Palm OS devices and the network capacity of the Mobitex network.

This chapter introduces the installation and features of Web clipping applications and the Clipper browser application. In addition, an outline is provided of the capacity and availability of the Mobitex network on Palm VII devices and the capacity and availability of other networks on other Palm OS–based wireless devices.

What Is Web Clipping?

Web clipping is the name Palm, Inc. created for their Web content delivery system designed for their line of Palm OS devices. Using the word *Web* in the title is obvious: HTML is the standard language to define content on the World Wide Web. *Clipping* is based off the name of the content browser application for Palm OS devices: Clipper.

Ultimately, Palm, Inc. wanted to deliver the complete World Wide Web on wireless devices with the same appearance, operation, and performance as desktop computers. However, they faced major design issues to make that a reality.

First, the screen size of Palm OS devices is significantly smaller than the size of a desktop computer screen. The screen size of Palm OS devices to date is 160 pixels wide (153 pixels plus the scroll bar) by 160 pixels high on a 2.5 inch square screen. Professional Web pages are typically designed to accommodate a browser window size of about 530 pixels wide by 400 pixels high on a 14-inch diagonal screen. Full-size Web pages will not translate well to the small screen on portable devices.

Compare the opening page of the Syngress Publishing Web site in the 640x480 pixel browser window in Figure 1.1, and the 160x160 pixel browser window on the Palm VII shown in Figure 1.2. Because of the limited size of the device, the page does not come close to displaying properly on the Palm OS device.

Figure 1.1 Sample Web Page on a Desktop Browser

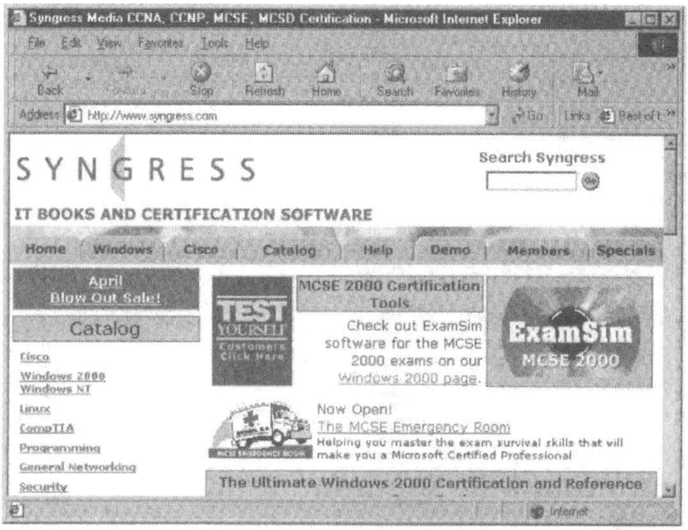

Figure 1.2 Same Sample Web Page on a Palm OS Device

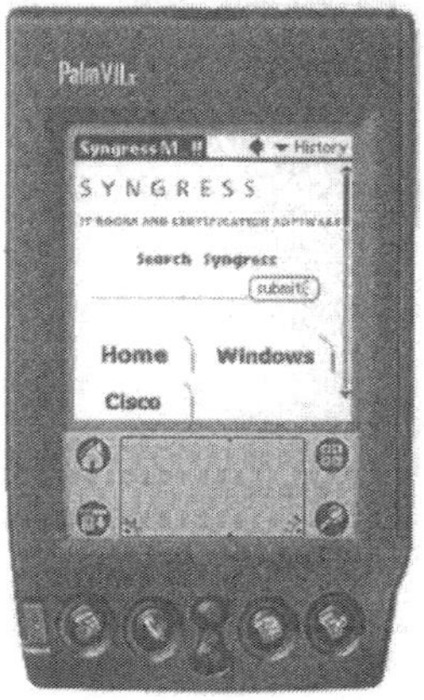

Second, the speed and expense of wireless networks does not come close to matching today's wired networks. In the year 2001, the maximum performance of the fastest wireless network, Cellular Digital Packet Data (CDPD), was 19.2Kbps, less than half the speed of most modem connections to the Internet. The Palm VII, which uses the Mobitex network designed for two-way paging, runs at 9.6Kbps. Analog modems seem like high performance automobiles in comparison with speeds of 56Kbps. T1, cable, and Digital Subscriber Line (DSL) networks run above 1Gbps. People who believe accessing the Web on an analog modem is slow will find that the Web delivered via a wireless network is excruciating.

Using the Syngress Web site again as an example, the number of bytes in the page source and images total about 197 kilobytes. A T1/DSL/cable connection presents this page in three to four seconds. A 56Kbps modem presents the page in about 30 seconds. At maximum speed on the Mobitex network of 9.6Kbps, a Palm VII presents this page in about three to four *minutes*.

Third, Palm OS devices have performance and memory issues for supporting every Web technology. The Palm OS device's Motorola 68000–based Dragonball processor and 2 to 8MB of memory provide adequate performance for the personal information management applications for which it was originally designed. However, providing full HTML support on a device that already has size and network limitations is beyond its capacity.

Due to these limitations, Palm, Inc. has created Web clipping to deliver as much of the Web experience as possible, redefine and package some components to perform better on Palm OS devices, and discard the rest. The biggest difference between Web clipping applications and standard World Wide Web applications is that Web clipping applications are started by launching an application database file installed by the user onto the device instead of typing a URL into a Web browser. A Web clipping database contains static HTML pages, document graphics and instructions for retrieving information from external servers.

By packaging these components into a single database file, Palm, Inc. significantly reduced the data transfer between a device and external server to only the dynamic components such as account numbers, store directions, or search results. The HTML and graphics for the page where a user enters her account number, ZIP Code, or search query is already on the device.

In addition to saving transfer time, Web clipping applications appear as icons in the Application Launcher alongside the Address Book, MemoPad, and other Palm OS applications. Because a user has learned how to launch a standard application from the Application Launcher, the user already knows how to launch a Web clipping application as well.

The primary disadvantage to Web clipping technology is that the static components in an application are not updated unless the user downloads and installs updates to the application. Content of a standard Web application is usually downloaded each time the application is referenced. Web clipping application developers should be prepared to support all revisions of an application, because developers cannot guarantee that the user base will diligently update the device-resident portions of the application on a timely basis.

Note that the screen size, network, and memory limitations of Palm OS devices are common to other similar devices, such as Microsoft's Pocket PC, Blackberry's RIM pagers, and Web-enabled phones. Palm, Inc. appears to have found the middle ground for delivering the Web experience.

Loading Web Clipping Applications on Your Device

New Web clipping applications can be added to Palm VII devices in the same fashion that Palm OS applications are installed. Web clipping applications can be added to a Palm VII by using the Install Tool application on a desktop computer and performing a HotSync operation with the device.

To learn how to install a Web clipping application with the Install Tool, we will add the Starbuck's Coffee Store Locator application to a Palm VII. In the future, you can rely on your Palm VII to lead you to hot fresh coffee.

Running the Install Tool

You can start the Install Tool by launching the Install Tool application or by launching the Web clipping application file to be installed. In this example, we launch the Install Tool application itself:

1. From the **Start** menu, select the **Install Tool** application from the **Palm Desktop** program group. The Install Tool dialog box appears, as shown in Figure 1.3.
2. Click the **Add** button. When the file selector dialog box appears, insert the companion CD from this book into the CD-ROM drive of your computer. Find the **Starbucks.PQA** file located in the Applications directory of the CD and click the **Open** button.
3. After the Starbucks application has been added, click **Done** to close the install tool.

Figure 1.3 The Install Tool Dialog Box

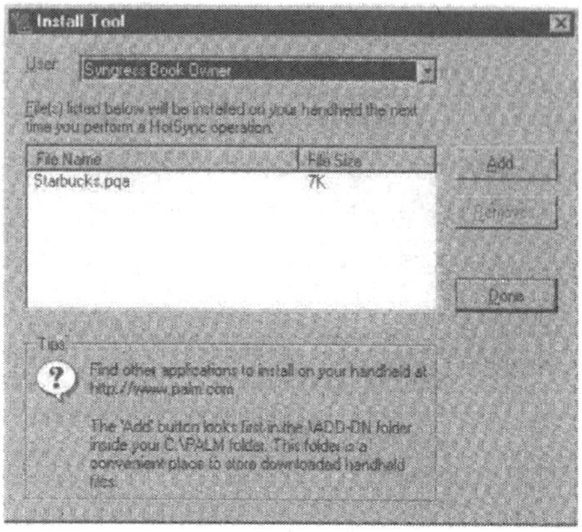

Performing a HotSync Operation on Your Device

The Starbucks application has been scheduled for installation on your device. To finish the installation, perform a HotSync operation as follows:

1. Place your Palm VII into its cradle.
2. Push the **HotSync button** on the cradle or run the HotSync application on the Palm VII.

After the HotSync operation is complete, find the Starbucks application in the Application Launcher of the Palm VII, as shown in Figure 1.4.

Figure 1.4 Starbucks Application Is Now Visible in the Application Launcher

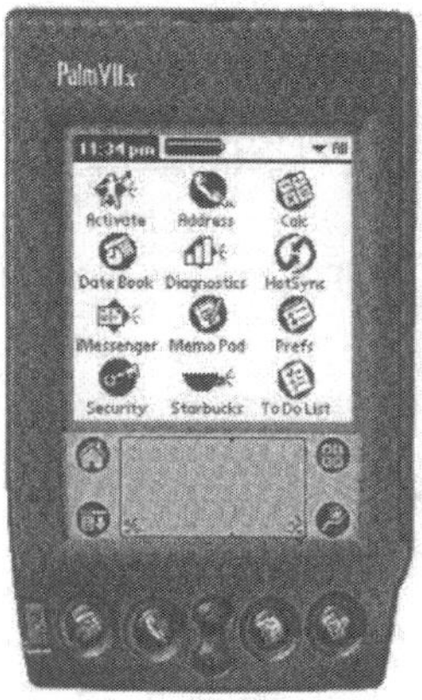

Developing & Deploying…

Beaming PQA Applications

In addition to installing Web clipping applications via a HotSync operation from your computer, Web clipping applications can be beamed via the infrared port to other Palm OS devices that support Web clipping.

To beam a Web clipping application to another device, bring up the Application Launcher, tap the **Menu** icon and tap the **Beam** menu option. Find and tap the name of the WCA in the list, and tap the **Beam** button to beam the application to another device. Enable reception of IR beams in the general panel of the Preferences application of the receiving device.

Loading Web Clipping Applications on the Palm OS Emulator

If you do not own one of the wireless Palm OS devices or simply want to evaluate this technology, an application called the Palm OS Emulator (POSE) simulates the operation of an actual Palm OS device on your desktop computer. The Palm OS Emulator is available for Microsoft Windows 95/98/Me/NT/2000, Apple Macintosh, and various flavors of Unix. The emulator is available at www.palmos.com/dev/tech/tools/emulator and requires a ROM image.

After downloading and unpacking the POSE archive, you will notice that POSE does not contain ROM image files. The ROM image files are copies of the Palm OS that permanently reside on a device. ROM image files can be obtained by transferring the ROM image from an actual device or by joining the Palm Alliance Program and downloading ROM images from the Palm OS Web site.

To transfer a ROM image from a device, refer to the section "Transferring a ROM Image From a Handheld" in the document entitled "Using POSE" supplied with the Palm OS Emulator. You will need an actual Palm VII, VIIx, m500, or m505 device for downloading the ROM.

To join the Palm Alliance Program and download ROM image files, visit www.palmos.com/alliance. Signup for the Alliance Program is free. After you have signed up and agreed to the terms of the agreement, find the link for the ROM Image Clickwrap Area and then the Special Downloads area for the Palm VII Family ROMs. At a minimum, download one ROM image file for the Palm

VII family (palmos32-en-ez.rom) and the Palm VIIx family (palmos35-en-ez-8mb-wc). You should also get the Palm m505 ROM images if you want to test on the Palm OS 4.0 version of Web Clippings. We recommend creating a directory called ROMS underneath the Palm OS Emulator directory and copying these image files into the ROMS directory.

After you have started the Palm OS Emulator for the first time, the startup dialog box should appear, as shown in Figure 1.5. Choose your ROM file, make sure that the device selected is correct, pick the appropriate memory size, and click **OK** to start the emulator.

Figure 1.5 Specifying Session Properties for a New Session in the Palm OS Emulator

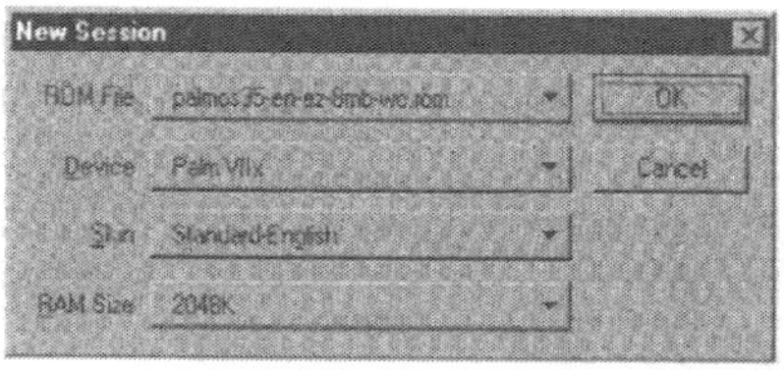

Now, the emulator should appear on-screen running the emulated Palm OS session. Before starting a Web clipping application, confirm the following session settings:

1. From the Application Launcher screen, tap the **Prefs** application, tap the category in the upper-right corner, and tap **Wireless** (labeled **Web Clipping** on Palm OS 4.0). With POSE version 3.1 and later, this setting should be automatically updated to point to the address of the Palm.Net proxy server. If you encounter problems later with not being able to reach Web sites, check Palm's Web Clipping pages and make sure that this panel is pointing to the correct proxy IP address.
2. From the POSE window, right-click and select **Settings** from the pop-up menu, select **Properties** from the next pop-up menu, and confirm that the **Redirect NetLib calls to host TCP/IP** is checked. When this option is checked, all Transmission Control Protocol/Internet Protocol (TCP/IP) requests by the device are forwarded to the computer's Internet connection. When this option is not checked, TCP/IP requests are sent directly to the device hardware that doesn't exist on the emulator.

To learn how to install a new Web clipping application on the Palm OS Emulator, we will add the Starbucks Coffee Store Locator application.

Installing a Web Clipping Application on the Emulator

You can use two different methods to install a Web clipping application on the Palm OS Emulator:

- Right-click the emulator application. From the pop-up menu, select the **Install Application/Database** menu option, select **Other**, and select the **Starbucks.PQA** file from the file browser.
- The Palm OS Emulator supports drag-and-drop operations. Simply drag and drop the **Starbucks.PQA** file onto the Palm OS Emulator window.

After the HotSync operation is complete, find the Starbucks application in the Application Launcher of the Palm VII. For either method of installation, you should *not* be in the launcher application when you install your Web clipping application. Due to how Palm OS devices normally handle program installation, the Launcher recognizes only changes in the list of available programs when it is started. If you install an application while it is active, it will not show the new icon, and you may have to reset the emulator session to get it to recognize the new program.

Using Clipper

The Clipper Web browser displays the text and graphics in Web clipping applications and performs the wireless communications to communicate over-the-air to Web servers on the Internet. Clipper is a permanent part of the Palm OS on Palm VII, VIIx, m500, and m505 devices and is installed separately for the OmniSky service or the Palm Mobile Internet Kit.

The Clipper application itself does not appear as an icon in the Application Launcher. Clipper is launched when a Web clipping application is selected from the Application Launcher. We outline the components of the Clipper application by using the Starbucks application installed in the previous section.

Navigating within Clipper

Tap on the Starbucks application icon in the Application Launcher to find a Starbucks located nearby. A window appears like the one shown in Figure 1.6.

Figure 1.6 The Starbucks Coffee Store Locator Window

The opening page appears immediately on the device without lifting the antenna. Remember that a Web clipping application is a Palm OS database that typically contains the static HTML pages and graphics for the application. In the Starbucks application, this opening document and its images are static and are stored within the Starbucks Web clipping application database.

Aside from this, many components of this page map to components of desktop Web browsers. The Type and State pop-up triggers mirror the operation of combo boxes in a desktop Web browser. The street, city, and ZIP fields provide a place for textual or numeric data entry. The Find, Clear, and Auto-Find buttons issue the appropriate commands. The About, Help, and Legal links redirect the application to show a different Web page.

In this application, tapping Find requires wireless communication with a Web server to determine Starbucks locations near to your specified location, to build an HTML page containing the addresses of those locations, and to send the HTML to the device.

Notice that the Find button contains a small "over-the-air" icon. This icon indicates that a wireless communication is required to complete the request. In addition to the over-the-air icon, you may sometimes see a secure over-the-air icon with a key to indicate Secure Hypertext Transfer Protocol (HTTPS) communication. These icons can be found in form buttons or at the end of the text of a hyperlink and are shown in Figure 1.7.

Figure 1.7 Examples of Nonsecure HTTP and Secure HTTP Icons

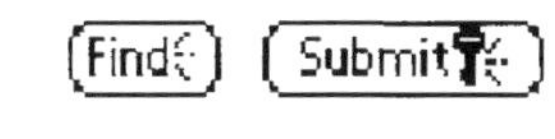

Enter an address or a ZIP Code into the appropriate fields. Keep an eye on the title bar and tap **Find**. On a Palm VII or VIIx device, you must raise the antenna to make a wireless connection. The device will remind you to raise the antenna if you try with the antenna down.

During the wireless communication, the title bar caption to the left changes to Connecting, a small pulsating circle in the center representing wireless activity and the signal strength indicator in the upper-right corner all indicate that wireless communication is in progress. Once complete, the Starbucks locations and their addresses are displayed as shown in Figure 1.8.

Figure 1.8 Starbucks Store Locator Addresses

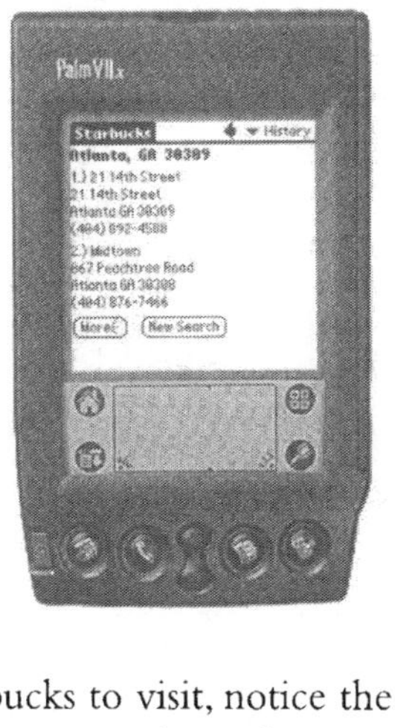

After deciding which Starbucks to visit, notice the right arrow and **History** pop-up trigger in the title bar. Tapping the right arrow displays the previous page.

Viewing the Clipper History

The History pop-up trigger contains a list of dynamically created pages that were wirelessly downloaded to the device. Tap **History**, find the entry containing the location list built earlier, and tap it. The location and address list reappears.

Notice that the opening address entry page does not appear in the History. Dynamically created pages that were wirelessly downloaded to the device are stored in the History. Static pages that reside in the Web clipping application itself are not held in a dynamic cache, but they can be accessed by using the Back button.

Using Clipper on Palm OS Devices

Although the Palm VII was the first device to merge Web applications on a Palm OS–based device, there are now several devices and solutions on multiple wireless networks for using Web clipping applications.

Using Clipper with Palm VII on Mobitex

The majority of Web clipping applications are designed with the Palm VII as the target device and the Palm OS Clipper application as the browser.

Palm VII and VIIx devices communicate via the Mobitex wireless network from Cingular Wireless. Mobitex coverage is widely available around most major urban areas and airports. Although Mobitex network coverage is widely available, expect a transfer rate of only about 2Kbps, out of a theoretical 9.6Kbps.

Using Clipper with Omnisky

OmniSky provides wireless network access and modems that connect to the Palm V, Palm Vx, and the entire line of HandSpring Visors.

OmniSky-enabled devices communicate via the Cellular Digital Packet Data (CDPD) network. This network leverages the original cellular data network to provide data speeds of up to 19.2Kbps. However, the CDPD access is not as widely available in the United States as the Mobitex network.

Using Clipper with the Palm Mobile Internet Kit

The Palm Mobile Internet Kit (MIK) from Palm, Inc. is a software solution that allows you to use your Palm OS handheld in combination with a mobile phone or modem to wirelessly access the Internet. It works by using the built-in data capability of your mobile phone or modem to establish a connection to the Internet for your Palm OS handheld. The Palm MIK works on any Palm OS device that runs Palm OS 3.5 or later, including the Palm m100, IIIxe, and Vx devices. The MIK comes with the Palm OS 3.5 upgrade to enable older devices.

The Palm m105 comes bundled with the MIK, whereas the new Palm m500 and m505 handhelds come with the Palm OS 4.0 version of the MIK built-in.

The performance of the MIK depends upon the performance of the mobile phone or modem. Using it with a GSM cell phone limits you to 9.6Kbps, whereas CDMA-based PCS phones have a native data rate of 14.4Kbps. With a wired modem, speeds vary from 14.4Kbps to 56Kbps.

Using Clipper to Get Access to Web Information

With the knowledge of installing and using Web clipping applications, sites on the Internet are available to find additional Web clipping applications to add to your Palm OS device.

The best place to start for finding Web clipping applications is from Palm, Inc. itself. Palm.Net has an ever-expanding library of applications available for download. Additionally, Palm.Net employees evaluate and rate Web clipping applications submitted to the site. The applications that receive a five-star rating comply with the standards Palm, Inc. has established for good Web clipping applications.

We have scanned the Palm.Net Web Clipping library and listed some of the applications we find useful. However, after you've looked at our selections, feel free to browse the Palm.Net library at http://wireless.palm.net/apps and find your own favorites.

- **Personal ThinAir e-mail client** www.thinairapps.com
- **UPS package tracking** www.ups.com
- **Real time traffic information** www.traffictouch.com
- **Price/product comparisons** www.barpoint.com

In the next chapter, we create our first Web clipping application.

NOTE

This book contains numerous Web clipping application development techniques and tricks to help make the application you develop a success. However, another way to get a feel for good Web clipping application development is to download, install, and use Web clipping applications. By using and evaluating these applications, you will quickly learn what works and does not work.

Summary

When presented the realities of slow wireless networks and limited screen and processor capabilities in handheld devices, Palm, Inc. created Web clipping technology to provide the best World Wide Web experience on wireless-capable Palm OS devices. By loading static content and images of a Web application directly on the device, the application accesses the wireless network to retrieve dynamic parts of an application. Title screens, company logos, and data entry forms that rarely change are available immediately from the device. Wireless communication is limited to the remote information retrieval to improve the application experience.

Static portions of a Web clipping application are installed onto a Palm OS device using the Install Tool. Web clipping applications appear in the Application Launcher alongside standard Palm OS applications. From a user's point of view, Web clipping applications are not that much different than the Address Book, Date Book, or Expense applications.

Web clipping technology is now available for a wide variety of Palm OS devices. The Palm VII family of devices has wireless capabilities built in. The Palm V family of devices and the entire Handspring line of Visor devices can use Web clipping applications through a wide variety of wireless modems. Finally, the Palm III series, V series, m100, and m105 modems can send and receive wireless data via an infrared port to the infrared port of a capable cell phone with the Palm MIK.

Solutions Fast Track

What Is Web Clipping?

- ☑ Web clipping is a technology created by Palm, Inc. for delivering Web content on its line of Palm OS devices.
- ☑ Web clipping is a subset of the HTML specification. The specification keeps elements from standard HTML that translates well to its devices, modifies elements to improve its delivery on its devices, and trims elements that do not translate well to its devices.
- ☑ Static elements of an application, such as HTML documents and graphics, are combined into a database that is loaded onto the device. This database also contains the programming for contacting servers to build and deliver dynamically created content.

Loading Web Clipping Applications on Your Device

☑ Use the Palm Install Tool to prepare a Web clipping application to be installed onto a device in the same manner that a standard Palm OS application is installed onto a device.

☑ Perform a HotSync operation to install the application.

Loading Web Clipping Applications on the Palm OS Emulator

☑ If you do not own one of the wireless Palm OS devices or simply want to evaluate this technology, an application called the Palm OS Emulator (POSE) simulates the operation of an actual Palm OS device on your desktop computer.

Using Clipper

☑ The Clipper browser is launched when a Web clipping application is selected from the Application Launcher.

☑ The History stores pages dynamically built from a Web server. Static pages are not listed because they are already stored in the Web clipping application on the device.

Using Clipper on Palm OS Devices

☑ The Clipper browser is part of the permanent software of the Palm VII and VIIx devices. Clipper can be installed as an add-on to the m100, m105, III, IIIx, IIIxe, IIIc, or V series devices.

☑ The Palm VII and VIIx use the Mobitex wireless network to communicate to the Internet. The OmniSky service provides a wireless modem that uses the CDPD network to communicate to the Internet. The Mobitex network is more widely available than CDPD, but the CDPD network is much faster than the Mobitex network.

Using Clipper to Get Access to Web Information

☑ Numerous Web clipping applications are available for download from Palm.Net and other file databases.

☑ You can use Web clipping applications to communicate with people, access the enterprise, manage finances, follow the news, travel the world, shop online, and refer to information.

Frequently Asked Questions

The following Frequently Asked Questions, answered by the authors of this book, are designed to both measure your understanding of the concepts presented in this chapter and to assist you with real-life implementation of these concepts. To have your questions about this chapter answered by the author, browse to **www.syngress.com/solutions** and click on the **"Ask the Author"** form.

Q: Do I need to purchase a Palm VII/VIIx, OmniSky wireless modem, or Palm MIK to develop Web clipping applications?

A: No. With the Palm OS Emulator, a Web clipping application can be completely developed and tested from your desktop computer. However, you should eventually test the applications on a real device for debugging and improving the real-time experience.

Q: Is there an appreciable difference between the Palm VII/VIIx, OmniSky, and Palm MIK?

A: Aside from the differing speeds of the wireless networks used, no. The same version of Clipper exists on all three types of solutions, and the end-user's experience is the same.

Q: How long does it take to develop a Web clipping application?

A: If you're using an existing Web application as a model, we have heard numerous stories of a single person taking a portion of the existing Web application functionality and creating a working prototype in a weekend. In these situations, management can easily determine the return on investment. If you're not using an existing application as a model, creating the full Web solution before creating the Web clipping solution may be a better idea.

Chapter 2

Building a Simple Web Clipping Application

Solutions in this chapter:

- Writing Simple Web Pages
- Running the Web Clipping Application Builder
- Unwired Widgets Product List Example

☑ Summary

☑ Solutions Fast Track

☑ Frequently Asked Questions

Introduction

If you have developed a standard Web application, the learning curve for developing Web clipping applications is short. The main difference between developing Web clipping applications and standard Web applications is that some parts of your site get stored locally on the device, whereas other parts of it stay on the Web server to be requested later. By installing the nonchanging parts of the application on the device, the wireless network transfer time is significantly reduced. By comparison, standard Web applications generally retrieve both static and dynamic components via the wired network.

To build a Web clipping application (WCA), Palm, Inc. has provided a utility called the Web Clipping Application Builder (WCA Builder). The WCA Builder parses and compresses static Hypertext Markup Language (HTML) and graphics into a format readable by Clipper, Palm Inc.'s limited Web browser.

This chapter shows you how to use the WCA Builder by building a "Hello, World!" example. In addition, we compare the differences between the 1.0 and 1.5 Versions of this utility. Finally, we step through the construction of a Web clipping application for the product list of the fictional company Unwired Widgets.

Writing Simple Web Pages

An introduction to a programming language isn't complete without the traditional "Hello, World!" example. The following is an HTML implementation of "Hello, World!", which is on the CD as the "hello world build 1" example.

```
<html>

<head>
      <title>Hello, World!</ title>
</head>

<body>
      Hello, World!
</body>

</html>
```

This example serves as a good point of reference for a refresher course on HTML:

- HTML documents are comprised of actual text to be displayed and *tags* that describe page elements or formatting changes. HTML tags are defined by the less than (<) and greater than (>) symbols. Examples of HTML tags in the document list above are <HTML>, <HEAD>, and <TITLE>.
- The text between the <HTML> and </HTML> tags identify the layout and design of the document in the browser window.
- The <HEAD> section provides a place to identify the title of the page and define META tags that define characteristics about the page.
- The <BODY> section provides a place to put the content of the page to be displayed in the browser window.

To start, create a temporary directory named *Hello*, type the HTML listed earlier in this section into your favorite text editor and save it into the temporary directory as *hello.html*. Load the page as a file into your favorite Web browser and you'll see "Hello, World!" proudly displayed. To show that Web clipping application development is virtually the same as standard Web application development, we use the HTML code for this example to build a Web clipping application.

Running the Web Clipping Application Builder

Palm, Inc. created a utility for building a Web clipping application called the Web Clipping Application Builder (WCA Builder). This utility takes the HTML files and graphics of a Web clipping application as input and combines them into a compressed database that is installed onto the device. To install the WCA Builder on your computer, download the latest version of the Web clipping tools from Palm, Inc. at www.palmos.com/dev/tech/webclipping.

These tools are also provided as part of the Palm OS Software Development Kit (SDK), which you may already have if you do custom Palm OS programming. The WCA Builder does not come with an installer application. Extract it to a directory along with all of its support files. Once installed, launch the WCA Builder executable file named WCABuild.exe. You should see a window that appears similar to Figure 2.1.

Figure 2.1 Opening Screen of the Web Clipping Application Builder

Picking Your HTML Files

To build a Web clipping application, the WCA Builder needs to know the index file in your application. The index file refers to the first HTML file that the Web clipping application will execute and display upon launch. In this example, index.html is the first HTML file that our example will display.

To identify the index file, select the **Open Index...** menu option from the **File** menu. From the file chooser dialog box, find the index.html file created earlier, select it, and click **OK**. The display should now look like Figure 2.2, showing the name of the file you just selected.

Figure 2.2 WCA Builder after Specifying Index File

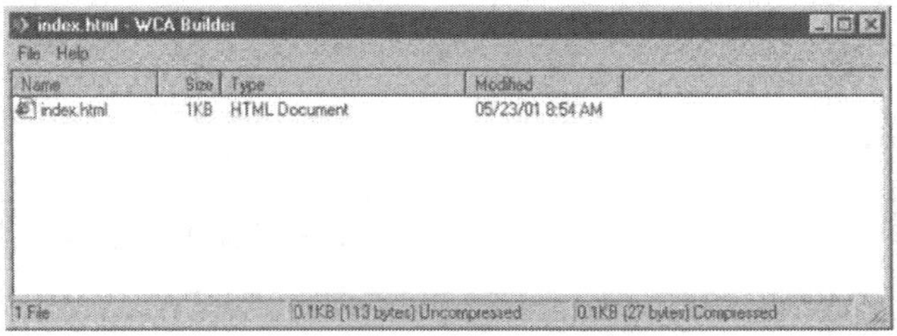

The WCA Builder scans hello.html for references to other HTML documents or graphic files. If a reference to another HTML document is found, the WCA Builder checks for the existence of that file, adds it to the list of files for this application, and opens the new HTML file looking for more references to graphics files or HTML documents. If graphic image references are found in an HTML document, the WCA Builder checks for the existence of this file and adds it to the list of files for this application. When it is finished, the file list window should show everything that can directly be reached by hyperlink or graphic reference from the initial HTML file.

In our example, the WCA Builder does not find references to other HTML documents or graphic files and reports that the file index.html is the only static component in this application. Now that the file list has been determined, it's time to build the application file. From the **File** menu, select the **Build PQA...** option. The application presents the Build PQA dialog box.

NOTE

WCA versus PQA—what's in a name? Actually, it's all marketing. When the Palm VII was introduced, the marketing name for the content delivery technology was Web clipping applications (WCA) but applications were named Palm Query Applications (PQA).

Palm, Inc. has recently begun referring to Palm Query Applications as Web clipping applications in both technical and marketing circles. However, the file extension .pqa remains the default extension for an application constructed by the WCA Builder utility.

Setting Options in the Build PQA Dialog Box

Before continuing with the "Hello, World!" example, take a moment to review each of the options available on this dialog box (Figure 2.3) before continuing.

Figure 2.3 Build PQA Dialog Box

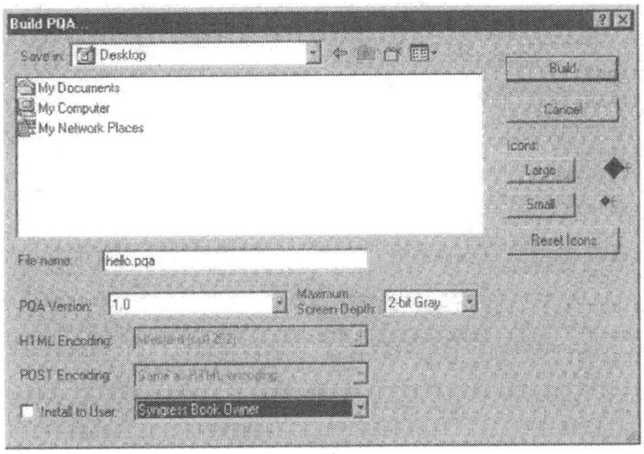

- **File name** File name of the PQA and the application name displayed on the Application Launcher of the device.
- **PQA Version** Build the application incorporating the features of Clipper 1.0 (Palm OS 3.2 and 3.5) or Clipper 2.0 (Palm OS 4.0 and greater).
- **Maximum Screen Depth** Maximum screen color depth to prepare images. The Clipper browser converts images at runtime that displayed on a screen depth lower than the screen depth selected. PQAs intended for Clipper 1.0 devices can use at most 2-bit grayscale, because some Palm VII devices support only four levels of gray.
- **HTML Encoding** Determines the character set to use to build the application. The cp1252 character set is Microsoft's extension of the ISO 8859-1 character set. The shift-jis character set is used for Japanese character set encoding. Choose cp1252 for English applications.
- **POST Encoding** When form data is sent from an application to a destination server, the data is first encoded in this format before being sent. Most applications will use the same encoding for the HTML encoding as the POST encoding.
- **Install to User** If the application should be immediately added to a HotSync user's folder, check this box and choose the appropriate user. This option is rarely used when testing an application using the Palm OS Emulator (POSE). However, if the test environment is the device, this step eliminates the need to find the PQA file and install it after building.
- **Large Icon** The **Large** button brings up a chooser dialog box for selecting the image to use for this application in the icon view of the Application Launcher. Once chosen, the selected image appears to the right of this button for review. Large icons in the Application Launcher are 32 pixels wide by 22 pixels high.
- **Small Icon** Same as the **Large** button except that this icon is shown for the list view of the Application Launcher. Small icons in the Application Launcher are 15 pixels wide by 9 pixels high.

To build the example application, type **hello** into the File name field and click **Build** to build the application. Once finished, locate the file hello.pqa in the directory specified in the Build PQA dialog box. Install the PQA onto your device or POSE using the methods described in Chapter 1, or use the shortcut provided by the **Install to User** checkbox if you're testing on an actual device. Once installed, a new application called *hello* is listed in the Application Launcher of your device, as shown in Figure 2.4.

Figure 2.4 "Hello, World!" Example Installed and Available from the Application Launcher

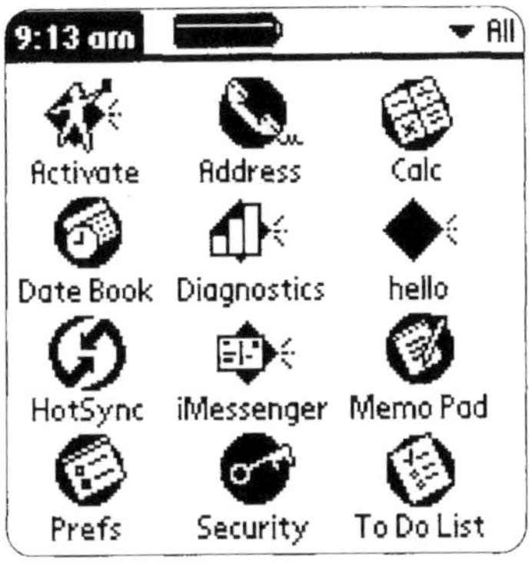

Tap the **hello** icon and feel the sense of accomplishment as the Clipper browser displays the intended greeting. Figure 2.5 shows the expected screen. You can return to the launcher by tapping the back arrow at the top of the screen.

Figure 2.5 "Hello, World!" Example Running in the Clipper Browser

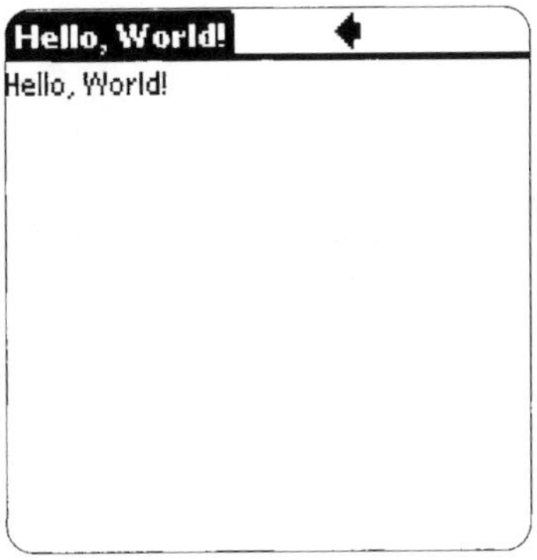

Setting Small and Large Icons

When the Build PQA dialog box was displayed, notice that the default icons were provided for the icon displayed in the Application Launcher. The default icons were used to build the example because no custom icons were specified.

In the next example, the "Hello, World!" example will be built using custom icons located on the CD accompanying this book, in the "hello world build 2" example for Chapter 2. Use the image files large.gif and small.gif from this directory.

From the WCA Builder, select the **Build PQA...** menu option from the **File** menu again. Confirm that the file name of the application is *hello*. Click the **Large** button and choose the large.gif file from the working directory. Next, click the **Small** button and choose the small.gif file from the working directory (see Figure 2.6).

Figure 2.6 Build PQA Dialog Box after Selecting Large and Small Icons

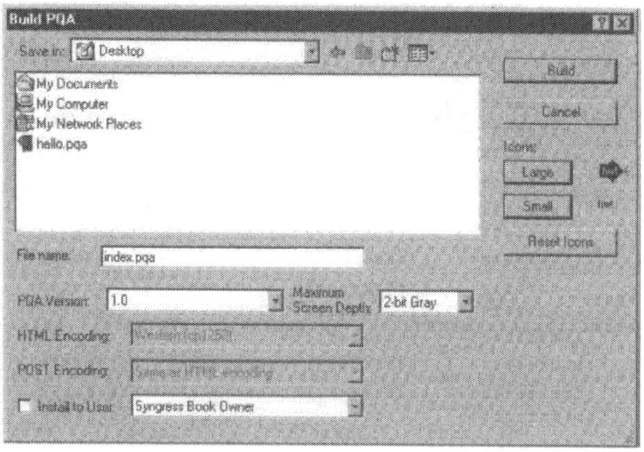

Click the **Build** button to rebuild the application with the new icons. Install the hello.pqa file again. From the Application Launcher, notice that the icon has changed in the Application Launcher to the "hw" icon supplied in the Build PQA dialog box, as shown in Figure 2.7. The large icon is used when the View By preference in the Application Launcher is set to Icon. The small icon is used when the View By preference is set to List. This preference can be changed in the **Preferences** menu selection in the **Options** menu of the Application Launcher.

Figure 2.7 "Hello, World!" Example with New Icon in the Application Launcher

Building a Multiple Document PQA

To expand the capabilities of the single page example, "Hello, World!" will become both multipage and multilingual. Create another temporary directory to preserve the first example, if you like. Type the following code into your favorite text editor and save it as index.html in the new directory (these files are also provided on the CD in the "hello world build 3" example):

```
<html>


<head>
      <title>Hello, World!</title>
</head>


<body>
      Tap your language below for your greeting.<p>


      <a href="english.html">English</a><br>
      <a href="spanish.html">Español</a><br>
      <a href="french.html">Français</a><br>
      <a href="german.html">Deutsch</a><br>
</body>
```

```
</html>
```

Next, type the following into your favorite text editor and save it as english.html:

```
<html>


<head>
      <title>Hello, World!</title>
</head>


<body>
      <h1>Hello, World!</h1>


      <a href="index.html">Back</a>
</body>


</html>
```

Finally, create spanish.html, french.html, and german.html by copying the structure of English.html. For spanish.html, the two changed lines are as follows:

```
<title>Hola, Mundo!</title>
<h1>Hola, Mundo!</h1>
```

For french.html, the two changed lines are as follows:

```
<title>Bonjour, Monde!</title>
<h1>Bonjour, Monde!</h1>
```

For german.html, the two changed lines are as follows:

```
<title>Hallo, Welt!</title>
<h1>Hallo, Welt!</h1>
```

After the five files have been created, launch the WCA Builder and choose the index file index.html by choosing the **Open Index...** menu option from the **File** menu. Because of the way that WCA Builder scans for links, your window should look like the one in Figure 2.8.

Notice that the WCA Builder scanned hello.html for references to other HTML files and added the language HTML files to the file list for the application.

Figure 2.8 File List in the WCA Builder

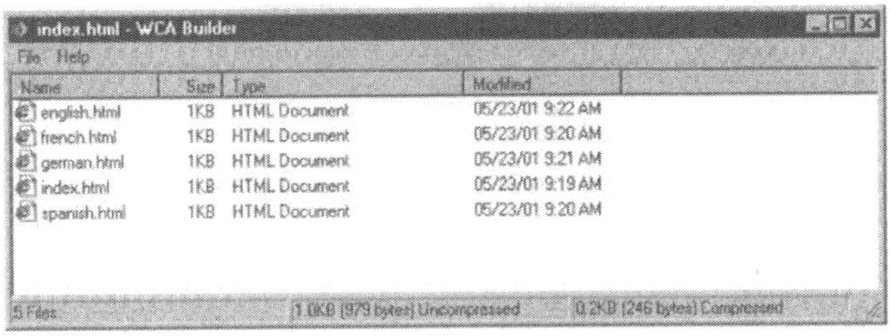

Build the application again by selecting the **Build PQA...** menu option from the **File** menu. Type **hello** for the file name, choose the same large and small icons used in the last example, and click **Build**. Install the application on your device or POSE and launch it. Your Palm OS device screen will show the initial index page, as in Figure 2.9.

Figure 2.9 Multilingual "Hello, World!" Example

Tapping one of the language links displays the appropriate page with the Headline 1 style applied to the greeting and a link for returning to the previous page. Figure 2.10 shows the results of clicking on the "Español" link.

Figure 2.10 "Hello, World!" in Spanish

Linking to Internet Web Sites

To reinforce the core concept in Web clipping that static HTML content is loaded from the device instead of over the wireless networks, the next example links to a standard Web site designed for the desktop computer with a screen significantly larger than Palm-sized devices. Make a copy of the previous example, edit hello.html, and create a link to the popular Yahoo! search engine (these files are also provided on the CD in the "hello world build 4" example). The change is listed boldface in the following code below:

```
<html>


<head>
     <title>Hello, World!</title>
</head>


<body>
     Tap your language below for your greeting.<p>


     <a href="english.html">English</a><br>
     <a href="spanish.html">Español</a><br>
     <a href="french.html">Français</a><br>
     <a href="german.html">Deutsch</a><br>
```

```
    <p>For more greetings, search <a
        href="http://www.yahoo.com">Yahoo!</a>
</body>

</html>
```

Rebuild the PQA with this change, install it on your device or POSE, and launch it. The link to Yahoo! is presented at the bottom of the document, similar to Figure 2.11.

Figure 2.11 Yahoo! Link Added to "Hello, World!"

Tap the Yahoo! link at the end of the page, and you will see the initial Yahoo! screen, similar to what is shown in Figure 2.12.

Figure 2.12 Yahoo! in Clipper

The layout of the opening page in Yahoo! has historically been a clean, simple design that views well on a variety of Web browsers on desktop computers. However, this example illustrates that this page does not translate well for the small screen.

The purpose of this example was to show that direct links to Web sites could be created in a Web clipping application. Clipper does its best to faithfully display the site, which is designed for the big screen, on the small screen. Web pages that contain few or no graphics and stick to standard HTML formatting tags such as <H1> and <P> actually translate surprisingly well. To continue this exercise, swap the link to Yahoo! in this example for some of your favorite Web pages and notice how the pages are rendered in Clipper.

Automating WCA through Command Line Parameters

In addition to building PQA files from the Windows client interface, the WCA Builder can also be used as a command line utility. After building a project for the tenth time, it comes in handy to create a batch file that builds the PQA file instead of selecting the same options repetitively with the mouse.

The command syntax is **WCABuild *HTML filename* [*commands*] [*options*]**. Table 2.1 provides a summary of the command line options.

Table 2.1 Command Line Options for the WCA Builder

Command	Description
/h	Displays a dialog box with the command line options for reference.
/pqa	Builds a query application from command line parameters. Launches the Windows user interface if not specified.
Options	
/d <value>	Maximum bit depth of application images. Valid values are "1", "2", "4", "8", and "16". Default value is "2" for black, white, light gray, and dark gray.
/e <value>	HTML encoding format to use. Values are cp1252 for Western encoding or shift_jis for Japanese encoding. Default value is cp1252.

Continued

Table 2.1 Continued

Command	Description
/l "largeicon.gif"	Graphic file (BMP, GIF, or JPG) to use as application icon for the Icon view of the Application Launcher. This file should be 32 pixels wide by 22 pixels high. Default value is plain diamond-shaped Web clipping icon.
/n "name"	Name of the query application to display in the Application Launcher. Double quotation marks are required. Default is the PQA file name.
/o "output.pqa"	File name of the query application to build.
/p <value>	POST-encoding format to use. Values are us-ascii, iso-8859-1, cp1252, shift_jis, EUC-JP, and iso-2022-jp. Default value is the HTML encoding format (/e).
/q <value>	Clipper version required for the application. Values are "1" for Version 1.0 (Palm OS 3.5 and below) or "2" for Version 2.0 (Palm OS 4.0). Default is "1".
/r <value>	Revision identifier of the query application to display in the Application Launcher. Double quotation marks are required. Default is "1.0".
/s "smallicon.gif"	Graphic file (BMP, GIF, or JPG) to use as application icon for the List view of the Application Launcher. This file should be 15 pixels wide by 9 pixels high. Default value is a plain, diamond-shaped Web clipping icon.
/u "username"	Specifies the user folder to install the query application to on the next HotSync operation. Double quotation marks are required. Default is no automatic installation.
/v	Verbose mode. WCA Builder displays errors. Default is no error display.

In our "Hello, World!" example, we identified the following components in the WCA Builder:

- The first HTML file to display (hello.html)
- The name of the output file (hello.pqa)
- The large icon file (large.gif) and small icon file (small.gif)

Assuming that the hello.html, large.gif, and small.gif files are located in the same directory as the WCABuild.EXE executable, the syntax for building "Hello, World!" via the command line is the following:

```
wcabuild hello.html /pqa /l "large.gif" /o hello.pqa /p "cp-1252" /s
     "small.gif" /v
```

Note the existence of the POST-encoding option in the command line (/p "cp-1252"). Without specifying this switch, Version 1.5 of the WCA Builder will not build on and be compatible with Palm OS 3.5 or earlier even if the Clipper Version option is set to "1" (/q "1"). When specifying launcher icons, both the large and small icons must be identified, or neither icon must be identified. For example, the large icon or small icon cannot be defined without defining the other icon as well.

Creating a batch file such as build.bat to build the Query Application Builder file turns a rebuild into two or three keystrokes instead of several clicks on the Windows user interface. The Windows user interface of the WCA Builder does not remember settings from one build to the next.

Using PQA Builder 1.0 and WCA Builder 1.5

Two different versions of the Builder utility exist for building Web clipping applications. The applications in this chapter have been built with Version 1.5 of the WCA Builder. Version 1.5 is the current release available as of this writing, available as part of the Palm OS SDK, Version 4.0.

Version 1.0 of the Builder utility is named the Palm Query Application Builder (PQA Builder). The acronym PQA reflects the marketing name first used for Web clipping applications (see the sidebar earlier in this chapter). It was first made available with the release of Palm OS 3.2 and the Palm VII device in 1999.

Aside from missing features that apply to the Palm OS 4.0 SDK, the use of the PQA Builder is identical to the WCA Builder. The index file is still established by the Open Index dialog box. An application is built by specifying the filename and the large and small icons in the Build PQA dialog box. The differences between the two applications are apparent from the Build PQA dialog box: Numerous options specific to Palm OS 4.0 are missing.

Which Version Should I Use?

If your target audience is exclusively for Palm OS 3.5 and earlier devices, the WCA Builder offers no additional features but you may encounter some bugs that might not be easily diagnosed as a new Palm OS developer. Use PQA Builder Version 1.0.

If your target audience exclusively uses Palm OS 4.0 devices and needs to take advantage of new Web clipping features (such as color bitmaps and icons and different HTML and POST encoding types), use WCA Builder Version 1.5. However, if your target audience includes those using Palm OS 3.5 and earlier devices, use the WCA Builder Version 1.5—but ensure that your applications are tested on Palm OS 3.5 and earlier devices to avoid being surprised by some known (and likely unknown) WCA Builder bugs.

NOTE

Before making PQA Builder your build utility of choice, note that a documented bug exists in the icon selection of the Build PQA dialog box. After selecting an icon with PQA Builder 1.0 running on Windows 2000, the application unexpectedly closes without warning. This problem does not exist when using the command line arguments to specify the build options.

Using QAB 1.5 (Palm OS 4.0 SDK)

WCA Builder Version 1.5 is part of the Palm OS 4.0 SDK. In addition to building applications compatible with versions of Clipper for the Palm OS 3.5 and earlier, WCA Builder supports the following features available in Clipper for Palm OS 4.0:

- Color icons for the Palm launcher
- Specifying the version of the PQA standard used
- Language used in the HTML documents
- Format for form text posted to the server
- Screen depth

Most of the new features are designed to support internationalization of Web clipping applications to countries that don't use the Western character set, such as Japan.

Color Icons

The WCA Builder supports 4-bit grayscale and 256-color bitmaps for both the application icon and the page graphics. The "hello world build 5" folder included on the companion CD has a multilingual "Hello, World!" example with large and small 256 color bitmaps for the icons.

Copy the color versions of these icons into your working directory, run the WCA Builder, and change the following options in the Build PQA dialog box:

- PQA Version set to 2.0 (Palm OS 4.0 or greater)
- Maximum Screen Depth set to (8-bit Color)

Don't forget to change the icons to the color versions using the **Large** and **Small** buttons. Note that when you select an icon, the WCA Builder shows the grayscale version of the colorized icons. Although this may be annoying, it is helpful to confirm how the icon will be displayed on a grayscale device. The command line version to build this application is as follows:

```
wcabuild hello.html /pqa /d "8" /l "large.gif" /o hello.pqa /q "2" /s
    "small.gif" /v
```

Debugging...

Using Color Icons in Web Clipping Applications

In addition to matching the blue tone of the other launcher icons, the blue color (#FF0000) used in the "Hello World!" color icon displays as black on Palm 3.5 and earlier grayscale devices. The WCA Builder does not create multiple versions of the icons for various display types. The Application Launcher and Clipper browser convert colors to gray shades before displaying them.

When adding color to launcher icons, be sure to check that the same icon will display properly on grayscale devices. Whether you check them by testing them on a grayscale device, in the Build PQA display, or with the Image Checker tool, some colors will not convert as you may expect. The light blue color used in most of the application icons (#639ACE) converts to white instead of black on the Application Launcher of grayscale devices.

After building this application, install it to see the colorized icon in the launcher. Figure 2.13 shows the Launcher from the Palm OS 4.0 ROM (this can be seen in color on the accompanying CD). Effective design and use of grayscale images and color will be covered in detail in Chapter 4.

Figure 2.13 Color Icon for "Hello, World!" in the Application Launcher

Unwired Widgets Product List Example

Although the single page "Hello, World!" example was a good introduction to developing a Web clipping application, a more complex and multiple page application is included in the "Unwired Widgets" folder on the CD for Chapter 2. To see it, you can install the prebuilt products.pqa file on your device or POSE.

The Product List application—shown in Figure 2.14—is a Web clipping application that identifies the widget product line. The entire product list can be browsed or filtered down to the widget's shape and size.

Figure 2.14 Unwired Widgets Product List Example

Clicking **product list** displays a table with the part ID, size, shape, and color for all widgets in the Unwired Widgets inventory. Clicking **shape, size and**

color first displays a page to choose the size (big or small) followed by a second page to choose the shape (round or square) followed by a list of widgets with the shape and size and its color.

Browse through some of the HTML files in this example and note the presence of formatting tags—such as the header tags <H1> and <H2> and table tags such as <TABLE> and <TR>—commonly found in standard Web applications. (Using tags will be covered in detail in Chapter 3.) For example, the body section of the file product list.html uses both of these typical HTML elements:

```
<html>

<head>
      <title>Product List</title>

      <meta name="palmcomputingplatform" content="true">
      <meta name="palmlauncherrevision" content="1.0">
      <meta name="historylisttext" content="(UW) Product List">
</head>

<body>
      <h1>Unwired Widgets</h1>

      <table>
            <tr>
                  <td width="42"><b><u>Part ID
                  <td width="32"><b><u>Size
                  <td width="38"><b><u>Shape
                  <td width="38"><b><u>Color</b>

            <tr><td>256-01 <td>Small <td>Round <td>Red
            <tr><td>256-02 <td>Small <td>Round <td>Green
            <tr><td>256-03 <td>Small <td>Round <td>Blue
            <tr><td>256-04 <td>Small <td>Round <td>Yellow
            <tr><td>256-11 <td>Small <td>Square <td>Red
            <tr><td>256-12 <td>Small <td>Square <td>Green
            <tr><td>256-13 <td>Small <td>Square <td>Blue
```

```
        <tr><td>256-14 <td>Small <td>Square <td>Yellow
        <tr><td>280-01 <td>Large <td>Round <td>Red
        <tr><td>280-02 <td>Large <td>Round <td>Green
        <tr><td>280-03 <td>Large <td>Round <td>Blue
        <tr><td>280-04 <td>Large <td>Round <td>Yellow
        <tr><td>280-11 <td>Large <td>Square <td>Red
        <tr><td>280-12 <td>Large <td>Square <td>Green
        <tr><td>280-13 <td>Large <td>Square <td>Blue
        <tr><td>280-14 <td>Large <td>Square <td>Yellow
    </table>
</body>

</html>
```

Browse this application in your desktop Web browser by opening the **index.html** file. Compare the look and feel of the text and formatting of this application in the desktop application and the Web clipping application.

Although this application does not have wireless interaction with the Internet, it does show that a standalone Web clipping application does not have to interact with the Internet to be useful. Web clipping applications can have static pages similar to these that provide company profiles, contacts, and help for the application itself.

Summary

The Web Clipping Application (WCA) Builder is a free utility from Palm, Inc. that creates Web clipping applications from the HTML and graphics you supply. The WCA Builder creates a database file to install on the Palm OS device for the nonchanging, or static, components of a Web application. By loading the nonchanging components on the device, the amount of data transmission over wireless networks is greatly reduced. This increase in performance and the improved user experience is a major component of Web clipping technology.

To create a Web clipping application with the WCA Builder, the first step is creating a Web application designed for the screen size and network capabilities of wireless Palm OS devices. Launch the WCA Builder, select the **Open Index...** menu option from the **File** menu and identify the index file of the Web application to build. The WCA Builder searches the index file and subsequent files for nonchanging documents and graphics to include in the Web clipping application.

After the index has been processed, select the **Build PQA...** option from the **File** menu to create the Web clipping application. Before building the application, several options such as the Application Launcher icons, Clipper version, screen depth setting, and HTML and POST encoding options can be established. After selecting the options, clicking the **Build** button creates the application.

In addition to using the Windows user interface for creating applications, the WCA Builder also supports command line options for automating the build process.

Palm, Inc. has two different versions of the builder application. The PQA Builder Version 1.0 was the first Web clipping application creation utility supplied with the release of the Palm VII. It is recommended for building applications targeted exclusively for the Palm OS 3.5 and earlier versions. The WCA Builder Version 1.5 is the version released with the Palm OS 4.0 SDK; use this if specific functionality in the Palm OS 4.0 is required. It supports new features available in Palm OS 4.0, such as incorporation of color icons and bitmaps and HTML and POST document encoding into your applications.

Solutions Fast Track

Writing Simple Web Pages

- ☑ HTML tags indicate document formatting and processing instructions. HTML tags are flanked by less than (<) and greater than (>) characters.
- ☑ The <HTML> tag indicates the beginning of an HTML document. HTML tags inside the <HTML> and </HTML> tags are processed by Web browsers.
- ☑ Text located between the <BODY> and </BODY> tags is displayed by a Web browser in its main window.

Running the Web Clipping Application Builder

- ☑ The filename of the utility is WCABuild.exe.
- ☑ Select the HTML file that will be the first HTML displayed in the application by selecting the **Open Index...** choice from the **File** menu.
- ☑ After the index file has been determined, build the application by selecting the **Build PQA...** choice from the **File** menu. Type a name for the file, select large and small icons (if desired), and click **Build**.
- ☑ Applications can be built with the WCA Builder from its Windows user interface or by supplying command line options. For the list of command line options, refer to Table 2.1 in this chapter or run the WCA Builder and add ***/h*** to the command line.
- ☑ WCA Builder supports new Web clipping features available in Palm OS 4.0 including color graphics and icons support and HTML and POST file encoding tags.

Frequently Asked Questions

The following Frequently Asked Questions, answered by the authors of this book, are designed to both measure your understanding of the concepts presented in this chapter and to assist you with real-life implementation of these concepts. To have your questions about this chapter answered by the author, browse to **www.syngress.com/solutions** and click on the **"Ask the Author"** form.

Q: How much does the PQA Builder cost?

A: It's free!

Q: Should I use the latest version of the Palm Query Application Builder 1.0 or Web Clipping Application Builder 1.5?

A: If your application audience has devices that are running Palm OS 3.5 or earlier, use PQA Builder 1.0. The additional features in WCA Builder 1.5 apply only to Palm OS 4.0 devices. If your application needs to use some of the features of Palm OS 4.0 devices, such as color icons and bitmaps or HTML and POST encoding, use WCA Builder 1.5.

Q: I get tired of creating the same setting each time I build an application. How can I make it remember the last build settings?

A: The Windows user interface for the WCA Builder does not remember the settings of the previous build. However, applications can be built with the WCA Builder via command line options.

Q: Do the builder utilities have any known bugs?

A: The application unexpectedly closes when selecting icons from PQA Builder 1.0 under the Windows 2000 environment. The command line requires the */p "cp-1252"* option to be set to build applications for Palm OS 3.5 and earlier with WCA Builder 1.5.

Chapter 3

Building WCAs Using HTML

Solutions in this chapter:

- Starting HTML Documents with a Header
- Providing HTML Content with Block and Text Markup Body Tags
- Linking to Application Pages and Web Sites

☑ Summary

☑ Solutions Fast Track

☑ Frequently Asked Questions

Introduction

Because of the small screen size and limited memory of Palm OS devices, Web browsers on these devices work differently from browsers on the desktop. Clipper understands a version of Hypertext Markup Language (HTML) based on the 3.2 standard, but with several additions that allow you to optimize pages for device display.

Some common features of desktop browsers are missing on the Palm OS. You will find no support for scripting on Web pages. There are no plug-ins for Flash or for playing Musical Instrument Digital Interface (MIDI) files. Frames are impractical and popping up another window doesn't work unless the user just happens to have an extra Palm OS device nearby. In many ways, it is a throwback to the early days of the Web when Mosaic was in, Java was for set-top boxes, and <BLINK> was a joke rather than a feature.

This may sound primitive, and in many ways it is. However, the lack of features isn't an obstacle to producing good Web clipping applications (WCAs). As a WCA author, you have some advantages a normal Web page author lacks. First, you can assume one page size for most devices. This simplifies the task of page layout and design. Second, user expectations are different. Fancy layout isn't as impressive as clarity of design and speed of accessing information. Finally, smaller and simpler pages are easier to maintain.

In this chapter, the subset of HTML 3.2 supported by Clipper and the elements of HTML 3.2 that are left out are identified. In addition, features to support optimized content for the Clipper browser are outlined. This chapter is organized by the different classes of HTML tags: first, we talk about the header and how you specify information about the document. We then look at the tags that are used to provide content, at both the block and text level. Finally, we focus of new features added to Palm Inc.'s version of HTML that differ from the standard HTML used on the desktop Web.

Starting HTML Documents with a Header

Tags in the header section of an HTML document define properties that apply to the entire document. This includes information such as the title of the page, who made it, and if it is a "Palm-friendly" document. These header tags are not shown directly to the user, although they might affect how the page is displayed. In later sections of this chapter, we talk about the body tags that hold the real content of the page.

For the Clipper browser, tags in the header section can indicate that a document was designed specifically for Clipper, the version of Clipper that the document requires, and the title of the document that appears in the upper left-hand corner of the Clipper browser window. Figure 3.1 shows our <HEAD> section from the Unwired Widgets example in Chapter 2 (also provided in the Unwired Widgets example for Chapter 2 on the accompanying CD).

The header is completely enclosed in a <HEAD> tag, starting with <HEAD> and ending with </HEAD>. If you specify the header-specific tags outside of a <HEAD> section, you will have an invalid HTML document, and the browser might ignore their values.

Figure 3.1 Sample HTML Header

```
<head>
     <title>Product List</title>

     <meta name="palmcomputingplatform" content="true">
     <meta name="palmlauncherrevision" content="1.0">
</head>
```

Setting the Title of the Page

The <TITLE> tag defines the text to be displayed in the title bar of the Clipper browser. If we refer to Figure 3.2, we will see that *Product List* is displayed in the title bar. The title is also used as the label in the history list that Clipper maintains of pages pulled from the Web.

Figure 3.2 Product List Title

Keep the length of this text short. The maximum length of the title extends to the middle of the screen. If the title is too long to fit, it is truncated and three periods are appended to indicate that the length of the title is longer than the space allocated.

You should supply a title in each document. If you had omitted the <TITLE> tag from the code shown earlier, you would get the display shown in Figure 3.3. Because a title was not supplied, the URL of the document is used in its place.

Figure 3.3 Title Set To Page URL (file:Products.pqa) When Not Specified

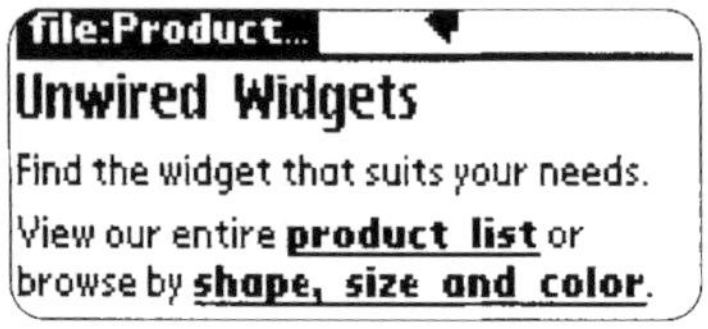

Using META Tags to Add Document-Level Information

META tags are a kind of an escape mechanism in HTML. These tags, located in the header, hold additional data about the document that isn't represented in other HTML tags. A META tag has three attributes, *http-equiv*, *name*, and *content*. The *http-equiv* attribute is used to emulate actions specified by Hypertext Transfer Protocol (HTTP) headers, such as automatic refreshing of the pages. Because Clipper doesn't handle special HTTP requests, META tags using this attribute are ignored. Palm, Inc. has defined a Palm-specific set of META tags that provide information to the Web Clipping Application Builder and to Clipper.

Marking Your Page as Palm-Friendly with the PalmComputingPlatform Tag

Some META tags with special Palm-specific names are honored, including the PalmComputingPlatform tag. This META tag tells the Palm.Net proxy that the page was designed specifically for the Clipper browser. The presence of this tag implies that the speed and availability of wireless networks and the screen size of the Palm OS device were taken into account for the page length and its images. The Palm.Net proxy does not reformat or redesign the page before sending it to the device.

When this tag is not present in a document, the proxy reserves the right to truncate page length and remove large images to deliver a page best formatted for the Palm OS device screen. This tag is used as shown here, with the *name* set to "PalmComputingPlatform" and the *contents* attribute set to "true":

```
<meta name="PalmComputingPlatform" content="true">
```

Providing Icon Information through META Tags

Several META tags can be added to your main page to affect how the Web clipping application appears in the Palm OS Launcher. These are the PalmLauncherName, PalmLauncherRevision, PalmLargeIconFilename, and PalmSmallIconFilename tags. Each of these affects some aspect of the appearance. By specifying PalmLauncherName, you can choose the displayed name for the WCA. The PalmLargeIconFilename and PalmSmallIconFilename tags let you pick graphics files to use for the large and small icon views. Finally, the PalmLauncherRevision tag lets you specify a version number for the WCA that will be shown when the user uses the Info menu command. All of these should be added to the index HTML page of your Web clipping application, so that they will be used by the WCA Builder application when building the Palm Query Application (PQA) file.

Only the PalmLauncherRevision tag is understood by the original Query Application Builder (QAB) executable. The other three tags aren't supported until you use WCA Builder 1.5 from the Palm OS 4.0 Software Development Kit (SDK). The version of Clipper used does not matter for these tags, because they affect only the properties of the built PQA file. The usage of these tags is as follows:

```
<meta name="PalmLauncherName" content="Unwired Widgets">
<meta name="PalmLauncherRevision" content="1.3.2">
<meta name="PalmLargeIconFilename" content="logo_large.gif">
<meta name="PalmSmallIconFilename" content="logo_small.gif">
```

Adding Unconnected Graphics Files

The LocalIcon META tag is used to add additional files to a Web clipping application that are not directly referenced. Because WCA Builder normally just includes the pages and graphics that can be reached from the index page of the site, it may leave out material that you want to use from your remote site but do not want immediately accessible. This tag is discussed in more detail in Chapter 4.

Overriding the History List

The HistoryListText META tag lets you specify an alternate string for the Web clipping history that Clipper saves. Normally, it uses the title of the page, along with the time it was received. Using this tag, you can specify your own text for this cache, including any combination of the current date and time you want. This is discussed in more detail in Chapter 6.

No Support for Other Standard META Tags

Clipper does not support many of the META tags that a desktop Web browser honors. As mentioned earlier, no META tags with the *http-equiv* attribute are honored, so using a META tag-style redirect will not work on the Palm OS. If you do wish to redirect the Web page to another location, the Palm.Net proxy does honor Redirect HTTP headers, although if you redirect more than twice, it will give up and return an error message to the user about excessive redirection.

Providing HTML Content with Block and Text Markup Body Tags

Body tags define the content and page presentation of a Web document. The most common body tags available in the HTML 3.2 specification are available in the Web clipping HTML definition.

Although the meaning of these tags match the meaning of the tags in the HTML 3.2 definition, content with these tags applied may render differently to fit the small Palm OS device's screen. As a Web developer, this should not come as a surprise; in practice, each Web browser shows HTML text differently.

The body of the HTML document is contained in a tag called <BODY>. Although this tag is required in HTML 3.2, in practice it can be left off a Web page unless you want to specify a special BODY attribute such as the background color. The body should start with a <BODY> tag, and close with </BODY>.

Block Markup

Within the <BODY> tag, you encounter two classes of HTML tags: *block markup* tags and *text markup* tags. Block markup is used to describe sections of text. A new block of text will be separated from the last block by whitespace. Text markup tags, such as <I> for italic text, should be entirely contained within blocks and should not span multiple blocks.

Paragraphs: <P>

Individual sentences or groups of sentences that should be formatted as paragraphs use the <P> tag appended to the beginning of the first sentence in the paragraph; at the completion of a paragraph, close the block by adding a </P>. The <P> tag supports the following tag attribute:

- *Align* for horizontal positioning of text. Values are *left*, *right*, and *center*.

In the following example code, provided in the build_01 example on the CD, four paragraphs are defined from the sentence provided using the different paragraph attributes. The results are illustrated in Figure 3.4.

```
<body>
    <p>Abraham Lincoln, November 19, 1863.</p>

    <p align=left>Four score and seven years ago, our fathers
    brought forth unto this continent a new nation.</p>

    <p align=center>Four score and seven years ago, our fathers
    brought forth unto this continent a new nation.</p>

    <p align=right>Four score and seven years ago, our fathers
    brought forth unto this continent a new nation.</p>
</body>
```

Figure 3.4 Using the *Align* Attribute in the <P> Paragraph Tag

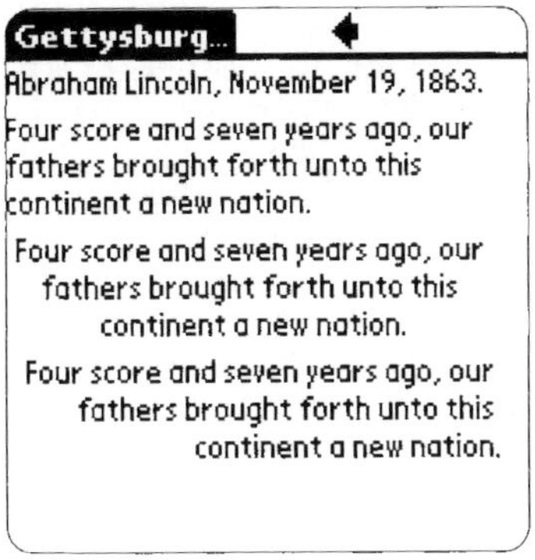

Large Headers: <H1>, <H2>, and <H3>

Headline text that identifies and separates major sections of content by using a large, boldface font are defined with the tags <H1>, <H2>, and <H3>. These header tags also support the *align* attribute with the values *left*, *right*, and *center*.

This example, provided in the build_02 example on the CD, illustrates the rendering of these headline tags compared to paragraph text. The final rendering is shown in Figure 3.5.

```
<body>
    <h1>Abraham Lincoln</h1>
    <p>Four score and seven years ago, our fathers
    brought forth unto this continent a new nation.

    <h2>Abraham Lincoln</h2>
    <p>Four score and seven years ago, our fathers
    brought forth unto this continent a new nation.

    <h3>Abraham Lincoln</h3>
    <p>Four score and seven years ago, our fathers
    brought forth unto this continent a new nation.
</body>
```

Figure 3.5 Clipper Rendering of Headline Tags <H1>, <H2>, and <H3>

Notice that the difference in font sizes for the headline and paragraph text is not as pronounced as the difference in font sizes for the same tags in Internet Explorer. These headline tags are one of the few formatting tags that render text significantly different than HTML 3.2 on a full-size screen. A full-size screen rendering is shown in Figure 3.6.

Figure 3.6 Internet Explorer Rendering of Headline Tags <H1>, <H2>, and <H3>

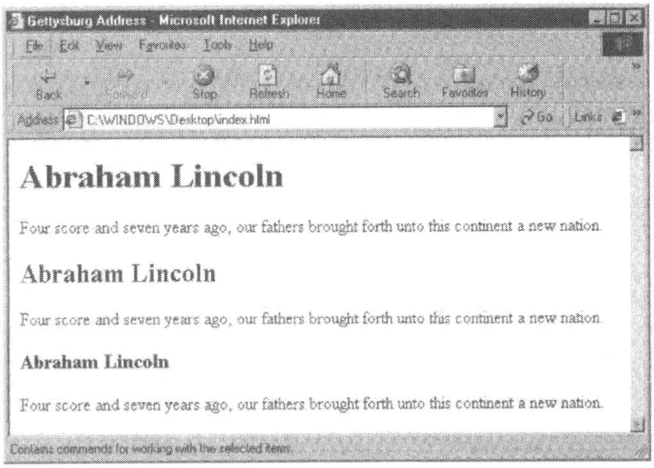

Small Headers: <H4>, <H5>, and <H6>

Although officially defined as headlines, these tags seem to de-emphasize text instead of emphasize them. These headline tags also support the *align* attribute.

The code example for showing headlines tags <H1>, <H2>, and <H3> has been edited to show headlines <H4>, <H5>, and <H6> (provided in the build_03 example on the CD). The results are shown in Figure 3.7.

Figure 3.7 Headline Tags <H4>, <H5>, and <H6> Are Small

Consider that many Palm OS device owners don't have 20/20 vision. Avoid the use of <H5> and <H6> in favor of the larger headline tags.

Horizontal Rule: <HR>

The horizontal rule tag <HR> draws a horizontal line across the screen. The <HR> tag supports the following attributes:

- *Align* for the horizontal justification of the text as *left*, *center*, and *right*. *Center* is the default.
- *Size* for the height of line in pixels (default is one pixel).
- *Width* for the horizontal length of the line in pixels (default is the entire screen width).

Horizontal rules are good for visually separating differing sections of content. In the Fidelity Investments application shown in Figure 3.8, the horizontal rule separates the document elements that initiate data retrieval from the document element that defines the use of the application. By providing a visual break between the two groups of visual elements, the user can easily and quickly determine where the first control group ends and the next control group begins.

Figure 3.8 Horizontal Rule Separator

Images: <IMG>

Sometimes text isn't enough, and you want to add a graphical image to a Web page. Most attributes of the image tag <IMG>are supported in Clipper. The <IMG> tag supports the following attributes for displaying images:

- *Src* for the URL of the image to display.
- *Alt* for the alternative text to display when the image is not available. The ALT text may be displayed on Clipper if your image is too large for the screen.
- *Height* and *width* define display dimensions in pixels for the source image in the document.
- *Align* specifies the horizontal alignment. Values are *left*, *right*, *top*, *middle*, and *bottom*.

For the first image example (provided in the build_04 example on the CD and shown in Figure 3.9), an image named palm.gif, of 108 pixels in length and 108 pixels in height, is displayed in the Clipper window. The code is as follows:

```
<html>

<head>
      <title>IMG tag</title>

      <meta name="palmcomputingplatform" content="true">
      <meta name="palmlauncherrevision" content="1.0">
</head>

<body>
      <img src="palm.gif">
</body>

</html>
```

Figure 3.9 <img src="palm.gif">

When the image width and/or height are redefined in the image tag, the Clipper browser resizes the image to the specified size. When the image height and width are *not* defined, the dimensions of the source image itself are used as the dimensions for the image in the document.

In Figure 3.10, the width and height of the image are redefined to 40 pixels by 40 pixels as follows (the code is provided in the build_05 example on the CD):

```
<img src="palm.gif" width="40" height="40">
```

Figure 3.10 <img src="palm.gif" width="40" height="40">

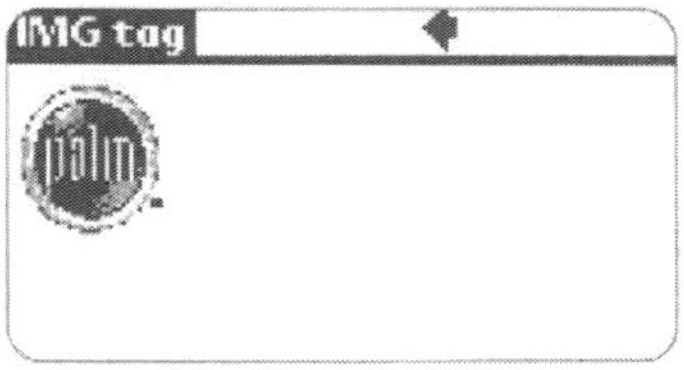

On desktop computers with high resolutions and millions of colors, a browser would retain more of the image detail when resizing this image. However, the Clipper browser will resize the image as quickly as possible because most device screen resolutions support a few shades of gray of a maximum or 256 colors.

If the dimensions of the image should be displayed on the document as 40 pixels by 40 pixels, design the image to be 40 pixels by 40 pixels—do not rely on the Clipper browser to resize the image.

The *align* attribute defines the horizontal positioning of an image in a document. The values *left* and *right* are commonly used in Clipper applications to align an image against the left or right margin and wrap text around the alternate side. The values *top*, *middle*, and *bottom* align the image along the top, middle, or bottom of the baseline compared to other images in the line. These three values are not commonly used in Clipper applications.

In the final image tag example (provided in the build_06 example on the CD and shown in Figure 3.11), the Palm logo is aligned against the right margin of the document, and text is wrapped around the left and bottom of the image. (Chapter 4 contains more discussion on creating good images for a Palm OS device.) The code is as follows:

```
<body>

    <img src="palm.gif" align="right">


    <p>Palm, Inc. sells the <b>world's favorite handheld
```

```
    computers</b>.

    <p>We also license the Palm OS® to <i>world-class
    companies</i> that create customized handheld solutions
    to meet specific market needs.

    <p>In May 1999, we launched our <u>Palm.Net™</u>
    wireless service, which provides on-the-go Internet
    access. No modems. No phone lines.
</body>
```

Figure 3.11 <img src="palm.gif" align="right">

Ordered and Unordered List: <OL> and <UL>

The ordered and unordered list tags are faithful to the HTML 3.2 specification in their use and rendering by Clipper. These tags format listlike information by displaying each list item indented out from the left margin on a separate line with an item marker prefixing each list item.

List items in ordered lists use incrementing numbers, letters, or roman numerals as the item marker. The <OL> tag for ordered lists accepts the following attributes:

- *Start* for the starting number in the list. The default starting number is 1.
- *Type* for the type of item marker. Values are *A* for uppercase letters, *a* for lowercase letters, *I* for uppercase Roman numerals, *I* for lowercase Roman numerals, and *1* for numbers. The default is *1* for numbers as the item marker type.

List items inside ordered lists are defined using the <LI> tag in the similar fashion that paragraphs are defined using the <P> tag. The end of an ordered list is defined with the </LI> tag.

The following example lists the different families of Palm OS devices as an ordered list. The following code is provided in the build_07 example on the CD and the results are shown in Figure 3.12.

```
<html>

<head>
      <title>Handhelds</title>

      <meta name="palmcomputingplatform" content="true">
      <meta name="palmlauncherrevision" content="1.0">
</head>

<body>
      <h1>Palm Handhelds</h1>

      <ol>
            <li>Palm m500 Series
            <li>Palm m100 Series
            <li>Palm III Series
            <li>Palm V Series
            <li>Palm VII Series
       </ol>
</body>

</html>
```

List items in unordered lists use a small shape (or bullet) as the item marker instead of letters or numbers. The <UL> tag for unordered lists accepts the following attribute:

- *Type* for the type of item marker. Values are *disc*, *square*, and *circle*.

List items are also defined using the <LI> tag in the same fashion as ordered lists.

Figure 3.12 Ordered List Example Using Numbers as the Marker Type

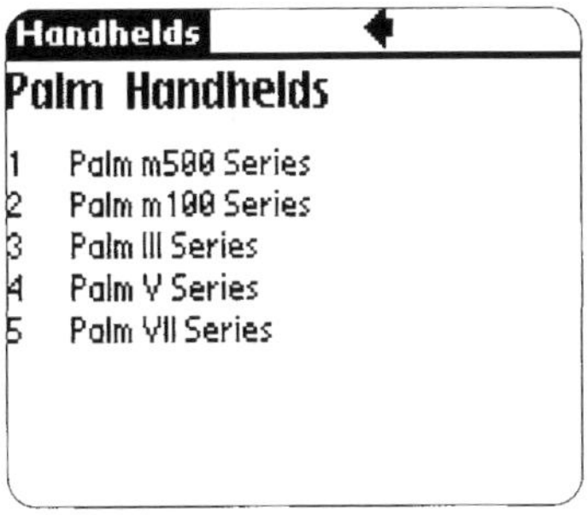

The following example (provided in the build_08 example on the CD and shown in Figure 3.13) lists the different families of Palm OS devices as an unordered list.

Figure 3.13 Unordered List Example Using Squares as the Marker Type

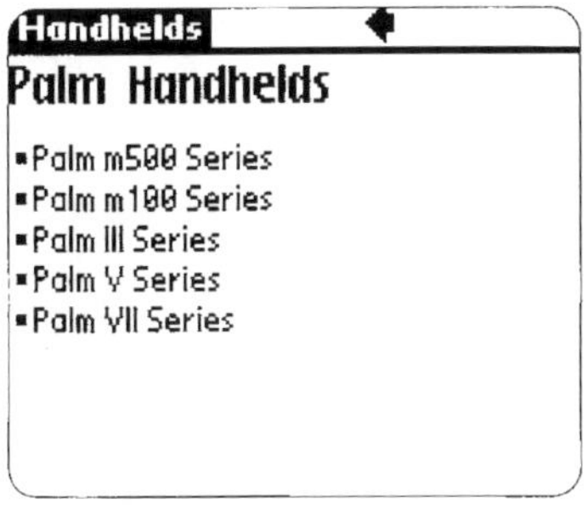

Structured Information: <TABLE>

The <TABLE> tag defines the start of data arranged into rows and columns. In addition to grouping numeric data or textual information that have similar properties, tables are often used in HTML to lay out images and text elements in a document. Using tables for effective layout of Web clipping pages is discussed in Chapter 6.

Tables are treated differently from a PQA file than from a Web site. If a page sent from a Web site is not marked as Palm-friendly using the PalmComputingPlatform META tag, any tables on the page will be ignored. Tables are always honored in pages compiled into a Web clipping application.

The <TABLE> tag indicates the start of a new table and defines properties for the entire table. The <TABLE> tag has the following attributes:

- *Align* for the horizontal alignment of the table. Values are *left*, *center*, and *right*. The default is *left*.
- *Width* for the horizontal width of the table in pixels. Percentage widths are not supported. The default is the entire length of the browser window.
- *Cellpadding* for the spacing between cells in pixels. The default is two pixels.
- *Cellspacing* for the spacing within cells in pixels. The default is two pixels.

The <TR> tag indicates the start of a new row in a table and defines properties for the row. The <TR> tag has the following attribute:

- *Align* for the horizontal alignment of the row in the table. Values are *left*, *center*, and *right*. The default is *left*.

The <TD> tag defines a cell inside a table row called a *data cell*. The <TD> tag has the following attributes:

- *Align* for the horizontal alignment of elements in the cell. Values are *left*, *center*, and *right*. The default is *left*.
- *Width* and *height* for the dimensions of the cell in pixels. When not specified, cells are automatically sized up or down to fit the contents of the cell.
- *Rowspan* for the number of rows spanned by the cell. The default is one row.
- *Colspan* for the number of columns spanned by the cell. The default is one column.

The <TH> tag defines a cell inside a table row called a *header cell*. Header cells are identical to data cells in all respects except that header cell text is boldfaced and has a default horizontal alignment of *center* instead of *left*.

The Unwired Widgets example in Chapter 2 contained several pages using tables to format the widget size, shape, and color properties into columns. Here is the HTML code for the entire product list using tables (see also the build_09 example on the CD):

```
<html>


<head>
```

```
    <title>Product List</title>

    <meta name="palmcomputingplatform" content="true">
    <meta name="palmlauncherrevision" content="1.0">
    <meta name="historylisttext" content="(UW) Product List">
</head>

<body>
    <h1>Unwired Widgets</h1>

    <table>
        <tr>
            <th width="42"><u>Part ID
            <th width="32"><u>Size
            <th width="38"><u>Shape
            <th width="38"><u>Color

        <tr><td>256-01 <td>Small <td>Round <td>Red
        <tr><td>256-02 <td>Small <td>Round <td>Green
        <tr><td>256-03 <td>Small <td>Round <td>Blue
        <tr><td>256-04 <td>Small <td>Round <td>Yellow
        <tr><td>256-11 <td>Small <td>Square <td>Red
        <tr><td>256-12 <td>Small <td>Square <td>Green
        <tr><td>256-13 <td>Small <td>Square <td>Blue
        <tr><td>256-14 <td>Small <td>Square <td>Yellow
        <tr><td>280-01 <td>Large <td>Round <td>Red
        <tr><td>280-02 <td>Large <td>Round <td>Green
        <tr><td>280-03 <td>Large <td>Round <td>Blue
        <tr><td>280-04 <td>Large <td>Round <td>Yellow
        <tr><td>280-11 <td>Large <td>Square <td>Red
        <tr><td>280-12 <td>Large <td>Square <td>Green
        <tr><td>280-13 <td>Large <td>Square <td>Blue
        <tr><td>280-14 <td>Large <td>Square <td>Yellow
    </table>
```

```
</body>

</html>
```

A rendering of this code is illustrated in Figure 3.14. Notice that the width of each column is defined in the header cells that define the category for each column. The width of data cells in the rows for each widget match the width defined in the header cells.

Figure 3.14 Table Example

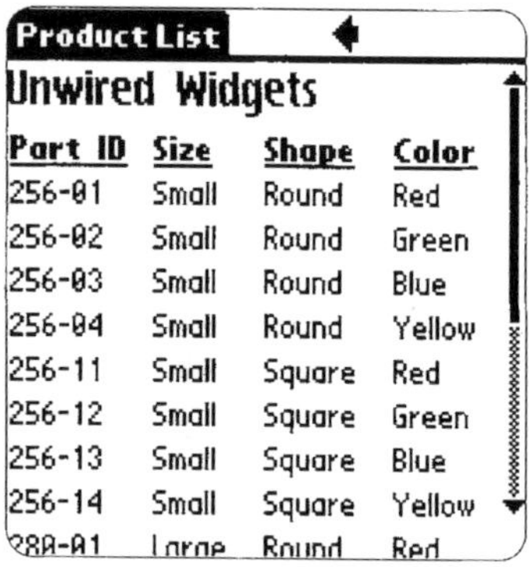

Part ID	Size	Shape	Color
256-01	Small	Round	Red
256-02	Small	Round	Green
256-03	Small	Round	Blue
256-04	Small	Round	Yellow
256-11	Small	Square	Red
256-12	Small	Square	Green
256-13	Small	Square	Blue
256-14	Small	Square	Yellow
288-01	Large	Round	Red

Table tags are faithful to the HTML 3.2 specification with one exception: Tables inside other tables (nested tables) are not supported.

Text Markup

Although block markup tags are used to handle logical chunks of text, the text markup tags let you change the appearance at the character and word level. These tags are generally used in short stretches of text to provide some sort of special effect, such as making the text bold or italic. In a proper HTML document, text markup tags are entirely contained within block tags. For example, you don't specify that an emphasized section starts at paragraph 5 and continues to paragraph 10. Instead, the text in each paragraph is individually marked as emphasized.

Physical Markup: Bold, Italics, and Underlining

Physical markup tags specifically change the display of textual information inside a block. The <B> tag marks text in a bold font, <I> marks text in an italic font, and <U> underlines text. No attributes exist for these tags.

The start of a physical markup is specified by one of these tags. The end of a physical markup is specified by its bookend tag </B>, </I>, or </U>.

Figure 3.15 Bold, Italic, and Underlined Example

The example that follows uses physical markup tags to highlight key phrases in the company profile for Palm, Inc. The "world's favorite handheld computers" phrase is set in boldface, "world-class companies" is set in italics, and "Palm.Net" is underlined. The code is provided in the build_10 example on the CD and the results are shown in Figure 3.15.

```
<html>

<head>
      <title>Palm, Inc.</title>
      <meta name="palmcomputingplatform" content="true">
      <meta name="palmlauncherrevision" content="1.0">
</head>
<body>
      <p>Palm, Inc. sells the <b>world's favorite handheld
      computers</b>.

      <p>We also license the Palm OS® to <i>world-class
      companies</i> that create customized handheld solutions
      to meet specific market needs.

      <p>In May 1999, we launched our <u>Palm.Net™</u>
```

```
    wireless service, which provides on-the-go Internet
    access. No modems. No phone lines.
</body>

</html>
```

Font Markup: <FONT>

You can directly control the font size of text in Clipper by using the <FONT> tag. This HTML 3.2 tag is used to change the size and color of text on a Web page. It uses the following attributes:

- *Size* which is a number from 1 to 6 that corresponds with the size of text used by the header tags <H1> through <H6>. Normal text has size 3.
- *Color* (an RGB value giving the red, green, and blue color levels). On grayscale devices, you should stay with normal black text, but with color devices, you can use this to emphasize text beyond bold, italics, and underlines. A color value looks like "#RRGGBB", where RR is the red value in hexadecimal, GG is the green value, and BB is the blue value. A higher number indicates a brighter version of the color. When all three components are the same, you have a grayscale color, ranging from black at "#000000" to white at "#FFFFFF".

Logical Markup: Strong and Emphasized Text

Whereas physical markup tags specifically define the type of formatting to represent text, *logical markup tags* format text for the content and meaning of text and leave it up to the browser to choose the specific formatting to use.

In the Clipper browser, the <STRONG> tag marks text with a strong meaning in bold. The <EM> tag marks text with an emphasized meaning in italic. In the following example, provided in the build_11 example on the CD, the physical tags from the physical markup example shown earlier have been removed and the <STRONG> and <EM> are now in their place. Figure 3.16 shows the bold and italic markup used for the strong and emphasized tags.

```
<body>
    <p>Palm, Inc. sells the <strong>world's favorite handheld
    computers</strong>.
```

```
        <p>We also license the Palm OS® to <em>world-class
        companies</em> that create customized handheld solutions
        to meet specific market needs.

        <p>In May 1999, we launched our Palm.Net™
        wireless service, which provides on-the-go Internet
        access. No modems. No phone lines.
</body>
```

Figure 3.16 Strong and Emphasized Example

Hyperlinks: <A>

As an essential part of HTML, the anchor tag, <A>, defines text that marks a hypertext link for presenting different parts of the current document or completely different HTML documents. The <A> tag has the following attributes:

- *Href* creates a hypertext link from the text between the opening and closing tags.
- *Name* creates an anchor that can be the target of another link.
- *Button* creates a Palm OS–style button to represent a hyperlink using the text between the opening and closing tags as the button's caption.

The opening page of the Unwired Widgets example from Chapter 2 is expanded here to demonstrate both text- and button-based hyperlinks using the anchor tag. The code is provided in the build_12 example on the CD and the changes are shown in Figure 3.17.

```
<html>

<head>
      <title>Product List</title>
      <meta name="palmcomputingplatform" content="true">
      <meta name="palmlauncherrevision" content="1.0">
</head>

<body>
      <h1>Unwired Widgets</h1>

      <p>Find the widget that suits your needs.

      <p>View our entire <a href="product%20list.html">
      <b>product list</b></a> or browse by starting with one of
      the following widget sizes.

      <p><a href="large.html" button>large</a>
      <p><a href="small.html" button>small</a>
</body>

</html>
```

Figure 3.17 Anchor Tag Example Using Both Text and Button Hyperlinks

As a general rule, links to a document containing other information in an application should use a textual hyperlink. Consider using a button as a hyperlink for links in a document that execute a command or submit data for processing. When Clipper shows hyperlinks, it will append a wireless icon or a secure wireless icon to the link text if the link is to something over the Internet. This is done automatically for you, and you can't disable this. Because all of the links in the example for Figure 3.17 are to local files, you do not see the wireless icon in the screen shot.

Line Breaks:

Similar to the paragraph tag, the break tag, <BR>, ends the current line and starts a new line below for the next document element. The length of the break is similar to the break between lines of sentences in a paragraph instead of the longer break in-between paragraphs.

Lines of text that are not considered first sentences for paragraphs can be separated by adding break tags to the end of each line. The following example, provided in the build_13 example on the CD, shows two sentences separated by paragraph tags and break tags. Notice the smaller spacing in the break tag. The results are shown in Figure 3.18.

```
<html>

<head>
    <title>Palm, Inc.</title>

    <meta name="palmcomputingplatform" content="true">
    <meta name="palmlauncherrevision" content="1.0">
</head>

<body>
    <p>Palm, Inc. sells the world's favorite handheld
    computers.<br>
    We also license the Palm OS® to world-class companies.<br>
    <p>Palm, Inc. sells the world's favorite handheld
    computers.</p>
    <p>We also license the Palm OS® to world-class
```

```
      companies.</p>
</body>


</html>
```

Figure 3.18 Break Tags versus Paragraph Tags

Linking to Application Pages and Web Sites

The attributes and values for the anchor tag were introduced earlier in this chapter. There are, however, some caveats when creating hyperlinks in Web clipping to elements in the same Web clipping application, different Web clipping applications, and external Web sites.

In the Unwired Widgets example in Chapter 2, two hyperlinks were presented for displaying the entire product list or selecting a widget by shape, size, or color. These hyperlinks presented two different pages within the same Web clipping application:

```
<a href="product list.html">product list</a>
<a href="browse.html">shape, size and color</a>
```

This example created and referenced all of the HTML documents in the application in the same directory. A Web clipping application can be developed and built with documents and images located in subdirectories. For example, suppose the product list document was placed in a subdirectory—called *products*—underneath the root application directory. The link for the product list would be as follows:

```
<a href="products/product list.html">product list</a>
```

Notice that the directory specification is relative to the root and not absolute to the physical location of the document on the local computer.

When a Web clipping application is built from a local file set with subdirectories, the Web Clipping Application Builder collapses all the subdirectories into a single directory to build the PQA file. The product list.html file in the last code example is now located and referenced in the root directory of the PQA instead of the products subdirectory.

In addition to linking to documents and images in the same Web clipping application, one Web clipping application can link to a different Web clipping application entirely. For example, Unwired Widgets might provide a link to the Web clipping application file for their edge distributor Edge Resources, named edge.pqa, also installed on the device. The link to the Edge Resources PQA would be the following:

```
<a href="file:edge.pqa">Edge Resoources</a>
```

However, if the developer for the Edge Resources PQA stored all documents in a subdirectory called *documents* off the root, the link for the company profile page in the application would *not* include the relative subdirectory. Web clipping application subdirectories are flattened into one directory when built by the WCA Builder. Therefore, a link to the profile.html page in the documents directory of the edge.pqa would not include the relative subdirectory:

```
<a href="file:edge.pqa/profile.html">Company Profile</a>
```

Hyperlinks can also be created for remote pages and graphics located over the air. For example, a link for the Palm OS Web page would be the following (provided in the build_14 example on the CD):

```
<a href="http://www.palmos.com">Visit the Palm OS page</a>
```

Notice that in Figure 3.19, the link to the Palm OS site adds an over-the-air icon to the end of the link to represent that a wireless transaction must occur to retrieve the page.

Figure 3.19 Link to the Palm OS Web Page

Secure links (Secure HTTP [HTTPS]) can also be defined. Notice that in Figure 3.20, the secure over-the-air icon—an over-the-air icon with a key to represent security—is added to the end of the link.

```
<a href="https://www.securesite.com">Secure Site</a>
```

Figure 3.20 Link to a Secure Web Page

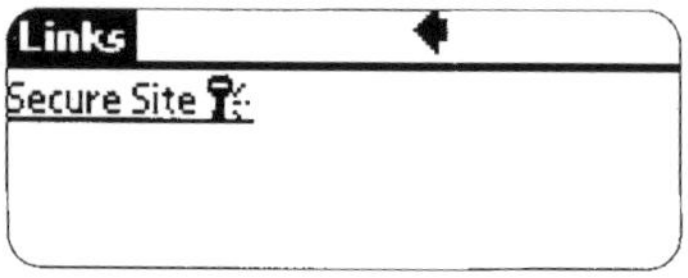

Finally, links can be created to launch Palm OS applications. Chapter 10 describes using *palm* and *palmcall* URL links to run other programs on the Palm OS device.

Example: Linking to www.unwiredwidgets.com

Because each tag defined in this chapter has an example to demonstrate its use, the example for this chapter focuses on adding a link to the Unwired Widgets Web page in the example from Chapter 2. Even though the static product information stored in the application is current, adding a link to the main Web page can keep customers up to date with recent company news and product specials.

The link to the main page will be added to the opening page below the product list and shape, size, and color links. To separate this local link from the new remote link, a horizontal line will be used to separate the two groups of links.

The following example is the revised HTML code for the application index, provided in the Unwired Widgets example for Chapter 3 on the CD. The rendering of the HTML is shown in Figure 3.21.

```
<html>

<head>
      <title>Product List</title>
      <meta name="palmcomputingplatform" content="true">
      <meta name="palmlauncherrevision" content="1.0">
</head>
```

```
<body>
      <h1>Unwired Widgets</h1>

      <p>Find the widget that suits your needs.

      <p>View our entire <a href="product list.html">product
      list</a> or browse by <a href="browse.html">shape, size
      and color</a>.

      <p><hr>

      <p>Visit the <a href="http://www.unwiredwidgets.com">Unwired
      Widgets</a> homepage for company news and product specials.
</body>

</html>
```

Figure 3.21 Unwired Widgets Example with Web Page Link

Tapping the Unwired Widgets link downloads the Unwired Widgets home page (shown in Figure 3.22). This page has been designed with the Clipper browser and Web clipping model in mind.

Figure 3.22 Unwired Widgets Home Page

Summary

The definition of HTML used in Web clipping applications and the Clipper browser closely mirrors the HTML 3.2 definition supported by most of today's Web browsers. Some elements of the HTML 3.2 specification are not included in Web clipping because they do not apply to the model or do not render well on the small screens of Palm OS devices. Some tags are added by Palm, Inc. to their Web clipping HTML that are Palm OS–specific, such as the META tags for defining document characteristics specific to the Clipper browser.

In both the HTML 3.2 and the Web clipping specification, the header section of an HTML document defines characteristics that are specific to the browser itself. Aside from the <TITLE> tag, definitions in the header section generally do not directly appear in the browser window itself. Instead, these tags define how the document is treated and rendered by both the Palm.Net proxy and the Clipper browser.

The body section defines the layout and content displayed in the browser window. Text and images are defined and formatted by a wide variety of HTML tags including block tags for formatting large blocks of text such as paragraphs, and text tags for small blocks of text such as formatting phrases or lines. Nearly all body tags in the HTML 3.2 specification are supported in the Web clipping specification by the Clipper browser, with minor changes.

Solutions Fast Track

Starting HTML Documents with a Header

☑ Tags in the header section of an HTML document define properties that apply to the entire document. This includes information such as the title of the page, who made it, and if it is a "Palm-friendly" document. These header tags are not shown directly to the user, although they might affect how the page is displayed.

☑ The header is completely enclosed in a <HEAD> tag, starting with <HEAD> and ending with </HEAD>. If you specify the header-specific tags outside of a <HEAD> section, you will have an invalid HTML document, and the browser might ignore their values.

☑ You should supply a title in each document and keep the length of this text short.

- ☑ The PalmComputingPlatform META tag tells the Palm.Net proxy that the page was designed specifically for the Clipper browser. The PalmLauncherName, PalmLauncherRevision, PalmLargeIconFilename, and PalmSmallIconFilename META tags can be added to your main page to affect how the Web clipping application appears in the Palm OS Launcher.

Providing HTML Content with Block and Text Markup Body Tags

- ☑ Body tags define the content and page presentation of a Web document. The most common body tags available in the HTML 3.2 specification are available in the Web clipping HTML definition. Content with these tags applied may render differently to fit the small Palm OS device's screen.
- ☑ The body of the HTML document should start with a <BODY> tag and close with </BODY>.
- ☑ Block markup tags are used to describe sections of text. A new block of text will be separated from the last block by whitespace. Block markup tags format paragraphs (<P>), small and large headline text (<H1>, <H2>, and so on), horizontal lines (<HR>), sizing and alignment of images (<IMG>), lists (<OL> and <UL>), and tables (<TABLE>).
- ☑ Text markup tags let you change the appearance at the character and word level. These tags are generally used in short stretches of text to provide some sort of special effect, such as making the text boldface or italic. Text markup tags include *physical markup tags* (bold <B>, italic <I>, and so on), font size and color, logical markup tags (strong <STRONG>, emphasized <EM>, and so on), hypertext links (<A>), and line breaks (<BR>).

Linking to Application Pages and Web Sites

- ☑ A Web application can link to documents and images in the same Web clipping application; it can be developed and built with documents and images in the same directory or located in subdirectories. The directory specification is relative to the root and not absolute to the physical location of the document on the local computer.

- ☑ When a Web clipping application is built from a local file set with subdirectories, the Web Clipping Application Builder collapses all the subdirectories into a single directory to build the PQA file.
- ☑ One Web clipping application can link to a different Web clipping application entirely.
- ☑ Hyperlinks can also be created for remote pages and graphics located over the air. Secure links (HTTPS) can also be defined.

Frequently Asked Questions

The following Frequently Asked Questions, answered by the authors of this book, are designed to both measure your understanding of the concepts presented in this chapter and to assist you with real-life implementation of these concepts. To have your questions about this chapter answered by the author, browse to **www.syngress.com/solutions** and click on the **"Ask the Author"** form.

Q: Is the Document Type Description (DTD) for the Web clipping HTML specification available?

A: Yes. Palm, Inc. has published both the 1.0 and 2.0 definitions in the appendix of its "Web Clipping Guide" document. For the uninitiated, the Palm OS HTML DTD defines the syntax used to develop HTML documents for the Clipper browser. A DTD itself is written in Standard Generalized Markup Language (SGML), a meta-language used to define other languages.

Q: What happens if the Clipper browser encounters a tag not in the Palm OS HTML specification?

A: Most of the time Clipper completely ignores the tag and any text inside the tag. If the rogue tag appears to be a block tag, Clipper ignores the tags and text between the tags. However, Clipper should rarely encounter tags that are not in the specification, because the Web Clipping Application Builder combs application documents and flags rogue tags as errors for the programmer to resolve. The only time Clipper would have to resolve an invalid tag is when it receives dynamic content from a remote Web server.

Q: Which tags in typical HTML documents deserve a review for the Web clipping environment?

A: First, take a look for header tags <H4> through <H6> and consider reorganizing the header structure to exclude these tags. Second, tables embedded inside tables are not permitted in Web clipping. Third, consider converting hyperlink images to a textual or button hyperlink. Finally, Clipper doesn't support any sort of browser-based scripting, so a site that depends on JavaScript or VBScript will need to be redesigned.

Q: Where can I find a template for a new Palm OS Web page?

A: For plain pages, start with this template:

```
<html>
<head>
<title>TITLE</title>
<meta name="PalmComputingPlatform" content="true">
</head>
<body>
<h1>TITLE<h1>
<p>TEXT</p>
</body>
</html>
```

Save this to a new file, then start replacing the boilerplate text and adding additional tags. If you are designing a large site, you probably should start by defining a more specific template and then build your pages based on that.

Chapter 4

Using Images in Web Clipping Applications

Solutions in this chapter:

- Dealing with Limited Screen Size
- Specifying Nonlinked Images
- Using Colors and Grayscale
- Optimizing Image Size
- Using the Palm Image Checker to Validate Your Images
- Adding Images to the Widget Catalog Example
- Widget Banner Ads Example

☑ Summary

☑ Solutions Fast Track

☑ Frequently Asked Questions

Introduction

Because of the Palm OS device's limited screen size and memory, coupled with the limitations of wireless bandwidth, developers need to be much more careful in the use of graphics in Web clipping applications (WCAs). However, in many cases, images can be used to good effect to convey information economically. Graphics can add a lot in terms of aesthetics and usability to your Web clipping application. Well-designed navigational graphics can make it easier and more intuitive for visitors to navigate around your site, and for applications such as Web catalogs, a single image may convey more information in a small space than a text description could.

If you're familiar with optimizing graphics for display on the Web, many of the same principles apply for Palm OS devices. You'll need to take extra care to keep size and color depth to an absolute minimum. Web clipping provides a mechanism for storing graphics on the device to avoid downloading them over a slow wireless link. You can link to these precompiled graphics both from local pages as well as from pages downloaded over the Internet. The Palm.Net proxy can also be of some help, because it will resample online graphics to monochrome if the device making the request does not support color.

Web clipping can use the two most common Web graphic formats: CompuServe Graphics Interchange Format (GIF) and Joint Photography Experts Group (JPEG). Although the first version of Web clipping didn't support color, Palm OS 4.0 adds color on those devices that support it. Devices running version 4.0 of the Palm OS send device capability information to the Palm.Net proxy server, which allows the proxy server to send images with the correct bit depth back to the device. But because a large percentage of the Palm OS devices currently in circulation have only monochrome screens, you'll want to make sure that your graphics also look good on these devices.

Dealing with Limited Screen Size

Most of the Palm OS-based devices currently available have a screen size of 160 by 160 pixels. When you subtract the areas reserved for the title/menu bar and the right-side scrollbar, you're left with an effective screen size of 153 pixels wide by 144 pixels high. In addition, Palm OS 3.5 and earlier didn't support horizontal scrolling. Any table content, for instance, that went beyond 153 pixels was simply cropped off; images wider than 153 pixels were simply removed by the Palm.Net proxy, so they were never even sent to the device. Although vertical scrolling is possible—either with the onscreen scrollbar or the rocker switch—you generally should avoid graphics larger than 144 pixels high. Palm OS 4.0 does add the capability to scroll horizontally, but this is awkward and should be avoided. This hard limit on screen size means that Palm OS developers need to be very creative in their use of page layout and graphics.

Throughout the rest of this chapter we refer to *remote* and *local* images and pages. *Remote* means files that reside on a Web server; they are downloaded to the Palm OS device every time they're needed on a Web clipping page. *Local* images and pages are compiled into the WCA when you run the WCA Builder. That means they're already available on the device and don't need to be downloaded. You can refer to local images from local pages as well as from pages stored on a Web server. This is a useful technique; on pages downloaded from the Internet, even those generated dynamically, you can refer to graphics already present on the device. Your visitors don't have to download the graphics over a slow wireless connection; all that's sent is the text of the <IMG> tag.

You include images in your Web clipping pages using the familiar Hypertext Markup Language (HTML) <IMG> tag. Table 4.1 details the required and optional attributes for the tag. Later, we look at when and how to use some of the optional attributes. Note that because Web clipping does not support imagemaps, the *ismap* and *usemap* attributes are not supported. You also can't use images as <FORM> submit buttons.

Table 4.1 Required and Optional Attributes of the <IMG> Tag

Attribute	Definition
Src	Required: Identifies the URL for the image file.
align	Optional: Identifies the alignment of the image in relation to any text around it.
alt	Optional: Describes the image in case graphics are turned off on the device.
border	Optional: Indicates the border width around the image; 0 (or no border) by default.
height/width	Optional: Specifies the height and width (in pixels) of the image file as displayed.
hspace/vspace	Optional: Specifies the amount of space—either horizontally or vertically—between the image as displayed and any text around it.

How you use the <IMG> tag depends on whether you intend to refer to local or remote images, and also on whether the link is on a local or remote page. The basic syntax for the tag is just the same as it is in regular HTML:

```
<img src="image01.gif">
```

This expects the file image01.gif to be present wherever the page referencing it is located. So if this link were on a remote page, the image file would also need to be in the same folder on your Web server. If this link is on a local page of the WCA, it will expect the image to also be available locally. Beware when using links to images in subfolders; Web clipping does not support subfolders, and it will flatten the local folder hierarchy when compiling the WCA. See the "Flattened Folder Hierarchy" sidebar for more information.

Developing & Deploying…

Flattened Folder Hierarchy

Web developers customarily keep images in subfolders to keep their root folders less cluttered. Sometimes they will use multiple subfolders. For example, this might be a typical structure:

```
Document Root/
              index.html
              about.html
              contact.html
                /images
                      /top_nav/
                              img01.gif
                              img02.gif
                              logo.gif
                      /bottom_nav/
                              img03.gif
                              img04.gif
                              logo.gif
```

Continued

However, Web clipping does not support subfolders. The folder hierarchy will be collapsed when you compile your WCA. This has a couple of ramifications that are important to remember when writing your <IMG> links.

If the images are referenced in any of the local WCA pages, the WCA Builder will move those graphics to the root folder level and alter any links on those pages so that they refer to images only in the root folder. However, if you refer to local graphics from your remote pages, make sure that you don't use folder names:

```
<img src="file:mywca.pqa/images/top_nav/img01.gif">
```

This tag will not work—that folder does not exist on the WCA. The correct way to write this link would be as follows:

```
<img src="file:mywca.pqa/img01.gif">
```

If you look again at the folder hierarchy, you may notice another potential problem. Two folders have an image with the same name (logo.gif). Moving these both to the root folder would result in two files with the same name. When the WCA Builder tries to compile a page referencing both of these, it will display an error due to the duplicate filenames.

Although the folder hierarchy is flattened in the local WCA, you can, however, continue to use subfolders on your remote pages. You just need to be careful when writing the <IMG> links. Consider the following link:

```
<img src="top_nav/image01.gif">
```

If this link is on one of the local pages compiled into the WCA, the Builder will move the image into the root folder, and rewrite the link accordingly. But if this code is on a remote page, your Palm OS device will download the image from the *top_nav* folder on your Web server.

Use of the LocalIcon META Tag

As we mentioned earlier, you can reference local graphics even in remote pages downloaded from the server. If the graphic in question is referenced even once in a local page (that is, one of the pages in the WCA), it will already be compiled into the WCA. But what if you want to store a graphic locally that's referenced only from remote pages? The Palm OS provides a special META tag for this purpose: LocalIcon. Use this tag to instruct the WCA Builder to compile graphics into the WCA that are not referenced in any of the local pages. This provides a very powerful means of preloading all the graphics you'll need, so that the user doesn't have to download them when viewed.

```
<html>
      <head>
            <meta name="palmcomputingplatform" content="true">
            <meta name="LocalIcon" content="widget01.gif">
            <meta name="LocalIcon" content="widget02.gif">
            <title>Unwired Widgets</title>
      </head>
<body>
... etc
```

Use the LocalIcon META tag in the <HEAD> section of your index page. Placing these tags on your index page isn't required—they can be on any local page—but keeping them all together on the main index page makes it easier to debug any image problems later. You'll need one tag for each graphic you want to include (see Figure 4.1).

NOTE

You can use the LocalIcon META tag to include HTML pages in your WCA that are not linked from any local pages. That way, you can refer to these pages from remote pages, exactly like you would for graphics. In this case, the format of the META tag would be as follows:

```
<meta name="LocalIcon" content="about.html">
```

You would refer to this page from a remote page with this link syntax:

```
<a href="file:mywca.pqa/about.html">About Us</a>
```

Figure 4.1 Referencing Images with the LocalIcon META Tag Includes Them in the Compiled WCA

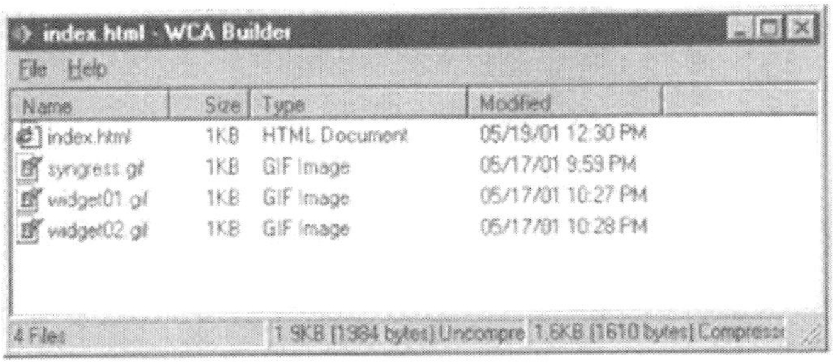

Specifying Nonlinked Images

We've used the LocalIcon META tag to include images in our WCA that are not referenced from any local files—now how do we reference these graphics from our remote pages? The syntax of the link is as follows:

```
<img src="file:mywca.pqa/widget01.gif">
```

Remember, we also discovered that the WCA Builder collapses the folder hierarchy, so don't include any folder names in the link. All images are assumed to be in the root folder of your WCA.

The use of nonlinked images compiled into the WCA is a powerful way to drastically reduce the amount of data your users need to download over a slow wireless link. All you need to send over the air is the link text, so the image will load almost instantly. For instance, we could precompile all of the Unwired Widgets product shots into the WCA, so that wireless visitors could browse the catalog and pull up product detail pages almost instantly. However, the drawback to this is that your available stock of images is frozen; the only way to add more images is to have your users download and install a new WCA. You'll need to weigh the benefits of speed against how often you think your product assortment is likely to change.

Figure 4.2 shows a sample page that you would place on the Web server. This file is also available on the accompanying CD as figure4_2.html.

Figure 4.2 Sample Remote Page Linking to Local and Remote Graphics (figure4_2.html)

```
<html>
     <head>
          <meta name="palmcomputingplatform" content="true">
          <title>Unwired Widgets</title>
     </head>
<body>
This page has been downloaded from the Web server, via the
    Palm.net proxy.
<hr>
<img src="file:mywca.pqa/widget01.gif"><br>
This graphic is local to the WCA,
    so it loads immediately.
<hr>
<img src="images/widget03.gif"><br>
This remote graphic is on the Web server, in the "images" folder, so it
    must first be converted by the Palm.net proxy, then downloaded to
    the Palm.
</body>
</html>
```

For the example in Figure 4.2 to work, you'll need to create a WCA that contains the graphic file widget01.gif, using the LocalIcon syntax we looked at in the previous section, and build this as mywca.pqa. This WCA is also included on the companion CD.

Table 4.1 listed the optional attributes of the <IMG> tag. The main ones of interest in this example are the *height* and *width* attributes. Generally, in regular Web pages, always including these attributes, as well as the ALT text, is a good idea. However, unless you're purposely resizing images, as we look at later, you can save on download times by omitting these attributes from your remote pages. You'll notice that in this code we left these attributes out entirely in order to save a few bytes of download. On a small page, this might not seem like a lot, but over a slow wireless link, where every byte counts, anything you can do to speed downloads is probably worth it. Web clipping under Palm OS 4.0 allows people to choose to switch off graphics completely, so if your images provide navigation, you may want to keep informative ALT tags on these, but you could omit ALT tags on purely decorative graphics or on product images.

The other attributes of the <IMG> tag work almost identically to regular HTML. One difference worth noting is that Clipper won't automatically put a border around images that are used as HREF links. If you want this, you need to set *BORDER="1"*. Currently, Web clipping supports only border widths of one pixel.

Using Colors and Grayscale

We take a slight detour here to briefly explain the intricacies of color bit depth. We take two factors into account when discussing bit depth: the bit depth of the image file and the capabilities of the display device.

Bit depth is a method used to describe the number of possible discrete colors that a graphic file is capable of producing. For instance, a 1-bit image has exactly one bit, or binary number, to describe the color of each pixel. The options are pretty limited: 0 or 1, which equates to either pure black or pure white. A 2-bit image, on the other hand, has a vastly expanded palette: four distinct shades, also referred to as grayscale. Four-bit grayscale allows us to display just 16 distinct shades of gray, whereas 8-bit grayscale allows us to display continuous-tone photographic images with 256 shades of gray. Figure 4.3 shows the levels of detail available with these four grayscale bit depths.

Figure 4.3 Bit Depth and Shades of Gray

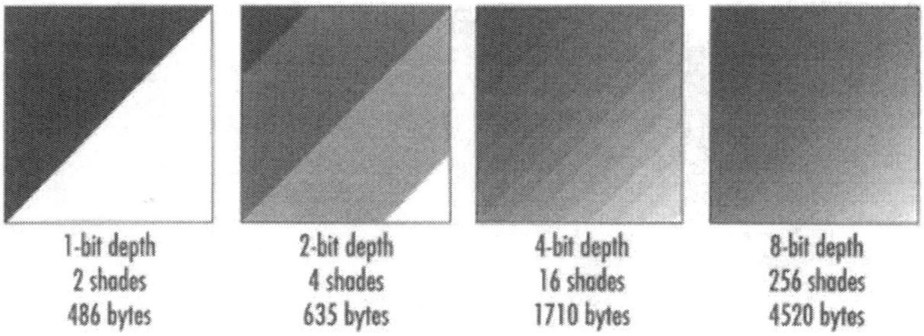

The early Palm OS models could display just black and white (or black and greenish, to be more exact). Any Palm OS device with the Dragonball EZ or VZ processor and with Palm OS 3.5 or later has the capability to do 4-bit grayscale.

(The exceptions are the Palm IIIc and the newer Palm m505, which we discuss later.) However, the original Web clipping specification allowed for only four shades of gray, presumably as a way of limiting the size of files downloaded to the slower Palm VII. The Palm.Net proxy actually converts any remote images to 2-bit grayscale before downloading to the device. The original Query Application Builder (QAB) also converted images to 2-bit before compiling into a WCA. The four colors you have available for most devices are black, silver, gray, and white. Table 4.2 lists these colors, along with their hexadecimal equivalents.

Table 4.2 Available Screen Colors with Hexadecimal Values

Color Name	Hex
Black	#000000
Silver	#C0C0C0
Gray	#808080
White	#FFFFFF

Palm OS 4.0 now allows for up to 4-bit grayscale and either 8-bit or 16-bit color on devices that support these bit depths. The WCA Builder included with the Palm OS 4.0 Software Development Kit (SDK) allows you to specify different bit depths in your WCA (see Figure 4.4).

Figure 4.4 Specifying the Bit Depth of Your WCA in the WCA Builder

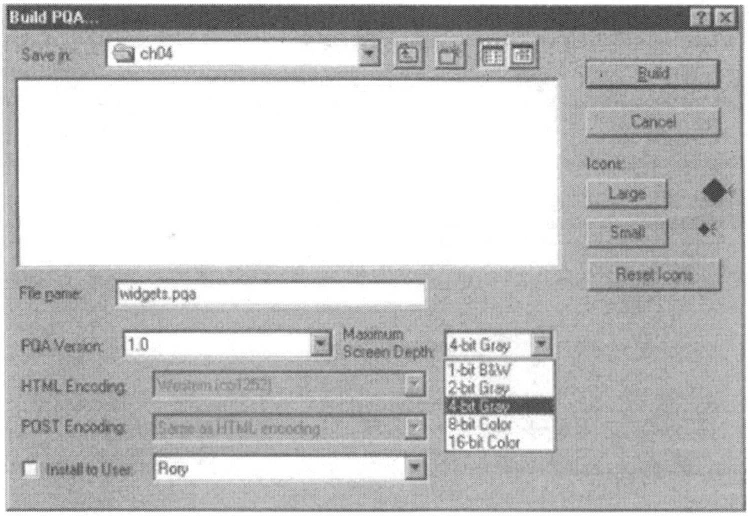

Eight-bit color will give you 256 colors, which on a screen the size of the Palm OS device should give you more than enough clarity to display full-color photographs. Eight-bit color yields a possible 65,000 colors, which takes full advantage of the new m505 Palm and Visor Prism.

Minimizing Bandwidth with Black and White

If you take a look back at Figure 4.3, you'll notice that file sizes increase significantly with added bit depth. If your visitors are using a device with Palm OS 3.5 or earlier, they will never see all of the shades of gray in the 4-bit and 8-bit images. However, the Palm.Net proxy is still going to have to download the full size image and reprocess it to 2-bit before sending down to the device.

Unless your images demand high resolution or full color, you can save your visitors a lot of time (and money, if they are using a per-kilobyte wireless plan) by restricting your graphics to the fewest possible colors. Line art images, for instance, seldom require the full range of grays. If your images are mainly line art or graphical text, consider restricting them to pure black and white. Doing so will increase the speed of download of your pages and result in a more responsive WCA. The Picture Viewer included with the Palm OS 4.0 SDK allows you to experiment with different bit depths and preview how they'll look after conversion by the Palm.Net proxy.

Smoothing Things Out with Grayscale

Photographic images generally won't work well in black and white. If you're using a device running Palm OS 3.5, you have the option of using 2-bit grayscale, which gives you four shades of gray. Although photographic images don't convert well to four shades of gray, at least with the default settings on the Palm.Net proxy, you can often improve the quality significantly by using the contrast and brightness controls in an image-editing program such as Adobe Photoshop or Jasc's Paint Shop Pro to convert the image to grayscale yourself. Good image-editing programs also allow you to apply *dithering,* which can approximate more shades of gray by using closely spaced dots of the available colors.

Using Full Color on Palm OS 4.0

Devices running Palm OS 4.0 can display higher bit depths and color images. Monochrome devices such as the Palm VIIx or Palm Vx are capable of displaying up to 16 shades of gray. The Palm m505 can display 65,000 different colors. As color Palm OS devices become more popular, you can design much more visually appealing mobile Web sites, but to accommodate the large current installed base of monochrome devices, you should ensure that your color images convert well to 4-bit grayscale. This is especially true of navigational images that use colored text on a colored background—when converted to four shades of gray, the text can effectively disappear, rendering your navigation useless to users with monochrome devices.

Optimizing Image Size

The size of files downloaded over the Internet should always be a concern to Web page designers, but this is even more critical when dealing with the extremely slow speeds of typical wireless links. Optimizing is the process of preparing your images so that their file sizes are as small as possible. You can achieve this in a number of ways.

The first and most obvious way to decrease file size is simply to decrease the physical dimensions of your image. The visible area of the Palm OS screen is 153 pixels wide by 144 pixels high. Versions prior to Palm OS 4.0, didn't support horizontal scrolling; the Palm.Net proxy server simply removed any images wider than 153 pixels before sending the page down to the device. You can make images taller than 144 pixels, but users then need to scroll to see them. Although there's no physical reason you can't fill the screen with an image, it's best to keep images as small as possible.

A major factor affecting image file size is the effectiveness of the compression scheme used to save it. *Compression* is the process of removing extraneous information from the image in order to make it take up less space. Both of the file formats supported by Web clipping perform some compression on the image as they save it. However, in this regard, all image-editing programs are not created equal. Certain programs perform a much better job of optimizing the quality of the image while simultaneously creating a smaller file size. Macromedia Fireworks is a program specifically designed for producing graphics that are optimized for the Web. At identical image quality, it will typically make significantly smaller file sizes than programs such as Adobe Photoshop. One especially useful feature in Fireworks is the Export Preview screen, which allows you to view the effects of varying file formats and color depths and make a visual comparison of image quality versus file size (see Figure 4.5).

Although optimizing images can make a major difference in regular Web pages, it's not quite so critical in Web clipping. The reason is that your actual GIF or JPG file is not downloaded directly to the device. All graphics downloaded to

Web clipping applications are first processed through the Palm.Net proxy, which converts them to its own 2-bit grayscale bitmap format before sending them over the air. The WCA Builder does the same for local graphics. The conversion process is actually quite efficient; identical graphics in either format, but with varying levels of compression, will generally convert down to the same size. However, your remote images still need to be downloaded to the Palm.Net proxy, so optimizing them for smaller file sizes is still a good idea.

Figure 4.5 Fireworks' Export Preview Screen Shows File Sizes for Various Color Depths

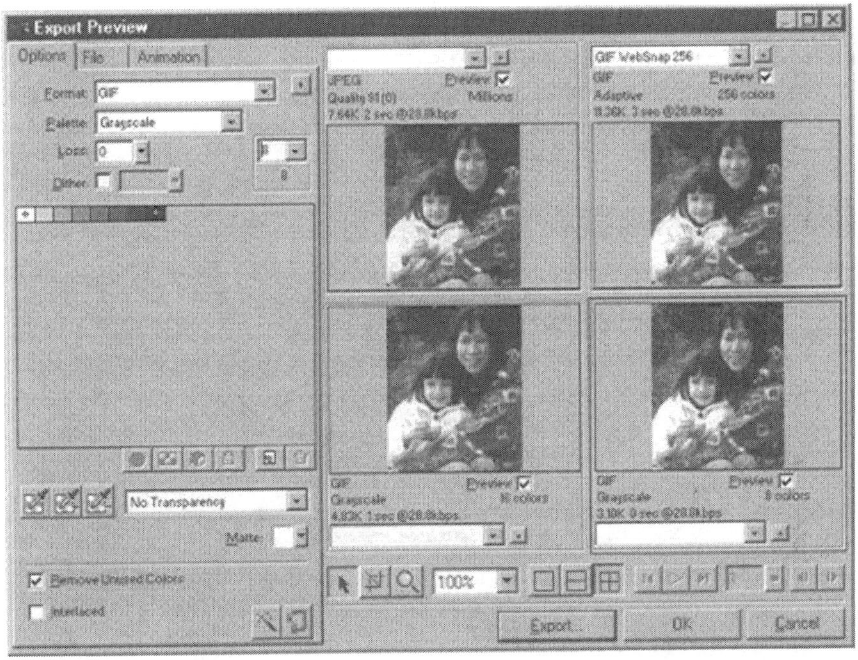

However, this efficiency does come at some cost. Although most small graphics, particularly line art and text, usually convert quite well, photographic images frequently look bad after conversion. This is especially true if the image you start with is in full color. The Palm.Net proxy will first need to convert the image to grayscale, discarding all color information. But, it has no way of knowing which colors are important or contain critical detail. It then attempts to represent the full range of tones in the original with just four shades of gray. If you intend to use photographic images or other graphics with very subtle shading, use an image-editing program to first convert the graphics to grayscale yourself. Most image-editing programs have sophisticated controls for brightness and contrast that allow you to get a much more pleasing conversion. In some cases, particularly with faces, it may be necessary to use image-editing tools to selectively convert some areas differently than others in order to end up with pleasing images.

Using the Palm Image Checker to Validate Your Images

Palm, Inc. includes a program with the WCA Builder called the Palm Image Checker (PIC), which allows you to preview how your images will look on a Palm OS device after the conversion process (See Figure 4.6). In the folder that includes the WCA Builder (or Query Application Builder, if you're using the 3.5 SDK), look for a file called pic.exe.

Figure 4.6 Previewing a Graphic in the Palm Image Checker

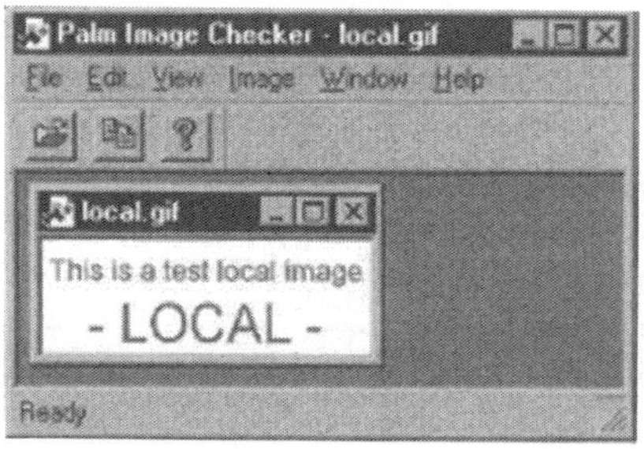

The Palm Image Checker is not a sophisticated program. In fact, all it does is show you the result of processing your images through the Palm.Net proxy. There's no option to save, although you can copy and paste into your image-editing program. PIC also allows you to resize images, but because it doesn't have a **Save** option, you're probably better off doing the resizing in your image-editing software.

Before compiling graphics into your Palm Query Application (PQA), or uploading to your Web server, particularly if image quality is critical, it's a good idea to quickly check them through PIC. Figure 4.7 shows a small JPG image and the result of previewing it through PIC. Although the subjects are vaguely recognizable, it's not the most pleasing rendition.

Figure 4.7 PIC's First Pass at Converting a JPG Image

Programs such as Adobe Photoshop or Jasc's Paint Shop Pro have sophisticated controls for selectively adjusting brightness and contrast. We used Macromedia Fireworks to convert the original image to grayscale, and then performed some minimal adjustments of brightness and contrast. Figure 4.8 shows the difference in PIC.

Figure 4.8 The Same Image Converted to Grayscale and Adjusted

Although you're still limited by having only four shades of gray to represent the full range of colors in the original image, you can see that even minimal changes to the image with an image-editing program can improve the final result.

When previewing images in PIC, bear in mind that this is still using your high-resolution desktop screen. When you display the image on your Palm OS device's greenish or grayish screen, it will look different. This is also subject to the brightness and contrast settings on the particular Palm OS device, something you may have no control over.

Experimenting with Color Depth

In the first version of the Query Application Builder, you had no choice regarding color depth; all images were reduced to 2-bit grayscale during the build process. The Palm OS 4.0 SDK ships with an updated PIC 1.5 that adds the capability to preview your images in different bit depths. Figure 4.9 shows the same image in 2-bit grayscale, 4-bit grayscale, 8-bit color, and 16-bit color, from left to right.

Figure 4.9 Previewing Different Bit Depths in PIC

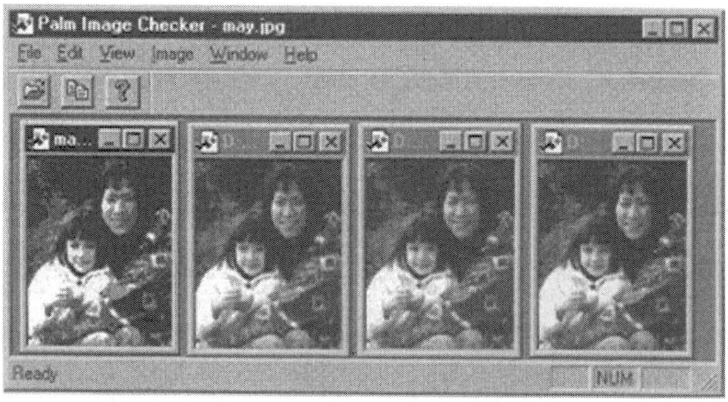

Bear in mind that images with higher bit depth will take more space to store in the WCA. If you just have a few images, this shouldn't be a problem, but if you have a lot of them, you could potentially end up with quite a large WCA. As an indication, a simple WCA with our earlier sample image encoded at the 4-bit depths shown yields the file sizes shown in Table 4.3.

Table 4.3 Relative File Sizes for Various Bit Depths

Bit Depth	File Size
Base JPEG	6.89KB
2-bit gray	2.06KB
4-bit gray	7.27KB
8-bit color	15.6KB
16-bit color	36.4KB

When building your WCA, you need to specify at what bit depth to store the images (see Figure 4.10). If all of your images are already 2-bit gray, you don't need to store them at any higher bit depth. But if your images are in color, and you would like suitably equipped visitors to see these at their best, select higher. Do bear in mind the relative file sizes for each, as shown in Table 4.3.

Note that these settings apply only to local images stored in the WCA. The Palm.Net proxy will still intercede and downshift remote graphics to the appropriate bit depth for the requesting device. Palm OS devices running Palm OS 4.0 now send device capability information to the proxy server, which allows the proxy server to send images with the correct bit depth back to the device.

NOTE

If you look at Figure 4.10, you'll also notice a drop-down box for **PQA Version**. The default is 1.0. You can also select 2.0, but doing so will build your WCA in such a way that it will work only on Palm OS devices running OS 4.0 or later. If you try to run it on version 3.5 or earlier, you'll get an error message. Unless your WCA takes specific advantage of some feature unique to OS 4.0 (such as cookies or cache control), we recommend using version 1.0. This makes your Web clipping application viewable by the largest number of people. A META tag specifies this version number, but this can only be used in local pages; it is ignored for remote pages downloaded over the Internet.

```
<meta name="PalmPQAVersion" content="2">
```

Figure 4.10 Specifying Bit Depth with the WCA Builder

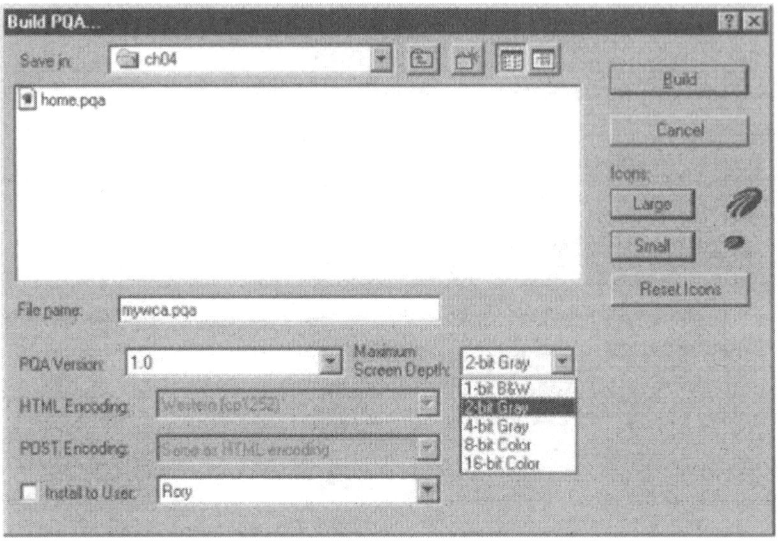

Resizing Images

A common trick in regular Web page design is to use a small graphic—often only 1 pixel in size—and "stretch" it by overstating the *width* or *height* attributes. This doesn't work the same way in Web clipping. You can reference stretched images in local pages, and the WCA Builder will resize the image before compiling it into the WCA. For example, let's say you have a graphic that's five pixels wide and reference it like this in a local page:

```
<img src="img01.gif" width="153">
```

When you run the WCA Builder, it will convert this graphic to 153 pixels wide before including it in the WCA. However, you can *not* reference the same image more than once with different *height* or *width* attributes. For example, this will not work:

```
<img src="img01.gif" width="100">
<img src="img01.gif" width="50">
```

Because each file in a WCA must have a unique file name, the WCA Builder will display an error if you try to compile these lines.

You can reference the same remote graphic with different sizes if it is downloaded over the Web. In this case, each remote graphic will be resized by the Palm.Net proxy before being downloaded to your device, so this doesn't necessarily save you any download time.

PIC allows you to resize images and preview how they will look on a Palm OS device (see Figure 4.11), but again, because it doesn't have a **Save** option within PIC, you should probably do this in your image-editing program.

Figure 4.11 Resize and Redepth Images in PIC

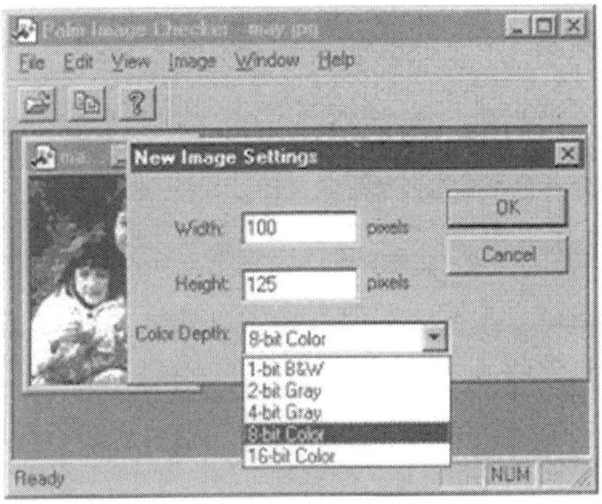

Adding Images to the Widget Catalog Example

Now that you know how to include both local and remote images in a WCA, let's put this to practical use. Because the Unwired Widgets company sells widgets in various shapes and sizes, wouldn't it be nice to allow visitors using a Palm OS device to browse the product catalog? We already discussed the possibility of storing all of the catalog images as local files on the WCA. For this example, we're going to assume that the product assortment changes too frequently to allow this, so we'll have to download those images over the Internet. But we'll still store some more-frequently used images locally. We'll also add a dash of color, so that visitors with color-enabled devices get to justify why they bought them.

The first task is to decide which images to include locally in the WCA. The obvious choice is the front "splash" page, which will have full-color images and serve as our home navigation page. We'll also make a title graphic for each subpage, again in full color. The code for this page is shown in Figure 4.12 and is also available on the companion CD.

Figure 4.12 Basic Code for Home Page (figure4_12.html)

```
<html>
  <head>
    <meta name="PalmComputingPlatform" content="true">
    <meta name="LocalIcon" content="hdr_about.gif">
    <meta name="LocalIcon" content="hdr_products.gif">
    <meta name="LocalIcon" content="hdr_contact.gif">
    <meta name="LocalIcon" content="hdr_square.gif">
    <meta name="LocalIcon" content="hdr_round.gif">
    <title>Unwired Widgets</title>
  </head>
<body>
<table width="153" border="0" cellspacing="0" cellpadding="0">
<tr>
    <td colspan="2">
        <img src="toplogo.gif" width="153" height="50">
    </td>
</tr>
<tr>
    <td>
        <a href="about.html">
         <img src="about.gif" width="63" height="30">
        </a><br>
        <a href="prod_menu.html">
         <img src="products.gif" width="63" height="30">
        </a><br>
        <a href="contact.html">
         <img src="contact.gif" width="63" height="30">
        </a>
    </td>
    <td>
```

Continued

Figure 4.12 Continued

```
        <img src="uw_logo.gif" width="90" height="90">
    </td>
</tr>
</table>
</body>
</html>
```

This page uses a simple table structure to hold several independent graphics that make up the image. (See Chapter 6 for more information on using HTML tables for laying out your WCA pages.) If you look at the image file dimensions, you'll see that this results in a page that's 153 pixels wide by 140 pixels high. We could, of course, have used a single full-screen graphic, but this page is also going to provide links to the other pages in the WCA, so we needed to be able to insert links; Web clipping does not support imagemaps. Figure 4.13 shows how this page would look on a color Palm device (see the color image on the CD that accompanies this book). The orange backgrounds of the independent graphics merge to give the impression of one large image with floating red text. A quick check with PIC ensures that these colors are still readable when converted to 2-bit grayscale. The HREF links wrapped around each of the navigation graphics means that these are clickable. When a user clicks one of these, the Palm OS device reverses the colors of that image to indicate that it has been clicked (a very neat feature that on a regular Web page would require several lines of JavaScript).

Figure 4.13 Our Colorful Home Page on a Palm m505 (figure4_13.tif)

Notice in the code in Figure 4.12 that we've also used LocalIcon to reference some graphics that are not used on this page, but that we'll want to refer to from some of our remote pages. If you'd like to construct this example, save the code in Figure 4.12 to your disk as home.html. You won't be able to build it just yet, until we create some of the linked pages.

Mindful of keeping over-the-air transmissions to a minimum, let's now add an intermediate product menu page (see Figure 4.14). This will allow visitors to choose whether they want square or round widgets before retrieving the product listing from our server. This code is available on the CD.

Figure 4.14 Intermediate Product Menu Page (figure4_14.html)

```
<html>
  <head>
  <meta name="PalmComputingPlatform" content="true">
  <title>Product Menu</title>
  </head>
<body bgcolor="#ffcc00">
<table width="153" border="0" cellspacing="0" cellpadding="0">
<tr>
  <td>
    <a href="home.html"><img src="hdr_uwlogo.gif"></a>
    <img src="hdr_products.gif" width="133" height="20">
  </td>
</tr>
<tr>
  <td height="100">
    We make a wide variety of widgets to suit all your needs.
    Choose from the links below to visit our site and view a
    full product listing.
    <p align="center">
    <a href="http://cgi.unwiredwidgets.com/product.cgi?type=square">
      Square Widgets</a>
    </p>
    <p align="center">
    <a href="http://cgi.unwiredwidgets.com/product.cgi?type=round">
```

Continued

Figure 4.14 Continued

```
        Round Widgets</a>
      </p>
    </td>
  </tr>
  <tr>
    <td>
      <a href="home.html"><img src="ftr_unwired.gif"></a>
    </td>
  </tr>
</table>
</body>
</html>
```

Notice a few things here. The <BODY> tag now has a *bgcolor* attribute. This allows us to set the background of the page to the same color as the header and footer graphics, resulting in a much more cohesive page layout. Do be careful with this attribute, because graphics aren't always converted to grayscale with the same colors as the page background. You may need to do a little experimenting here to get a scheme that works well in both grayscale and color. If you have a color Palm OS device, this page will give you a full-screen, light orange background with a red text header and footer. The page content is just black text. The header includes a miniature version of the Unwired Widgets logo we created earlier. On a monochrome Palm OS device, the background should be a light silver, with heavier gray for the header and footer text. Again, we used PIC to quickly verify that the screen would be readable in grayscale.

We've also broken the top header graphic into two pieces. The left-side small logo now links back to the home page, a convention we'll repeat throughout the WCA. Likewise, the footer graphic also links back to the home page. If you click on either of these graphics, the device will briefly reverse the colors—to signify that you've clicked the graphic—before returning you to the home page. Because this page is quite short and would not fill the device screen, we've added the attribute *height="100"* to the middle table cell to force the page to fill the screen.

If you're constructing these examples yourself, save the code in Figure 4.14 as prod_menu.html. You'll also find this on the companion CD as figure4_14.html.

Now, we'll construct a sample product-listing page that might be returned by the Web server (see Figure 4.15, also on the CD). Here we'll begin to see the benefit of storing images locally and referring to them from remote pages.

Figure 4.15 Product Listing Code Returned from the Server (figure4_15.html)

```
<html>
  <head>
  <meta name="PalmComputingPlatform" content="true">
  <title>Products</title>
  </head>
<body bgcolor="#ffcc00">
<table width="153" border="0" cellspacing="0" cellpadding="0">
<tr>
  <td>
    <a href="file:widgets.pqa/home.html">
      <img src="file:widgets.pqa/hdr_uwlogo.gif"></a>
      <img src="file:widgets.pqa/hdr_square.gif">
  </td>
</tr>
<tr>
  <td height="100">
    34345  
    <a href="http://cgi.unwiredwidgets.com/prod_detail.cgi?sku=34345">
     round-hole adapter</a>   Red<br>
    34875  
    <a href="http://cgi.unwiredwidgets.com/prod_detail.cgi?sku=34875">
     round-hole adapter</a>   Green<br>
    34876  
    <a href="http://cgi.unwiredwidgets.com/prod_detail.cgi?sku=34876">
     round-hole adapter</a>   Blue<br>
    34691  
    <a href="http://cgi.unwiredwidgets.com/prod_detail.cgi?sku=34691">
     round-hole adapter</a>   Yellow<br>
  </td>
</tr>
```

Continued

Figure 4.15 Continued

```
<tr>
  <td>
    <a href="file:widgets.pqa/home.html">
      <img src="file:widgets.pqa/ftr_unwired.gif"></a>
  </td>
</tr>
</table>
</body>
</html>
```

Remember, this is code that would be returned from the server and downloaded to the device. In a real application, the listing section of this page would likely be generated from a Common Gateway Interface (CGI) script, based on the query string sent from the prod_menu.html page (Figure 4.14). Notice in the first table row we use the *src="file:.."* format of the <IMG> tag to refer to graphics resident on the Palm OS device, saving our visitors the need to download these files. We also use this format for the link back to the home page, which is also local to the WCA:

```
<a href="file:widgets.pqa/home.html">
```

Further links on each individual product would lead to a product detail page, which would likewise use local graphics, as well as probably a link to a remote product shot. We've used <TD HEIGHT="100"> on this page again, so that if there are just a few products, the footer graphic is placed at the bottom of the screen. Had there been more products than would fit on one screen, this attribute would be overruled and the page would simply push down as far as was needed.

Widget Banner Ads Example

Banner advertisements are either the bane or the savior of the Web, depending on whom you ask. Either way, a lot of sites depend on these little HTML snippets for revenue or to drive traffic. Over time, some standards have evolved in the Web world for dimensions and file sizes for these little ads. No such standardization has taken place yet on the Palm OS. Moreover, the screen size and bandwidth limitations of wireless means that developers need to make extra efforts to ensure that banner ads don't interfere with the Web clipping's main function and don't overly inconvenience our wireless site's visitors.

Unwired Widgets wants to include banner ads for a select few partners on their wireless Web site. They considered using banner ads generated on a remote server, as is typically the case with Web banners, but decided this would negatively affect the experience of their site visitors using slow wireless links. Consequently, they decided to embed the banner ads into the WCA, so that they would load instantly. The drawback to this is that adding new banner ads isn't easy—other than having people install a new WCA.

We first need to decide on dimensions for these banners. Obviously, width is decided for us—153 pixels is as much as we can use. Most banner ads tend to be placed towards the top of the page, or "above the fold." Given that we have only 144 pixels of visible space, we need to make a hard decision about how many of these pixels we can spare for banner ads. For this example, let's say we'll make our banners 153 by 25 pixels.

The next thing to do is go back to our home page and use the LocalIcon META tag to include the banners we'll use. Add these lines to the <HEAD> section of home.html (the code shown in Figure 4.12):

```
<meta name="LocalIcon" content="banner01.gif">
<meta name="LocalIcon" content="banner02.gif">
<meta name="LocalIcon" content="banner03.gif">
```

You could continue like this for however many banners you want to preinclude in the WCA. You don't have to use all of these right away—if you know that you'll be doing a special deal or running a promotion with a partner in a few months, you could compile these banners into the WCA to be used later.

Now we're going to put these banners on some pages. Because Unwired Widgets has weekly specials on their regular Web site, we'll put a banner ad for the Palm-friendly version of this page on the WCA. Because this is a constant feature, we'll put this first banner on a local page of the WCA, the prod_menu.html we constructed in Figure 4.14. The modified HTML is shown in Figure 4.16, which is also available on the companion CD.

Figure 4.16 Revised Product Menu Page with Banner Ad (figure4_16.html)

```
<html>
  <head>
  <meta name="PalmComputingPlatform" content="true">
  <title>Product Menu</title>
  </head>
<body bgcolor="#ffcc00">
<table width="153" border="0" cellspacing="0" cellpadding="0">
<tr>
  <td>
    <a href="home.html"><img src="hdr_uwlogo.gif"></a>
    <img src="hdr_products.gif" width="133" height="20">
  </td>
</tr>
<tr>
  <td height="75">
    We make a wide variety of widgets to suit all your needs.
    Choose from the links below to visit our site and view a
    full product listing.
    <p align="center">
    <a href="http://cgi.unwiredwidgets.com/product.cgi?type=square">
      Square Widgets</a>
    </p>
    <p align="center">
    <a href="http://cgi.unwiredwidgets.com/product.cgi?type=round">
      Round Widgets</a>
    </p>
  </td>
</tr>
<tr>
  <td>
  <a href="http://www.unwiredwidgets.com/mobile_specials.html">
    <img src="banner01.gif"></a><br>
    <a href="home.html"><img src="ftr_unwired.gif"></a>
```

Continued

Figure 4.16 Continued

```
  </td>
</tr>
</table>
</body>
</html>
```

Note two changes here. As you can see in Figure 4.16, we added our first banner just above the footer graphic. The link associated with this graphic links to a fictitious mobile_specials.html page we might have on our server. Because both this page and the banner graphic are local to the WCA, we just link directly—no need for the *src="file:.."* syntax. The other change we made was reducing the *height* of the central <TD> tag so that everything still appears on one screen. Our completed page is also available on the companion CD as prod_menu.html, ready to be compiled into a WCA.

Now, as shown in Figure 4.17, let's put an ad on the remote dynamically generated product listing page. We'll modify the code from Figure 4.15 to add a different banner. Note also that we need to decrease the *height* of the <TD> tag so that this banner appears on the first screen. Of course, if the product listing returned is longer than one screen, the banner will be pushed down "below the fold." Figure 4.17 is provided on the CD.

Figure 4.17 Product Listing Code Returned from the Server, with Local Banner Ad (figure4_17.html)

```
<html>
  <head>
  <meta name="PalmComputingPlatform" content="true">
  <title>Products</title>
  </head>
<body bgcolor="#ffcc00">
<table width="153" border="0" cellspacing="0" cellpadding="0">
<tr>
  <td>
    <a href="file:widgets.pqa/home.html">
      <img src="file:widgets.pqa/hdr_uwlogo.gif"></a>
      <img src="file:widgets.pqa/hdr_square.gif">
```

Continued

Figure 4.17 Continued

```
  </td>
</tr>
<tr>
  <td height="75">
    34345  
    <a href="http://cgi.unwiredwidgets.com/prod_detail.cgi?sku=34345">
     round-hole adapter</a>   Red<br>
    34875  
    <a href="http://cgi.unwiredwidgets.com/prod_detail.cgi?sku=34875">
     round-hole adapter</a>   Green<br>
    34876  
    <a href="http://cgi.unwiredwidgets.com/prod_detail.cgi?sku=34876">
     round-hole adapter</a>   Blue<br>
    34691  
    <a href="http://www.unwiredwidgets.com/prod_detail.cgi?sku=34691">
     round-hole adapter</a>   Yellow<br>
  </td>
</tr>

<tr>
  <td>
    <a href="http://cgi.unwiredwidgets.com/ad_redirect.cgi?02">
    <img src="file:widgets.pqa/banner02.gif"></a><br>
    <a href="file:widgets.pqa/home.html">
     <img src="file:widgets.pqa/ftr_unwired.gif"></a>
  </td>
</tr>
</table>
</body>
</html>
```

The result of this code is shown in Figure 4.18. One important point to note here is that we added the "over the air" marks to the banner graphic to indicate to people that this is an online link (these are the little radiant lines that Web clipping automatically adds to any links that will require an Internet connection). Providing these marks is a courtesy to our site's visitors to let them know that clicking on this banner will incur some cost—either in airtime charges or simply the time taken to download the page.

Figure 4.18 Product Listing Screen with Local Banner Ad

You may have noticed the CGI link around the banner advertisement in Figure 4.17:

```
<a href="http://cgi.unwiredwidgets.com/ad_redirect.cgi?02">
<img src="file:widgets.pqa/banner02.gif"></a>
```

In a real application, because the actual code for the page is retrieved from a Web server each time, this would allow us to dynamically change out banner ads. The script that dynamically produces the product listing page could also be designed to periodically change the code number for both the banner graphic and the CGI link. A CGI on the server would then redirect the Palm OS device to the appropriate page that corresponds with the banner (a Palm-friendly page, we hope). This is close to how banner ads are handled on regular Web sites and allows you quite a lot of flexibility in changing and rotating banner ads. The only limitations are that you need to precompile all the banners you'll need into the WCA and can't easily add new ones.

Summary

Images can add to the aesthetics and usability of your wireless Web site. If used properly, they can make for very efficient navigation, and they often take the place of longer text descriptions. However, the limited screen size and bandwidth available on a wireless Palm OS device present some unique challenges for wireless developers. Web clipping applications can use the same graphics file formats used on regular Web pages: GIF and JPEG.

The available screen size is 153 pixels wide by 144 pixels high. However, this would be a very large graphic to send over a wireless connection, so it's best to keep graphics as small as possible. Palm OS 4.0 adds the capability to scroll horizontally in Web clipping, but this should be avoided. Graphics are not downloaded directly to the device. Rather, the Palm.Net proxy first converts them to a proprietary bitmap format and then sends them over the air to the Palm OS device.

You include graphics on Web clipping pages similar to the way you would on regular HTML pages. However, the WCA Builder flattens the folder hierarchy, so you need to be careful with image links and use unique file names. By using the special LocalIcon META tag, you can precompile images into the WCA, which are then linked to from online pages, saving greatly on download time.

Most of the current Palm OS devices can reproduce only four shades of gray in Web clipping applications. Palm OS 4.0 adds the capability to use 4-bit grayscale, which yields 16 shades, as well as 8-bit or 16-bit color, which is supported on some devices. Bit depth has a significant impact on downloaded file sizes, so these options should be used only when necessary. The Palm OS 4.0 SDK provides a very basic graphics program that allows you to preview images at different bit depths. Photographic images reproduce better at the higher bit depths, but it's also possible to enhance the Palm.Net proxy's default conversion by converting images first in a separate image-editing program. When producing graphics for use in Web clipping, you need to take care to optimize file sizes and color depth; you may often need to make a tradeoff between higher image quality and faster download speeds.

The single-pixel GIF trick doesn't work the same way in Web clipping as it does in HTML. You can stretch images, but you need to ensure that each has a unique filename. This does work for remote graphics, but because each must be converted by the Palm.Net proxy and downloaded separately, it doesn't provide any savings.

Our example demonstrated how to use the various image options to include both remote and local images in Web clipping pages. By using HTML tables to lay out individual graphics, you can produce full-screen, full-color graphical navigation menus that are very quick to download. When using color graphics, constantly check is that these do not degrade badly to grayscale. PIC is useful for quickly checking that your navigational graphics are still readable in four shades of gray.

Banner ads offer special challenges on the Palm OS device. The severely limited screen real estate means that you have to carefully choose where these are placed. Here again, the LocalIcon META tag can help by compiling banner graphics into the WCA itself, saving considerably on downloads. With careful coding, you can use server-side code to rotate banner ads that are stored locally, offering many of the features of traditional Web ad tracking in a Palm-friendly format.

Solutions Fast Track

Dealing with Limited Screen Size

☑ The available screen size on a Palm OS device is 153 pixels wide by 144 pixels high.

☑ Web clipping can use both local and remote images.

☑ Use the LocalIcon META tag to include images that are not referenced from local pages.

☑ The WCA Builder flattens the folder hierarchy when compiling, so be sure to use unique file names.

Specifying Nonlinked Images

☑ Use local images compiled into the WCA to save on download times.

☑ Remote pages can refer to local images with the syntax <img src="file:mywca.pqa/image.gif">.

☑ Save on downloaded text by omitting the *height*, *width*, and *alt* attributes of <IMG>.

Using Colors and Grayscale

- ☑ Palm OS 3.5 Web clipping applications support only four shades of gray.
- ☑ The WCA Builder in SDK 4.0 allows you to save in several bit depths, including color.
- ☑ Ensure that color graphics are still readable in 2-bit grayscale.

Optimizing Image Size

- ☑ Keep image dimensions as small as possible to keep file sizes down.
- ☑ Some image-editing programs optimize much better than others.
- ☑ The Palm.Net proxy image conversion can reduce image quality.

Using the Palm Image Checker to Validate Your Images

- ☑ Use PIC to preview images at different bit depths before building your WCA.
- ☑ Convert graphics to grayscale in an image-editing program to increase image quality.
- ☑ Bit depth can have a significant effect on the size of your WCA.

Frequently Asked Questions

The following Frequently Asked Questions, answered by the authors of this book, are designed to both measure your understanding of the concepts presented in this chapter and to assist you with real-life implementation of these concepts. To have your questions about this chapter answered by the author, browse to **www.syngress.com/solutions** and click on the **"Ask the Author"** form.

Q: Can I use imagemaps for navigation?

A: No, this is not supported. Use multiple images laid out with tables to simulate this effect.

Q: I just built a WCA with color images, so why do they show up only as grayscale?

A: Be sure to select the **Screen Depth** option in the WCA Builder dialog box. This defaults to 2-bit Gray.

Q: Can I make WCAs that work only on Palm OS 4.0?

A: Yes. When building your WCA, select 2.0 from the **PQA Version** drop-down box.

Q: Can I have different table cell background colors?

A: No, Web clipping supports the *bgcolor* attribute for the <TABLE> tag only, not for <TD>.

Q: Why don't my images show up when I link to remote pages?

A: Be sure that you have the PalmComputingPlatform META tag on all pages.

Q: Do I have to use LocalIcon for every image I want to use in my WCA?

A: No. If the images are used on any of the pages within the WCA, the WCA Builder will find and include them.

Q: My WCA uses only grayscale images. Does it matter whether I build it as 2-bit gray or 8-bit color?

A: Yes, the file size of the WCA roughly doubles for each higher bit depth.

Chapter 5

Interacting with Forms

Solutions in this chapter:

- Using Standard HTML Forms
- Tracking Widget Inventory Example
- Placing a Widget Order Example
- Enhancing Forms for Clipper
- Setting Delivery Dates for Widget Orders Example

☑ Summary

☑ Solutions Fast Track

☑ Frequently Asked Questions

Introduction

When you add forms to a Web clipping application, it ceases to be a one-way read-only channel and becomes something that allows user interaction. Forms are the basis for interaction on the Web, and their availability on Palm handheld computers expands the range of possibilities for Web clipping applications. Any application that needs to let users request and/or respond to information can be supported, including applications for travel, finance, sports, weather—the list goes on and on.

Adding form elements to a Web clipping application requires new coding. Clipper supports most of the <FORM> tag specification from HTML 3.2; it also supports some additional types that take advantage of the built-in controls for setting times and dates, namely *timepicker* and *datepicker*. In this chapter, you will learn how to use each form element that Clipper supports, including correct syntax, sample code, and screen shots. Bandwidth considerations will also be presented to maximize your use of wireless data transfers.

In addition to changing Web pages, handling forms requires scripting on the server. To process form submissions, you can use many different languages and systems, but popular choices include Perl, C, PHP, Microsoft's Active Server Pages (ASP), and Sun's Java Server Pages (JSP). Approaches to server-side scripting are discussed in enough detail in this chapter to get you "up and running" quickly, and example server-side scripts are provided.

Tying all subject matter together are three progressive examples that cover the following: first, updating the Unwired Widgets company inventory database; second, placing a widget order; and third, setting an order delivery date and time. In each example, the user is allowed to enter a widget of interest (size, shape, and color) and quantity. A password/key is also available for user authentication to either lock out unauthorized users or to identify a customer. **Submit** and **Reset** buttons are provided for control. All <FORM> tags supported by Clipper are used, along with a robust server-side Perl script for data processing. The software was tested under both Unix and Windows. (You can find information about the build process in Chapter 1 and in Chapter 4.)

Using Standard HTML Forms

The <FORM> tag and its associated attributes are used to create Web Clipping Applications (WCAs) capable of capturing user inputs and sending information to a server. Most of the associated attributes are centered on capturing user inputs, providing the developer with a feature-rich environment for creating robust user interfaces. A wide variety of user interface elements/controls can be represented, from text boxes to multiple selection lists. The <FORM> tag and its associated attributes take full advantage of Palm display resources, providing a valuable tool for creating WCAs.

For sending information to a server, Clipper's form processing provides standard HTML communication support. Whether in response to previously retrieved data, or as an initial request, Clipper's form processing provides a mechanism by which clients can send strings of concatenated data to a server. Clipper's form processing closes the WCA/server communication loop, providing WCAs their ability to be complete interactive applications rather than simple read-only Web access portals. The general syntax of the <FORM> tag is as follows:

```
<form method="mymethod" action="myurl" enctype="myenctype">
...
</form>
```

NOTE

We will use the following conventions in the code snippets shown in this chapter to indicate types of input: **Bold** variables indicate required information; *italics* indicate user information. For example, ***bold italics*** indicate required user information, whereas *nonbold italics* indicate optional user information. Also, no information is case-sensitive. This convention is not applied to complete code listings.

The optional *method* attribute is GET or POST (default GET), depending on whether the *action* is used to retrieve data or if the *action* changes the state of the server. For the GET *method*, form data is used as a list of attributes to the specified retrieval *action*. The resulting *action* URL is of the form:

```
http://cgi.unwiredwidgets.com/cgi-bin/your_script.pl?item1=A&item2=B
```

GET operations can be cached, and they should not change the state of the server.

In contrast, POST operations send form data in the post body. As a result, POST operations cannot be cached, and they usually change the state of the server. POST operations are especially useful for sending large amounts of data that would otherwise overflow the URL length constraints of the HTTP server or client.

The required *action* attribute is a valid URL that will handle your form's submission. This is often a server-side Common Gateway Interface (CGI) script.

The optional *enctype* attribute is the encoding type for your form. The default is application/x-www-form-url-encoded, and it is the only *enctype* supported by Clipper.

You need to make sure that any <FORM> tags you use are properly nested within the HTML. For example, if you start a form, start a paragraph, close the form, and then close the paragraph, you will have improperly nested HTML tags. This can cause your page to be rejected by the Web Clipping Builder software or by the Palm.Net proxy server.

WARNING

Note the <TABLE> and <FORM> restriction that you can't have a form within a table cell, although a table can be within a form.

The <FORM> tag and its associated attributes are a subset of the HTML 3.2 standard for forms. The following tags associated with forms are supported:

- <INPUT>
- <SELECT/OPTION>
- <TEXTAREA>

NOTE

Tags are case insensitive in standard HTML. For example, <form> is the same as <FORM>.

Accepting User Input

As its name suggests, the <INPUT> tag is used to capture user inputs. It can be used to capture a wide variety of inputs ranging from radio button selections to directly-input text. It can even maintain data that is never seen by a user. The general syntax of the <INPUT> tag is:

```
<input type="see below" name="input_name" value="input_value">
```

The <INPUT> tag typically has three attributes:

- ***Type*** Required for all types, except *text*.
- ***Name*** Required for all types, except *submit* and *reset*.
- ***Value*** Optional for all types, except *checkbox* and *radio*.

NOTE

Type is not syntactically required if you have a text input field, because **type="text"** is the default. Explicitly specifying it for text fields makes your HTML more maintainable, because the reader doesn't need to know about the default type to understand what kind of <INPUT> tag you are using.

The *type* attribute indicates what kind of user input can be captured. It is the most significant attribute for the <INPUT> tag, because it controls both the operation and appearance of the <INPUT> tag. The *type* attribute defines the capabilities of the <INPUT> tag, allowing it to act in a multitude of ways. The valid values for the *type* attribute are as follows (each is discussed in greater detail in the following section):

- *Text*
- *Password*
- *Checkbox*
- *Radio*
- *Hidden*
- *Submit*
- *Reset*

The usually required *name* attribute identifies an <INPUT> tag so that it can be distinguished from other tags. This is especially important when sending data to a server. The server needs to be able to determine which data came from which <INPUT> tag. However, note that the specific meaning of the *name* attribute is dependent on the contents of the *type* attribute. The following sections discuss the meaning of the *name* attribute as it pertains to the various types of <INPUT> tag.

The optional *value* attribute specifies a default value for the <INPUT> tag. This is useful for pre-populating fields with suggested entries. However, note that the specific meaning of the *value* attribute is dependent on the contents of the *type* attribute. The following sections discuss the meaning of the *value* attribute as it pertains to the various types of <INPUT> tag.

NOTE

The <INPUT> tag must be embedded within the <FORM> tag, as in <FORM> ... <INPUT> ... </FORM>.

The <FORM><INPUT></FORM> sequence does not have to be contiguous. Other tags can come between the <FORM> and <INPUT> tags and between the <INPUT> and </FORM> tags.

Handling Textual Input

The *text* type indicates that the corresponding <INPUT> tag can accept ASCII data, and that both the field and the data (when entered) are to be displayed. Any valid character can be entered, so this type of <INPUT> tag is extremely powerful. *Text*-type <INPUT> is typically used to capture information that is too broad for more constrained types of <INPUT>, such as *checkbox* and *radio*. Examples of *text*-type <INPUT> include names, addresses, and telephone numbers. Note that the numeric data in a *text* field is stored as an ASCII string. The syntax of *text*-type <INPUT> is shown in Figure 5.1.

Figure 5.1 *Text*-Type <INPUT> Syntax

```
<input type="text" name="mytxt" value="abc" size="10" maxlength="20">
```

The *type* attribute indicates that the <INPUT> is of *text* type (such as "text"). The <INPUT> tag can accept any ASCII string, including strings of digits for numeric input.

The required *name* attribute identifies an <INPUT> tag so that it can be distinguished from other tags. In Figure 5.1, "mytxt" was chosen arbitrarily to illustrate a possible choice. For *text*-type <INPUT>, the *name* attribute is used to identify data to a server so that the server will know from which field the data originated. The *name* should be lowercase and short to minimize the bandwidth required to send data to the server.

The optional *value* attribute specifies a default value for the <INPUT> tag. This is useful for pre-populating fields with suggested entries. As shown in Figure 5.1, the string "abc" will be initially displayed as data within the *text*-type <INPUT>. And as with *name*, the *value* should be lowercase and short for bandwidth conservation.

The optional *size* attribute is an extra attribute available for *text*-type <INPUT>. *Size* indicates the width—in number of ASCII characters—of the displayed *text*-type field. *Size* in Figure 5.1 is "10", indicating that up to ten characters of the field contents will be displayed. Note that this is different from the *maxlength* (the maximum number of ASCII characters that the field can hold). In WCAs, the *size* attribute is typically set to a value less than that used for the *maxlength* attribute.

The optional *maxlength* attribute is an extra attribute available for *text*-type <INPUT>. *Maxlength* indicates the maximum number of ASCII characters that the *text*-type <INPUT> can hold. *Maxlength* in Figure 5.1 is "20", indicating that up to twenty characters can be contained in the field. Note that this is different from the *size* (the number of ASCII characters of the field that are displayed). *Maxlength* should be kept to a minimum to limit the bandwidth required to send data to the server.

A complete WCA source code listing and Palm OS device screen shot illustrating the use of *text*-type <INPUT> are shown in Figures 5.2 and 5.3.

Figure 5.2 *Text*-Type <INPUT> Example

```
<html>
<head>
<title>Text</title>
<meta name="PalmComputingPlatform" content="true">
</head>
<body>
<center>
<form method="GET"
    action="http://cgi.unwiredwidgets.com/cgi-bin/input_text.pl">
<font size="4">TEXT-type &lt;INPUT&gt;</font>
```

Continued

Figure 5.2 Continued

```
<br>
<input type="text" name="mytxt" value="abc" size="10" maxlength="20">
</form>
</center>
</body>
</html>
```

Figure 5.3 *Text*-Type <INPUT> Example

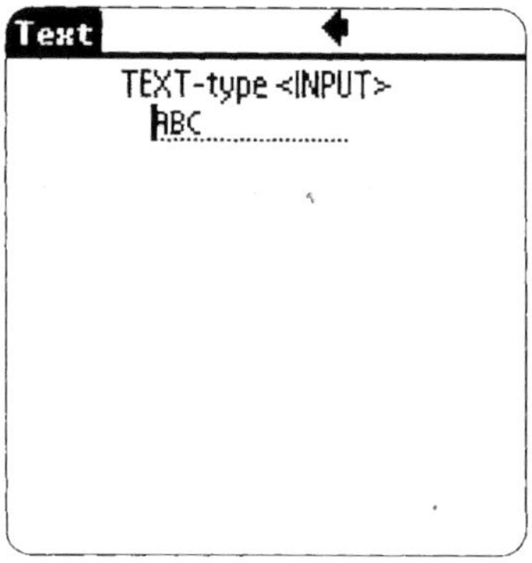

Retrieving Sensitive Passwords

A *password*-type <INPUT> tag is typically used to capture security code information, although it can be used to capture any information that is not to be directly displayed. The *password* type indicates that the corresponding <INPUT> tag can accept any valid ASCII data, and that the data itself should not be displayed. Only an indication about whether data has been entered should be displayed. A password field that contains data will read "-Assigned-", whereas one that does not will read "-Unassigned-". The actual data is sent to a server to determine whether the corresponding request should be processed. To the server, *password* data looks just like *text* data—it's only in the Palm's user interface where the appearance differs. The syntax of *password*-type <INPUT> is shown in Figure 5.4.

Figure 5.4 *Password*-Type <INPUT> Syntax

```
<input type="password" name="mypw" value="guest" maxlength="12">
```

The *type* attribute indicates that the <INPUT> is of *password* type (such as "password"). That is, the <INPUT> tag can accept any ASCII string that is subsequently hidden from view. "-Assigned-" or "-Unassigned-" is displayed, depending on whether data has or had not been entered into the field, respectively.

The required *name* attribute identifies an <INPUT> tag so that it can be distinguished from other tags. In Figure 5.4, "mypw" was chosen arbitrarily to illustrate a possible choice. For *password*-type <INPUT>, the *name* attribute is used to identify data to a server so that the server will know from which field the data originated. The *name* should be lowercase and short to minimize the bandwidth required to send data to the server.

The optional *value* attribute specifies a default value for the <INPUT> tag. This is useful for specifying a default password for the <INPUT> tag. One example application is the creation of guest accounts. And as with *name*, the *value* should be lowercase and short for bandwidth conservation.

The optional *maxlength* attribute is an extra attribute available for *text*-type <INPUT>. *Maxlength* indicates the maximum number of ASCII characters that the *password*-type <INPUT> can hold. *Maxlength* in Figure 5.4 is "12", indicating that up to twelve characters can be contained in the field. *Maxlength* should be kept to a minimum to limit the bandwidth required to send data to the server.

SECURITY ALERT!

Entering a password into a *password*-type <INPUT> field causes a dialog box to be displayed. The dialog box accepts the password entry and then is closed via **OK** or **Cancel**. If **OK** is selected, the password entry is retained as the field's value.

When the password is being entered into the dialog box, it is not masked. Anyone looking over your shoulder will see your password as you enter it.

A complete WCA source code listing and Palm OS device screen shot illustrating the use of *password*-type <INPUT> are shown in Figures 5.5 and 5.6.

Figure 5.5 *Password*-Type <INPUT> Example

```
<html>
<head>
<title>Password</title>
```

Continued

Figure 5.5 Continued

```
<meta name="PalmComputingPlatform" content="true">
</head>
<body>
<center>
<form method="GET"
    action="http://cgi.unwiredwidgets.com/cgi-bin/input_password.pl">
<font size="4">PASSWORD-type &lt;INPUT&gt;</font>
<br>
<input type="password" name="mypw" size="6" maxlength="12">
</form>
</center>
</body>
</html>
```

Figure 5.6 *Password*-Type <INPUT> Example

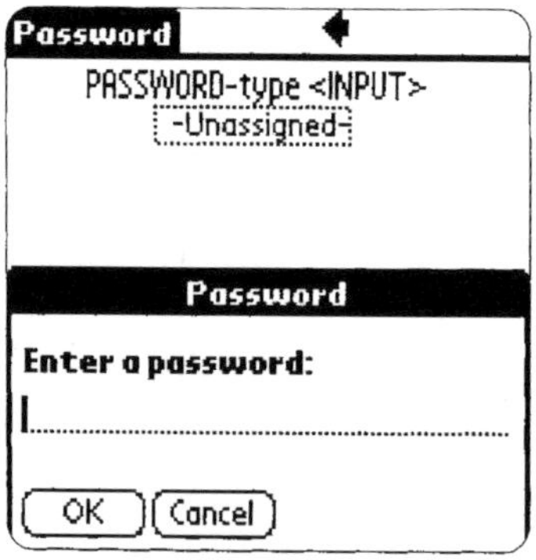

Making a Choice Using a Checkbox

The *checkbox* type indicates that the corresponding <INPUT> tag can accept multiple on/off (binary) user inputs. Each *checkbox* can be individually selected or unselected, and the value associated with a selection can be assigned a descriptive value. Also, as you might have guessed, any user inputs are displayed as a check-mark inside a box.

Developing & Deploying…

Why Doesn't Password Obscure My Input?

When you enter your password, rather than echoing asterisks like desktop Web browsers do, Clipper pops up a dialog box in which you enter the password in the clear. This is done to address the problem of using the Palm OS graffiti input scheme. Showing the characters is necessary for the user to know what they are actually scribbling. Without that feedback, you could easily enter wrong data. Palm's compromise is to show this password input for only the brief time that the user is entering the text. After the user hits the **OK** button, the dialog box is dismissed, and the only indication that a password has been entered is the "-Assigned-" string.

Checkbox-type <INPUT> is typically used to capture selections from a small list of choices, where any number of selections may need to be made. For example, in terms of the Unwired Widgets company, a widget delivery could optionally be specified as overnight and/or insured. Because any combination of the overnight/insured options is valid, one *checkbox*-type <INPUT> could be used for the overnight selection, and another could be used for the insured selection. The user can tap anywhere on the box or descriptive text to toggle the value of the checkbox. The syntax of *checkbox*-type <INPUT> is shown in Figure 5.7.

NOTE

Assigning descriptive values to *checkbox*-type <INPUT> is an effective tool toward making WCAs more robust and maintainable. Don't make your values too long, however, as lengthy values require additional bandwidth when being sent to a server.

Figure 5.7 *Checkbox*-Type <INPUT> Syntax

```
<input type="checkbox" name="myckboxa" value="a" checked>Multi-Option #1
<input type="checkbox" name="myckboxb" value="b">Multi-Option #2
<input type="checkbox" name="myckboxc" value="c" checked>Multi-Option #3
```

The *type* attribute value of "checkbox" indicates that the <INPUT> is displayed as a typical checkbox control (that is, a small box that can contain a checkmark). Tapping on the displayed box turns the checkmark on and off.

The required *name* attribute identifies an <INPUT> tag so that it can be distinguished from other tags. In Figure 5.7, "myckboxa," "myckboxb," and "myckboxc" were chosen arbitrarily to illustrate possible choices. The *name* should be lowercase and short to minimize the bandwidth required to send data to the server.

NOTE

As seen in Figure 5.7, the *name* attribute can be the same for different *checkbox*-type <INPUT> tags. This allows different *checkbox*-type <INPUT> tags to be identified by the server as part of the same group. The default data shown in Figure 5.7, when sent to the server, looks like the following:

```
myckbox="1"&myckbox="3"&myckboxa="a"&myckboxc="c"
```

Although CGI.pm recognizes only the first value of *myckbox* (such as myckbox="1"), both values of *myckbox* are available to be parsed.

The *value* attribute specifies the data to be associated with an individual selection. As seen in Figure 5.7, the value associated with "Multi-Option #1" is *a*. Values can be virtually any string, limited only by length, of valid ASCII characters. If no *value* is provided, the default "*on*" is sent to the server if the checkbox is selected. And as with *name*, the *value* should be lowercase and short for bandwidth conservation.

WARNING

If the same *name* attribute is assigned to different *checkbox*-type <INPUT> tags, each should have a unique *value* attribute to identify to the server, which is selected.

The optional *checked* attribute specifies that the default state for the corresponding *checkbox*-type <INPUT> be selected ("checked"). This feature can be used to enhance the user's experience by providing default selections that match typical choices.

NOTE

Take care when using the *checked* attribute to make sure that the selection doesn't unnecessarily obligate users. You are making a decision for your users here, and you have a responsibility to not abuse the privilege. Users need to have reasonable actions take place when they use your WCA as-is, defaults included. For example, don't assume that all of your users will want overnight delivery. Even if a user catches (and unchecks) a default selection, he will become irritated if he has to uncheck the default selection every time he uses your WCA.

A complete WCA source code listing and Palm OS device screen shot illustrating the use of *checkbox*-type <INPUT> are shown in Figures 5.8 and 5.9.

Figure 5.8 *Checkbox*-Type <INPUT> Example

```
<html>
<head>
<title>Checkbox</title>
<meta name="PalmComputingPlatform" content="true">
</head>
<body>
<center>
<form method="GET"
    action="http://cgi.unwiredwidgets.com/cgi-bin/input_checkbox.pl">
```

Continued

Figure 5.8 Continued

```
<font size="4">CHECKBOX-type &lt;INPUT&gt;</font>
<br>
<br>
<input type="checkbox" name="myckbox" value="1" checked>Uni-Option #1
<br>
<input type="checkbox" name="myckbox" value="2">Uni-Option #2
<br>
<input type="checkbox" name="myckbox" value="3" checked>Uni-Option #3
<br>
<br>
<input type="checkbox" name="myckboxa" value="a" checked>Multi-Option
#1
<br>
<input type="checkbox" name="myckboxb" value="b">Multi-Option #2
<br>
<input type="checkbox" name="myckboxc" value="c" checked>Multi-Option
#3
</form>
</center>
</body>
</html>
```

Figure 5.9 *Checkbox*-Type <INPUT> Example

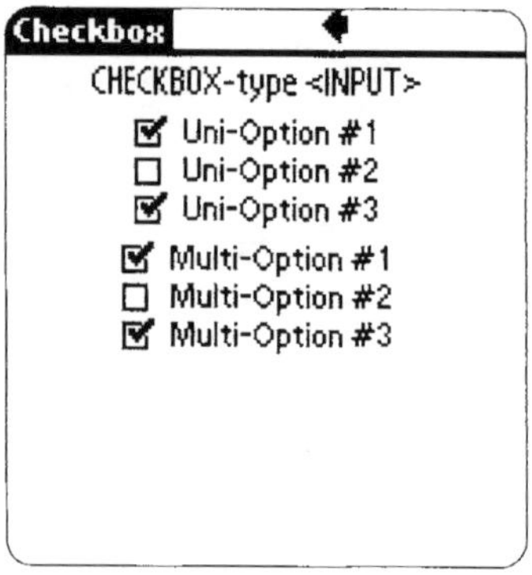

Selecting from Several Items with Radio Buttons

The *radio* type indicates that the corresponding <INPUT> tag can accept a single selection from a list of choices. Each *radio* button can be individually selected, the result of which is that all other related *radio* buttons are deselected. Each *radio* button can also be assigned a descriptive value.

Radio-type <INPUT> is typically used to capture a single selection from a small list of choices, where only a single selection makes sense. For example, in terms of Unwired Widgets, the payment method for widgets will either be cash, check, money order, or credit card. Only one choice at a time makes sense. Because only one choice at a time should be allowed, the *radio*-type <INPUT> is the appropriate tag. The syntax of *radio*-type <INPUT> is shown in Figure 5.10.

Figure 5.10 *Radio*-Type <INPUT> Syntax

```
<input type="radio" name="myradio" value="1" checked>Option #1
<input type="radio" name="myradio" value="2">Option #2
<input type="radio" name="myradio" value="3">Option #3
```

The *type* attribute indicates that the <INPUT> is of *radio* type (such as "radio"). The <INPUT> tag can accept a single entry. Actually, only a single entry can be accepted from a group of related *radio*-type <INPUT> tags.

The required *name* attribute determines which *radio* tags are related. In Figure 5.10, "myradio" was chosen arbitrarily to illustrate a possible choice. Note that each of the <INPUT> tags in Figure 5.10 has the same name. This is to identify the <INPUT> tags as a single group. Clipper will only allow one radio button in each group to be selected at one time.

When data is sent to a server, this naming convention enables the server to discern from which group a particular data item originated. The *name* should be lowercase and short to minimize the bandwidth required to send data to the server. The required *value* attribute specifies the data to be associated with an individual selection. As seen in Figure 5.10, the value associated with "Option #1" is "1". The value is an ASCII string, in this case chosen to be the ASCII representation of the number 1. Values can be virtually any string, limited only by length, of valid ASCII characters. And as with *name*, the *value* should be lowercase and short for bandwidth conservation.

The optional *checked* attribute specifies that the default state for the corresponding *radio*-type <INPUT> be selected (such as "checked"). This feature can be used to provide a default selection for the user.

NOTE

Assign values to each *radio* option to identify to the server the specific option selected. Otherwise, data will be sent to the server in the form "myradio=on", indicating only that a *radio* option was selected. The specific option will not be discernable in this case.

A complete WCA source code listing and Palm OS device screen shot illustrating the use of RADIO-type <INPUT> are shown in Figures 5.11 and 5.12.

Figure 5.11 *Radio*-Type <INPUT> Example

```
<html>
<head>
<title>Radio</title>
<meta name="PalmComputingPlatform" content="true">
</head>
<body>
<center>
<form method="GET"
    action="http://cgi.unwiredwidgets.com/cgi-bin/input_radio.pl">
<font size="4">RADIO-type &lt;INPUT&gt;</font>
<br>
<input type="radio" name="myradio" value="1" checked>Option #1
<input type="radio" name="myradio" value="2">Option #2
<input type="radio" name="myradio" value="3">Option #3
</form>
</center>
</body>
</html>
```

Figure 5.12 *Radio*-Type <INPUT> Example

Developing & Deploying…

Radio Buttons and the Palm OS UI

As a Web designer, you might expect that radio buttons will appear like they do on the desktop, with a series of circles and labels, the selected item indicated by a filled circle. As you can see in the screen shots, this isn't the case; Clipper uses the Palm OS convention for selection boxes, where the buttons appear as boxes with the label text inside, and inverting the entire box highlights the selected button.

Palm chose this interface style because of the small screen size on the Palm device. Checkboxes and traditional radio buttons looked too similar in the limited resolution and screen space of the Palm device, so the user-interface designers created this push-button format.

Because of this change, you should make sure your forms that use radio buttons appear correctly when shown on Clipper. In general, you should have the buttons adjacent to each other on a vertical line to follow Palm's user interface standards. If you have more choices than will fit in a single line, you probably should use a selection list to allow the user to pick a choice from a drop-down list.

Storing State in Hidden Fields

The *hidden* type indicates that an <INPUT> field contains data, but that the data is not displayed. The data is hidden from the user. This does not imply that the data is protected via some security mechanism, but rather that the data is not displayed in Clipper's user interface but is just stored locally to be submitted with the form.

SECURITY ALERT!

Data in a *hidden* field is not protected from the user. While Clipper doesn't support a **View Source** command, it does cache away Web pages in a page cache that can be browsed using other Palm OS software. By looking directly at the binary data, an attacker can possibly see sensitive information that is stored as a *hidden* field in a form. Also, an attacker could just imitate Clipper from a standard Web browser and then view the fields using normal mechanisms.

The *hidden* type is particularly useful for storing context within a Web session, including data submitted on previous pages. It also servers as a placeholder for sending back ZIP Code and device ID information from the Pocket PC. The syntax of *hidden*-type <INPUT> is shown in Figure 5.13. The *type* attribute indicates that the <INPUT> is of *hidden* type.

Figure 5.13 *Hidden*-Type <INPUT> Syntax

```
<input type="hidden" name="myhidden" value="abc">
```

The required *name* attribute identifies an <INPUT> tag so that it can be distinguished from other tags. In Figure 5.13, "myhidden" was chosen arbitrarily to illustrate a possible choice. For *hidden*-type <INPUT>, the *name* attribute is used to identify data to a server so that the server will know from which field the data originated. The *name* should be lowercase and short to minimize the bandwidth required to send data to the server.

Although the *value* attribute is optional, having a hidden input with no value is useless, because there is no other way to specify what the <INPUT> tag will return. This attribute specifies the value for the <INPUT> tag. As shown in Figure 5.13, the string "abc" will be stored as the value of the *hidden*-type

<INPUT>. And as with *name*, the *value* should be lowercase and short for bandwidth conservation.

NOTE

%ZIPCODE and %DEVICEID must be used in *hidden*-type <INPUT> tags to ensure proper translation. They can also be used at the end of any URL in a WCA.

SECURITY ALERT!

%DEVICEID is considered useless by many, except for applications where security is not a factor. Although it may be suitable for accessing nonprotected data, it is unwise to use it in a secure environment. Chapter 8 covers these problems in more detail.

Chapter 8 talks in more detail about using hidden fields to store state information; Chapter 9 covers location based services using the %ZIPCODE code. A complete WCA source code listing illustrating the use of *hidden*-type <INPUT> is shown in Figure 5.14.

Figure 5.14 *Hidden*-Type <INPUT> Example

```
<html>
<head>
<title>Hidden</title>
<meta name="PalmComputingPlatform" content="true">
</head>
<body>
<center>
<form method="GET"
    action="http://cgi.unwiredwidgets.com/cgi-bin/input_hidden.pl">
<font size="4">HIDDEN-type &lt;INPUT&gt;</font>
<br>
```

Continued

Figure 5.14 Continued

```
<input type="hidden" name="myhidden" value="abc">
</form>
</center>
</body>
</html>
```

Submitting Completed Forms

The *submit* type indicates that the corresponding <INPUT> tag is a button. The button is used to initiate communication with the server named in the <FORM> tag's attributes. The syntax of *submit*-type <INPUT> is shown in Figure 5.15.

Figure 5.15 *Submit*-Type <INPUT> Syntax

```
<input type="submit" value="Submit">
```

The *type* attribute indicates that the <INPUT> tag will be displayed as a button and when pressed will send the form data to the server.

The *name* attribute is not used for *submit*-type <INPUT> tags/buttons.

The optional *value* attribute specifies a label for the <INPUT> tag/button. This is useful for customizing the WCA display. As shown in Figure 5.15, the string "Submit" will be displayed as the button label for the *submit*-type <INPUT> tag/button.

A complete WCA source code listing and Palm OS device screen shot illustrating the use of *submit*-type <INPUT> are shown in Figures 5.16 and 5.17.

Figure 5.16 *Submit*-Type <INPUT> Example

```
<html>
<head>
<title>Submit</title>
<meta name="PalmComputingPlatform" content="true">
</head>
<body>
<center>
```

Continued

Figure 5.16 Continued

```
<form method="GET"
    action="http://cgi.unwiredwidgets.com/cgi-bin/input_submit.pl">
<font size="4">SUBMIT-type &lt;INPUT&gt;</font>
<br>
<input type="submit" value="Submit">
</form>
</center>
</body>
</html>
```

Figure 5.17 *Submit*-Type <INPUT> Example

Starting with a Clean Slate

The *reset* type indicates that the corresponding <INPUT> tag is a button used to reset the form to its initial state, clearing some fields, and restoring default values to others. The syntax of *reset*-type <INPUT> is shown in Figure 5.18.

Figure 5.18 *Reset*-Type <INPUT> Syntax

```
<input type="reset" value="Reset">
```

The *type* attribute indicates that the <INPUT> tag will be displayed as a button, and will accept button clicks to clear form contents and to re-initialize all fields possessing a default value.

The *name* attribute is not used for *reset*-type <INPUT> tags/buttons.

The optional *value* attribute specifies a label for the <INPUT> tag/button. This is useful for customizing the WCA display. As shown in Figure 5.18, the string "Reset" will be displayed as the button label for the *reset*-type <INPUT> tag/button.

A complete WCA source code listing and Palm OS device screen shot illustrating the use of *reset*-type <INPUT> are shown in Figures 5.19 and 5.20.

Figure 5.19 *Reset*-Type <INPUT> Example

```
<html>
<head>
<title>Reset</title>
<meta name="PalmComputingPlatform" content="true">
</head>
<body>
<center>
<form method="GET"
    action="http://cgi.unwiredwidgets.com/cgi-bin/input_reset.pl">
<font size="4">RESET-type &lt;INPUT&gt;</font>
<br>
<input type="reset" value="Reset">
</form>
</center>
</body>
</html>
```

Selecting from Many Choices

The <SELECT> and <OPTION> tags, like the <INPUT> tag, are used to capture user inputs. Unlike the <INPUT> tag, the <SELECT> and <OPTION> tags accept a limited range of inputs. Specifically, the <SELECT> and <OPTION> tags are used to allow the selection of either one or several items from a predefined list. Examples include address information (city, state, and so on), date information (month, day, and so on), and payment method (check, credit card, and so on). Almost any list can be implemented in this manner; the limiting criteria are system memory and the user's tolerance for scrolling through a long list of choices. The syntax is as shown in Figure 5.21.

Figure 5.20 *Reset*-Type <INPUT> Example

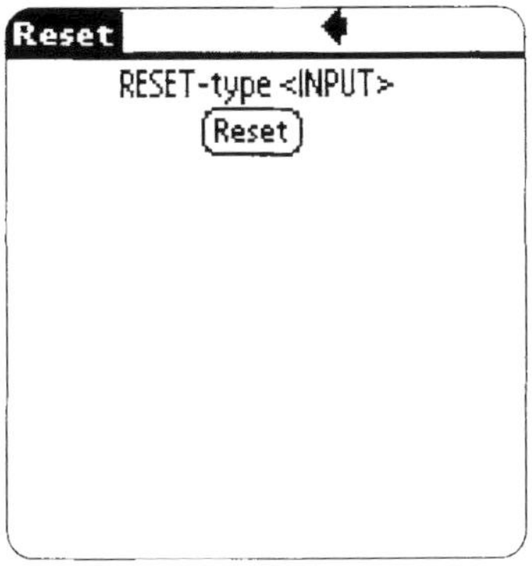

Figure 5.21 <SELECT>/<OPTION> Syntax

```
<select name="myselect" size="1">
    <option selected>Big Square Widget</option>
    <option>Small Square Widget</option>
    <option>Big Round Widget</option>
    <option>Small Round Widget</option>
</select>
```

NOTE

<OPTION> tags should be alphabetized by label, and labels should not contain any special characters and/or spaces. This is so the Palm OS UI can quickly jump to <OPTION> labels as graffiti characters are entered.

The required *name* attribute identifies the <SELECT> and <OPTION> tags so that they can be distinguished from other tags. In Figure 5.21, "myselect" was chosen arbitrarily to illustrate a possible choice. For <SELECT> and <OPTION> tags, the *name* attribute is used to identify data to a server so that the server will know from which field the data originated. The *name* should be lowercase and short to minimize the bandwidth required to send data to the server.

The optional *size* attribute indicates the number of options to be simultaneously displayed. *Size* in Figure 5.21 is "1", specifying that only one option is displayed at a time. (Setting *size* to "1" is the way to create a pop-up menu.) This is a common setting for WCAs given the Palm OS device's limited screen real estate.

An optional attribute not shown in Figure 5.21 is *multiple*. The *multiple* attribute is available, as in <SELECT ... MULTIPLE>, to indicate that the corresponding <SELECT>/<OPTION> tags can accept more than one choice at a time. When using the *multiple* attribute, make sure that *size* is set to at least "2" so that a scrolling list will be visible. This facilitates making more than one selection. Keep in mind, however, that *multiple* can adversely affect bandwidth requirements for server communication should several choices be made before form submission.

The optional *selected* attribute is an extra attribute available to <OPTION> tags. *Selected* indicates that the corresponding item (as in "Big Square Widget" in Figure 5.21) is the default selection. That is, if a user makes no selection, "Big Square Widget" is used. If you are using a multiple-selection list, you can have multiple <OPTION> tags selected with this mechanism.

An optional *value* attribute can be used with the <OPTION> tag, as in <OPTION ... VALUE="myvalue">. This is not necessary, however. The <OPTION> label is the default value and is usually adequate. In Figure 5.21, <OPTION> labels are: "Big Square Widget," "Small Square Widget," and so on.

WARNING

Within Web clippings, setting the *value* attribute for <OPTION> tags produces undesirable results—namely Proxy Server Error Code C2010005.

<OPTION> tags should be terminated with the closing tag. Failing to close these tags may be tolerated by the Web Clipping Builder application but has occasionally caused problems at the Palm.Net proxy server when it is translating the options into its compressed HTML format.

A complete WCA source code listing and Palm OS device screen shot illustrating the use of the <SELECT> and <OPTION> tags are shown in Figures 5.22 and 5.23.

Figure 5.22 <SELECT>/<OPTION> Example

```
<html>
<head>
<title>Select/Option</title>
<meta name="PalmComputingPlatform" content="true">
</head>
<body>
<center>
<form method="GET"
    action="http://cgi.unwiredwidgets.com/cgi-bin/select_option.pl">
<font size="4">&lt;SELECT/OPTION&gt;</font>
<br>
<select name="myselect" size="1">
    <option selected>Big Square Widget</option>
    <option>Small Square Widget</option>
    <option>Big Round Widget</option>
    <option>Small Round Widget</option>
</select>
</form>
</center>
</body>
</html>
```

Figure 5.23 <SELECT>/<OPTION> Example

NOTE

Sometimes it is useful for the first <OPTION> tag to contain a prompt. For example, **<OPTION>Please Make A Selection**. This provides a mechanism for users and servers alike to know whether an entry has been made, while circumventing the need to assign a superfluous default selection. If you use this, you should make sure that your server script acts sanely if the user submits this default value.

Handling Large Amounts of Input Text

The <TEXTAREA> tag, like the <INPUT> tag, is used to capture user inputs. Specifically, the <TEXTAREA> tag is used to allow users to enter multiple lines of text. One application of the <TEXTAREA> tag is to allow users to provide feedback about your WCA. The syntax of the <TEXTAREA> tag is shown in Figure 5.24.

Figure 5.24 <TEXTAREA> Syntax

```
<textarea name="mytextarea" rows="2" cols="16"></textarea>
```

The required *name* attribute identifies a <TEXTAREA> tag so that it can be distinguished from other tags. In Figure 5.24, "mytextarea" was chosen arbitrarily to illustrate a possible choice. For <TEXTAREA> tags, the *name* attribute is used to identify data to a server so that the server will know from which field the data originated. The *name* should be lowercase and short to minimize the bandwidth required to send data to the server.

The required *rows* attribute indicates the height of the text area in number of horizontal lines. *Rows* in Figure 5.24 is "2". This indicates that two rows of text can be entered.

A reasonable value for *rows* is eight or less. The Palm device display can accommodate up to 13 rows, but more than eight is visually cumbersome. Besides, if more text is entered than can be displayed at a time, scroll bars automatically appear for navigation.

The required *cols* attribute indicates the width of the text area in number of ASCII characters. *Cols* in Figure 5.24 is "16". This indicates that 16 characters can be entered on each row of the <TEXTAREA>.

A reasonable value for *cols* is twenty or less. The Palm OS device display can accommodate up to 28 columns, but more than 20 is visually cumbersome. Besides, if more text is entered than can be displayed at a time, scroll bars automatically appear for navigation.

WARNING

The <TEXTAREA> tag can result in significant bandwidth consumption, depending on how much data is entered before form submission.

If you want default text to be displayed in the text area control when its initially displayed, you should put the text between the start and end tags. This can be useful for prompting the user or for showing values previously entered if the user has to revise a form submission. You could also put some sort of prompt in the initial text that the user will delete and replace with his or her own text.

A complete WCA source code listing and Palm OS device screen shot illustrating the use of the <TEXTAREA> tag are shown in Figures 5.25 and 5.26.

Figure 5.25 <TEXTAREA> Example

```
<html>
<head>
<title>Textarea</title>
<meta name="PalmComputingPlatform" content="true">
</head>
<body>
<center>
<form method="GET"
    action="http://cgi.unwiredwidgets.com/cgi-bin/textarea.pl">
<font size="4">&lt;TEXTAREA&gt;</font>
<br>
<textarea name="mytextarea" rows="2" cols="16"></textarea>
</form>
</center>
</body>
</html>
```

Figure 5.26 <TEXTAREA> Example

Tracking Widget Inventory Example

To tie together the form tags discussed thus far (<INPUT>, <SELECT>/<OPTION>, and <TEXTAREA>), consider an inventory-update WCA for Unwired Widgets. A WCA is needed that will assist shipment receiving personnel in logging the receipt of widgets. The data that must be logged are as follows:

- Widget Type (size, shape, color)
- Quantity
- Receiving Attributes (bad invoice, missing widgets)
- Notes

The corresponding form tags that are needed to handle the data are as follows:

- <SELECT>/<OPTION> Widget Type (size, shape)
- *Radio*-type <INPUT> Widget Type (color)
- *Text*-type <INPUT> Quantity
- *Checkbox*-type <INPUT> Receiving Attributes (bad invoice, missing widgets)
- <TEXTAREA> Notes

A complete WCA source code listing and Palm OS device screen shot are shown in Figures 5.27 and 5.28. Note how the WCA flows from top to bottom, allowing the user to enter the widget of interest (size, shape, color), quantity, and receipt information (bad invoice, missing widgets, notes). Finally, a password/key is available for user authentication by the server—you don't want everyone updating your inventory database! **Submit** and **Reset** buttons complete the example, providing necessary control operations. Note, however, that the Notes (<TEXTAREA>) are for illustration only and are not particularly efficient!

Figure 5.27 Inventory Example (WCA)

```
<html>
<head>
<title>Inventory</title>
<meta name="PalmComputingPlatform" content="true">
</head>
<body>

<center>
<form method="GET"
    action="http://cgi.unwiredwidgets.com/cgi-bin/inventory.pl">

<font size="4">Inventory Update Form</font>

<br>
<br>
<select name="item" size="1">
    <option selected>Big Square Widget</option>
    <option>Small Square Widget</option>
    <option>Big Round Widget</option>
    <option>Small Round Widget</option>
</select>
<br>
<input type="radio" name="color" value="r" checked>Red
<input type="radio" name="color" value="g">Green
<input type="radio" name="color" value="b">Blue
<input type="radio" name="color" value="y">Yellow
<br>
Recv'd Quantity:
```

Continued

Figure 5.27 Continued

```
<input type="text" name="qty" value="" size="4" maxlength="6">

<hr>
<input type="checkbox" name="status" value="b_inv">Bad Invoice
   
<input type="checkbox" name="status" value="m_wid">Missing Widgets
<hr>

Note:
<textarea name="note" rows="2" cols="16"></textarea>

<input type="hidden" name="dev" value="%deviceid">

<br>
<br>
Key:
<input type="password" name="pword" size="6" maxlength="6">
<br>
<input type="submit" value="Submit">
<input type="reset"  value="Reset">
<br>
<font size="1">unwiredwidgets.com</font>

</form>
</center>

</body>
</html>
```

Figure 5.28 Inventory Example (WCA)

Processing Forms on the Server

To process form data on a server requires server-side software to receive, interpret, and act on the data. This can be accomplished via a variety of programming languages, with one common choice being Perl. The Perl script in Figure 5.29 (inventory.pl) illustrates how to process form data—specifically how to process form data for the Inventory Example (WCA) in Figure 5.27. Figure 5.29 receives form data and uses it to update an inventory database (inventory.db), shown in Figure 5.30. A Web clipping is also created and returned to the Palm VII to indicate the status of the operation. Keep in mind that clippings should be kept to a minimum to conserve communication bandwidth.

Figure 5.29 Inventory Script (inventory.pl)

```
#!/usr/bin/perl
use CGI;
&update_inventory;

sub update_inventory {

    # parse incoming parameters as per either "GET" or "POST"
    $q = new CGI;

    # isolate parameter names
    @name_list = $q->param;
```

Continued

Figure 5.29 Continued

```
# extract values
foreach $name (@name_list) {

    # decode encoding
    $value = $q->param($name);

    # save pertinent data
    if    ( $name eq "item"  ) { $item_value  = $value; }
    elsif ( $name eq "color" ) { $color_value = $value; }
    elsif ( $name eq "qty"   ) { $qty_value   = $value; }
}

# open inventory database
open (inventory, "inventory.db") or
    die "Couldn't open inventory.db!";

# process inventory database one record at a time
$updated_db = "";
$flag       = 0;
while (<inventory>) {

    # read database record
    readline;

    # process database record
    ($field_0, $field_1, $field_2) = split /,/;
    if (($field_0 eq $item_value) && ($field_1 eq $color_value)) {

        # update database record
        $updated_db .= $field_0 . "," . $field_1 . "," .
            ($field_2 + $qty_value) . "\n";
        $flag = 1;
```

Continued

Figure 5.29 Continued

```
        }
        else {

            # update database record
            $updated_db .= $_;
        }
    }

    # close inventory database
    close (inventory) or die "Couldn't close inventory.db!";

    # return results header
    print "Content-type: text/html\n\n";
    print "<html>\n";
    print "<head>\n";
    print "<title>Inventory</title>\n";
    print "</head>\n";
    print "<body>\n";
    print "<center>\n";
    print "<font size='4'><b>Inventory</b></font>\n";

    # report success, or lack thereof
    if ($flag eq 1) {
        print "<br>Successful Update\n";
    }
    else {
        print "<br>UNSUCCESSFUL UPDATE; TRY AGAIN!\n";
    }

    # return results footer
    print "</center>\n";
    print "</body>\n";
    print "</html>\n";
```

Continued

Figure 5.29 Continued

```
    # update inventory database
    if ($flag = 1) {

        # open inventory database
        open (inventory, ">inventory.db") or
            die "Couldn't open inventory.db!";

        # update contents
        print (inventory $updated_db);

        # close inventory database
        close (inventory) or die "Couldn't close inventory.db!";
    }
}
```

Figure 5.30 Inventory Database (inventory.db)

```
inventory.db
Big Square Widget,r,11
Big Square Widget,g,12
Big Square Widget,b,13
Big Square Widget,y,14
Small Square Widget,r,21
Small Square Widget,g,22
Small Square Widget,b,23
Small Square Widget,y,24
Big Round Widget,r,31
Big Round Widget,g,32
Big Round Widget,b,33
Big Round Widget,y,34
Small Round Widget,r,41
Small Round Widget,g,42
```

Continued

Figure 5.30 Continued

```
Small Round Widget,b,43
Small Round Widget,y,44
```

Debugging...

What Environment Is Useful for Debugging My WCA?

Using the Palm OS Emulator's ability to redirect network requests, combined with Microsoft's Internet Information Server (IIS) or the Apache Web server, provides a robust development environment for debugging WCAs. This approach avoids the need for both a Palm OS device and Palm.Net account and the associated charges. Also, this approach allows you to test full server communication, including server-side form data reception and parsing.

The following server-side Perl script (found on the CD as debug.pl) returns HTML code showing all of the parameters submitted from a form; it can be very useful for debugging form submissions.

```
#!/usr/bin/perl

use CGI;

&debug_client_interface;

sub debug_client_interface {

    # parse incoming parameters
    $q = new CGI;

    # isolate parameter names
    @name_list = $q->param;
```

Continued

```
    # return results header
    print "Content-type: text/html\n\n";
    print "<html>\n";
    print "<head>\n";
    print "<title>Debug</title>\n";
    print "</head>\n";
    print "<body>\n";
    print "<center>\n";
    print "<font size='4'><b>Data Received</b></font>\n";

    # extract values
    foreach $name (@name_list) {

        # decode encoding
        $value = $q->param($name);

        # output received data
        print "<br>";
        print $name;
        print "=";
        print $value;
        print "\n";
    }

    # return results footer
    print "</center>\n";
    print "</body>\n";
    print "</html>\n";
}
```

NOTE

A common problem associated with Perl scripts is installing them on a server where Perl isn't located in /usr/bin, as with Apache running under Windows NT. For such installations, change the first line of the script to refer to the Perl interpreter. For example, #!/usr/bin/perl might be changed to #!/usr/local/bin/perl. The name of the Perl interpreter might also need to be changed, as in #!/usr/bin/perl5. This is the case with some installations as a prerequisite to including the CGI package (such as "use CGI").

On a Windows box where the Perl interpreter is in the server's executable path, you can just specify "#!perl" with no path information.

Placing a Widget Order Example

On the customer side of business for Unwired Widgets, consider an order-processing WCA. A WCA is needed that will assist customers in placing widget orders. The data that must be collected are as follows:

- Widget Type (size, shape, color)
- Quantity

The corresponding form tags that are needed to handle the data are as follows:

- <SELECT>/<OPTION> Widget Type (size, shape)
- *Radio*-type <INPUT> Widget Type (color)
- *Text*-type <INPUT> Quantity

A complete WCA source code listing and Palm OS device screen shot are shown in Figures 5.31 and 5.32.

Figure 5.31 Order Example

```
<html>
<head>
<title>Order</title>
<meta name="PalmComputingPlatform" content="true">
</head>
```

Continued

Figure 5.31 Continued

```
<body>

<center>
<form method="GET"
    action="http://cgi.unwiredwidgets.com/cgi-bin/order.pl">

<font size="4">Order Form</font>

<br>
<br>
<select name="item" size="1">
    <option selected>Big Square Widget</option>
    <option>Small Square Widget</option>
    <option>Big Round Widget</option>
    <option>Small Round Widget</option>
</select>
<br>
<input type="radio" name="color" checked>Red
<input type="radio" name="color">Green
<input type="radio" name="color">Blue
<input type="radio" name="color">Yellow

<br>
<br>
<br>
Order Quantity:
<input type="text" name="qty" value="" size="4" maxlength="6">

<input type="hidden" name="dev" value="%deviceid">

<br>
<br>
<br>
```

Continued

Figure 5.31 Continued

```
Customer Key:
<input type="password" name="pword" size="6" maxlength="6">


<br>
<br>
<br>
<input type="submit" value="Submit">
<input type="reset"  value="Reset">
<br>
<font size="1">unwiredwidgets.com</font>


</form>
</center>


</body>
</html>
```

Figure 5.32 Order Example

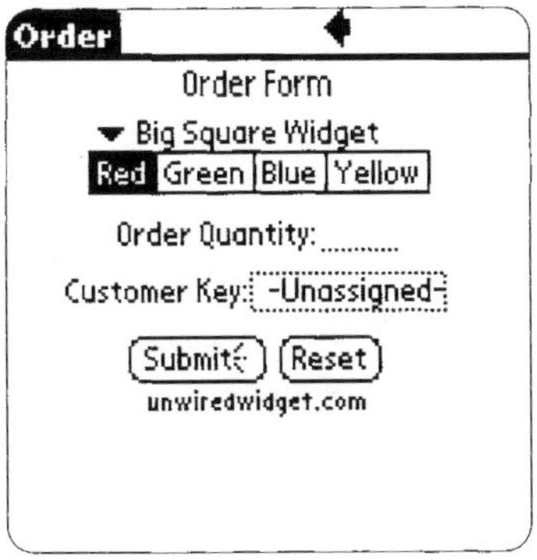

Enhancing Forms for Clipper

The <INPUT> tag, as has been previously discussed, is enhanced by its wide variety of types. Additional enhancement is also available via two Palm-specific types: *timepicker* and *datepicker*. As their names suggest, they are used to handle time and date data, respectively. Applications include time/date stamping of <FORM> data and displaying the current time and date.

Using the *Timepicker* Type

The *timepicker* type indicates that the corresponding <INPUT> tag can display time data. *Timepicker* displays the current or specified time in the 12-hour format "HH:MM am/pm", although a different display format can be specified in the Preferences application. Time data is submitted to, and received from, the server in 24-hour format, "HH:MM". Note that the *value* attribute can be used to set the time to be displayed. The syntax of *timepicker*-type <INPUT> is shown in Figure 5.33.

Figure 5.33 *Timepicker*-Type <INPUT> Syntax

```
<input type="timepicker" name="mytmpckr" value="08:29 AM">
```

The *type* attribute indicates that the *timepicker*-type <INPUT> tag is of *timepicker* type (such as "timepicker"). That is, the <INPUT> tag can display the current or specified time.

The required *name* attribute identifies an <INPUT> tag so that it can be distinguished from other tags. In Figure 5.33, "mytmpckr" was chosen arbitrarily to illustrate a possible choice. For *timepicker*-type <INPUT>, the *name* attribute is used to identify data to a server so that the server will know from which field the data originated.

The format of the optional *value* attribute is either 12-hour ("HH:MM am/pm") or 24-hour ("HH:MM"). If *value* is not specified, the current time is displayed. The display format defaults to 12-hour ("HH:MM am/pm"), although the user can change this using the Preferences application. Note that time data is sent to, and received from, the server in 24-hour "HH:MM" format.

NOTE

A *value* attribute that is not understood is treated as if it had not been specified at all. For example, in *value*="mytime," "mytime" is not understood as a valid time and is ignored. The current time is displayed.

A complete WCA source code listing and Palm OS device screen shot illustrating the use of the *timepicker*-type <INPUT> are shown in Figures 5.34 and 5.35.

Figure 5.34 *Timepicker*-Type <INPUT> Example

```
<html>
<head>
<title>Timepicker</title>
<meta name="PalmComputingPlatform" content="true">
</head>
<body>
<center>
<form method="GET"
    action="http://cgi.unwiredwidgets.com/cgi-bin/input_timepicker.pl">
<font size="4">TEXT-type &lt;TIMEPICKER&gt;</font>
<br>
<input type="timepicker" name="mytmpckr">
</form>
</center>
</body>
</html>
```

Figure 5.35 *Timepicker*-Type <INPUT> Example

Using the *Datepicker* Type

The *datepicker* type indicates that the corresponding <INPUT> tag can display date data. *Datepicker* displays the current or specified date in the format MM/DD/YY, although a different display format can be specified in the Preferences application. Date data is submitted to, and received from, the server in YYYY-MM-DD format. Note that the *value* attribute can be used to set the date to be displayed. The syntax of *datepicker*-type <INPUT> is shown in Figure 5.36.

Figure 5.36 *Datepicker*-Type <INPUT> Syntax

```
<input type="datepicker" name="mydtpckr" value="08/28/62">
```

The *type* attribute indicates that the *datepicker*-type <INPUT> tag is of *datepicker* type (e.g., "datepicker"). That is, the <INPUT> tag can display the current, or specified, dates.

The required *name* attribute identifies an <INPUT> tag so that it can be distinguished from other tags. In Figure 5.36, "mydtpckr" was chosen arbitrarily to illustrate a possible choice. For *datepicker*-type <INPUT>, the *name* attribute is used to identify data to a server so that the server will know from which field the data originated.

The optional *value* attribute specifies the date to be displayed. If *value* is not specified, the current date is displayed. The format of the *value* attribute is MM/DD/YY, which is also the default display format; the display format can be changed by the user using the Preferences application. Date information is sent to/from the server in YYYY-MM-DD format.

NOTE

Other undocumented formats can be used to specify a date value, such as "Aug 28, 1962" and "08/28/1962". Note, however, that a *value* attribute that is not understood is treated as if it had not been specified at all. For example, in *value*="1962-08-28", "1962-08-28" is not understood as a valid date and is ignored. The current date is displayed.

A complete WCA source code listing and Palm OS device screen shot illustrating the use of the *datepicker*-type <INPUT> are shown in Figures 5.37 and 5.38.

Figure 5.37 *Datepicker*-Type <INPUT> Example

```
<html>
<head>
<title>Datepicker</title>
<meta name="PalmComputingPlatform" content="true">
</head>
<body>
<center>
<form method="GET"
    action="http://cgi.unwiredwidgets.com/cgi-bin/input_datepicker.pl">
<font size="4">TEXT-type &lt;DATEPICKER&gt;</font>
<br>
<input type="datepicker" name="mydtpckr">
</form>
</center>
</body>
</html>
```

Figure 5.38 *Datepicker*-Type <INPUT> Example

Setting Delivery Date for Widget Orders Example

An example application of both *timepicker-* and *datepicker*-type <INPUT> tags, and a Palm OS device screen shot, are shown in Figures 5.39 and 5.40, including a complete source code listing. Note that no time and/or date information is preset via the *value* attribute, implying that the current time and date will be used.

WARNING

The danger in using *timepicker-* and *datepicker*-type <INPUT> tags for display only is that the user will think that they are dynamic controls and that changing them will affect form submission.

Figure 5.39 Order Time/Date Example

```
<html>
<head>
<title>Order Time/Date</title>
<meta name="PalmComputingPlatform" content="true">
</head>
<body>

<center>
<form method="GET"
    action="http://cgi.unwiredwidgets.com/cgi-bin/order_tm_dt.pl">

<font size="4">Order Form</font>

<br>
<br>
<select name="item" size="1">
    <option selected>Big Square Widget</option>
    <option>Small Square Widget</option>
```

Continued

Figure 5.39 Continued

```
    <option>Big Round Widget</option>
    <option>Small Round Widget</option>
</select>
<br>
<input type="radio" name="color" checked>Red
<input type="radio" name="color">Green
<input type="radio" name="color">Blue
<input type="radio" name="color">Yellow

<br>
<br>
<br>
Order Quantity:
<input type="text" name="qty" value="" size="4" maxlength="6">

<br>
<br>
<br>
Delivery Approx. 2 Weeks From:
<br>
<input type="timepicker" name="mytmpckr">
<input type="datepicker" name="mydtpckr">
<br>

<input type="hidden" name="dev" value="%deviceid">

<br>
<br>
<br>
Customer Key:
<input type="password" name="pword" size="6" maxlength="6">

<br>
```

Continued

Figure 5.39 Continued

```
<br>
<br>
<input type="submit" value="Submit">
<input type="reset"  value="Reset">
<br>
<font size="1">unwiredwidgets.com</font>

</form>
</center>

</body>
</html>
```

Figure 5.40 Order Time/Date Example

Summary

This chapter illustrates how forms provide the mechanism for WCAs to become more than just a one-way read-only communication channel. Forms provide the means by which user interaction can be supported, thus providing the basis for WCA interaction with the Web.

Based on HTML 3.2, Clipper supports most standard HTML form tags:

- <INPUT>
- <SELECT/OPTION>
- <TEXTAREA>

These tags are illustrated in two examples: "Tracking Widget Inventory" and "Placing A Widget Order." The most flexible of the supported tags is <INPUT>, as it supports all of the following *types*:

- *Text*
- *Password*
- *Checkbox*
- *Radio*
- *Hidden*
- *Submit*
- *Reset*

Clipper also supports Palm-specific input types, most notably *timepicker* and *datepicker*. This is illustrated in a third example, "Setting Delivery Dates For Widget Orders."

Communication with a server is accomplished via form GET and PUT methods, depending on the application. GET appends form data to the *action* URL, whereas POST sends form data in the post body. Keep in mind that *name* and *value* attributes for all tags should be kept short to minimize the bandwidth required to send them to a server.

Solutions Fast Track

Using Standard HTML Forms

- ☑ HTML forms enable data to be sent to a server or received from a server.
- ☑ Three main form tags exist to capture user input: <INPUT>, <SELECT>/<OPTION>, <TEXTAREA>.
- ☑ Tags are case-insensitive in standard HTML.
- ☑ HTML form tags typically have a *name* and *value* attribute. Other attributes are tag-specific. *Name* and *value* attributes are lowercase and short.
- ☑ <INPUT> tags have many various types, including: *text*, *password*, *checkbox*, *radio*, *submit*, *reset*, and *hidden*.
- ☑ <OPTION> tags do not typically need the *value* attribute within WCAs.
- ☑ <OPTION> tags should be alphabetized by label, and labels should not contain any special characters and/or spaces. This is so the Palm OS UI can quickly jump to <OPTION> labels as graffiti characters are entered.

Tracking Widget Inventory Example

- ☑ Many form tags can be incorporated into a single WCA.
- ☑ Many choices exist in applying form tags to a particular application.
- ☑ When applying form tags, several rules of thumb exist to optimize server communication.
- ☑ Using POSE's network redirection coupled with IIS is a reasonable environment in which to develop WCAs. This approach avoids the need for both a Palm OS device and Palm.Net account—including associated charges. Also, this approach allows you to test full server communication, including server-side form data reception and parsing.

Placing a Widget Order Example

- ☑ Using a WCA similar to that in the Inventory Example enhances the user's experience, not to mention providing the developer the benefits of code reuse.
- ☑ Customer Key is one application of a *password*-type <INPUT> tag that can be used to identify existing customers. The net effect is to minimize the interaction necessary to conduct a transaction. This benefits both customer (the UI experience) and WCA (bandwidth conservation).

Enhancing Forms for Clipper

- ☑ *Timepicker* and *datepicker* are Palm-specific types of <INPUT>.
- ☑ *Timepicker* data can be specified in either 12- or 24-hour format. The display format is specified in the Preferences application, with the default being the 12-hour "HH:MM am/pm" format. Server communication is done using the 24-hour "HH:MM" format.
- ☑ *Datepicker* display format is specified in the Preferences application, with the default being the same as that for directly specifying a date: MM/DD/YY. Server communication format is YYYY-MM-DD.
- ☑ Current time and date can be accessed, or a specific time and date can be set via the *value* attribute.

Setting Delivery Dates for Widget Orders Example

- ☑ *Timepicker* and *datepicker* can be used to augment WCAs.
- ☑ *Timepicker* and *datepicker* can be used for several applications, including time stamping activity logs, scheduling, and so on.

Frequently Asked Questions

The following Frequently Asked Questions, answered by the authors of this book, are designed to both measure your understanding of the concepts presented in this chapter and to assist you with real-life implementation of these concepts. To have your questions about this chapter answered by the author, browse to **www.syngress.com/solutions** and click on the **"Ask the Author"** form.

Q: What development package is most useful for creating WCAs (for example, .htm and/or .html files) and server-side scripts (for example, .pl files)?

A: A simple text editor (such as WordPad under Windows) is a reasonable tool for WCA and script creation.

Q: How are server-side scripts, such as the Perl sample in this chapter, compiled?

A: Server-side Perl scripts are interpreted and do not have to be compiled. Other server-side languages do have compilers—you must consult each language's particular documentation for additional information.

Q: How are WCAs installed?

A: WCAs are installed in the same fashion as any other Palm OS application, regardless of whether installation is occurring within the emulator or on an actual device.

Q: How are server-side scripts installed?

A: There is no single answer to this question. However, the Perl scripts used as examples in this chapter were transferred via FTP (ASCII mode) to a Unix Web hosting account. A chmod had to be done to insure that execution privileges were set on the script. Also, "use CGI" within the script required specifying "#!/usr/bin/perl5" as the first line of the script.

Q: Where is a good starting point for additional information?

A: You can always find additional information at Palm, Inc.'s Web site at www.palmos.com.

Chapter 6

Optimizing WCAs for Palm OS Devices

Solutions in this chapter:

- Making Pages Useful on Both Desktop and Palm Devices
- Making Unwired Widgets Pages for Both Desktop and Palm Devices
- Using Tables for Page Layout
- Specifying History Text
- Using MAILTO Links to Send E-Mail

☑ Summary

☑ Solutions Fast Track

☑ Frequently Asked Questions

Introduction

In today's wireless Web, you can seldom specify only one device for accessing your Web content. As the Internet becomes increasingly central to business and recreation, the variety of ways to access the Internet is increasing. In Japan, more people already access the Net from mobile devices than from fixed or "landline" computers. As the number of mobile devices grows, people are demanding that they be able to access all Web content from their wireless PDAs.

Building pages for the Palm OS is quite different from building pages for the desktop. A lot of the experience you may have in creating standard Web pages applies here, but there are several tricks that can enhance the user experience on a handheld device, and there are also many pitfalls. The first and most obvious difference is the limited screen size, but just as critical is the very limited download speeds of current wireless devices. The Palm VII has a nominal speed of 9.6Kbps, while the Palm V or Handspring with an OmniSky modem tops out at 19.2Kbps. The screen has a viewing width of 153 pixels. In comparison, most modern Web sites are designed for a minimum speed of 56Kbps and expect a screen resolution of at least 800x600 pixels in full color.

However, with some careful planning, you can create pages that are universally accessible. Among the optimization possibilities are special Hypertext Markup Language (HTML) tags that allow you to make pages useable from a standard Web browser and from the Palm OS Clipper. We look at how to modify your pages to make this easier. If you're building pages just for the Palm OS, you may find it easier to lay out your presentation using HTML tables. Later in this chapter, we look at how you can use tables to position items within the Web clipping page. This is a powerful technique and can help you make efficient use of the limited screen size, but it's subject to limitations not seen on the desktop. We also look at some special tags that allow your visitors to navigate around the local cache, and we also show you how to send e-mail from within your Web clipping pages.

Making Pages Useful on Both Desktop and Palm Devices

Back in the early days of the Web, developers often resorted to writing completely separate pages for both of the major browsers. These days, your Web site may be visited by people using everything from a WAP phone to a Palm device to a Pocket PC to a full-screen Web browser. Although you have no choice but to write separate code for WAP phones, wouldn't it be nice if you could use the same pages for both full-size Web browsers and Palm devices? Web Clipping Applications (WCAs), after all, use regular HTML, so there's no reason your pages can't be displayed on a desktop browser (or even Pocket Explorer on a Windows CE device). The obvious difficulty here is that you need to design pages to be 153 pixels wide (or less) in order to display properly on a Palm OS device. Optimizing pages for this format isn't going to give you a very pleasing view in a desktop browser. However, with careful planning, you can design pages that look good in both formats.

What's needed, of course, is a way to tell Palm OS devices to ignore content that can't be displayed properly. Fortunately, Palm anticipated this need and provided us with a very useful tag: <SMALLSCREENIGNORE>. This tag tells the Palm.Net proxy to throw away all markup (that is, HTML tags) within this tag set. You can use this to "mask" markup that you don't want to appear on a Palm OS device, such as large graphics or banners. Full-size browsers, meanwhile, will just ignore this tag and display all valid HTML within it.

However, you need to keep a few limitations in mind. Although you can use the <SMALLSCREENIGNORE> tag to hide HTML code from the Palm device, HTML doesn't have a corresponding tag to tell desktop browsers to ignore WCA-only content. Provided that you keep your code well-formed by having no unclosed or improperly nested tags, most browsers will totally ignore any Palm-proprietary tags or attributes. This means that if you use, for instance, the Palm-proprietary *button* attribute of the <A HREF> tag to display links as buttons, these will revert to normal hypertext links in a desktop browser. However, desktop browsers will still attempt to parse and display content within unknown tags. There's no easy way to tell a browser to skip over a block of code that you intended only for Palm OS devices. As we'll see, there are some creative ways around this that will allow you to create universally good-looking pages, but we may need to slightly "bend" the rules of good HTML.

Using the <SMALLSCREENIGNORE> Tag

<SMALLSCREENIGNORE> is a proprietary tag, meaning it's not part of the official HTML specification. However, it's used just like a normal HTML tag; it has an opening and corresponding closing tag but no attributes.

Say, for example, that you have a graphical banner advertisement on your main page. The typical size for a Web banner ad is 470 pixels wide by 60 pixels high. As you learned in Chapter 4, both the Query Application Builder and the Palm.Net proxy will simply discard images wider than 153 pixels, replacing them with "[image]" or the text in the *alt* attribute. However, banner ads are typically surrounded by a link leading to the advertiser's Web site. This will not be removed, so you'll end up with a text link to a Web site that's most likely not Palm OS-friendly. The solution is to surround the entire banner code with <SMALLSCREENIGNORE>, shown as follows:

```
<smallscreenignore>
   <a href="http://www.verylargewebpage.com">
     <img src="banner.gif" width="470" height="60" alt="Click Here">
  </a>
</smallscreenignore>
```

Making Unwired Widgets Pages for Both Desktop and Palm Devices

As you learned in Chapter 3, Web clipping doesn't support nested tables (that is, a table within a table). Nested tables are one of the main techniques Web designers use to provide a sophisticated page layout in standard desktop browsers. The Query Application Builder will happily compile a page with nested tables, but it will ignore any <TABLE> tags nested within the first one, giving you unpredictable, and usually unsatisfactory, results.

Now, HTML purists (and I count myself among them) may want to check their hats at the door in this section. What I describe—a very neat way to construct pages that look good in standard desktop browsers and Palm OS devices alike—is not strictly "good" HTML. In fact, if you run your HTML code through a validator, it will complain about "nesting errors" and illegal tags. In technical jargon, you will not have *well-formed* HTML.

Debugging...

Well-Formed HTML and HTML Validation

As you may know, HTML is based on Standard Generalized Markup Language (SGML). SGML defines a set of rules that detail what tags are allowed, what attributes they should have, and so forth. This is called a Document Type Definition (DTD). The World Wide Web Consortium

Continued

(W3C) is the group charged with creating these DTDs and publishing the HTML specifications. Web clipping supports a subset of the HTML 3.2 definition. Validating your code against the official specification is always a good idea. (*Validation* is the process of comparing your HTML against the official specification. You can do this online at the W3C's Web site at http://validator.w3.org.) Many professional Web design tools, such as Allaire's HomeSite, have built-in validators.

Valid HTML is code that has been checked against the standard to confirm that tags are used correctly. Because <SMALLSCREENIGNORE> is a proprietary Palm OS tag and not in the official specification, a validator will complain that this is not a legal tag. However, browsers are programmed to ignore any tags they don't recognize, so you can disregard this particular warning.

You can avoid some of these validation errors by specifying the correct DTD to be used. Most validators allow you to specify where the DTD is located, in order to override their default DTD. One way to do this is to include the following tag (all on one line) as the first line in your HTML file:

```
<!DOCTYPE HTML PUBLIC "-//POS//DTD WCA HTML 1.1//EN"
"http://www.palm.com/dev/webclipping-html-dtd-11.dtd">
```

This is called an *SGML declaration*. It's a way of telling the browser where it can find the official version of the DTD that this document conforms to. In reality, modern browsers have this DTD built in; they already know the major HTML DTDs. But a validator will use this tag to go out and download the specific DTD it should validate the document against. In the tag preceding this paragraph, the document is declaring that it conforms to the WCA HTML version 1.1 DTD, located on Palm Inc.'s Web site at the URL specified.

We say markup is well-formed when all tags are closed properly (every tag has a matched opening and closing tag pair). They must also be nested properly, so that the opening tag for a one tag pair cannot be inside another open/close tag pair:

```
<td>This is not <b>well-formed</td></b>
<td>This is <b>correct</b></td>
```

Unfortunately, you may occasionally need to bend this "well-formed" rule in your use of <SMALLSCREENIGNORE>.

Starting with a Desktop-Oriented Page

Let's construct a page (see Figure 6.1) for the Unwired Widgets main Web site that uses tables to lay out a typical left-hand navigation menu, with another central table to display a list of available products.

Figure 6.1 Nested Table Construction in HTML

```
<html>
<head>
    <meta name="palmcomputingplatform" content="true">
    <meta name="historylisttext" content="Products">
    <title>Unwired Widgets - Products</title>
</head>

<body bgcolor="#FFFFFF">
<table width="750" border="0" cellspacing="0" cellpadding="2">
  <tr>
    <td colspan="3" align="center">
    <a href="http://www.erbaviva.com">
    <img src="http://www.erbaviva.com/img/banner1.gif" width="468"
    height="60" border="0"></a>
    </td>
  </tr>
  <tr>
    <td valign="top" width="100">
    <table width="100" border="0" cellspacing="0" cellpadding="0">
      <tr>
        <td><img src="image/unwired_logo.gif" width="100"
            height="75"alt="Unwired Widgets"></td>
      </tr>
      <tr>
        <td><a href="about.html">About Us</a></td>
      </tr>
      <tr>
        <td><a href="products.html">Products</a></td>
```

Continued

Figure 6.1 Continued

```
    </tr>
    <tr>
      <td><a href="shop.html">Shop Online</a></td>
    </tr>
    <tr>
      <td><a href="contact.html">Contact Us</a></td>
    </tr>
  </table>

  </td>
  <td width="550">
  <hr>
  <h2 align="center">Welcome to Unwired Widgets</h2>
  <p>We've got a wide range of products to meet all of your
  widget needs. Click on the item that interests you below
  to view a picture and further details.</p>
  <h3>Products</h3>
  <table width="100%" border="1" cellspacing="0" cellpadding="0">
    <tr>
      <th>SKU</th>
      <th>Description</th>
      <th>Color</th>
    </tr>
    <tr>
      <td>34345</td>
      <td>Square widget round-hole adapter</td>
      <td>Red</td>
    </tr>
    <tr>
      <td>34875</td>
      <td>Square widget round-hole adapter</td>
      <td>Green</td>
    </tr>
```

Continued

Figure 6.1 Continued

```
        <tr>
          <td>34876</td>
          <td>Square widget round-hole adapter</td>
          <td>Blue</td>
        </tr>
        <tr>
          <td>34691</td>
          <td>Square widget round-hole adapter</td>
          <td>Yellow</td>
        </tr>
      </table>
      </td>
      <td width="100" valign="top">
      <a href="http://www.unwiredwidgets.com/sizeguide.html">
      <img src="image/rt_advert1.gif" width="100" height="125"
       border="0"></a>
      <br>
      Try our Interactive Sizing Guide
      </td>
    </tr>
    <tr>
      <td colspan="3">
      <!-- bottom text-only navigation menu ->
        <p align="center">
        <a href="about.html">About Us</a> |
        <a href="products.html">Products</a> |
        <a href="shop.html">Shop Online</a> |
        <a href="contact.html">Contact Us</a></p>
        <p align="center">&copy;2001 Unwired Widgets<br>
        <a href="mailto:info@unwiredwidgets.com">
         info@unwiredwidgets.com</a>
        </p>
      </td>
```

Continued

Figure 6.1 Continued

```
  </tr>
</table>
</body>
</html>
```

WARNING

If you try to compile the code that was shown Figure 6.1 with the Query Application Builder (QAB), it will give you an error when it hits the first navigation menu item. This is because it expects the linked pages about.html, shop.html, and contact.html to exist in the same folder because they are "local" to the WCA. If these are server-side pages, then we would link to them with the full <A HREF="http://..."> syntax. For clarity, I removed that code. So in order to compile a WCA, you'll need to either insert the full http://www.unwiredwidgets.com/ part of the links, as I did with the right-hand sizeguide.html link, or make three empty pages, in the same folder, with these names.

If you save the code in Figure 6.1 to disk as products.html and then load it into a browser, you'll see that it's a fairly typical (if uninspired) Web page, laid out with a traditional three-column grid: a banner advertisement across the top, left-side navigation menu, central content area, and right-side column with special offers. (In the code, I've omitted the hyperlinks around each product line for clarity—we add these later in the chapter.) The whole page is laid out in one three-column table, and both the navigation menu and product listing use nested sub-tables to control their appearance. Figure 6.2 shows a diagram of the table layout, and Figure 6.3 shows how this page will look in a desktop browser.

Figure 6.2 Layout of Nested Table Construction

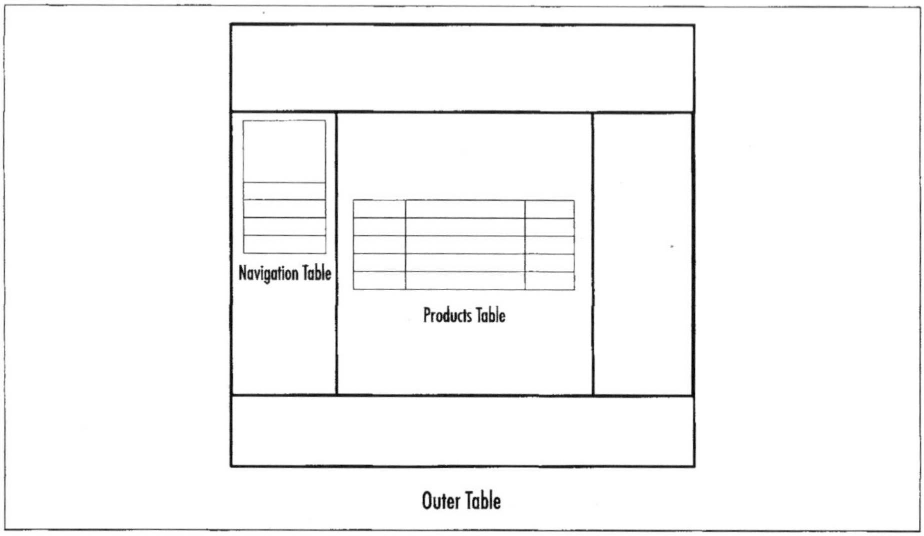

Figure 6.3 Nested Table Construction in a Desktop Browser

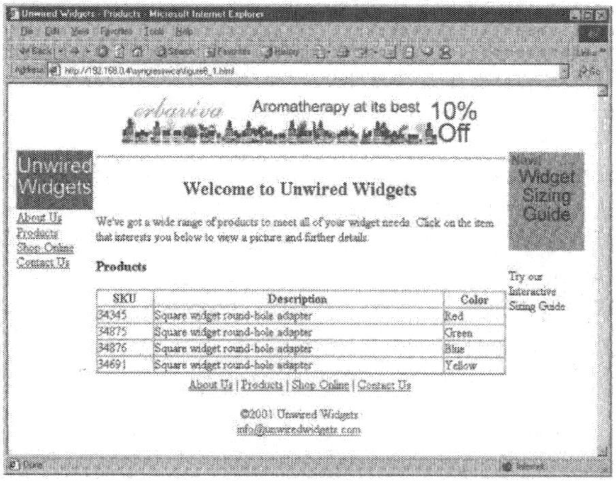

Redesigning the Page for Both Desktop and Handheld

We've already seen how to mask the banner advertisement so that it won't appear on a Palm OS device. In this case, we could wrap the entire table row containing the banner in <SMALLSCREENIGNORE>, because it doesn't contain anything that's needed on a Palm device.

```
<smallscreenignore>
  <tr>
    <td colspan="3">
    <a href="http://www.erbaviva.com">
     <img src="http://www.erbaviva.com/img/banner1.gif" width="468"
      height="60" border="0"></a>
    </td>
  </tr>
</smallscreenignore>
```

However, if you look at the navigation menu section of the code, you'll notice an immediate problem: The Unwired Widgets logo is 100 pixels wide. On a Palm device screen, that leaves you just 50 pixels or so for the actual content. The next problem is that the real content of the page—the product listing—is within a sub-table that's set at 550 pixels wide. Remember, Web clipping pages don't currently provide a horizontal scrollbar, so everything beyond the right margin is gone forever. Horizontal scrolling is possible in Palm OS 4.0, but it's difficult to use and should be avoided.

So how do we go about redesigning this page so that it looks good on a Palm device or the desktop? First, let's look at what content we really need to be on the Palm OS version. Obviously we want the product listing, and we probably want to link each to a more detailed description page. But we also need some sort of navigation around the Web site. Beyond that, most of the code that is shown Figure 6.1 is superfluous on a Palm device.

The left-side navigation menu is the first, and easiest, problem to deal with. Because it's in a self-contained table, we just surround it with <SMALLSCREENIGNORE>:

```
<smallscreenignore>
<td valign="top" width="100">
  <table width="100" border="1" cellspacing="0" cellpadding="0">
```

```
    <tr>
      <td>
       <img src="image/unwired_logo.gif" width="100"
       height="75" alt="Unwired Widgets">
      </td>
    </tr>
    <tr>
      <td><a href="about.html">About Us</a></td>
    </tr>
    <tr>
      <td><a href="products.html">Products</a></td>
    </tr>
    <tr>
      <td><a href="shop.html">Shop Online</a></td>
    </tr>
    <tr>
      <td><a href="contact.html">Contact Us</a></td>
    </tr>
    </table>
  </td>
  </smallscreenignore>
```

What we did was surround both the nested table itself, as well as the enclosing <TD> column with <SMALLSCREENIGNORE>. This effectively removes this whole left-side column from the page when viewed on the Palm OS device. Now, do the same for the right-side column:

```
<smallscreenignore>
  <td width="100" valign="top">
    <a href="http://www.unwiredwidgets.com/sizeguide.html">
    <img src="image/rt_advert1.gif" width="100"
     height="125" border="0"></a>
    <br>
    Try our Interactive Sizing Guide
  </td>
</smallscreenignore>
```

What we now have, after this code passes through the Palm.Net proxy, is a main table with one single column. Now things begin to get tricky. Because we've already had an opening <TABLE> tag, the Palm.Net proxy will ignore the opening <TABLE> tag wrapping the product listing, so it will interpret the columns within this table as just a string of content text, all in the same cell. But then it comes upon a closing </TABLE> tag and promptly closes the table, leaving us with an "orphan" table row at the bottom. We could continue to wrap bits and pieces of code in more and more <SMALLSCREENIGNORE> tags, but this would rapidly get unmanageable—and it would result in very bloated code for desktop browsers. A better way to handle this would be to reformat the original code a little so that it looks the same on the desktop but is easier to mark up for the Palm device.

Because what we're really interested in is the product listing, let's surround everything except this with <SMALLSCREENIGNORE>. We probably want to maintain the introduction text, so leave this. We also need to change some of the table width settings, because the Palm.Net proxy will happily obey these and give us a 550-pixel-wide table. An easy way to do this is to replace the absolute pixel values with percentages. Unfortunately, WCA pages don't allow percentage widths for the <TABLE> tag. We could set the width to 153 pixels, but this would not look good on a regular browser. One way around this is to leave the inner table width at 100 percent. Web clipping will ignore this attribute, but still use its "best fit" algorithm to size the table appropriately.

NOTE

Generally, Web clipping pages need to conform to the HTML 3.2 specification. HTML 3.2 does not allow percentage widths for the <TD> tag. Web clipping does—but it does not allow percentage widths for the <TABLE> tag, something that *is* valid in HTML 3.2. Instead, the Web Clipping Application Viewer will use a "best fit" algorithm to determine the optimum size for the Palm screen.

There is one other way to force a table to be 153 pixels wide on a Palm device, while using a different measurement on a desktop browser: by using Cascading Style Sheets (CSS).

```
<table width="153" border="1" cellspacing="0" cellpadding="0"
    style="width: 100%;">
```

Because Web clipping doesn't support CSS, it will ignore the style tags and render the table width as 153 pixels. Conversely, Internet Explorer and other CSS-compliant desktop browsers will favor the CSS style and ignore the other width setting. However, beware: CSS is notoriously difficult to use reliably across the two main desktop browsers: Internet Explorer and Netscape Navigator. The designers of Web clipping wisely chose to avoid it totally.

Of course, we also need some way of navigating around the Web site. Luckily, the designer of the original Web page believed in designing pages accessible to those with text-only browsers and incorporated an alternate text-only navigation bar across the bottom of the page. If we move this outside of the main table, it will still show up, nicely centered. We can then add the Palm OS-proprietary *button* attribute of the <A HREF> tag to format these links as buttons. A regular Web browser will ignore this and format them normally. (Note that I added a <SMALLSCREENIGNORE> around one of the vertical bars separating the bottom navigation links in order to hide this on the Palm device.) Figure 6.4 lists the new code.

Figure 6.4 The Unwired Widgets Code Redesigned to Work in Both Palm OS and Desktop Browsers

```
<html>
<head>
    <meta name="palmcomputingplatform" content="true">
    <meta name="historylisttext" content="Products">
    <title>Unwired Widgets - Products</title>
</head>

<body bgcolor="#FFFFFF">
<smallscreenignore>
<table width="750" border="0" cellspacing="0" cellpadding="2">
  <tr>
    <td colspan="3" align="center">
     <a href="http://www.erbaviva.com">
     <img src="http://www.erbaviva.com/img/banner1.gif" width="468"
     height="60" border="0"></a>
    </td>
  </tr>
```

Continued

Figure 6.4 Continued

```
  <tr>
    <td valign="top" width="100">

    <table width="100" border="0" cellspacing="0" cellpadding="0">
    <tr>
      <td><img src="image/unwired_logo.gif" width="100"
       height="75" alt="Unwired Widgets"></td>
    </tr>
    <tr>
      <td><a href="about.html">About Us</a></td>
    </tr>
    <tr>
      <td><a href="products.html">Products</a></td>
    </tr>
    <tr>
      <td><a href="shop.html">Shop Online</a></td>
    </tr>
    <tr>
      <td><a href="contact.html">Contact Us</a></td>
    </tr>
    </table>

    </td>
    <td width="550">
</smallscreenignore>
<!— Palm-friendly HTML begins here —>
    <h2 align="center">Welcome to Unwired Widgets</h2>
  <p>We've got a wide range of products to meet all of
     your widget needs. Click on the item that interests
     you below to view a picture and further details.</p>
    <h3>Products</h3>
    <table width="100%" border="1" cellspacing="0" cellpadding="0">
    <tr>
```

Continued

Figure 6.4 Continued

```
        <th>SKU</th>
        <th>Description</th>
        <th>Color</th>
      </tr>
      <tr>
        <td>34345</td>
        <td>Square widget round-hole adapter</td>
        <td>Red</td>
      </tr>
      <tr>
        <td>34875</td>
        <td>Square widget round-hole adapter</td>
        <td>Green</td>
      </tr>
      <tr>
        <td>34876</td>
        <td>Square widget round-hole adapter</td>
        <td>Blue</td>
      </tr>
      <tr>
        <td>34691</td>
        <td>Square widget round-hole adapter</td>
        <td>Yellow</td>
      </tr>
      </table>

<smallscreenignore>
      </td>
      <td width="100" valign="top">
      <a href="="http://www.unwiredwidgets.com/sizeguide.html">
      <img src="image/rt_advert1.gif" width="100" height="125"
       border="0"></a>
      <br>
```

Continued

Figure 6.4 Continued

```
    Try our Interactive Sizing Guide</td>
  </tr>
</table>
</smallscreenignore>

<p align="center">
<a href="about.html" button>About Us</a> |
<a href="products.html" button>Products</a>
<smallscreenignore> | </smallscreenignore>
<a href="shop.html" button>Shop Online</a> |
<a href="contact.html" button>Contact Us</a>
</p>
<p align="center">&copy;2001 Unwired Widgets<br>
  <a href="mailto:info@unwiredwidgets.com">info@unwiredwidgets.com</a>
</p>
</body>
</html>
```

What we're left with is a page that looks almost identical in a standard Web browser (see Figure 6.5), but which also formats quite nicely on the Palm OS device, as you can see in Figure 6.6.

Figure 6.5 Redesigned Unwired Widgets Page in a Desktop Browser

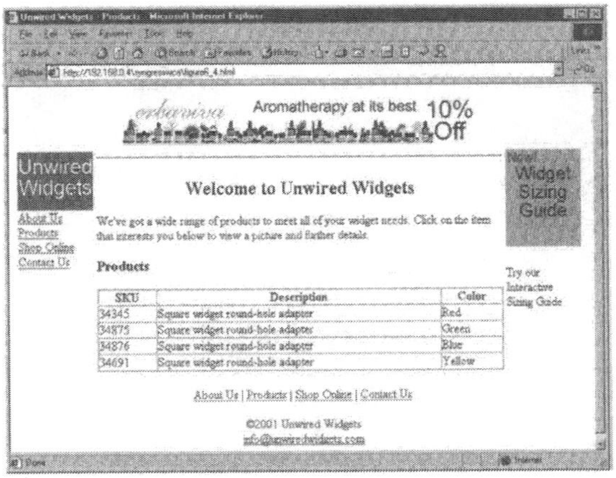

Figure 6.6 Redesigned Unwired Widgets Page on the Palm OS Device

Remember, as you provide links to other pages on the Web site, these pages too will need to be formatted to be "Palm-friendly." Of course, Web pages these days are usually a lot more complicated than this example, but this shows how a little planning, and some simple changes, can give you universally accessible Web pages. With the new Palm.Net proxy, more and more pages that aren't Palm OS–friendly get reformatted to better suit the device. However, licensees of Palm, Inc.'s proxy, such as OmniSky, may not have the current code and may suffer poor performance in this area. Regardless of the capabilities of the proxy, pages designed for large screens and faster connection speeds are always going to be problematic for the small Palm OS screen and slow wireless links. If you expect your visitors to be using these devices, making the extra effort to make your pages universally accessible can simplify your Webmaster's life—and give you happier Web site visitors.

Using Tables for Page Layout

Tables are one of the chief tools used to lay out HTML pages when you want to precisely control where items appear on the page. Web pages designed for desktop browsers sometimes use very complex nested tables for sophisticated page layout. Unfortunately, the designers of Web clipping chose not to support nested tables. Tables, in fact, require quite a lot of processing on the client side to render, and they add a significant amount of nondisplayed text to be downloaded. Because Web clipping was specifically designed to minimize download file sizes over slow wireless connections, the decision to not support nested tables makes sense.

Nested tables won't necessarily cause an error. The Palm.Net proxy will attempt to process the table tags, but it will completely ignore the nested table and render any content as if it was the content of the parent <TD> cell. This rarely gives you the effect you were looking for.

Considering the limited space available on a Palm OS screen, you can't get very complex with layouts anyway, so the loss of nested tables is not a real problem. You can, however, still use tables to control how content is displayed on your pages. The first thing to be aware of is that your tables need to be no more than 153 pixels wide. Clipper will quite happily accept a table width wider than 153 and render it properly, but because there is no horizontal scroll bar, any content beyond 153 pixels is lost.

Web clipping supports the *width* attribute of both the <TABLE> and <TD> tags. However, as mentioned earlier in the chapter, the <TABLE> tag allows only absolute pixel widths—percentages are not accepted. If you enter percentage widths, or no width at all, the Web Clipping Application Viewer will use a "best fit" algorithm to size the table appropriately. Percentage widths *are* supported for the <TD> tag.

Web clipping also supports some other common <TABLE> attributes that allow you to more accurately get the look you want for your pages. *Border* is the size of the lines around the table and between individual table cells. The default, if you don't specify anything for this attribute, is no border. To add a border to your table, use the following:

```
<table border="1">
```

On such a small screen, table borders can look quite heavy, so use them judiciously. You can also specify borders larger than 1, but these tend to look overpowering. Figure 6.7 shows the effect of changing the *border* attribute of the <TABLE> tag.

Figure 6.7 Effect of the *Border* Attribute of the <TABLE> Tag

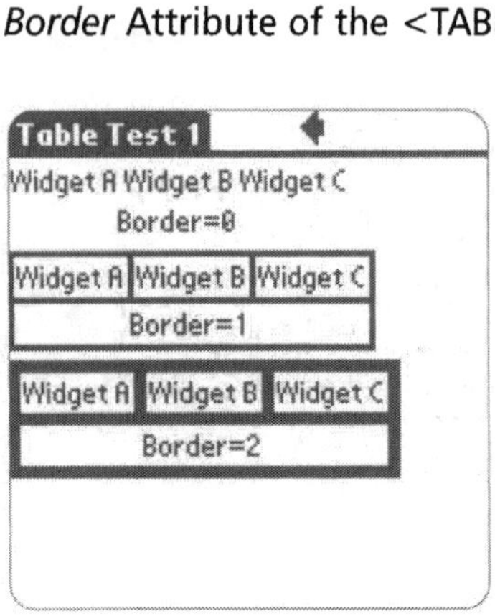

NOTE

The *border* attribute behaves a little differently on a Palm OS device than in a regular browser. In Netscape or Internet Explorer, as you increase the value of *border*, the lines between the table cells stay at the default 1, with the extra being added around the *outside* of the table to create a beveled look. In a Web clipping, increasing the value of border adds thick black lines *around* and *between* all table cells. This usually looks too heavy, although you may be able to use it for effect in some cases.

Cellspacing controls the amount of space between table cells. This amount is in addition to what you can define with the *border* attribute. If you have already specified **border="1"**, then adding **cellspacing="1"** will increase the width of your column dividers. One good use for this attribute is to set **border="0"** so that the borders are invisible, then add **cellspacing="2"** to create some breathing room between the content of your table cells.

Cellpadding, which is similar to *cellspacing*, controls the amount of space around the text *within* a <TD> cell. One likely place to use this is when you have a table with **border="1"** and want to add some space around the content without increasing the width of the dividing lines. In most cases, *cellpadding* will give you better results than *cellspacing* and is the best choice if your table has a visible border. Note that *cellspacing* and *cellpadding* affect all cells in the table, so you should use other mechanisms if individual control is needed. Figure 6.8 shows the effect of changing *cellpadding* on a Palm OS screen.

Figure 6.8 Effect of Changing the *Cellpadding* Attribute of the <TABLE> Tag

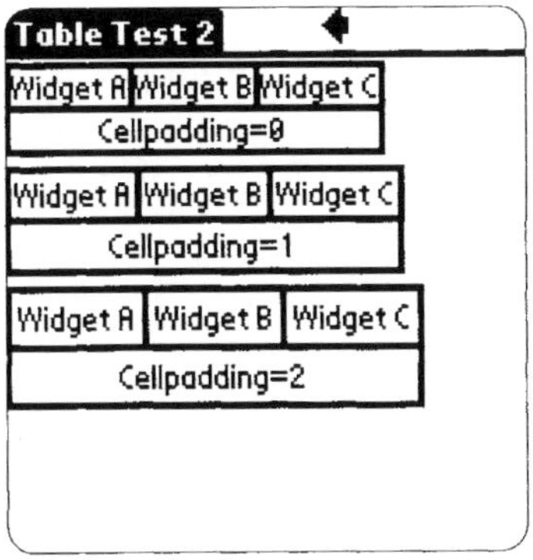

Let's take another look at the product-listing table we created earlier as part of Figure 6.1.

```
<table width="100%" border="1" cellspacing="0" cellpadding="0">
<tr>
    <th>SKU</th>
    <th>Description</th>
    <th>Color</th>
</tr>
<tr>
    <td>34345</td>
    <td>Square widget round-hole adapter</td>
    <td>Red</td>
</tr>
<tr>
    <td>34875</td>
    <td>Square widget round-hole adapter</td>
    <td>Green</td>
</tr>
<tr>
    <td>34876</td>
    <td>Square widget round-hole adapter</td>
    <td>Blue</td>
```

```
</tr>
<tr>
    <td>34691</td>
    <td>Square widget round-hole adapter</td>
    <td>Yellow</td>
</tr>
</table>
```

This works fine on the Palm device, as you can see from Figure 6.6, and of course on a desktop browser, too. But it's not the most attractive table; the border makes it look heavy, and the text is a little too crowded. What's more, if you make a WCA with just this table (adding the necessary head and body tags, of course), you'll notice that the Web Clipping Application Viewer has used its "best fit" algorithm to make the table less than full-screen width, crowding the text even more. So let's see if we can clean up the appearance of this table a little, while still making sure it will work well on a desktop browser.

First, let's remove the border by setting **border="0"**. This will crowd all the text together, so let's also add a little white space for breathing room around the text with *cellpadding*. Notice that *cellpadding* adds space both top and bottom as well as left and right. (Adding too much here can make your tables too spaced out.)

```
<table width="100%" border="0" cellspacing="0" cellpadding="2">
```

We now have a more pleasing-looking table; the heavy border has been removed, and text is nicely spaced apart for readability, as you can see in Figure 6.9. To complete it, let's put back in the <A HREF> links to product detail pages that we omitted earlier for clarity. In an actual Web site product listing, each item would typically link to another page that would offer expanded product details. One way to do this would be to call a Common Gateway Interface (CGI) program, a server-side program that would perform a database query and return the relevant information for the product based on the stockkeeping unit (SKU), a unique ID commonly used to identify products. In this case, we link to a fictitious CGI called *products*. We tell this CGI which product we're interested in by passing the SKU as part of the URL. The syntax for doing this is:

```
<a href="http://www.unwiredwidgets.com/cgi-bin/
    products.cgi?sku=34345">Square widget round-hole adapter</a>
```

Figure 6.9 Products Table with Extra White Space

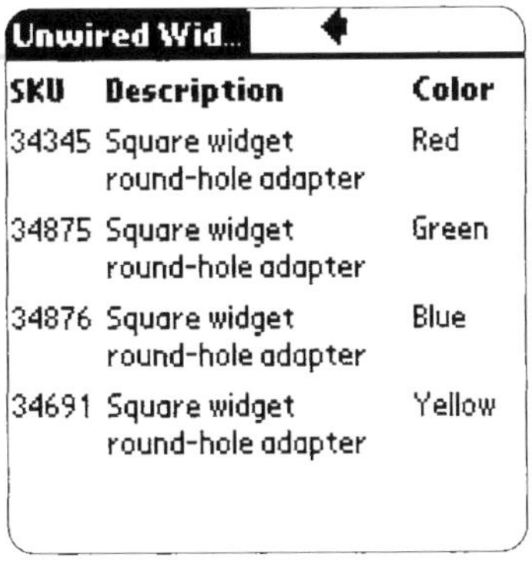

Because these are links to off-device items, Web clipping displays the "over the air" symbol next to them, as well as the conventional underline. The resulting page is shown in Figure 6.10.

Figure 6.10 Products Table with "Over the Air" Symbols

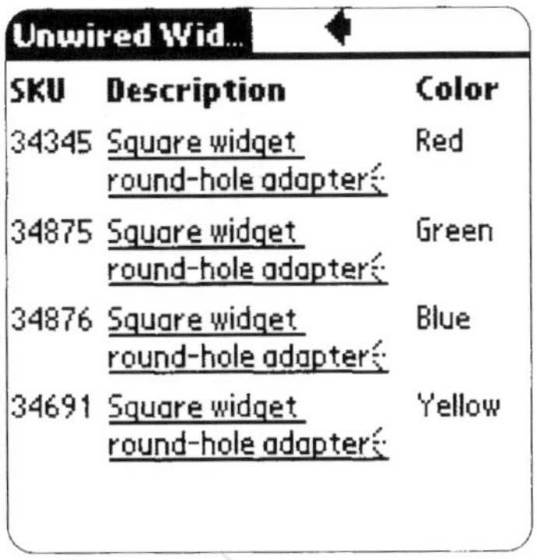

Typically, the product listing itself would also be generated from a database query. Most companies will have quite a few products, in several categories, that they want to display to visitors. We could, of course, extend this fairly simple table to any length, but this would give us a very long, unwieldy table. Because widgets come in several categories, let's organize the table by category to increase readability. For this, we can use the *colspan* attribute of the <TD> tag.

```
<table width="100%" border="0" cellspacing="0" cellpadding="2">

    <tr>
```

```
          <th colspan="3"><font color="#808080">Square
Widgets</font></th>
     </tr>
     <tr>
          <td>34345</td>
          <td><a href="http://www.unwiredwidgets.com/products?sku=34345">
               round-hole adapter</a></td>
          <td>Red</td>
     </tr>
     <tr>
          <td>34875</td>
          <td><a href="http://www.unwiredwidgets.com/products?sku=34875">
               round-hole adapter</a></td>
          <td>Green</td>
     </tr>
     <tr>
          <td>34876</td>
          <td><a href="http://www.unwiredwidgets.com/products?sku=34876">
               round-hole adapter</a></td>
          <td>Blue</td>
     </tr>
     <tr>
          <td>34691</td>
          <td><a href="http://www.unwiredwidgets.com/products?sku=34691">
               round-hole adapter</a></td>
          <td>Yellow</td>
     </tr>
     <tr>
          <th colspan="3"><font color="#808080">Round Widgets</font></th>
     </tr>
     <tr>
          <td>44345</td>
          <td><a href="http://www.unwiredwidgets.com/products?sku=44345">
               square-hole adapter</a></td>
          <td>Red</td>
```

```
    </tr>
    <tr>
        <td>44875</td>
        <td><a href="http://www.unwiredwidgets.com/products?sku=44875">
            square-hole adapter</a></td>
        <td>Green</td>
    </tr>
    <tr>
        <td>44876</td>
        <td><a href="http://www.unwiredwidgets.com/products?sku=44876">
            square-hole adapter</a></td>
        <td>Blue</td>
    </tr>
    <tr>
        <td>44691</td>
        <td><a href="http://www.unwiredwidgets.com/products?sku=44691">
            square-hole adapter</a></td>
        <td>Yellow</td>
    </tr>
</table>
```

This gives us a much more readable table. Also, because the text under the product descriptions is now shorter, the table is more compact so that we can see more items at a time on the screen. We've also added a different text color for the category names to add some differentiation for the headers. See Figure 6.11 for the completed table.

This approach works well if you have one or two screens full of items. If your product assortment contains a larger number of items, or several categories and sub-categories, you might want to organize them into two or more screens with sub-menus. Remember, the basic concept of Web clipping is targeted access to specific information, rather than the "browsing" mode of Web navigation. Visitors are accessing your pages over a slow link and often paying per kilobyte downloaded, so design your navigation so that people see only the items they're looking for. Palm, Inc. recommends that you keep the size of downloaded files to less than 360 bytes. On the Palm VII, which has less memory, even a file of this size can make the device appear to "freeze" as the Palm device attempts to decompress and display the entire page.

Figure 6.11 The Completed Products Table

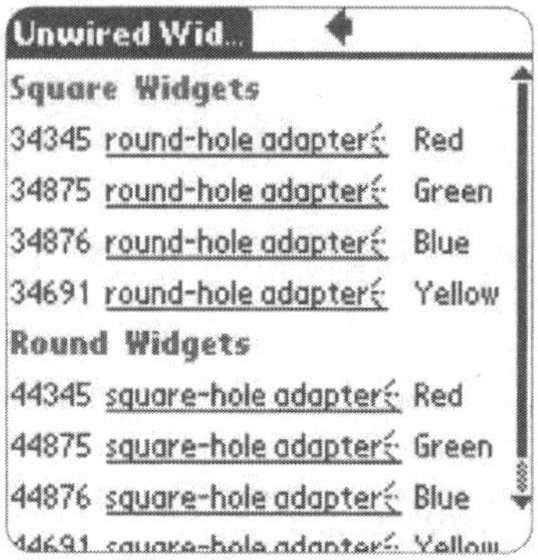

Another way to use tables is for laying out images and text on the same page. The ESPN WCA, which probably came preinstalled on your Palm VII or PalmV with OmniSky, shows one good example of this technique.

Figure 6.12 shows the first page of the ESPN WCA. This uses tables to display quite a lot of links in the available space, without it seeming crammed. Across the top, a table row uses *colspan* to display the site logo, as well as two links: one to breaking news online and one to a local "About" page. Below this are four columns: the first and third are icons that link to live scores in each of the sports; the second and fourth lead to local sub-menu pages. Again across the bottom, *colspan* is used to allow for a longer piece of hint text.

Figure 6.12 ESPN Home Screen

Figure 6.13 shows the result of tapping on the underlined NFL text link. This takes you to a local page that provides expanded links to more online data on the

chosen sport. The large graphic loads quickly because it's precompiled into the local WCA. (See Chapter 4 for how to compile graphics into your WCA.)

This is a fairly simple table, but used to good effect to create an attractive and readable page. The top and bottom rows use **colspan="2"** to house the section header and site logo respectively. The center of the screen uses two columns to display a graphic and the links with plenty of white space around them. Also, the ESPN logos top and bottom both link back to the home page, making this a very effective use of space.

Figure 6.13 NFL Sub-Menu

NOTE

One of the best ways to improve your WCA design skills is to look at what other people have done—both the good and the bad. Palm, Inc. maintains a directory of Web clipping applications you can freely download at http://wireless.palm.net/apps.

Particularly useful are the companion WCAs for major Web sites. Several sites now offer a downloadable Web clipping application to access their pages; usually you'll find it under the "Wireless" link on the home page.

Several tools are available to turn downloaded WCAs back into HTML text; Palm Inc.'s Web clipping information page links to some of them. Reverse engineering WCAs is similar to using **View Source** in a desktop browser to examine the underlying HTML of a page—it can be a good source of ideas, but directly copying the work of others may violate copyright laws.

Specifying History Text

On a desktop browser, you can navigate to pages previously visited by clicking on the little arrow next to the **Back** button, creating something like a trail of bread-crumbs. As you navigate through a Web site and around the Web, the browser also keeps a record of your travels that allows you to retrace your steps. This is known as the *History* list. One improvement it offers over breadcrumb trails is that you can jump randomly to specific pages in the history, rather than having to work your way back link by link.

Web clipping offers the same history feature, but with one improvement: You can specify the text to be displayed in the History list. You can access this history by either clicking the left arrow in the center of the top margin of the screen to step back page by page, or you can access it by clicking on the word **History** that appears in the upper-right corner of the screen. This will reveal a drop-down list of recently visited pages, and you can jump directly to any page by clicking on the History list entry. One advantage of using the history is that the pages will be loaded from local cache, if available, which makes them load much more quickly. One disadvantage, at least until Palm OS 4, is that you can't prevent a page from being cached and entered into the History list.

Using the HistoryListText META Tag

The tag that enables this is the HistoryListText META tag. A META tag is a special form of HTML tag that generally provides information to the browser or the Web server, rather than being displayed on-screen.

```
<meta name="historylisttext" content="Unwired Widgets">
```

Remember that this META tag goes in the <HEAD> section of your HTML page. Whatever you put in the *content* attribute is what will display in the History list. However, you can only have about 12 characters displayed here, so keep the text short. Each successive page you visit is added to the top of the History list, and previous pages scroll down to accommodate them. Only about 12 history items can appear in the drop-down list, but if there are more, scroll arrows appear within the drop-down listing. The size of the HistoryListText cache is about 50K. When this becomes full, items are removed based on a "least recently used" algorithm.

Web clipping will append not only the text you supply but also the current time (as set in your device preferences) when you accessed the page. The text you supply for this History list doesn't have to be the same as the title of the page.

Because you only have such a limited space, you might want to use abbreviations or some other shortened text that still clearly identifies what the page contains.

If you don't supply a HistoryListText META tag on your pages, Web clipping will use whatever is in the <TITLE> tag, again truncated to about 12 characters, and append the time. If your page also doesn't have a <TITLE>, then the history will display the page URL, which probably won't be very readable in this format, so it's best to supply both a <TITLE> tag and the HistoryListText META tag.

NOTE

The history is attached directly to the relevant Web clipping. If you're in the ESPN Web Clipping, you'll see only your history of navigation around that particular WCA. Backing up all the way will take you back to the Applications screen, just as if you had clicked the Home icon on the touch screen.

This history is maintained between invocations of the WCA. You could view a page, switch to another program, return to your WCA, and go back to the page you were viewing by clicking on the History list.

Also, the history is maintained only for pages retrieved over the air. If you navigate around pages local to the WCA, these are not added to the History list.

Using Date and Time Variables with the History Text

As we saw earlier, Web clipping automatically appends the time to whatever you supply as the *content* attribute of the HistoryListText META tag. One side effect of this is that it will truncate your HistoryListText at about 12 characters in order to be able to display the time. You can control this somewhat by using two special variables—*&date* and *&time*—within the text of the *content* attribute. If you supply either of these variables, Web clipping will not truncate your text, and you can get labels of about 22 characters to display here; however, this will push the actual date or time off the right-hand side, so it will be invisible.

In actual use, *&date* and *&time* will be replaced by the date or time from your device. The display format will be as you have it set in your device preferences. For example, if you use the following META tag, the resulting display would be as shown in Figure 6.14.

```
<meta name="historylisttext" content="Products &date &time">
```

The first item shows the default when you don't specify any variables; the text is truncated at 11 characters to make room for the time. The middle history item shows the effect of extending the length of the HistoryListText; the date and time are pushed off the right-hand side. The bottom item is the result of the aforementioned tag.

Figure 6.14 HistoryListText Displayed

Developing & Deploying…

Clearing Your HistoryListText Cache with the Palm OS Easter Egg

What is an Easter Egg? This is a secret mini-application that programmers sometimes put in a program or OS. A special and unusual sequence of keystrokes is usually required to activate it, and the egg may do something funny, list credits for the programming team, or occasionally let you perform some unusual developer trick. Palm OS programs have numerous Easter Eggs, but one in particular is of use when playing with the settings for HistoryListText.

There's normally no way to clear the History cache, but a variation of the famous "Taxi" Easter Egg will allow you to. Here's how:

1. Activate the Taxi Easter Egg by opening up the Preferences page. Select the **General** screen.

Continued

2. In the bottom-right corner of the screen, above the calculator, draw a tiny circle (clockwise or counterclockwise—either should work).
3. An Easter Egg graphic will pop up on the screen. (You can perform an extra step to have a little taxi drive across your screen, but we'll assume you're not that starved for entertainment.)
4. Go into any Web clipping application.
5. Tap four times in rapid succession right over the **Calculator** silkscreen button.
6. Tap the **Menu** silkscreen button.
7. If you do it right, you'll see a new selection under the Options menu called **Preferences**.
8. Open this, and set the History list storage to **0**. This effectively clears the cache.
9. Click **OK**.

After it's cleared, change it back to the default 50K to begin testing again. A word of warning: Do not change the Proxy setting on this screen.

The Easter Egg works on the Palm VII and VIIx and the Handspring Visor with OmniSky modem. It does not seem to work on the Palm V or Vx with OmniSky modem. This Easter Egg also gives you another menu item called Page. Using this, you can go to any arbitrary URL on the Web—not just Palm OS-friendly pages. But beware—using this can seriously deplete your per-byte transfer allowance on Palm.Net.

Using MAILTO Links to Send E-Mail

You may have noticed the e-mail address at the bottom of Figure 6.6. Depending on how your computer is set up, clicking on these kinds of links in a regular browser will usually launch your default mail program, with this e-mail address loaded into the "To:" field. This is a useful way of providing feedback links, usually at the bottom of your pages or on a contact page. It saves people from having to cut and paste your e-mail address into their mail program.

E-mail is a tremendously powerful tool to add to your Web pages. Because wireless-enabled Palm OS devices also have e-mail capabilities, you might want to consider putting MAILTO links on your Web clipping pages, too.

So what happens if you click on one of these links from within a Web clipping page on a Palm device? On the Palm VII and VIIx devices, the MAILTO construct will immediately launch iMessenger, an e-mail application that works with special Palm.Net e-mail accounts. iMessenger stores messages in an "outbox" to be sent the next time your device has a connection and you click on the **Check and Send** button.

The format of the MAILTO link is exactly the same as on a regular Web page:

```
<a href="mailto:info@unwiredwidgets.com">Display Text</a>
```

Replace *Display Text* with the text you want to be highlighted as a link. Unlike an HTTP link, you don't place the "//" after the colon. You type this link exactly as in the example above.

Clicking on this link in a Web clipping on a Palm VII or VIIx launches iMessenger with the e-mail address already loaded into the "To:" field. You can then type a subject and message and put it in the Outbox. As soon as your message is put in the Outbox, iMessenger closes and you're back at the original Web clipping page you came from. Because iMessenger is a separate program residing on your Palm OS device; what you're actually doing is calling an external program from within your WCA. This will be explored in more depth in Chapter 10.

You can also call iMessenger with some of the other parameters already specified. Netscape pioneered this enhanced MAILTO scheme when they integrated a mail client into the browser back in the mid-1990s, and Palm, Inc. continues its support with MAILTO links in Clipper.

```
<a href="mailto:info@unwiredwidgets.com?subject=Feedback&body=Your
   website is wonderful.">Send a Compliment</a>
```

NOTE

The section on MAILTO in the original version of Palm, Inc.'s Web Clipping Developer's Guide contains a typo. The example shown here is the correct syntax for these links.

This would load iMessenger with the "To:," "Subj:," and "Body:" fields already filled in with your text. Unfortunately, there's no way to insist that people send only compliments; they can still modify the message contents before sending. Figure 6.15 shows the display after someone selects the link on their Palm VII or VIIx.

Figure 6.15 iMessenger Called with Parameters

Because this is a regular <A HREF> tag, you can also use the proprietary *button* attribute to have this link appear as a graphical button:

```
<a href="mailto:info@unwiredwidgets.com?subject=Feedback&body=Your
    website is wonderful." button>Send a Compliment</a>
```

Using Other Mail Handlers with Palm OS 4.0

In Palm OS 3.5, iMessenger is hard-wired to the MAILTO link. This also works only on Palm VII and VIIx devices under Palm OS 3.5. Palm OS 4.0 will allow other applications to register themselves to handle MAILTO, so bear in mind that iMessenger may not always be the application called when you insert a MAILTO in your Web clipping page. For instance, developers could write a custom application that would detect calls from the MAILTO tag and divert into their own mail client. Hopefully, the developers would be careful to maintain backward compatibility with the current function, but you probably can't rely on this always being the case.

Summary

Nowadays, visitors may arrive at your Web site using anything from a WAP phone to a PDA to a full-screen desktop browser. Developing one set of pages for both desktop browsers and PDAs offers a huge saving in effort for developers. Although you need to bear in mind certain limitations, with careful planning you can construct pages that work well on any size screen.

In this chapter, you learned how to modify your pages to make them work well on both desktop browsers and a Palm OS device. Although using the special <SMALLSCREENIGNORE> tag may require you to bend the rules of good HTML, you can minimize this by adjusting your page layout slightly. Desktop browsers will ignore the unknown tag, but using the tag allows you to cordon off areas of your HTML code that wouldn't work on a Palm device.

Tables are useful for creating a pleasing layout on the very limited screen of Palm devices. This is particularly good for mixing text and graphics. Adjust table borders and padding to give your text some "breathing room" and lighten the look of the pages. With this approach, you can make optimum use of the available space, while making a much more readable page. The ESPN Web Clipping shown is one example, but look at the other samples provided with your Palm device and those available for download from the Palm, Inc. Web site to see how other developers approached the problem.

We examined how to use the special HistoryListText tag to allow your visitors to navigate freely among pages stored in the local cache. We also saw how to control this history text and to use special variables for date and time. Lastly, we saw how to insert MAILTO links that allow you to send e-mail directly from within your Web clipping page in a format that also works well on a desktop browser. Mail links work well for providing a feedback mechanism for your Web sites.

Solutions Fast Track

Making Pages Useful on Both Desktop and Palm Devices

☑ You can write pages that work well on both desktop browsers and Palm OS devices.

☑ Ensure that pages and graphics are no more than 153 pixels wide.

- ☑ Use the <SMALLSCREENIGNORE> tag to mark off sections of HTML you don't want displayed on the Palm device.

Making Unwired Widgets Pages for Both Desktop and Palm Devices

- ☑ Some minor modifications to your HTML can make it easier to optimize for Palm devices.
- ☑ Use alternate text-only navigation links with the special *button* attribute.
- ☑ Decide on what content is truly crucial and put this in one table, because Palm OS does not support nested tables.
- ☑ Minimize nesting errors, although some are unavoidable. Modern browsers will ignore these.

Using Tables for Page Layout

- ☑ Tables must be formatted to be no more than 153 pixels wide.
- ☑ Nested tables are not supported.
- ☑ Use *border* and *cellpadding* to create "breathing room" around your content.
- ☑ Use tables to lay out text and images to create a more pleasing arrangement.

Specifying History Text

- ☑ Palm OS appends the time automatically if you do not specify it.
- ☑ The HistoryListText META tag is limited, so keep your labels concise.
- ☑ Use *&date* and *&time* variables in the HistoryListText.
- ☑ Specifying *&date* and *&time* allows you to use longer history text.

Using MAILTO Links to Send E-Mail

- ☑ Use MAILTO links to allow visitors to send e-mail from within your Web clipping.
- ☑ Append arguments to the MAILTO to prefill the "To:," "Subj:" and "Body:" fields.
- ☑ iMessenger is the default mailer on Palm VII, but Palm OS 4 will allow other applications to handle this.

Frequently Asked Questions

The following Frequently Asked Questions, answered by the authors of this book, are designed to both measure your understanding of the concepts presented in this chapter and to assist you with real-life implementation of these concepts. To have your questions about this chapter answered by the author, browse to **www.syngress.com/solutions** and click on the **"Ask the Author"** form.

Q: Can I specify an alternate banner graphic to be used on Palm OS pages and one for desktop browsers?

A: Not easily; although <SMALLSCREENIGNORE> allows you to mark areas you don't want to see on a Palm device, there is no corresponding tag to tell desktop browsers to ignore Palm OS–only markup. However, one solution, if you're familiar with server-side scripting languages such as ASP or Perl, would be to detect the incoming browser and display different markup in the banner section according to which browser is accessing the page.

Q: What happens if my table is wider than 153 pixels? Will Web clipping accept it?

A: Yes, Web clipping will happily process a table wider than 153 pixels, but because the Web Clipping Application Viewer does not provide a horizontal scroll bar, everything beyond the right border is lost. If you're making pages just for the Palm OS, you can control this, but if you're making universally accessible pages, try to avoid absolute measurements for <TABLE> and <TD> tags. Web clipping will do its best to format your table to best fit in the available space. Palm OS 4 adds horizontal scrolling ability, but it is difficult to use and should be avoided.

Q: Can I have table background colors?

A: No, Web clipping does not allow background colors for <TABLE> or <TD> tags. It will simply ignore these. But be careful if you have a table that uses a black background and white text for a desktop browser. Web clipping will ignore the background color, but it will accept font colors, which would make your text invisible.

Q: Can I have MAILTO links launch a different program?

A: In Palm OS 3.5, MAILTO is linked only to iMessenger. Palm OS 4.0 will allow applications to register themselves to handle these and other links.

Q: How long do items stay in the History cache?

A: Items stay in the History cache until it becomes full. The size is about 50K. When this becomes full, items are removed from the cache based on a "least recently used" algorithm. There is no easy method of clearing these history items yourself, but you can use third-party tools such as Cobweb to clear your device's Clipper cache. Also see the sidebar on the Easter Egg that allows you to clear this cache.

Chapter 7

Debugging Web Clipping Applications

Solutions in this chapter:

- Emulating Web Clipping by Using the Palm OS Emulator
- Understanding the Palm.Net Proxy
- Using Tools to Debug WCAs

☑ Summary

☑ Solutions Fast Track

☑ Frequently Asked Questions

Introduction

You need to test and debug your Web clipping application (WCA) before sending it out to the world. As an alternative to burning batteries doing exhaustive testing on a real device, Palm, Inc. supports using the Palm OS Emulator (POSE). This is a program that emulates a real Palm OS device using a copy of the actual operating system code. You interact with POSE on your desktop, with mouse clicks taking the place of pen strokes and the keyboard acting as a quick substitute for graffiti entry of text.

Even with POSE testing, you will sometimes find applications acting very oddly. Your pages display as blanks, you get odd error messages with cryptic numbers, and your server shows too many hits. These are all artifacts of the Palm.Net proxy server, so understanding how it talks to the device and to your Web server can help you avoid problems like these.

In debugging, having a good set of tools is important. We close this chapter talking about software to help you find problems. Among the invaluable part of your toolkit are programs that will validate your Hypertext Markup Language (HTML), check your links, decompile your code, and send arbitrary requests to your Web server. Some of these run on the desktop, some run on the Palm OS device—using them can really help you out.

Emulating Web Clipping by Using the Palm OS Emulator

The *Palm OS Emulator* (POSE) is a standalone software application that mimics the behavior of Palm OS devices. Supported by Palm, Inc. for both Windows and Macintosh, POSE allows you to verify the operation of your Web clipping application without being burdened with using an actual device. You don't even need a cradle to download your new WCA for its first trial run! With its Internet connectivity, POSE offers one of the best ways to test a WCA.

Because POSE lets you run Palm OS applications on your desktop computer, it lets you check WCAs without going through batteries, as you would when testing on a real Palm VII device. POSE lets you reuse your existing Internet connection as a substitute for wireless service, so you don't need to pay connection fees, and you can test your software when you are out of wireless coverage. You also can mimic different device types, letting you see what your pages would look like on everything from the grayscale Palm VII to a 16-bit color Visor Prism.

POSE also offers the capability to easily make screen shots. One of the menu options lets you save the current screen as a bitmap; most of the screens shown in this book were captured this way. Because it runs on a PC, you can also use it for presentations by hooking up a projector to a laptop computer and letting the whole room see what is on the emulated Palm OS device's screen.

An implicit benefit of using POSE is that it allows you to test your server-side script's ability to handle default values for Palm OS–specific variables. For example, POSE produces a %DEVICEID of 0.0.0 and a %ZIPCODE of 00000 (see Chapter 9). Of course, *real* %DEVICEID and %ZIPCODE values need to be tested from an actual device, but that can be deferred until you gain some confidence in the overall WCA operation.

POSE's shortcomings are relatively minor. For example, graffiti input with a mouse is not easy. But then again, POSE has a keyboard available to do it! The appropriate time to use POSE is any time from the initial creation of your WCA through and including the performing of field tests. It can identify problems early in the software lifecycle, verify that bug fixes have been properly implemented, and reproduce problems identified on actual devices. In a nutshell, POSE represents one of the most valuable tools available for debugging your WCA.

Getting a Copy of POSE

The latest version of POSE can be downloaded from Palm, Inc.'s emulator Web site at www.palmos.com/dev/tech/tools/emulator. POSE is provided in binary form, ready to run on either Windows or the Macintosh, and in source form, with projects to build Windows, Macintosh, and Unix versions of the emulator. The emulator is provided under the GNU Public License, which requires that people distributing versions of the software include the source code—including any modifications that they've made—and that the software can be freely distributed. Download POSE, unpack the archive, and install the files into a separate directory. Be sure to review the release notes, which are packed with the emulator in the files _News.txt and _OldNews.txt.

NOTE

Check the POSE Web site frequently to make sure that you are using the most up-to-date version of POSE. At the time this book was completed, POSE 3.1 was the current version, with POSE 3.2 with support for the Palm m500 and m505 devices about to be released.

Developing & Deploying...

Dealing with POSE Errors That Don't Occur on Actual Devices

Among the many features of POSE is its ability to detect application errors and warn the user. This is designed to help programmers build robust Palm OS software by catching problems that could crash a device or corrupt user data. Unfortunately, the developers of Clipper didn't have this error-catching available to them when they were developing their code, and there are some latent bugs that POSE catches. A message you might see is: "Web Clipping 3.2 has just read directly from memory manager data structures. This problem indicates an error in the application. Users should upgrade this product immediately to safeguard their data."

One possible cause for this message is activating a Secure Hypertext Transfer Protocol (HTTPS) link from within your WCA. Unless the **Free Chunk Access** debug option is turned off within POSE, the transaction cannot be completed. However, this message is not displayed when running the same scenario on an actual device.

Although this is an error in Clipper, it is generally harmless. POSE is being picky, but it should not cause any problems in real operations. To silence the warning, you can turn off the corresponding debugging options within POSE. Also, newer versions of POSE often have special code to silence warnings like this for known but harmless bugs in the Palm OS ROMs.

If, like most techno-type personalities, you *must* do something to correct the problem, you can try the following procedure. Use an HTML Validator (see "Using Tools to Debug WCAs" later in this chapter) to verify that your HTML conforms to the Web clipping Document Type Definition (DTD). Some Clipper errors are caused by malformed HTML, so making sure that you have clean input can go a long way towards silencing POSE's warnings.

NOTE

When POSE keeps responding with "no interfaces (Net 120C)," check POSE's configuration to make sure that NetLib requests are being directed to the desktop's Transmission Control Protocol/Internet Protocol (TCP/IP) connection. According to Palm's documentation, "Right-click on the Emulator window and select **Properties** (or if you're on Mac OS, use the **Preferences** menu item from the Edit menu)." Then, "check the box **Redirect NetLib calls to host TCP/IP"** and "reset the emulated device."

Obtaining Palm OS ROM Images

By itself, POSE does very little. Although it does emulate the hardware in a Palm OS device, it requires a copy of the operating system to perform any useful work. Because the OS is stored in read-only memory (ROM) on the device, the copy of the OS is referred to as a ROM image.

ROMs are not freely distributable. They contain the copyrighted code of Palm, Inc. and its licensees, and there are only two legal ways to obtain ROM images. The first is to download a ROM from the Palm, Inc. Web site. When you do this, you agree to Palm's legal agreement that outlines what you can and cannot do with the OS image. The second method is to download a copy of the ROM from an actual device, which is the quickest way to get POSE running when you cannot access Palm's site.

NOTE

ROMs running inside POSE cannot operate *exactly* as they would on an actual device. For example, the execution speed of a ROM within POSE will most likely be different than the execution speed of a ROM within an actual device. POSE also does not support infrared (IR) beaming.

Downloading the ROMs from Palm's Web Site

From the Palm, Inc. developer Web site, you can join the Palm Alliance Program to gain access to ROM images. You have to wait a few days while Palm, Inc. processes your application, but after you have an account, you can enter the resource pavilion and agree to the Palm, Inc. clickwrap agreement, letting you immediately download ROM images for all of Palm, Inc.'s released devices. People accessing Palm, Inc.'s site from outside the United States may have problems downloading the ROMs this way; Palm, Inc. does not have legal assurances that the Web site license would be valid outside the U.S., so they require citizens from other countries to complete a paper agreement in order to get access to the ROMs. Palm, Inc. also has tighter access control to the images with Web clipping software, because it contains encryption software that has restrictions on export.

Obtaining ROM images from Palm, Inc. has several advantages. First, you can get ROMs from several devices, not just the Palm OS device you own. Second, Palm, Inc. supplies both release and debug ROMs, where the debug versions contain extra checks that help you catch bugs in your programs. Third, ROM images downloaded from Palm, Inc. are guaranteed to work. If you have modified your device ROM using a flash programming tool, you won't be able to upload it to the desktop and use it in POSE, because the ROM checksum will be invalid.

Grabbing a ROM Image from a Palm OS Device

Another means of obtaining a ROM is grabbing it from an actual device. Currently, POSE supports uploading ROM images through serial cradles only, so if you are using a Handspring Visor, Sony Clie, or Palm m500–series device, you won't be able to transfer your ROM with this method.

The procedure for downloading a device ROM is straightforward. Within POSE, select the **Transfer ROM...** command. This will prompt you to download the ROM Transfer.prc file to the device, to turn off HotSync Manager, and to run the new ROM Transfer program on your device. POSE and the device will now talk over the serial link, and a few minutes later, you will have the ROM image of the Palm OS device on your desktop.

Understanding the Palm.Net Proxy

The Palm.Net proxy is a server farm that provides an interface between your WCA and the Internet. All of your online activities, wireless or not, flow through the Palm.Net proxy. This is significant because as you come to understand how the proxy functions, you come to understand how your device talks to the rest of the world. A typical flow of data is as follows:

- User initiates a request by selecting a link or clicking on a submit button, for example.

- Data request is sent to the Palm.Net proxy. If the transfer is secure, the data request is first encrypted using Certicom's Elliptic Curve Cryptosystems (ECC) process.
- Palm.Net proxy interprets the data request, making an equivalent HTTP/HTML request of the specified destination server. If the transfer is secure, the data request is first decrypted. Upon interpretation, an equivalent encrypted request is made via a Secure Sockets Layer (SSL) connection to the destination server.
- Destination server interprets the data request, responding to the proxy with an HTML page as part of the HTTP or HTTPS transaction.
- Palm.Net proxy interprets the HTML, translating it into the compressed form used by Clipper. If the transfer is secure, the proxy encodes the response using the ECC encryption scheme. This response is now sent back to the device.
- Requesting device receives the Web clipping. If the transfer is secure, the Web clipping is first decrypted. The Clipper application then renders the Web clipping.

In this data flow, two interfaces to the Palm.Net proxy exist. The first is the interface between POSE/device and the proxy. This interface is characterized by a custom protocol and the WCA data format—a compressed subset of the HTML 3.2 standard. The second is the interface between the proxy and the Internet, which uses standard HTTP and HTML. Each of these interfaces is discussed in the following sections.

Communicating between POSE/Devices and the Proxy

Communication between either POSE or an actual device and the Palm.Net proxy is accomplished using a compressed subset of HTML 3.2, called the Compressed Markup Language (CML). Both device-resident WCAs and clippings sent back from the Palm.Net proxy servers are represented in this format, making Clipper's rendering task the same regardless of the data source. The WCA Builder produces this format from HTML pages on your hard drive, whereas the Palm.Net proxy produces this format from the HTML pages returned by Web servers.

A full description of the device-resident version of this format is included in the document "Palm File Formats," available from www.palmos.com. This file also describes the .prc and .pdb formats used for Palm programs and databases, but the last two chapters are dedicated to the CML and how it is used inside Palm Query Application (PQA) files.

Understanding how the WCA format is processed and transferred is the key to understanding how POSE/device communicates with the proxy. In addition to basic compression, the WCA format is processed and transferred by a variety of mechanisms:

- Hashing links
- Converting images
- Securing data using ECC
- Talking to development and production servers

Hashing Links

Link hashing is a process whereby links are not sent verbatim from the proxy to the device. Links are replaced with an index and checksum. The index is the output of a hashing scheme and indicates the relative position of the link within the Web clipping. The checksum is based on the link's full URL, protocol, and parameter data. The index and checksum are generated as part of the compression process.

Sending an index/checksum pair in lieu of a link minimizes the bandwidth required for POSE/device-to-proxy communication. Granted, this is more of a concern when the proxy is communicating with an actual device, although it is still the method employed when the proxy is communicating with POSE. After all, the point of using POSE is to test your WCA in an environment that mimics a *real* environment as closely as possible.

The effects of link hashing on pages dynamically generated by your Web server are explored in the Chapter 8 discussion of session management using URL rewriting.

Converting Images

Images are converted to the 2-bit depth Palm bitmap format for inclusion into Web clippings. This is consistent with the processing performed by the WCA Builder, which also converts images to conform to the WCA format. With Palm OS 4.0 and later devices, the proxy may convert images to higher bit depths, depending on the settings in Clipper. The proxy will also resize some pictures to fit the 153-pixel wide clipping area.

Securing Data Using Elliptic Curve Cryptosystems

Certicom's *Elliptic Curve Cryptosystems* (ECC) technology is used to protect data transferred between the device and the proxy. Data is encrypted using Certicom's Security Builder product and is kept in an encrypted state until decrypted by the proxy. Decryption is also performed with Certicom's technology.

The ECC approach combines the speed of symmetric-key cryptography with the power of public-key cryptography. Symmetric-key cryptography is used to encrypt message data. The speed of this algorithm is beneficial given unknown and potentially large message size. The symmetric key is randomly generated for each transmission.

The key is then protected by slower, yet more powerful, public-key encryption. An Elliptic Curve Diffie-Hellman (ECDH) function generates a Data Encryption Standard Extended (DESX) key. Represented as a 163-bit ECC key, the protection this key offers is approximately the same as that provided by a 1024-bit Rivest Shamir Adelman (RSA) key. And because encryption performed with this key can only be decrypted using the corresponding private key, the private key is kept only on the proxy server for added protection.

A public key transaction is not made every time the Palm OS device talks to the proxy. Instead, public key updates occur occasionally, when either the proxy or device thinks that it has used the current symmetric key for too long and that it should be invalidated.

Talking to Development and Production Servers

Two types of servers exist for POSE and device communication with the Palm.Net proxy servers: development servers and production servers.

Development Servers

Development servers are available for POSE-to-proxy communication. They communicate between POSE and the proxy over a TCP/IP connection, using sockets to facilitate data transfer. To facilitate the use of POSE, Palm, Inc. makes available two dedicated development proxy servers:

- content-dev.palm.net
- content-dev2.palm.net

Their addresses are available from the Web clipping proxy (WCP) server status page, http://oasis.palm.com/dev/proxy. To use one of them, first verify that POSE is pointed to the appropriate server by running the Prefs application and going to the wireless page. Next, verify that POSE is set to **Redirect NetLib calls to host TCP/IP** by examining the POSE Settings/Properties dialog box. These development proxy servers mimic Palm.Net for WCA testing, with the exception that they do not support iMessenger. However, note that content-dev2.palm.net is also used for testing prereleases of the proxy server.

NOTE

The status of Palm, Inc.'s development servers needs to be checked periodically, because the addresses associated with each is subject to change. Check the proxy status page for more details.

Production Servers

Production servers are available for device-to-proxy communication. They communicate between actual devices and the proxy over a User Datagram Protocol (UDP) connection, using sockets to facilitate data transfer. Their actual IP address is usually unimportant, because the device-to-proxy connection is managed as part of the Mobitex network. In contrast to using POSE, an explicit address does not have to be specified for communication to occur.

On non-Mobitex devices, such as those using the Palm Mobile Internet Kit, the official proxy server is at "proxy.palm.net". On Palm OS 3.5 devices, you will need to get the IP address of this server and use it directly.

NOTE

The IP address of the Palm.Net proxy must sometimes be known in order for your WCA to gain access to a destination server. This occurs when the destination server is behind a firewall that requires a priori knowledge of IP addresses to which it will grant access. The IP addresses associated with Palm.Net can be obtained from the WCP server status page.

Communicating between the Proxy and Your Web Server

Communication between the proxy and a destination server is conducted using standard Internet interfaces such as HTTP and HTML. The proxy employs standard techniques and practices to take advantage of the efficiencies and security of existing technologies. Two such examples are caching and SSL.

Caching

The proxy server does not cache Web clippings per se, although it does cache static Internet HTML pages. When the proxy server determines that the cache contains the static page corresponding to a Web clipping request, it responds to the request with a Web clipping version of the cached page.

The determination about whether a page has been cached is made using the HTTP date header. This field is retrieved from the content server and used to indicate the last modified date for the static page. If this date is later than the corresponding date in the proxy cache, a request for an updated copy of the page is sent. The content server responds with the latest copy of the page, which is used to overwrite the corresponding page in the proxy cache.

When considering *dynamic clippings,* however, caching does not apply. Dynamic clippings—clippings generated on the fly—are not available to be cached because they are not stored on a content server. Comparison of modification dates cannot be done. This applies to all nonstored pages, including those generated by Common Gateway Interface (CGI) scripts, Active Server Pages (ASPs), and so on.

Because the proxy server cannot determine whether a page is dynamically generated, the page content itself must specify whether this is the case. To make certain that the proxy server does not attempt to cache dynamically generated pages, the pages should always include the PRAGMA: NO-CACHE header in the HTTP response. This should be done in lieu of CACHE-CONTROL: NO-CACHE, which may not be honored by the proxy server.

Secure Sockets Layer Encryption

As a protection mechanism for communication between the proxy server and your Web server, SSL is employed. Information, or requests for information, received from WCAs is decrypted from its ECC form and re-encrypted using SSL. No data is stored in its decrypted form.

Before data is sent to a content server, however, the server must identify itself by providing a credential certificate. The proxy server verifies the credentials by verifying that the server has the private key matching the public key embedded within the certificate. The certificate is also verified as having been issued by a trusted Certification Authority (CA). The certificate chain is verified to be complete and all certificates in the chain are verified to be current and active (for example, nonrevoked). After the content server's identify is verified, SSL-encrypted data is sent. Encryption is performed using a 128-bit strong RSA encryption. Decryption is performed on the content server.

NOTE

When changing your WCA during the test-modify-retest cycle, introduce temporary characters into your code in conspicuous places. For example, add a leading alphanumeric character to the title of your WCA. This will help you verify that your changes are being properly compiled and loaded into POSE and/or your actual device. You don't want to be testing old code! Keep in mind that this trick works for server-side software as well.

Detecting Proxy Problems

Various problems may arise during the debugging of your WCA. Some of the more likely issues you will have to address are the following:

- Using valid development proxy servers and HTTP port numbers
- Having a valid security certificate
- Failing due to invalid HTML
- Diagnosing image problems
- Detecting server errors
- Getting multiple Web server hits

NOTE

Several valuable resources exist for developing and debugging your WCA:

- **Developer Forums** www.palmos.com/dev/tech/support/forums
- **Developer Exchange** www.palmos.com/dev/tech/support/devexchange.html
- **Developers' Nation** www.devnation.net

Using Valid Development Proxy Servers and HTTP Port Numbers

Using an incorrect development proxy server and/or HTTP/HTTPS port number for the proxy server creates a potential source of proxy problems. Palm.Net has specific proxy servers for development, and it restricts the number of open ports available to URLs within Web clipping applications. Valid development proxy servers and ports follow:

Development Proxy Servers

content-dev.palm.net

content-dev.palm.net

HTTP Port Numbers

80	8000	8080	8801
81	8001	8083	
82	8002		
	8003		
	8004		
	8005		

HTTPS Port Numbers

443	8003	10443

NOTE

POSE requires port 5002 to be open in both directions through a firewall.

Having a Valid Security Certificate

Palm.Net recognizes only some authorities for signed server certificates; having one from a nontrusted authority will prevent secure communications. Certificates must conform to the X.509 certificate format, and be verifiable using one of the following certificate authorities:

- VeriSign
- Thawte
- Keywitness Canada, Inc.
- GTE Cybertrust ROOT
- Root Server Gated Cryptography (SGC) Authority
- Microsoft Root Authority

Additional information can be obtained from www.ietf.org/html.charters/pkix-charter.html, the home page of the Internet Engineering Task Force (IETF) Public-Key Infrastructure group.

NOTE

Do not require a certificate from the proxy server when establishing an SSL connection, because Palm.Net does not supply user certificates.

Failing Due to Invalid HTML

The WCA Builder catches HTML errors during the WCA build process, but the proxy server must catch errors when it is generating its CML data from the returned Web pages.

Due to the complexity of pages returned over the Web, sometimes the proxy will produce invalid CML and send that to the device, although the proxy does a much better job now than it did in the past due to software upgrades. Invalid pages can be generated from HTML that does not belong in the Web clipping or that would not validate due to missing tags. Examples include the following:

- Protocols being used other than http, https, file, mailto, palm, and palmcall
- Forgetting to include PalmComputingPlatform META tag

- Using embedded scripting
- Using tables wider than 153 pixels on pre–Palm OS 4.0 devices
- Using references of the form file:mine.pqa/about.html from the root page
- Attempting to redirect to a page stored on the device (a maximum of three Internet redirects is allowed)
- Using relative references to pages stored on the device

NOTE

Forgetting to include the PalmComputingPlatform META tag within the HEAD container allows automatic truncation of the Web clipping to occur. Truncation occurs at 10KB with the current proxy servers.

Diagnosing Image Problems

You may encounter the following common problems associated with images:

- Accessing images that exceed the memory and display limits imposed on WCAs
- Not being able to see an image at all

With regard to WCAs, images are limited to 64KB of storage and must be 153 pixels wide or less. The storage limit is imposed as a result of Palm OS database file restrictions. As a part of a Palm OS database file (for example, the database file containing the Web clipping), images are storage-limited to ensure that the entire Web clipping does not exceed what the Palm OS can handle. Keep in mind, then, that the 64KB limit represents a best-case scenario. The width limit is imposed to ensure that images will fit on the Palm OS device's screen. No height limit is imposed because vertical scrolling is supported.

If an image cannot be seen at all, the PalmComputingPlatform META tag is probably missing from within the HEAD container. When this is the case, automatic truncation of the Web clipping occurs. The result is truncation to 1KB, which can easily cut off any image data from the Web clipping.

NOTE

Packet flow control between a Palm OS device and the underlying wireless data network can limit the practical image size to between 5 and 13KB.

Detecting Server Errors

Several different types of server errors are possible when using WCAs. The list is difficult to enumerate, because each WCA and the corresponding server interface is different. However, the following errors are representative of those you may encounter:

- **Getting an "Access Forbidden" error when attempting to access a server configured for Basic Challenge Response authentication** Challenge and response authentication is not supported by the Web clipping proxy server.
  - **Corrective Action:** Reconfigure your WCA so that challenge and response authentication is not attempted.
- **Getting errors when activating a link within a dynamically generated Web clipping** A link within a Web clipping is not a link per se, but rather an index referring to the link. This efficient representation is used in Web clippings to minimize bandwidth consumption between the proxy and device. However, with dynamic content, the number and order of links sometimes changes. When this occurs, the links (for example, link indexes) previously created are invalidated—that is, the checksum used to verify them fails.
  - **Corrective Action:** One possible solution could be for each link to include an instance ID. It could uniquely identify which revision of each link was being activated. The server could then determine whether a previously generated Web clipping was being requested, and if so, which one. The challenge with this approach would be to make sure that the instance ID is not updated during each request to the content server, because more than one request is required to serve a single link activation (for example, link hash resolution requires more than one content server hit per link activation).

Debugging...

Link Activation Errors

Errors associated with link activation in dynamically generated Web clippings pose unique challenges to debugging WCAs. One tempting correction is to dynamically produce a root Web clipping that always contains the same links in the same order. Any variations in Web clipping data would be represented in clippings referred to by the root clipping. Unfortunately, this approach does not eliminate the problem—it only buries it a level deeper in the Web clipping access chain.

- **Getting incomplete and/or incorrect data when parsing parameter data that contains empty form fields** When parsing parameter data, empty form fields confuse the process, making the data seem incomplete and/or incorrect. Empty form fields are sent to the proxy server in the following form:

```
fld_1=&hfld_2&pfld_3&fld_4=
```

The & character separates parameter data definitions, thus causing the previous line to be interpreted as the following:

```
fld_1=
hfld_2
pfld_3
fld_4=
```

The fields *fld_1* and *fld_4* represent empty text fields. The fields *hfld_2* and *pfld_3* represent a hidden field and password field, respectively. The hidden and password fields, when empty, have data definitions that *do not* include the & character. This confuses some server-side parameter processing software.

  - **Corrective Action:** Test your server-side parameter processing software to determine whether or not it has a problem parsing empty field data. If it does, you will have to write a wrapper for it to anticipate empty fields. Of course, you may want to look into your server-side software documentation to make sure that it doesn't have the ability to handle the WCA empty-field format before developing this wrapper.

NOTE

Fields associated with radio buttons and checkboxes are not represented at all in the parameter string when their value is empty/NULL.

- **Getting a garbled %DEVICEID** The %DEVICEID string is being received in the form "[dbjrnva.poldyr]". The %DEVICEID string is probably being used as a parameter at the end of a URL, and it isn't being properly expanded (for example, %DEVICEID is a Palm OS–specific variable/macro). This is a byproduct of link hashing.
  - **Corrective Action:** Use %DEVICEID within a hidden form field.

NOTE

Palm-specific variables can have uninteresting values that must be anticipated on the server. Examples are %DEVICEID=0.0.0 and %ZIPCODE=00000. Some of these are POSE-specific, whereas others can occur on the device. In any event, POSE produces each of these, making it a valuable tool in testing WCA robustness.

Getting Multiple Web Server Hits

The proxy server caches static HTML pages from content servers in an attempt to efficiently serve Web clippings to Palm OS devices. However, this does not preclude the proxy server from having to perform multiple Web server hits on content servers.

Due to the link hashing scheme, the proxy may refetch the original page when the user tries to follow a link, so it retrieves the original URL string. If the page is cached, the proxy may not have to go back to your server to get the original text, but if the user waits too long, the page may leave the cache.

Another reason for multiple server hits is cache coherency. Sometimes, Palm.Net will request a page to see if its copy in the cache is still current. This is necessary to ensure that the proxy server will produce a Web clipping from the latest copy of the page. If the content server has an updated copy of the page (that is, its modification date is later than that for the cached page), a full copy of the updated page must be obtained. This results in an additional Web server hit.

Understanding POSE Transaction Errors

Several types of error are possible when dealing with your WCA, proxy servers, and the server. This section classifies, and provides a brief explanation of, each documented error message. These error codes can be categorized as follows:

- Device
- Proxy server
- HTTP
- Miscellaneous

NOTE

The latest version of the Web Clipping Guide is an invaluable resource for understanding POSE transaction errors.

Device Error Codes

Device error codes specific to POSE and/or an actual device are described in Table 7.1.

Table 7.1 POSE Device Error Codes

Code	Text	Description
Net 1205	No more sockets	An attempt was made to exceed the maximum number of allowable open sockets (four). **Remedy:** Check the number of currently open sockets before attempting to open another one. Also, close sockets when they are no longer needed.
Net 1206	No interfaces	POSE has not been configured to redirect iNetLib requests to the desktop's TCP/IP connection. **Remedy:** Within POSE, modify Properties to redirect iNetLib requests to the desktop's TCP/IP connection and then reset POSE.

Continued

Table 7.1 Continued

Code	Text	Description
Net 1410	Your handheld could not connect to the server. Wait a few minutes and try again.	A problem has been encountered connecting to the Web clipping proxy server. The server may be down or operating slowly. **Remedy:** If you are using POSE, try the other proxy server. Otherwise, you may need to take the advice given in the error message and wait a few minutes.
Net 1413	Your handheld could not connect to the server. Wait a few minutes and try again.	A connection was established to the Web clipping proxy server and/or your destination server. However, the attempt to read data timed out before any data was received. **Remedy:** If you are using POSE, try the other proxy server. Otherwise, you may need to take the advice given in the error message and wait a few minutes.
Net 145D	Your handheld lost connection with the server. Wait a few minutes and try again.	The connection to either the Web clipping proxy server and/or your destination server has been closed. **Remedy:** Palm OS closes a connection after data (or a request for data) is sent. If a firewall is involved in your connection (if you are using POSE behind a firewall and/or your server is behind a firewall), the firewall may be closing the connection with Palm.Net and/or your destination server. Some firewalls consider leaving an incoming connection open to be a security risk.

Proxy Server Error Codes

Proxy server error codes specific to POSE and/or an actual device are described in Table 7.2.

Table 7.2 POSE Proxy Server Errors

Code	Text	Description
00002AF9 or 503	Host not found or unavailable or Service Unavailable	The Web clipping proxy server could not find a host for a URL, or the host was busy. **Remedy:** Check the validity of the URL. As an alternative, check the HTTP Content-Location header value string—redirection links can cause this type of error if this header is improperly formatted.
0000274C	Timed out	A response was not received before the connection waiting time expired. Standard wait-time is 30 seconds. **Remedy:** Try again.
0000274D or 503	Connection refused Service Unavailable	A connection could not be made, possibly resulting from the destination server being located behind a firewall. **Remedy:** The firewall will have to be reconfigured to allow the proxy server to have access (either direct or indirect) to the destination server.
C100000C	The remote machine closed the connection	The destination server closed the connection between the proxy server and the destination server. **Remedy:** Try again. If the problem persists, contact the system administrator of the destination server.
C2010005	An invalid CTP request was received	A problem was detected with data transferred between the device and proxy server. One possible cause is the transfer of an HTML form within a clipping that contains value attributes within OPTION tags. Value attributes are incorrectly interpreted as link hash codes by the proxy server. **Remedy:** Until there is a ROM fix for this officially-logged problem, create server-generated HTML that does not set the value attribute with OPTION tags.

Continued

Table 7.2 Continued

Code	Text	Description
C201000D	Attempt to reference an indirect hyperlink with out of date base document	A URL link seems to be stale. One possible cause is that the hashed link sent to the device does not match the current Web clipping. This can be a problem, particularly with dynamically generated clipping. For example, if a link's position in the current Web clipping is different than it was when the clipping was initially downloaded to the device (hashed), then this error will be generated. **Remedy:** Verify that the Web clipping in question remains unchanged, at least with respect to the relative position of links, over the life of a user's access.
C201001D	Content conversion error – unsupported content type	A type of media has been referenced that is not supported by the proxy server. Currently, the supported types are "text/html", "text/plain", "image/gif" and "image/jpeg". **Remedy:** Correct the HTML media type string being sent to the proxy server.
C201001E	The requested content contained an unsupported encoding type	The HTML contains an HTTP "Content-encoding" header. Content encoding is not supported for Web clippings. **Remedy:** Produce HTML that does not contain an HTTP "Content-encoding" header.
C2020004	The HTTP response is not formatted correctly	The response probably contains an invalid HTTPS header field. **Remedy:** Make sure that response header fields conform to the RFC 2616 standard, Hypertext Transfer Protocol—HTTP/1.1.

Continued

Table 7.2 Continued

Code	Text	Description
C202000A	Received a request with an unsupported encoding type specified	An encoding type other than "application/x-www-form-urlencoded" was received. **Remedy:** Make sure that the encoding type "application/ x-www-form-urlencoded" is used.
C202000B	There are no active HTTP or HTTPS proxies available to handle the request	The proxy server was unable to connect to a proxy cache. **Remedy:** Notify Palm.Net technical support of this (internal) problem: support@palm.net or (407) 531-4400
C2060001	Could not correctly recognize Internet date string	The response contains an invalid HTTPS date header field. **Remedy:** Make sure that the response header field conforms to the RFC 2616 standard, Hypertext Transfer Protocol—HTTP/1.1.
C2060002	Could not correctly parse an Internet string	The proxy server had one of several problems: parsing a requested URL string, interpreting an HTTP header string format, or dealing with a blank HTTP header field value. **Remedy:** Make sure that the response header field conforms to the RFC 2616 standard, Hypertext Transfer Protocol—HTTP/1.1.

HTTP Error Codes

HTTP error codes are not specific to POSE, actual devices, or Palm.Net. They are standard error codes for HTTP(S) messages and can be found at Hypertext Transfer Protocol—HTTP/1.1.

Miscellaneous Error Codes

Miscellaneous error codes specific to POSE and/or an actual device are described in Table 7.3.

Table 7.3 Miscellaneous POSE Errors

Text	Description
Web Clipping 3.2 has just read directly from memory manager data structures.	These types of error typically indicate Clipper problems recognized by POSE. They do not indicate WCA problems. **Remedy:** Hit **Continue**; this type of error won't show up on an actual device.

Using Tools to Debug WCAs

The following tools are available to support WCA testing:

- HTML validators
- Link checkers
- WCA decompilers
- Palm's InetLow application

HTML validators are designed to work with Palm's DTD to provide robust HTML checking for your WCA. This is in addition to the checking that the WCA Builder performs and is helpful to examine any Web content under your control that will reside on a destination server. One option is A Real Validator, http://arealvalidator.com; another is the validation service provided by the World Wide Web Consortium (W3C) at http://validator.w3.org.

Make sure that the HTML being validated references the correct DTD for WCA validation. The following line of code tells the validator where to find the DTD to use to verify the encompassing HTML file:

```
<!DOCTYPE HTML PUBLIC "-//POS//DTD WCA HTML 1.1//EN"
    "http://www.palm.com/dev/webclipping-html-dtd-11.dtd"
```

WARNING

Directly validating all dynamically generated HTML content is impossible. As an attempt, however, save representative examples of dynamically generated HTML content and validate it. This will provide at least basic confidence that the dynamically generated HTML content does not suffer from glaring errors.

Link checkers can scan a set of HTML pages for dead links, allowing you to make sure that your WCA is not stale. Several packages are available, including one from Netmechanic at www.netmechanic.com.

WCA decompilers allow you to extract significant details from compiled WCAs. Basically, decompilers put a .pqa in a format that is more easily read. Palm, Inc.'s Web clipping tools Web page links to several tools that can turn PQA files into text or HTML.

Palm's InetLow application demonstrates how to use the INetLib API for obtaining and displaying raw data from a URL. It can be used to test communication with a destination server, including data transfers and server-side processing. InetLow helps verify that the WCA-to-server interface is functioning properly, including the ability to navigate through firewalls. It can be downloaded from the Palm Knowledge Base at http://oasis.palm.com/dev/kb/samples/1709.cfm.

NOTE

Some testing tools can be ignored, because they are not particularly applicable to WCAs. For example, Gremlins within POSE are a useful mechanism for testing Palm OS applications. However, the Palm OS application associated with WCAs is Clipper, which has already been tested.

Summary

Debugging Web clipping applications (WCAs) can seem like a daunting task. Fortunately, many tools and techniques are available to assist you. From emulators to online discussion groups, it is difficult to find a circumstance that has not or cannot be addressed to your satisfaction.

One of the first tools that you should consider is the Palm OS Emulator (POSE). Built on the actual Palm OS, this tool allows you to test your WCA without even owning a device. No batteries are required, no wireless connection fees are incurred, and multiple types of Palm OS devices can be tested anytime and anywhere. You can even test your WCA right on your desktop without so much as a single HotSync operation.

After you have a working knowledge of POSE, consideration must be given to behind-the-scenes operation of the Palm.Net proxy. This server farm coordinates communication between WCAs and the Internet, providing access to a multitude of content servers. The proxy communicates with POSE and your device using Transmission Control Protocol/Internet Protocol (TCP/IP) and User Datagram Protocol (UDP), respectively, securing data using Elliptic Curve Cryptosystems (ECC) technology. Data is sent using a compressed subset of HTML 3.2 (the WCA format). Communication between the proxy and destination servers takes place using TCP/IP, securing data using Secure Sockets Layer (SSL) encryption. Data is sent using the HTML 3.2 standard.

The WCA format is used to represent both POSE/device-resident WCAs and Web clippings. Web clippings, when generated dynamically, require special attention during debugging because they can confuse the proxy server's link hashing algorithm.

Turning attention back to tools, advanced utilities exist to support your advanced software development tasks. HTML validators, link checkers, WCA decompilers, and Palm's InetLow application are all available to assist in various ways. HTML validators check HTML source code for compliance with the WCA Document Type Definition (DTD). Link checkers verify that no hypertext links are stale. WCA decompilers help verify that what is actually contained within a WCA and/or Web clipping reflects what was specified in the corresponding source code. And Palm, Inc.'s InetLow application demonstrates how to use the INetLib API for obtaining and displaying raw data from a URL.

In conclusion, remember to take advantage of all resources available when debugging your WCA. The chances are good that others have already faced any problem you face. So try out the tools, think about whether your WCA is in tune with Palm.Net's operational characteristics, and then plug into online resources and forums.

Solutions Fast Track

Emulating Web Clipping by Using the Palm OS Emulator

- ☑ POSE mimics the operation of a Palm OS device using actual Palm OS software.
- ☑ POSE allows WCAs to be tested without using an actual device, and it requires no batteries, no wireless connection, and no connection charges.
- ☑ POSE operation is not limited to the wireless coverage area.
- ☑ POSE is tightly integrated with the desktop, providing for widely visible presentations and/or demonstrations and easily obtained screen shots.
- ☑ POSE can emulate multiple types of device.

Understanding the Palm.Net Proxy

- ☑ Palm.Net is a server farm that facilitates WCA connections to the Internet.
- ☑ Palm.Net protects data between itself and POSE/device using ECC, and between itself and content servers using SSL.
- ☑ Palm.Net responds to requests with Web clippings in the WCA format (a compressed form of HTML 3.2).
- ☑ Web clippings are not cached.
- ☑ Dynamically generated Web clippings can cause problems for Palm.Net relative to Palm.Net's link hashing algorithm.
- ☑ Given the broad scope of Palm.Net's responsibilities, it is susceptible to a variety of problems.

Using Tools to Debug WCAs

- ☑ HTML validators check HTML source code for compliance with the WCA Document Type Definition (DTD).
- ☑ Link checkers verify that no hypertext links are stale.
- ☑ WCA decompilers help verify that what is actually contained within a WCA and/or Web clipping reflects what was specified in the corresponding source code.
- ☑ Palm's InetLow application demonstrates how to use the InetLib API for obtaining and displaying raw data from a URL.

Frequently Asked Questions

The following Frequently Asked Questions, answered by the authors of this book, are designed to both measure your understanding of the concepts presented in this chapter and to assist you with real-life implementation of these concepts. To have your questions about this chapter answered by the author, browse to **www.syngress.com/solutions** and click on the **"Ask the Author"** form.

Q: Where should proxy server problems be reported?

A: Visit the Proxy Server Feedback page at http://oasis.palm.com/dev/support/ask.cfm?page=38 and include pertinent information, such as the steps required to produce the problem, date and time of the first occurrence (including time zone), and so on.

Q: What can I do to stay abreast of the latest developments in WCA debugging technology?

A: A good first step is to join the Web Clipping Announcement list and Web Clipping Forum using the forms at www.palmos.com/dev/tech/support/forums.

Q: Where are additional resources for WCA debugging?

A: Palm, Inc.'s Web clipping development site, www.palmos.com/dev/tech/webclipping, contains additional information related to both development and debugging of WCAs.

Chapter 8

Identifying Users and Sessions

Solutions in this chapter:

- Using %DEVICEID to Uniquely Identify a Device
- Identifying Sessions Using URL Rewriting
- My Unwired Widgets Order Example
- Identifying Sessions Using Cookies in Palm OS 4.0
- Cookie Explorer Example

☑ Summary

☑ Solutions Fast Track

☑ Frequently Asked Questions

Introduction

In a word processing program, you have a document with words, images, and formatting commands. In a spreadsheet, you have a table of cells, each with its own value or formula. In an adventure game, you have the player's current location and the inventory of objects that the character is carrying. Although this data is all different, it is united by a common concept called *state*. The state of a system is the information that differentiates one instance of the system from another. State can be very simple: a light bulb is either *on* or *off*. It can also be very complex: the air traffic control system's state includes the position and velocity of every aircraft in the sky, along with information about each airport.

Computer programs can be seen as processors of state. They all start the same way, then they change states based upon the input of the user, eventually using that state to produce output. State has lots of different names: *memory, storage, databases,* and *variables* are just four terms that describe different forms of state.

Maintaining State on the Web

On the Web, state is a problem. Hypertext Transfer Protocol (HTTP), which is used to communicate between Web browser and Web server, is a *stateless* protocol: Each page served by a Web site is independent of the others, and the server does not remember anything from one transaction to another. This is done intentionally; building a server with no state lets you perform tasks more efficiently, and it lets you improve your network by adding servers or moving services from one box to another. It also means that you can build very simple Web servers that exist only to handle a single request, then go away.

For many applications, this works perfectly. This is because the state regarding the session is maintained on the client devices. When a Web browser requests a page, it gets back a document that might have links to other documents on the same server. The client has the memory about what has been requested and what should be fetched, but the server cares about the requests only while it is processing them.

This scheme of shifting state from server to client works well for more complex situations. In the case of a search engine, a user using a Web browser asks the Web server to search its database for a term. The server performs the search, and then returns a document that has the first twenty matches. In that document, the server also provides a link that gives instructions on how to ask the server for the next twenty matches. If the user wants more matches, they request a new search, showing items 20 to 40. As long as the searches can be done efficiently, this shifts the role of keeping track of where the user is in a search from the Web server to the Web client. It also means that different machines could do each set of matches, which helps simplify a network because the computational task of doing a search can be balanced between several Web servers. At the time this chapter was written, Google (www.google.com), a popular Web search engine, uses this kind of setup to distribute search requests to over 8,000 different Web servers on its network, according to an April 27, 2001 *Internet Week* story.

Sometimes, having the user maintain all of the system's state is a bad idea. Many applications use the Web browser as a user interface into a larger system that is not completely open to the user. In an e-commerce system, you might want to keep track of the user's orders and preferences. If you store this information in the Web server, then you cannot trust the quality of the data sent back to you. Perhaps you want to make a special offer that customers can use only one time. If you store the state of the offer in the Web browser, then it's simple for the user to access your site from a different browser or to change the state in the current one to reactivate the coupon.

Using %DEVICEID to Uniquely Identify a Device

Many Web applications rely on uniquely identifying a user. This can be used for several purposes, such as allowing the presentation of the site to be customized for each viewer or to prevent unauthorized access to financial transactions. The primary technique used by Palm's Web clipping application for identifying a user is the special string %DEVICEID. This string can be embedded in a Web page, where it will be replaced by Clipper with another string that uniquely identifies the device.

Reasons to Avoid %DEVICEID

Before we explain how %DEVICEID works, we want to warn you that using this for the purpose of authenticating a user is not a good idea. If you need a secure solution, we urge you to use one of the other methods explored in this chapter.

The problem with using %DEVICEID is that it is the device's "true name." Each device has only one device ID, and the user cannot change it. Therefore, if it gets compromised, the problem can't be fixed without replacing the device.

When a site requests this string, it gets returned the actual device ID string, not a version of it created especially for the site. This means that any site you visit with Clipper can capture this information. The "Wireless/Web Clipping" panel has an option in the system preferences that allows the user to turn off sending identifying information, but if this flag is turned off, the user isn't alerted when this identifying information is sent.

Here is the security issue: Suppose evilsite.com distributes a Palm Query Application (PQA) for the purpose of grabbing device ID strings. Evilsite.com might disguise this Web clipping application (WCA) as a useful reference. A user uses this PQA file to visit the site, and now the administrators of evilsite.com know the user's device's ID. If mybankaccount.com uses the device ID to authenticate the user, then the administrators of evilsite.com can make a custom INetLib application that will impersonate Clipper but send the captured device ID, letting them log in to mybankaccount.com, impersonating one of their users. They have access to any of the accounts of people who have used both evilsite.com and the bank site, because the bank is using information shared with evilsite.com to prove what user is accessing its site.

Suppose the mybankaccount.com just uses the device ID to maintain a session after the user has logged into the site. Now, evilsite has it a bit harder, because they don't know the username and password. However, they just need to wait for the user to log in to the bank and set up a session, then they can hijack the session because the bank is using the device ID.

Palm, Inc. should have used some methods that would have reduced the effectiveness of an attack like this. Having the device return a unique ID string that was hashed against the requesting site's hostname would have allowed sites to remember users while limiting the portability of those strings between sites and preventing this attack.

Because Palm, Inc. has introduced cookies with the Palm OS 4.0 version of Clipper, the %DEVICEID support seems unlikely to change. Cookies solve this problem because they allow sessions and identification of the user using data created on the server. Because that data is unique to the site that creates it, it cannot be taken by other sites and used to impersonate the user.

Because of this security problem, the authors of this book do not want to encourage use of this feature. A few situations exist where a user would want personal data available to the operators of any site the user visits. If you want to use the device identifier, you should make sure that it, by itself, is insufficient to authorize actions on behalf of the user or to get to personal data of the user.

Using %DEVICEID in a PQA

You can use the %DEVICEID variable in your HTML page, either as a hidden input field to a form or as part of a URL in a hyperlink. In Figure 8.1, we create a simple form that will submit the device ID to the server. Figure 8.2 has the server-side Common Gateway Interface (CGI) script that echoes the device ID string to the user. Figure 8.3 shows the output of this when run in the Palm OS emulator, which always has an ID of 0.0.

Figure 8.1 Using %DEVICEID in a Hidden <INPUT> Tag

```
<html>
<head>
    <title>DEVICEID Test</title>
</head>
<body>
    <p>Press the button to submit your device identifier.</p>
    <form
     action="http://cgi.unwiredwidgets.com/cgi-bin/echo-deviceID.cgi"
     method="POST">
        <input type="HIDDEN" name="ID" value="%DEVICEID">
        <input type="SUBMIT">
    </form>
</body>
</html>
```

Figure 8.2 CGI Script to Echo the Device ID (echo-deviceID.cgi)

```
#!perl -w
use CGI;
$q = new CGI;
print $q->header,
    $q->start_html("Your %DEVICEID"),
    $q->p("Your %DEVICEID is " . $q->param("ID")),
    $q->end_html;
```

Figure 8.3 PQA Screen and Output of Echo Device ID Script

On static pages that are part of a Web clipping application file, you can use the %DEVICEID string in both forms and hyperlinks. However, for dynamic pages, use it only as a hidden field in a form. The problem is link hashing, which causes the proxy server to not send complete URL strings to the device. Because the device never sees the string "%DEVICEID", it doesn't insert its special codes with the device identifier in its output, so your site will not see the string in the URL that follows.

Formatting a Device Identifier

In their Web Clipping Guide, Palm, Inc. published a specification for how device identifiers are sent to the server. A %DEVICEID string starts with one of three numbers: –1, 0, or 1, then a period follows, and then you have a string of digits that provide a unique value derived from the device. You have no guarantees as to the format of this string, but you should assume that the string contains no white space. The leading number is treated as a namespace for interpreting the following string. Right now, all Palm VII/VIIx devices report an ID in the "1" space, whereas requests from the Palm OS Emulator always show up as "0.0.0". The device IDs produced by the Palm Mobile Internet Kit (MIK) and OmniSky devices all start with –1. Palm, Inc. has reserved the other leading numbers for expansion as they and their licensees introduce new device types (Table 8.1).

Table 8.1 Device ID String Formats

Device Type	ID String Format
Palm VII/VIIx	1.nnnnnnnn.nnnnnnnn (8 digits per bundle)
Palm OS Emulator, device with no flash ID	0.0.0
Palm OS device with a flash ID	-1.nnnnnnnn.nnnnnnnn (8 digits per bundle)

Developing & Deploying...

How Device IDs Are Sent from the Device

Palm.Net's proxy does not derive your device ID from the network. Instead, the proxy relies on data sent by the device in a special format. This string looks like "[dhjljlas.awejola]". It represents two 32-bit values, rendered in Base 26 notation where a = 0, b = 1, ... z = 25. To translate this back to a number, you have to convert each letter to a digit and add the values together, shifting as you go. The delimiters for this string are "[d" at the beginning, "." in the middle, and "]" at the end. If you're sending raw data through the Palm.Net proxy using INetLib (as explained in Chapter 11), you need to be careful to use a proper Multipurpose Internet Mail Extension (MIME) content type or the proxy could translate data that looks like these device identifiers into strings such as "1.2242.21245". It is unclear why Palm, Inc. used this encoding format, although a likely explanation is that they wanted an encoding which would compress effectively in their 5-bit CML encoding scheme. This encoding scheme is explained in more detail in the Palm Knowledge Base technical note "Why is data sent from a Palm device url-encoded...," available at http://oasis.palm.com/dev/kb/faq/1816.cfm.

Building Device Identifiers on Mobitex Devices

The Palm VII was the original platform where Web clipping was deployed. Because these devices all communicated on Cingular Wireless' Mobitex network, each one had a built-in unique identifier called the Mobitex Access Number (MAN). This is the address that the Mobitex network uses to route messages to the device and identify transmissions from the device. If you look at a Palm VII, it is the three-part number printed below the bar code on the back of the unit. Because this identifier was required for the network, the Palm.Net team decided to also expose this to Web clipping developers. This device identifier is guaranteed to be unique among Palm OS devices.

Building Device Identifiers on the Palm OS Emulator

The Palm OS Emulator can do Web clipping using ROM images from devices that have INetLib and Clipper installed, such as the Palm VIIx and Palm m505. However, the Emulator has no radio or flash identifier from which it can derive its ID, so it always uses a default ID of "0.0.0", which is represented over the air as "[da.a]".

Building Device Identifiers with the Mobile Internet Kit

The Mobile Internet Kit (MIK) provides INetLib and Web clippings over a normal Transmission Control Protocol/Internet Protocol (TCP/IP) connection. Because nothing in the connection provides a consistent, unique identifier, the MIK produces this ID from the flash identifier. If your device does not have a flash ID, like the Palm m100 and m105 handhelds, then the MIK reverts to the value used by the Palm OS emulator, "0.0.0".

Building Device Identifiers with the OmniSky CDPD Modem

OmniSky's wireless Internet service uses the Cellular Digital Packet Data networks of AT&T, Verizon Wireless, Cingular Wireless, and ALLTEL to provide 19.2Kbps wireless data service. Their modems come bundled with a custom version of INetLib and Clipper. With the OmniSky version of INetLib, the device ID is derived from an internal identifier in the wireless modem. This means that even on devices with no flash, such as the Handspring Visor handhelds, you will have a unique ID.

Developing & Deploying...

HTTP Access Control

One of the earliest features added to HTTP was user access control at the protocol level. In this scheme, a site would isolate some pages into controlled areas where the client would have to send a valid username and password with each request or not get access to the pages.

When the user tried to access a page that was off-limits, the server would return a special error code rather than the page. The browser would then ask the user for his or her username and password, and it would request the page again, passing this information as additional headers on the HTTP GET operation. If the username and password were valid, the server would send the page, and the browser would remember the values the user entered and use them to retrieve future pages on the same server.

Web clipping on the Palm OS device does not support this mechanism. If you try to access a page that uses HTTP-level access control, you will get back an unauthorized access error message, but you have no way to send a username and password back to the site. This is not a big obstacle to controlling site access, because a site can use other methods that don't rely on these headers to control who can see a Web page. But you should be aware of this if you are converting a site that uses HTTP authentication to wireless access over Palm OS devices.

Building Device Identifiers on the Kyocera QCP-6035 Smartphone

In the spring of 2001, Kyocera, the Korean company that had bought Qualcomm's PCS phone business in 1999, introduced its next-generation cellphone, the QCP-6035. This phone incorporated a Palm OS PDA into the normal cell phone functions; it also supported wireless data access, using both NetLib and INetLib. The %DEVICEID value used by Clipper is based on a network identifier given to the phone by the service provider, so it is unique.

However, users of the phone have noticed that this identifier has changed since they first received their phones, which indicates that the PCS carriers (Sprint PCS and Verizon Wireless, at the time this was written) have the ability to change the %DEVICEID remotely.

Identifying Sessions Using URL Rewriting

A useful method for tracking user sessions is to encode a server-generated identifier in the URLs used to access data. This method is called *URL rewriting,* because normal URLs that are used to get to a resource are modified to include the custom information. Unlike cookies, URL rewriting does not require special support in the Web browser, making it quite appropriate for the limited capabilities of Web clipping.

This information can take several forms. It could be a copy of the information your scripts will need on the next page; this method works poorly in practice due to security problems and verboseness. To give an example of what can go wrong, consider what happened to some Internet retailers in the early days of online commerce. The retailers used shopping cart systems that stored all of the information about a user's order in form variables that got resubmitted on each user action. When the user added items to the shopping cart, the item list being stored on the user's PC held the item, quantity, and price. System abusers discovered that they could change this information and resubmit their orders with the prices changed to give everything a huge discount. Because these retailers had automated the entire order system, this fraud wasn't detected until well after the "free" items had been sent off, and the corrupt user had disappeared.

NOTE

The BugTraq mailing list hosted by SecurityFocus.com serves as a forum for exposing security problems in widely used software. One example of the kind of pricing vulnerability discussed in this section is documented in the BugTraq archives at www.securityfocus.com/archive/1/136764. A summary of the kinds of attacks that have been made against shopping carts is included in an article at www.securityfocus.com/archive/1/44785.

A better method of tracking user sessions is to use a *session ID,* which is a unique identifier that does not contain any information other than the name of a user session. All of the session data is kept on the server where it is secure. The user could alter her session ID, but unless she had special knowledge of which sessions were open, doing so would only result in a rejected session from the server.

A good session identifier has several properties: It should be of sufficient length and randomness that an attacker would not be able to guess an active session ID. The server should have some mechanism to invalidate and remove old sessions from the server after a period of nonuse. When using session IDs with Palm's Web clipping, the ID should stay the same through the entire user session; if it does not, issues arise with link caching (which we discuss later). The session ID should also be valid in the standard URL character set without using URL-encoding escapes, because this simplifies the session-handling logic on the server.

Developing & Deploying...

Rewriting in the Real World

The idea of encoding identifying information into an address isn't new with the Web. This practice has been used for years, especially in big mail centers. The next time you look at rebate coupons, notice that many rebates—even from different companies—all go to a similar address, often a place such as Young America, Minnesota. Other parts of the address, such as the department number, are actually used to identify which rebate it is, what retailer sold the product offering the rebate, or what region of the country the purchaser lives in. A similar technique is used for record clubs, where the same offer might be in four different publications, but each one has its own toll-free number so that the record club can tell which ads are generating which calls.

Encoding a Session ID in a URL

Typically, the session ID is added to all of the internal URLs on the page using an automated mechanism. This discussion is a bit abstract, applying to session IDs as used on many different systems. Although session IDs are independent of the Web browser, their implementation is specific to the back-end system you use on your Web site. Later in this chapter we show you how to implement session IDs using PHP: Hypertext Processor (PHP), a popular and free system for dynamically creating Web pages.

Typically, a session ID is added as a form variable to the end of every URL on the page. Remembering the form request syntax from Chapter 5, a GET action acts just like a normal request, except that extra text is added to the end of the URL to indicate the choices made by the user. This text takes the form "name=value", with a leading question mark and ampersands separating the name/value pairs. However, you don't need a form to use this syntax. For a fixed query, you can specify everything in the hypertext link. In effect, a page fetch with a session ID is a fixed query, with the one parameter being the session identifier.

The device doesn't know the session ID when it first connects to the server. An access without a session ID causes the server to generate a new one to be used while the user is accessing the site. The server should produce a long, random string that cannot be easily guessed, but that also can be sent easily as part of a URL string.

For example, if you were connected to the Unwired Widgets Web site and your connection was given the new session ID "3HSS678B", then links on that initial page would be encoded to include the session ID. A link to the home page might show up as "http://www.unwiredwidgets.com/?sid=3HSS678B", as shown in Figure 8.4. Notice that we've taken a normal link and appended the form variable *sid* with the value "3HSS678B". We also modified the link to the sales page in the same manner. We did not modify the link to Palm, Inc., because that goes to another company's site that is not running the same session identification scheme we are using.

Figure 8.4 Hypertext Links with and without Embedded Session IDs

```
<a href=" http://www.unwiredwidgets.com/?sid=3HSS678B">
Unwired Widgets Home Page</a>
<a href=" http://www.unwiredwidgets.com/sales/index.html?sid=3HSS678B">
Unwired Widgets Sales Information</a>
<a href=" http://www.palm.com">Palm, Inc. Home Page</a>
```

This embedding of the ID at the end of a hypertext link works fine for standard hyperlinks. However, if you want to actually use an HTML form, you need to use an alternate scheme. The way to go in this case is to add a hidden input field to your forms, with a variable named the same as the name you gave your session ID, and with its value set to the session identifier. If you do this, the session ID will be transmitted along with the rest of the user responses when the form is submitted. Figure 8.5 shows this technique as used in a simple form that gets the user's name.

Figure 8.5 HTML Form with Embedded Session ID

```
<form method="GET"
    action="http://cgi.unwiredwidgets.com/cgi-bin/username.cgi">
<p>Please enter your name:
    <input type="hidden" name="sid" value="3HSS678B">
    <input type="text" name="username" maxlength="30">
    <input type="submit" value="OK">
</p>
</form>
```

If you use this method, you should be sure your scripts that handle the form submissions also work with your session management code. Most form processing packages will ignore extra variables, but you may want to look up user information using the session ID or just return it in the hyperlinks for the output page.

Managing Sessions with PHP 4

In the free software world, PHP, the recursively named PHP: Hypertext Processor, has become the dominant dynamic content system for Web servers, due to its combination of ease-of-use, speed, flexibility, and availability. PHP is available in binary and source form for a variety of systems, include Linux, Solaris, BSD Unix, and Windows. For these reasons, this chapter will use PHP as the example to show how to perform session handling. There are many different systems available that help you generate dynamic content, including Microsoft's Internet Information Server (IIS) with Active Server Pages (ASP) and Allaire's ColdFusion. If you are using one of these systems, you should be able to apply the concepts shown here, although the syntax and operation details will be different.

Developing & Deploying…

Installing Apache and PHP on Windows

The CD that accompanies this book includes the current Apache and PHP distributions; the code for this chapter was developed on a Windows 2000 system running Apache 1.3.19 and PHP 4.0.4. Apache's installation on Windows is very straightforward; the installation file is a ".msi" archive, which is used by the Microsoft Windows Installer. If you are using Windows 2000 or Windows Me, you already have Windows Installer as part of your system. If you're running an older Microsoft operating system, you may need to download the Windows Installer binary from Microsoft at www.microsoft.com/msdownload/platformsdk/instmsi.htm.

PHP is shipped as a ZIP file. To install it, you should unzip the PHP binary distribution file into a directory like C:\PHP\, and then you should follow the instructions in Chapter 2 of the PHP Manual to change the appropriate files to get Apache to launch the PHP processor on files with the PHP extension.

PHP can also install into Microsoft IIS and other popular Windows Web servers. See the PHP manual for details. To get the latest version of the Apache server, visit the Apache Group's Web site at www.apache.org. They have source distributions, along with prebuilt binaries for Windows and Linux systems. The latest releases of PHP are available at the PHP site, at www.php.net.

Understanding PHP Syntax

When using PHP, you have an HTML file with special embedded directives that direct the processor to perform special actions. These actions vary from simple substitutions of variables to complex database manipulations. PHP directives are isolated from standard HTML by the delimiters <?PHP and ?>. Anything between these strings is considered a PHP command, whereas the rest of the text is passed directly as output. You can also use just <? to start a PHP directive block, but this usage is discouraged, because it is incompatible with XHTML, the next-generation HTML standard based around XML.

Page processing has several phases. Any PHP directives that appear before your <HTML> tag get executed before headers are output, so they can affect how the page is transmitted and cached. This is also a good place to put PHP functions that you've defined to be used later in the page. After you've started your HTML text, directives get executed as they are seen.

NOTE

For more information on PHP's syntax, refer to the PHP Reference Manual, downloadable from www.php.net/docs.php. The current copy of this manual in Adobe Acrobat PDF format is provided on the bundled CD. This manual is not the easiest way to learn PHP syntax, because it is designed as a reference. If you want more information about PHP, the PHP site has an extensive book list at www.php.net/books.php.

Figure 8.6 shows a small "Hello, World" example of a PHP page. When you access this page, you will get back an HTML document saying "Hello" and telling you what Web browser you used to access the page.

Figure 8.6 "Hello, World" and Browser Identification Using PHP

```
<html>
<head>
    <title>PHP Hello World Example</title>
</head>
<body>
<p>
<?php
    echo "Hello, PHP user!<BR>\n";
    echo "Your browser is ", $HTTP_USER_AGENT, ".\n"
?>
</p>
</body>
</html>
```

In this example, we use two echo statements to output a hello greeting in the middle of our HTML page. The first echo just outputs plain text, but the second one used a predefined variable, HTTP_USER_AGENT. Variables in PHP start with the dollar sign character. This prefix prevents conflicts between variable names and function names, because functions cannot start with a dollar sign. HTTP_USER_AGENT is an environment variable set by the Web server based on the User-Agent HTTP header, which is a header sent by Web browsers to identify what software was used to access the site. Figure 8.7 shows the result of accessing this PHP page from Clipper.

Figure 8.7 Output of PHP "Hello, World" Example in Clipper

Configuring PHP for URL Rewriting

Out of the box, PHP is set up to use cookies to manage sessions. This method doesn't work for most of the user base of Web clipping, because cookie support wasn't added until Palm OS 4.0. To configure PHP to use URL rewriting to manage sessions, you should alter the PHP.INI file by adding the line:

```
session.use_cookies = 0
```

Another setting you might want to change for use with Web clipping is the name used for the session variable. The default value is "PHPSESSID", but the *session.name* variable in the PHP.INI file controls what name is used. Using a shorter name can save transmission time and characters, because it can get sent many times in one page. If you wanted to use the name "SID", you would add the line:

```
session.name = "SID"
```

To prevent naming conflicts, you should pick a name that is not used in any of your forms.

Starting a Session

There are two ways to tell a PHP page that it should use PHP's session management scheme. Before you have any HTML text on your PHP page, you should add the directive **session_start**. This command causes the PHP server to re-establish the session from the submitted session ID or to create a new session ID if one was not available. See Figure 8.7 for an example of this usage. You also can also use the **session_register** command, which will also begin a session if one has not yet been established. This command is also used to associate PHP variables with the session, so their values will be preserved from page to page.

PHP can also be set to always start sessions when a page is loaded, which may be useful if your site will always be managing user sessions. The configuration setting is called *session.auto_start*, and it is set in the PHP.INI configuration file. To activate this, add this line to your PHP.INI file:

```
session.auto_start = 1
```

Saving System State in a Session

Just having a session is not very useful. You need to be able to store data with the session. PHP does this by associating variables with the session object. The values of these variables are saved on the server, and their values are available to other pages that will be generated in the session.

Lots of values are candidates for saving as part of the session. In a shopping cart application, you could save the list of items the user had added to the cart in the session variables. After the user has selected several items and navigated to the checkout form, a PHP script would display all of them along with their current prices, as pulled from a database.

To get a PHP variable saved from session to session, you use the **session_register** command to add the variable's name to the list of those whose values will be saved. When you use **session_register**, you provide a comma-separated list of the variable names as strings, not the actual variables themselves. Consider this example: You have stored the result of a list of shipping methods in the variable $SHIPPING_METHOD. To register this as a session variable so your later forms could use it, you would write:

```
<?PHP session_register("SHIPPING_METHOD") ?>
```

Later pages in the same session would then see a variable called $SHIPPING_METHOD. Variables have to be registered to the session only once. After the initial registration, changes to the variables will be automatically saved.

PHP saves the session just before it exits, writing any variables that have been registered, using **session_register**, back to the server in a file named after the session ID. PHP never accepts session IDs from the user; it creates these session files only when the user accesses a page that uses sessions without an existing ID. The PHP documentation describes where these session files are saved and how you can alter the session save-and-restore process to store this data into a database.

Using Automatic URL Rewriting

PHP can automatically change URL strings to include the session identifier. When you have sessions enabled, any relative URLs (ones without schemes or site names) will be automatically rewritten to include the session ID name and value. For example, if your hyperlink looks like this:

```
<a href="page2.html">Go to page 2</a>
```

PHP will automatically rewrite it to read like this:

```
<a href="page2.html?SID=sessionid">Go to page 2</a>
```

PHP also recognizes several other kinds of links. Links to images within your page will also have the session ID appended. PHP also automatically inserts hidden fields into any forms on the page to preserve the session identifier when you make a form submission.

Adding Session IDs to Hyperlinks and Forms

Sometimes, PHP cannot automatically add the session ID to your hyperlink. If you try to link to another page using a full URL, PHP will not add the session ID to avoid passing sensitive session information to other sites. In this situation, you can explicitly add this identifier by using the SID variable. An example of how to write a hyperlink with an embedded session ID is as follows:

```
<a href="http://unwiredwidgets.com/home.html?<?=SID?>">Home</a>
```

To output the variable value, we use "<?=SID?>" The "<?=" starts the PHP directive and is a shortcut for "<?PHP echo". **SID** is a special session command that outputs either "PHPSESSID=*session*" or a blank string, depending on whether the session ID has been set. "?>" closes the directive. We prefixed this with a question mark; without it, PHP wouldn't see the session ID string as a form variable.

If you have a form that submits to an absolute URL, you cannot rely on the automatic URL expansion either, because the URL specified by the *action* attribute is not modified by PHP's automatic rewriting. To fix this, you can either add the same "?<?=SID?>" construct to your URL string, or you could make the session ID an explicit form variable by specifying it as a hidden input to the form, using code like this:

```
<input type="hidden" name="<?= session_name() ?>"
    value="<?= session_id() ?>">
```

This input tag uses two of PHP's session-handling calls, **session_name** and **session_id**, to fill in the name and values of the hidden field. This will be part of the variables sent to the server when the form is submitted.

Palm.Net Proxy URL Hashing and Session IDs

The Palm.Net proxy, by default, saves URL strings on the server and sends a hashed form of the URL to the device. Instead of sending the long URL string, the proxy turns each string into a much smaller number produced by taking the string and performing computations on it, such as taking its length, adding the values of all the characters, or performing a Cyclic Redundancy Check (CRC). When the device wants to follow a URL, it sends the address of the current document and the hash value of the URL. The proxy goes and refetches the original page, reruns the hash function on each URL, finds the one that matches the request, and then follows it to fetch the new page for the device.

As an example, consider a Web page that has a hyperlink to the URL http://www.unwiredwidgets.com/salesflyer/page4/specialoffer2.html. If this were sent directly over the air, you would have 65 characters just to represent the complete URL. With hashing, this could be reduced to a 32-bit number, which is made of only 4 characters. If you have half-a-dozen links of that length on a page, your transmission size has just been reduced from 360 characters to 24, a major savings when the users are paying by the byte for data, like they do with some of the Palm.Net plans for the Palm VII and VIIx.

When this works, it does a good job of reducing the bandwidth used between the proxy and wireless Palm OS devices. Web sites have gotten into the habit of sending long URLs to desktop Web browsers, where the length of the text is overwhelmed by the size of associated graphic files.

However, you should be aware of two possible failure points. First, sometimes the hash function that the Palm.Net proxy uses doesn't produce unique values. For this hash to work, each link on the page should have a unique hash value so that when you follow a link, it finds the correct one at the server. Early versions of Palm.Net proxies used a hashing scheme that ignored characters at the end of long URLs. Some systems that had deep directory structures or long session IDs produced pages with multiple links that matched to the same value. The best way to avoid this bug is to make sure that your URL strings have sufficient differences to trigger different hash values.

NOTE

As an example of a long URL, a recent visit to one of the book pages at Amazon.com produced the URL http://www.amazon.com/exec/obidos/ASIN/1928994326/ref%3Dnosim/searchbyisbn/104-4588797-9911941, a total of 95 characters. This link seems to encode the name of Amazon's book lookup software, an ISBN code, a string that identifies the referring site, and finally a session ID.

Second, you have to be concerned about the initial creation of the session. The problem is that when you grab the first page in a session, you get a unique ID handed back to the device. When you follow a link, the proxy server may use a cached copy of that page with the session ID, but it also could go back to the server and request the original page again. If the proxy does the latter, it will now get a different session ID, so the link hashes will not match, causing a connection error.

To solve this problem, you need to prevent the server from using link hashing on your initial session page. You can do this in two ways. The most reliable is to always generate the start page with an HTTP POST event. You could do this from a Web clipping application by making your page a form that uses the POST action to submit its query to the server. The Palm.Net proxy does not do link hashing for posts, it instead passes the text of the URLs to the device; this is because of the HTTP semantics for a post, which indicate that a post cannot be resent to the server. Because Palm cannot guarantee that it will keep the result of the posting in its cache, it sends the full URLs to the device so that the links will be able to be followed in the future.

The other method available to solve this problem involves adding a special attribute to your Web pages to specify that link hashing should not be done. This can be done using either a META tag, which controls the entire document, or by tagging individual hyperlinks. Adding the following line to the <HEAD> tag of your HTML page will cause the Palm.Net proxy to send full URL strings back to the device:

```
<META NAME="PalmHREFStyle" CONTENT="FULL">
```

If you have only some hyperlinks where this hashing will be an issue, you can leave the page with the default scheme and tag individual hyperlinks with the *PalmStyle* attribute, like this:

```
<a href="hyperlink" palmstyle="FULL">hyperlink</a>
```

This method does work well, but the *PalmStyle* attributes are understood only on recent versions of the Palm.Net proxy. If you are using Clipper through a service provider using an older proxy, the POST method is the only one guaranteed to work.

My Unwired Widgets Order Example

Let's take a look at an example using two PHP files that together form a session-based order system. This example is a very simplified version of a real-world shopping cart program, but it does show how sessions let us keep information in variables for later processing.

The entry page, order.php, shown in Figure 8.8, represents a simple HTML form for ordering widgets. In this form, you enter a quantity, and then choose the color, size, and shape of the widgets you want to order. When you hit the **Add** button, the order gets submitted back to the server, which reruns the original PHP page. We also have a form link that goes to the companion PHP page, checkout.php, which shows the user a list of all the widgets he has ordered.

All of the order data is stored in one variable, the multidimensional array $ORDER. We use PHP to store all of the orders as items in a simple array, where each individual order is an associative array holding the order details. In our session management code, we have to establish the $ORDER variable as an array before registering it as a session variable, or it will be registered as a string, and the array operations when we add to it will cause PHP to indicate an error.

In this page, we use the presence of the $COLOR variable to tell if we're processing a form submission or just showing the page for the first time. We process the submission late in the page because we are also giving you feedback about what you just ordered, and it's convenient to add the order to our array at the same time as we tell you what we added.

Figure 8.8 Unwired Widgets Order Script (order.php)

```
<?php
    session_start();

    // force $order to be an array if it doesn't exist
    if (empty($order)) { $order=array(); }

    session_register("order");
?>
<html>
<head>
<title>UW: Order Widget</title>
<meta name="PalmComputingPlatform" content="TRUE">
</head>
<body>
<h1>Unwired Widgets</h1>

<p>Choose a widget style and quantity and hit "Add"
to add it to your order, or hit "Checkout" to
confirm your selection.</p>

<form method="post" action="order.php">

<table>

<tr>
<td>Quantity:</td>
<td>
<input name="quantity" maxlength="5" size="5" value="1">
</td></tr>

<tr>
<td>Color:</td>
<td>
```

Continued

Figure 8.8 Continued

```
<select name="color" size="1">
<option>red</option><option>blue</option>
<option>green</option><option>yellow</option>
</select>
</td></tr>

<tr>
<td>Size:</td>
<td>
<select name="size" size="1">
<option>big</option><option>small</option>
</select>
</td></tr>

<tr>
<td>Shape:</td>
<td>
<select name="shape" size="1">
<option>square</option><option>round</option>
</select>
</td></tr>

</table>

<input type="submit" value="Add">

</form>

<form method="post" action="checkout.php">
<input type="submit" value="Checkout">
</form>

<?php
```

Continued

Figure 8.8 Continued

```
    echo "<p>Already seen ", count($order), " orders</p>";

    // if we're responding to a POST, add the new
    // order to the list, and let the user know what
    // was added
    if (isset($color) && is_numeric($quantity))
    {
        $order[] = array(
            "color" => $color,
            "size" => $size,
            "shape" => $shape,
            "quantity" => $quantity);

        printf("<p>Added %d %s, %s, %s widget(s)</p>",
            $quantity, $color, $size, $shape);
    }
?>
</body>
</html>
```

Figure 8.9 shows our checkout.php script. When you access this page with an active session, it shows you everything that we've stored away in the $ORDER variable by generating an HTML table from the items in the array.

Figure 8.9 Unwired Widgets Checkout Script (checkout.php)

```
<?php session_start(); ?>
<html>
<head>
<title>UW: Order Checkout</title>
<meta name="PalmComputingPlatform" content="TRUE">
</head>
<body>
```

Continued

Figure 8.9 Continued

```
<h1>Unwired Widgets</h1>

<p>Here is your order:</p>

<table>
<tr>
<th>Qty.</th> <th>Color</th> <th>Size</th> <th>Shape</th>
</tr>

<?php
    for ($i = 0; $i < count($order); $i++)
    {
        echo "<tr>\n";
        echo "<td>", $order[$i]["quantity"], "</td>\n";
        echo "<td>", $order[$i]["color"], "</td>\n";
        echo "<td>", $order[$i]["size"], "</td>\n";
        echo "<td>", $order[$i]["shape"], "</td>\n";
        echo "</tr>\n";
    }
?>

</table>
</body>
</html>
```

This example has several problems that should be addressed in real-world code. The first problem is data validation. If you enter nothing or a non-number for the quantity field, you don't get any sort of error message. Also, no validation exists to make sure that the selections from the <SELECT> tags are valid. Although you would not expect Clipper to send back bad data, someone trying to break the security of the system could send anything as an imitation of Clipper.

This system also needs to be expanded to provide order editing. At the least, the user should be able to clear all pending orders, but giving the user the ability to edit individual items would be nice. When designing systems for Palm OS devices, you should remember that you have limited bandwidth and screen space, so some features that may be appropriate for a desktop shopping cart would be excessive on the handheld.

Finally, to be useful, you would need to track additional information, such as the name and address of the customer. This would be a good opportunity to use PHP's huge library of functions to access your customer list, validate credit card numbers, and communicate with other network systems to let your order fulfillment personnel know about the new order.

To complete the example, we need a WCA that will launch the user into the order system. Because we don't want caching problems, our WCA will enter this system using an HTTP form submission. Figure 8.10 shows the HTML source used to make this WCA.

Figure 8.10 Unwired Widgets Order System WCA

```
<html>
<head>
<title>UW: Enter Order System</title>
</head>
<body>
<h1>Unwired Widgets</h1>
<form method="post"
    action="http://www.unwiredwidgets.com/order.php">
<input type="submit" value="Enter Order System">
</form>
</body>
</html>
```

In a more secure system, you may want to put a username and password field on this form, then use those to set up the user session before letting the user add items to her shopping cart.

Identifying Sessions Using Cookies in Palm OS 4.0

Cookies, in the Web sense, are an invention designed to deal with HTTP's lack of state. Online privacy advocates hate cookies, going as far as disabling them in their Web browsers. Web designers find them extremely useful, often making sites that won't allow access without them. As with many things in life, cookies are neither a plight nor a savior for the Web, but to understand that, we need to first understand what cookies are.

To explain, we will use the analogy of a *pass*. In real life, a pass is granted from some issuing authority to a person. To use the pass, the passholder presents it back to the authority. Passes usually have an expiration date—after some amount of time they are no longer good. Passes often carry some sort of information that is useful to the issuer. Sometimes this information is very brief—consider a parking pass that just has the year and the parking area allowed. Sometimes this information is very detailed: A driver's license can be considered as a kind of pass that had the name of the issuing state, the name of the driver, a license number, the driver's personal traits, and the expiration date of the license. Finally, a pass usually means nothing to an authority that isn't associated with the issuer.

Cookies share many of the properties of a pass. A cookie is just a pair of strings: a name and a value. They are issued by a Web site as part of the site returning a Web page. Once issued, the Web browser will send the cookie back as part of any Web page requests made at the issuing site. A cookie has an expiration date; the issuing site can set some time in the future where the cookie will no longer be valid, or the site can leave it at its default, which is until the Web browser session is finished. A cookie can be very short, or it can be up to 4K long (short is encouraged). Finally, a cookie can be returned only to the site that issued it, although there are some exceptions.

One area where cookies and passes differ is their voluntary nature. When you're given a pass in real life, you have the ability to reject it before ever receiving it, and once you've received it, you can ignore it, never showing it to anyone. Because the Web browser automatically handles cookies, a user is not given a choice to accept cookies sent from a site. Palm Inc.'s cookie implementation in Palm OS 4.0 is this way; the user cannot use a setting to turn cookie handling off, and the user has no control over accepting or declining cookies from Web sites. Some desktop Web browsers, such as Microsoft's Internet Explorer 6.0 and the open source Mozilla, give users more control over cookies, but this capability is very new to the Web.

Sending Cookies from a Web Server

The formal specification for cookies is RFC 2109, which is a formalization of the specification originally designed by Netscape for the Netscape Navigator 1.0

browser back in 1995. Palm's documentation claims compliance with Netscape's document, so use it as your primary reference.

NOTE

The text of RFC 2109 is available from www.cis.ohio-state.edu/cgi-bin/rfc/rfc2109.html. Netscape's document describing cookies is available at http://home.netscape.com/newsref/std/cookie_spec.html.

To set a cookie, a Web server returns one or more special "Set-Cookie" headers. Each header sets one cookie in the Web browser. The contents of this header follow a set format. First, you have the name and value for the cookie in the form "name=value". This can be the complete cookie, but usually it is followed by optional attributes that modify the cookie from its default behavior.

The full syntax is as follows:

```
Set-Cookie: NAME=VALUE; expires=DATE; path=PATH; domain=DOMAIN_NAME;
   secure
```

Anything after the "name=value" part is optional, but for compatibility, it should be presented in the order shown here. Both the *NAME* and *VALUE* strings are limited to non-whitespace, non-comma, non-semicolon ASCII characters. The standard recommends using URL encoding to include the prohibited characters, but this convention isn't required.

The *expires* attribute describes a date when the cookie is no longer valid. The format for this date is very specific:

```
Wdy, DD-Mon-YYYY, HH:MM:SS GMT
```

This format is similar to the required date format specified in RFC 822, RFC 850, RFC 1036, and RFC 1123, the specifications that describe e-mails and newsgroup postings. The difference between those specifications and the dates described in the cookies document is that cookies require the Greenwich Mean Time (GMT) time zone, and they allow only the dash to separate parts of the date. A sample date might look like this:

```
Sun, 13-May-2001, 19:02:00 GMT
```

This requirement for GMT time offers a clue as to why Palm, Inc. didn't support cookies until Palm OS 4.0. Before that version of the operating system, no global setting existed to describe the time zone in which the device was operating. Because of that, cookies could not be reliably expired, because the Palm couldn't map the GMT time into a local operating time. With OS 4.0, Palm added a time zone setting, so this is no longer a problem.

The *path* attribute is used to describe the set of URL paths on a Web site over which the cookie operates. The default is for the cookie to be sent back only to the page that originally sent it. By setting a path of "/", the cookie would be sent on a request for any page at the site. Other path settings are more restrictive: Setting it to "/foo/bar/" would cause the cookie to be sent on a request for "/foo/bar/baz.html" but not for "/foo/quux.html".

The *domain* attribute is like path, because it regulates what sites the cookie will be sent to. Again, the default is the most restrictive, allowing the cookie to be sent back to only the original machine it was sent from. You can loosen this requirement by specifying a more top-level domain. For example, if your Web server machine was "www.unwiredwidgets.com", you could set the domain of your cookie to be "unwiredwidgets.com", and the cookie would now be sent to any machine whose name ended with "unwiredwidgets.com", such as "www2.unwiredwidgets.com" or "alpha.beta.unwiredwidgets.com". The domain of the sending machine limits this attribute—a Web server at "foo.net" could not set the domain attribute to be "bar.com". Also, it wouldn't be able to set it to be ".net"; the domain attribute requires at least a second-level domain (or a third-level domain if the TLD is a two-letter country code such as "uk" or "de").

The final attribute is *secure*. If this keyword is listed, then the cookie will be sent back only over secure connections, as in ones that use the HTTPS protocol. Normally, cookies will be sent over any HTTP connection type.

Servers can also delete cookies that are already on the browser by sending a name-value pair with an empty value. The cookie has to match the one on the client exactly—name, path, and domain information all must be exact matches for the stored forms in the Web browser. Also, the same restrictions apply for deleting as do for creating; "foo.net" is unable to delete a cookie stored by "bar.com".

Including Cookies in a Web Browser Request

A Web browser keeps a local database of all the cookies it has seen along with the restriction information it has stored to tell it when to send back the stored cookies. Most browsers have some sort of built-in limit as to how many cookies they will store and how large each cookie can be. The original minimums specified in

Netscape's document were 300 total cookies, each up to 4K in size, with at most 20 cookies per specified domain. Microsoft's Internet Explorer does not seem to limit the total number of cookies, but it does limit each domain to 30 total cookies. On the Palm OS, the limitation is expressed in terms of database size: By default, Clipper allows the cookie database to grow to 50K; any new cookies cause older cookies to be removed.

When the Web browser is ready to request a Web page, it goes through its cookie list, trying to find any cookies that might match the domain name of the site it's going to access. This is also usually when it removes any expired cookies from the local database. After it collects this list, it then weeds out any cookies whose paths don't match the path of the request. Now, the browser has a list of cookies to send. It formats the list into an HTTP "Cookie" header in the following form:

```
Cookie: NAME=VALUE; NAME=VALUE; … NAME=VALUE
```

It has no trailing semicolon, and no cookies are found, this header is not sent. The order of the name-value pairs is significant. If more than one cookie has been sent for a particular name, all of the cookies will be sent, but the one with the closest match to the site will be sent first, followed by the next-closest match, and so on until all cookies have been sent. Usually, you will get your expected behavior if your cookie processing script just uses the first value seen for any particular name.

Using Cookies to Enhance Web Sites

Web designers have invented many different uses for cookies throughout the lifetime of the Web. Most uses fall into one of several categories:

- Username and password storage
- User preferences
- Shopping carts
- User tracking
- Session management

Username and password tracking is natural for cookies. When the user successfully logs in to the site for the first time, the site returns a cookie with an encoded form of the username and password the user entered. When the user returns to the site, these get sent automatically, and the site can log in the user without interaction. Usually, sites that do this offer a logout option that deletes the cookie, and they make saving the cookie in the browser optional through a checkbox that enables saving it on the user's machine. This may be a good candidate for the "secure" attribute, so the cookie with the username and password doesn't ever get sent in the clear.

Rather than storing a user database on the server, you may find it easier to save user preferences in cookies on the device. Although you could store each preference in its own variable, it's better to represent all of the preferences in one string that you can parse at the beginning of your server script. Site preferences can be anything. On the Palm, some preferences might be the maximum length of pages to return, displayed fields and sort keys for database tables, or the user's home town for a location-based service.

Cookies can store quite a bit of data. Netscape's original specification allowed a single cookie to grow to 4K of storage. For a Palm OS device, you should limit your cookies to a few hundred bytes at most, because they get sent for every page transaction, and some wireless services charge by the byte. Still, it's possible to store a shopping cart in a very small number of bytes if you use the right encoding. The key is to save your shopping cart as a compact string, with just the item quantities and part numbers. You should heed the security warnings from the "Identifying Sessions Using URL Rewriting" section earlier in this chapter and not store any sensitive data that you wouldn't want the user to change in a cookie; just store the user's choices and keep recomputing everything else on your Web server.

Using cookies to track users is a common task but one that has given cookies a bad name among computer users concerned about their privacy. The idea is for a site to issue a cookie with a random string. Then, every time that site sees that cookie again, it knows that the original user has returned. Because cookies are returned only to the site that issued them, this doesn't seem so bad. However, with the growth of advertising networks, Web programmers realized that many different Web sites would be showing images served from a single advertiser domain. Because the ads are fetched over HTTP, it's possible for the advertising company to send a cookie when you view an ad on site A, then get that cookie returned when you visit unrelated sites B and C. The advertising company now knows that this one user has visited all three sites.

In the previous section, we talked about managing sessions using URL rewriting. You can also track a session by using cookies, storing the session ID in the cookie but keeping all of the session variables on the server. This is the default mode for sessions when using PHP, and it can be explicitly enabled using the following in the PHP.INI file:

```
session.use_cookies = 1
```

Unless your site also uses cookies for other purposes, you should probably use URL rewriting if it's available, because cookies are not available on Palm OS devices running Palm OS 3.5 or earlier.

Cookies versus URL Rewriting

The biggest advantage cookies have over URL rewriting is that cookies can be preserved from one session to another. If you set a cookie with an expiration date, it will be kept on the device, even when other applications are running instead of Clipper. When the user relaunches the Web clipping application and goes back to your site, she won't need to re-establish context, because the cookies set in a previous session will be automatically returned if they haven't expired.

Cookies also work with nondynamic pages. If you use cookies, you don't need to generate every page on your site with a script, because you aren't relying on altering the URL strings to maintain the session. Cookies will always be sent, as long as the address being loaded matches the cookie criteria.

On the Palm OS device, the big disadvantage of cookies is support in Clipper. Cookie support didn't get added until Palm OS 4.0, so the majority of Web clipping users will not be able to use pages that rely on cookie support. If you have to support a user base that includes Palm VII and VIIx users, cookies just aren't part of your Web site toolbox.

Another disadvantage to using cookies is the bandwidth used, especially on the request side. Cookies can burden every request to your site with hundreds of bytes of cookie data that have to be sent every time a user follows a link. With the slow and expensive connections that Palm OS devices use to connect to the Web, this is a factor against using complicated cookie schemes.

Cookie Explorer Example

This example doesn't build on the Unwired Widgets site, but it is useful for playing with cookies and seeing how they work on a Palm OS device. Cookie Explorer is a PHP page that lets you set cookies in your browser using simple HTML forms. The page will tell you what it sent in its Set-Cookie header and will also let you see all the cookies that were sent to it from your Web browser.

To use this site, you navigate to the initial page; on the Palm OS device, a simple Web clipping application that just links to the Cookie Explorer page is sufficient. If this is the first time you've used this page, it should show that no cookies have been set and give you an input screen like the one shown in Figure 8.11. If you enter parameters for a cookie and submit it, you will get the original input form repeated, with the addition of a line saying that the server sent back a cookie with your values. At this time, you should be able to reload the page by following its link back to itself. When you do that, the PHP script is run again, but now it has your first cookie sent back as another input. Figure 8.12 shows Clipper's view of the page after it has been run several times, setting multiple cookies.

Figure 8.11 Cookie Explorer: Initial Page

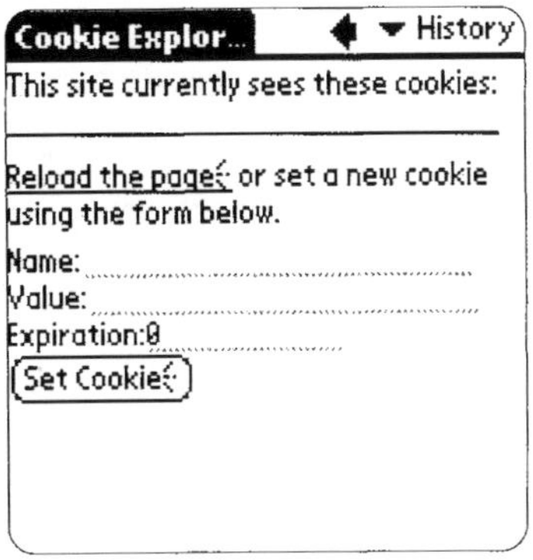

Figure 8.12 Cookie Explorer: After Several Cookie Submissions

Using Cookie Explorer, you can leave the expiration at 0 to make a session-only cookie, or you can give it a positive number, which is treated as the number of seconds past the current time to set the expiration. When we were using this, we found out that the Palm OS device didn't seem to deal with expirations in the very near future. When we set the number of seconds to expire a cookie within a minute of it being sent, the cookie never got sent back to the server. Based on this, we'd recommend setting the expiration time of your cookies at least five minutes from the time you sent it.

The code for the Cookie Explorer page is listed in Figure 8.13. This PHP page does not do extensive error checking—it is possible for you to give illegal cookie names or values, although it looks like PHP automatically URL encodes and decodes cookies, so it never really sends anything illegal.

Figure 8.13 Cookie Explorer PHP Script (cookietest.php)

```
<?php
    if (isset($cookie_name))
    {
        // adjust non-zero value expirations
        // using the input as an offset from the
        // current time
        if ($cookie_expires != 0)
        {
            $cookie_expires += time();
        }

        SetCookie(
            $cookie_name,
            $cookie_value,
            $cookie_expires);
    }
?>
<html>
<head>
    <title>Cookie Explorer</title>
</head>
```

Continued

Figure 8.13 Continued

```
<body>
    <?php
        if (isset($cookie_name))
        {
            echo "<p>Just set cookie ", $cookie_name;
            echo " with value \"", $cookie_value, "\".  ";
            if ($cookie_expires != 0)
            {
                echo strftime("It expires at %H:%M:%S " .
                    "on %m/%d/%y.  ", $cookie_expires);
            }
            echo "Reload to see it in cookie list.</p>";
        }
    ?>
    <p>This site currently sees these cookies:</p>
    <ul>
    <?php

        reset ($HTTP_COOKIE_VARS);
        while (list ($key, $val) = each ($HTTP_COOKIE_VARS))
        {
            echo "<li><b>", $key;
            echo "</b> = \"", $val, "\"</li>\n";
        }
    ?>
    </ul>
    <hr>
    <p><a href="cookietest.php">Reload the page</a> or
    set a new cookie using the form below.</p>

    <form action="cookietest.php" method="POST">
    Name: <input type="text" name="cookie_name" size=20><br>
    Value: <input type="text" name="cookie_value" size=20><br>
```

Continued

Figure 8.13 Continued

```
    Expiration: <input type="text" name="cookie_expires" value="0"
        size=10><br>
    <input type="submit" value="Set Cookie">
    </form>
</body>
</html>
```

This script is great for experimenting. In testing cookies, we modified this to send a lot of cookies in a loop every time the page was loaded. Although Internet Explorer will keep only the last 30 cookies sent, Palm's Clipper in OS 4.0 kept track of 100 different cookies on one of my tests, sending them all back to the site. We think it actually was able to keep track of more cookies than could be returned, causing my Apache server to abort the transaction with an internal error thrown by having a cookies header that was much too long.

Also, we tested this script without building any PQA files; instead, we directly navigated to the site using the "go to URL" feature of iKnapsack, as described in Chapter 10. The CD included with this book contains both this source file and a small source file that you can change and point at your server to run this Cookie Explorer.

Summary

Sophisticated techniques have overcome the stateless nature of HTTP, allowing complex applications to be implemented on the Web. This chapter showed three different technologies that allow a Web site developer to find out more about the site's users and to provide a customized user experience.

The first mechanism was to use the unique identifier that Clipper can be asked to return to track a user's identify. However, because the unique ID isn't treated as a secret, using it invites people to break into your site, representing themselves as other users by hijacking their device IDs. The ID can be used for nonsecure applications, but should never be used as the sole authentication authority.

A better approach is to use the links that a user follows to store information about his or her session. By rewriting each URL to include a tracking string, you can associate data stored on the server with a particular user. This technique doesn't require any specific device support, because it uses standard links that have extra information encoded in the Web addresses. PHP 4.0 proved to be a useful tool for implementing URL rewriting, with built-in support for modifying all the local hyperlinks on a Web page to include the session ID variable.

With Palm OS 4.0, you can use cookies to provide context and state to Web transactions. By storing data on the device that gets automatically sent back to the server, you can identify users, manage Web sessions, and provide a better user experience. However, cookies can be misused, and you need to be aware that older devices are not capable of sending and receiving them.

Solutions Fast Track

Using %DEVICEID to Uniquely Identify a Device

☑ Many devices that support Web clipping will send unique identifiers when the string %DEVICEID is used in a URL or form.

☑ Because the device ID can be spoofed, you should not rely on it to give the users access to sensitive data.

Identifying Sessions Using URL Rewriting

- ☑ By adding a server-generated identifier to all of your page's URLs, you can track a user across pages on a Web site.
- ☑ PHP 4 provides a powerful system for generating content for the Web.
- ☑ To use PHP's session rewriting, each page must enable sessions using the **session_start** or **session_register** commands.
- ☑ PHP's sessions allow you to preserve the values of variables across multiple page loads without directly exposing the values of those variables to the user.

My Unwired Widgets Order Example

- ☑ PHP sessions can be used to implement a simple shopping cart system.
- ☑ When implementing a real system, you should pay close attention to user authentication and the security of form submissions.

Identifying Sessions Using Cookies in Palm OS 4.0

- ☑ Cookies let you store data on the device that can be retrieved at a later time.
- ☑ Cookies are supported only in Web clipping on Palm OS 4.0 and later devices.
- ☑ Although cookies can be used to make the user's life much easier, by storing preferences or login information, they can also be used to secretly track which sites a user visits.

Cookie Explorer Example

- ☑ The Cookie Explorer PHP script can be used to set and delete cookies on your Palm OS 4.0 device.
- ☑ The script can be customized to automate your cookie explorations.

Frequently Asked Questions

The following Frequently Asked Questions, answered by the authors of this book, are designed to both measure your understanding of the concepts presented in this chapter and to assist you with real-life implementation of these concepts. To have your questions about this chapter answered by the author, browse to **www.syngress.com/solutions** and click on the **"Ask the Author"** form.

Q: Does every device have a unique identifier?

A: No. Although you can request a %DEVICEID string through Web clipping, this string always has the same value for every user of the Palm OS emulator or for devices that do not have a flash ID, such as the Palm m100 and m105 handhelds.

Q: My %DEVICEID request returned the actual string "%DEVICEID". What went wrong?

A: You can only put this string in a link URL under three circumstances. First, if it is used in a PQA file local to the device, this will work. Second, you can put it on a link returned by the HTTP POST form transaction. Finally, if you are using the new proxy and you have specified that either the page or the link not be hashed, this will work. Otherwise, you need to just put it in a hidden field on a form submission.

Q: I'm using PHP session management with URL rewriting. Why do I lose the user's session when they go to one of my static pages?

A: The PHP session is maintained only as long as the user keeps following links that contain the session ID. If the user goes to a nondynamic page, that page will lack rewritten URLs, and any links followed will not be tagged with a session ID.

Q: Which method is more bandwidth efficient: URL rewriting or cookies?

A: If you're using the standard Palm.Net proxy and your pages are mostly returned as the result of following normal links, URL rewriting is very efficient, because the URLs containing the session IDs are not sent in full to the device, and the device doesn't have to send back a cookie with every request. However, for a forms-heavy site where link hashing doesn't happen, it's better to send just one cookie than to repeat the session ID string over and over.

Q: How do I look at the cookies stored on my device?

A: At the time this book was written, there weren't any specialized cookie viewers. However, an on-device resource editor such as Insider or Onboard RsrcEdit can be used to open the database "CookieDB" and directly view the cookie records. There is one cookie per database entry, and the entries' name, value, path, and domain attributes are all easy to identify as ASCII strings.

Q: Can I use cookies on my Palm VII or VIIx?

A: No. Cookie support requires Palm OS 4.0 or later, and although an OS upgrade is available for some older Palm OS devices, the Palm VII and VIIx handhelds do not have sufficient flash memory to hold Palm OS 4.0, the Mobitex radio libraries, and the new Web clipping tools.

Chapter 9

Locating Mobile Users

Solutions in this chapter:

- Finding a User's Position with the Palm VII
- Address Locator Example
- Mapping ZIP Codes to Coordinates
- Determining the Closest Address
- Locating the Closest Widget Outlet Example
- Using Enhanced %LOCATION Information in Palm OS 4.0

☑ Summary

☑ Solutions Fast Track

☑ Frequently Asked Questions

Introduction

One of the unique capabilities of mobile Web access is the ability it affords the user to tailor his or her experience based on physical location. Palm OS Web clipping supports this through U.S. Postal Service Zone Improvement Plan (ZIP) Code information that can be provided for the device.

Each Palm VII device communicates with Palm.Net via a BellSouth Mobitex base station. The wireless system keeps track of the base station with which a Palm VII device is communicating, and also the ZIP Code of each base station. By correlation, the wireless system can determine the ZIP Code of a Palm VII device.

Using ZIP Code information is a way to make your applications position-sensitive. You will find that despite some technical challenges, ZIP Code interpretation can greatly improve the user experience. Technical challenges include the need to turn ZIP Codes into coordinates and searching through a database to find coordinate-based information (for example, the closest address). It can be quite complicated, but the challenges are typically justified by the outcome.

Already, many useful position-based systems exist. Weather applications use your local ZIP Code to tell you about conditions nearby. Store and bank locators can tell you the closest branch position. News sites can tailor the coverage to include both local and national stories.

In this chapter, you will learn how to make your WCA position-sensitive, including both obtaining and processing position information. You will learn how to find a Palm VII device's ZIP Code and how to map that ZIP Code to latitude/longitude coordinates; these coordinates will be used to determine which address in a database is closest to the Palm VII device's current position. This chapter will also explain how to use the new Palm OS variable %LOCATION. You will learn enough about Palm VII position-based WCA development to give your users a new level of performance.

Finding a User's Position with the Palm VII

The Palm OS-specific variable %ZIPCODE is the mechanism available to WCAs to determine the current position of a Palm VII device. The %ZIPCODE variable provides a rough estimate of a device's position by referring to the ZIP Code of the base station with which it is currently communicating. Its use can make possible the existence of new and exciting applications, while enhancing others.

Position-based applications include, among others, weather information, ATMs, car repair and gas, entertainment, airline arrival/departure information, real-time traffic, realty information, boating services, and news information. However, %ZIPCODE is not a perfect answer to the position question, and an understanding about its operation and limitations must be gained in order to use it appropriately.

Understanding %ZIPCODE Operation

As with any other server, the server for your Palm VII device (that is, Palm.Net) is aware of the identity of specific computers with which it communicates. Palm.Net knows how to identify each computer, usually via IP address. Fortunately, this ability carries over to base stations. Palm.Net can identify specific base stations with which it communicates.

Because base stations are stationary, it is a direct correlation for Palm.Net to associate a base station with its encompassing ZIP Code. And, because a Palm VII device typically communicates with the nearest base station, the base station ZIP Code is a reasonable estimate of the Palm VII device's encompassing ZIP Code. However, *reasonable* estimates are not always accurate.

NOTE

In the headers of Mobitex packets forwarded to Palm.Net is information about the Mobitex Access Number (MAN) of both the base station and the Palm VII device that is communicating. The base station's MAN is cross-referenced with a current server list, finding the server's ZIP Code. Server ZIP Code is inherited by the Palm VII device as the value of %ZIPCODE. This explains why sometimes you get 00000 as the ZIP Code when you're talking to a base station about which Palm.Net has not learned.

Understanding %ZIPCODE Limitations

Base station coverage areas cannot follow ZIP Code boundaries, especially because ZIP Codes do not always have well defined boundaries. This is not to say that ZIP Codes have no meaningful geographic description, rather that the ZIP Code geographic description is not always an enclosed geometric shape. For example, ZIP Codes associated with rural areas may simply be represented by a group of lines. Also note that ZIP Codes can exist across state, county, and city boundaries.

Even if enclosed geometric shapes characterized ZIP Codes, gaps and/or overlaps would still exist between base stations. This would confuse how a reported ZIP Code should be interpreted. If coverage *gaps* exist, it may not be possible for any reported ZIP Code to ever match the actual ZIP Code of the Palm VII device's position. If coverage *overlaps* exist, more than one reported ZIP Code possibility might exist for a given Palm VII device position.

Additional considerations include both natural and man-made obstacles. Natural obstacles include mountain ranges and vegetation, whereas man-made obstacles include buildings and bridges. Any natural or man-made obstacle can block the line of sight between a Palm VII device and the closest base station, which will result in a Palm VII device having to communicate with a base station that is farther away. The net effect is that the ZIP Code of the more distant base station will be reported as the ZIP Code of the Palm VII device, even though the ZIP Code is *not* that of the closest base station.

Additionally, even if an obstacle doesn't affect the base station with which a Palm VII device communicates, it may affect application-specific interpretation of the reported ZIP Code. For example, if an Unwired Widgets WCA is used to locate the nearest store/kiosk, the interpretation of "nearest" will be based on the reported ZIP Code. The nearest store/kiosk may actually be in or near the reported ZIP Code, only in an area difficult to access from the Palm VII device's current position (for example, across a bay or down the busiest streets).

Keep in mind that even an exact ZIP Code determination is a coarse measurement at best, because ZIP Codes typically cover areas measured in square miles rather than square inches. The main rule of thumb is to use caution when interpreting reported ZIP Codes. Even with its inherent limitations, %ZIPCODE can satisfy a wide variety of applications. In fact, for some applications such as weather reporting, which do not rely on an *exact* location, the ZIP Code position accuracy is quite sufficient.

WARNING

For some applications, ZIP Code positioning does not provide enough accuracy. In the case of moving map software, for example, the ZIP Code associated with a person or vehicle may not change even though the person or vehicle has traveled several miles.

Understanding %ZIPCODE Syntax

The syntax of %ZIPCODE is straightforward, as shown in Figure 9.1.

Figure 9.1 %ZIPCODE Syntax

```
<input type="hidden" name="zip" value="%zipcode">

-OR-

<form method="get"
    action="http://www.unwiredwidgets.com/cgi-bin/zip.pl?zip=%zipcode">
```

The *type* qualifier indicates that the <INPUT> tag is of *hidden* type. For a full explanation of the <INPUT> tag, see Chapter 5.

The *name* qualifier identifies an <INPUT> tag so that it can be distinguished from other tags. In Figure 9.1, *zip* was chosen arbitrarily to illustrate that the *hidden* type <INPUT> tag will contain a ZIP Code.

The *value* qualifier specifies the default value for the *hidden* type <INPUT> tag. In the case of %ZIPCODE, the *value* qualifier indicates that the *hidden* type <INPUT> tag contains a placeholder for the current base station ZIP Code.

Within URLs, %ZIPCODE is appended to the end, as shown in the <FORM> example in Figure 9.1.

Complete WCA source code for a %ZIPCODE example is shown in Figure 9.2, and the server-side script is shown in Figure 9.3. Before and after screen shots are shown in Figures 9.4 and 9.5.

Figure 9.2 %ZIPCODE Example

```
<html>
<head>
<title>ZIP Code</title>
<meta name="PalmComputingPlatform" content="true">
</head>
<body>
<center>
<font size="4">ZIP Code (%zipcode)</font>
<form method="GET"
    action="http://cgi.unwiredwidgets.com/cgi-bin/zip_code.pl">
```

Continued

Figure 9.2 Continued

```
     <input type="hidden" name="zip" value="%zipcode">
     <input type="submit" value="Get ZIP Code">

</form>
</center>
</body>
</html>
```

Figure 9.3 %ZIPCODE Example (zip_code.pl)

```
#!/usr/bin/perl

use CGI;

&extract_n_display_zipcode;

sub extract_n_display_zipcode {

     # parse incoming parameters as either "GET" or "POST"
     $q = new CGI;

     # isolate parameter names
     @name_list = $q->param;

     # return results header
     print "Content-type: text/html\n\n";
     print "<html>\n";
     print "<head>\n";
     print "<title>ZIP Code</title>\n";
     print "</head>\n";
     print "<body>\n";
     print "<center>\n";
     print "<font size='4'><b>ZIP Code</b></font>\n";
```

Continued

Figure 9.3 Continued

```
    print "<br><br>\n";
    print "<i>(As Interpreted By Palm.net)</i>\n";

    # extract values
    foreach $name (@name_list) {

        # decode encoding
        $value = $q->param($name);

        # output received data
        print "<br>";
        print $name;
        print "=";
        print $value;
        print "\n";
    }

    # return results footer
    print "</center>\n";
    print "</body>\n";
    print "</html>\n";
}
```

Address Locator Example

To illustrate the concepts discussed thus far, consider an address locator example that looks for a store address for Unwired Widgets that has the same ZIP Code as the Palm VII device. This example demonstrates how to obtain the %ZIPCODE value and how to perform a direct match between it and a store address database. Although the direct match approach may work, keep in mind that no match is guaranteed.

Figure 9.4 The Before Screen Shot

Figure 9.5 The After Screen Shot

A complete WCA source code listing, server-side script, and sample store address database are shown in Figures 9.6, 9.7, and 9.8, respectively. The WCA before and after screen shots are shown in Figures 9.9 and 9.10. Note that your application should be able to handle ZIP Code strings of 00000.

Figure 9.6 Address Locator Example

```
<html>
<head>
<title>Address Locator</title>
<meta name="PalmComputingPlatform" content="true">
</head>
```

Continued

Figure 9.6 Continued

```
<body>
<center>
<font size="4">Address Locator Example</font>
<form method="GET"
    action="http://cgi.unwiredwidgets.com/cgi-bin/address_locator.pl">

    <input type="hidden" name="zip" value="%zipcode">
    <input type="submit" value="Get Address">

</form>
</center>
</body>
</html>
```

Figure 9.7 Address Locator Example (address_locator.pl)

```
#!/usr/bin/perl

use CGI;

&find_store_by_address;

sub find_store_by_address {

    # parse incoming parameters as either "GET" or "POST"
    $q = new CGI;

    # isolate parameter names
    @name_list = $q->param;

    # extract values
    foreach $name (@name_list) {
```

Continued

Figure 9.7 Continued

```
        # decode encoding
        $value = $q->param($name);

        # save pertinent data
        if ($name eq "zip") {$zip_value = $value;}
    }

    # check for a ZIP Code of 00000
    if ($zip_value eq "00000") {

        die "ZIP Code value is unavailable (e.g. 00000).";
    }

    # open store address database
    open (store_addresses, "store_addresses.db") or
        die "Couldn't open store_addresses.db!";

    # process store address database one record at a time
    $store_name = "";
    $store_addr = "";
    $store_city = "";
    $store_st   = "";
    $store_zip  = "";
    while (<store_addresses>) {

        # read database record
        readline;

        # process database record
        ($field_0, $field_1, $field_2, $field_3, $field_4) = split /,/;
        $zip_read = substr($field_4, 0, 5);
        if ($zip_read eq $zip_value) {
```

Continued

Figure 9.7 Continued

```
            # keep the matching store address
            $store_name = $field_0;
            $store_addr = $field_1;
            $store_city = $field_2;
            $store_st   = $field_3;
            $store_zip  = $field_4;
        }
    }

    # close store address database
    close (store_addresses) or die "Couldn't close
        store_addresses.db!";

    # return results header
    print "Content-type: text/html\n\n";
    print "<html>\n";
    print "<head>\n";
    print "<title>Address Locator</title>\n";
    print "</head>\n";
    print "<body>\n";
    print "<center>\n";
    print "<font size='4'><b>Address Locator Results</b></font>\n";

    # return matching store address
    if ($store_name ne "") {

        print "<br><br>\n";
        print "Store Address Match\n";
        print "<br><br>\n";
        print $store_name;
        print "\n";
        print "<br>\n";
        print $store_addr;
```

Continued

Figure 9.7 Continued

```
          print "\n";
          print "<br>\n";
          print $store_city;
          print ", ";
          print $store_st;
          print "  ";
          print $store_zip;
          print "\n";
     }
     else {

          print "<br><br>\n";
          print "No Store Address Matches\n";
          print "<br><br>";
          print "ZIP Code ";
          print $zip_value;
          print "\n";
     }

     # return results footer
     print "</center>\n";
     print "</body>\n";
     print "</html>\n";
}
```

Figure 9.8 Store Address Database (store_addresses.db)

```
store_addresses.db
The Widget Outlet,123 Your Street,Toney,AL,35773
Widget Emporium,456 Your Street,Springville,AL,35146
Widgets-R-Us,789 Your Street,Center Point,AL,35235
Unwired Widget Outlet #1,ABC-1 Your Street,Decatur,AL,35601
Get Unwired,DEF-2 Your Street,Hazel Green,AL,35750
```

Continued

Figure 9.8 Continued

```
Unwired Widget Outlet #2,GHI-3 Your Street,Laceys Spring,AL,35754
ABC Widgets,JKL-4 Your Street,Meridianville,AL,35759
John's Widgets,MNO-5 Your Street,Valhermoso Springs,AL,35775
Widgets 123,PQR-6 Your Street,Huntsville,AL,35801
```

Figure 9.9 The Before Screen Shot

Figure 9.10 The After Screen Shot

Mapping ZIP Codes to Coordinates

As seen in the previous example, performing direct ZIP Code matching is not robust. Of course, ZIP Codes were not designed with intelligent WCA processing in mind, so a different, better approach is needed.

Latitude/longitude measurements provide a robust, global description of position information. Used for centuries, latitude/longitude measurements denote positions in a generic, country-independent format. They offer a numeric description of positions (free from arbitrarily assigned codes and identifiers) that lends itself to automated processing. Latitude/longitude measurements are the standard position descriptors for applications in mapping, navigation, aviation, and global positioning. By converting ZIP Codes to their corresponding latitude/longitude, a wide spectrum of new opportunities arises for robust position processing.

Considering Available Data Sources

Several data sources exist for mapping ZIP Codes to their corresponding latitude/longitude. Two significant sources are the U.S. Census Bureau and the U.S. Postal Service. Their corresponding links are:

- **U.S. Census Bureau Files** http://ftp.census.gov/geo/www/gazetteer/places.html
- **U.S. Postal Service Files** www.usps.gov/ncsc/products/tiger.htm

Additional data sources are available from several commercial vendors, including the following:

- **GreatData.com** www.emory.com/progress/US-Zips.htm
- **HALLoGRAM** www.hallogram.com/mailers/zipdata
- **ZIP Code USA** www.tpsnet.com/html/zipcode.html and also www.zipcodedatabases.com
- **ZIPList5 Geocode** http://zipinfo.com/products/z5ll/z5ll.htm

For the purposes of this book, the U.S. Census Bureau's data source was selected for illustration. This is due in large part because it is free—it is not the most up-to-date, but it serves the intended purpose well. You should consider other data sources for more recently updated, albeit costly, alternatives.

Extracting Coordinates

As of this writing, the U.S. Census Bureau offers four views of its data source, each contained in a downloadable .zip file. The .zip files are as follows:

- counties.zip
- mcds.zip
- places.zip
- zips.zip

Each .zip file contains a single ASCII.txt file of the same name, written one line per record, and containing both latitude and longitude data. Each file also contains various references to the Federal Information Processing Standard (FIPS) codes for states' various census unit subdivisions.

The *counties.txt* file contains all counties included in the 1990 U.S. Census, specified in the following format:

- **Columns 1–2** State FIPS Code
- **Columns 6–8** County FIPS Code
- **Columns 10–75** County Name
- **Columns 77–78** State Abbreviation
- **Columns 80–88** Total 1990 Population
- **Columns 90–98** Number of 1990 Housing Units
- **Columns 100–109** Land Area
- **Columns 111–120** Water Area
- **Columns 122–130** Latitude
- **Columns 132–141** Longitude

Note that columns 10 through 75 contain the county name, including a "County" suffix. Also, columns 100–109 and 111–120 (Land Area and Water Area) are measured in thousandths of a square kilometer. Columns 122–130 and 132–141 (Latitude and Longitude) are measured in millionths of a degree (10^6 units = 1 deg). Latitude begins with either a plus sign (+) or a minus sign (-), indicating North or South respectively; longitude begins with either a plus sign (+) or a minus sign (-), indicating East or West respectively. An excerpt from counties.txt looks as follows:

```
01    089 Madison County
AL 000238912 000097855 0002084844 0000020532 +34760002 -086548777
01    103 Morgan County
AL 000100043 000040419 0001508018 0000043624 +34453298 -086857298
```

The *mcds.txt* file contains all subcounties, or Minor Civil Divisions (MCD) and Common Core of Data (CCD) (county subdivisions record type 060) places in the U.S. included in the 1990 U.S. Census. The format is:

- **Columns 1–2** State FIPS Code
- **Columns 4–8** County Subdivision FIPS Code
- **Columns 10–75** Place Name
- **Columns 77–78** State Abbreviation
- **Columns 80–88** Total 1990 Population
- **Columns 90–98** Number of 1990 Housing Units
- **Columns 100–109** Land Area
- **Columns 111–120** Water Area
- **Columns 122–130** Latitude
- **Columns 132–141** Longitude
- **Columns 143–145** County FIPS Code

Note that columns 10 through 75 contain the place name, including the type of place (city, town, borough, village, or Census-designated place [CDP]). Also, columns 100–109 and 111–120 (Land Area and Water Area) are measured in thousandths of a square kilometer. Columns 122–130 and 132–141 (Latitude and Longitude) are measured in millionths of a degree (10^6 units = 1 deg). Latitude begins with either a plus sign (+) or a minus sign (-), indicating North or South; longitude begins with either a plus sign (+) or a minus sign (-), indicating East or West. An excerpt from mcds.txt follows:

```
01 90171 Autaugaville division
AL        2983        1117 0000478289 0000013428 +32458063 -086728471 001
01 90315 Billingsley division
AL        2282         887 0000387786 0000000947 +32603561 -086763221 001
```

The *places.txt* file contains all *places* (incorporated and unincorporated settlements) in the U.S. and outlying areas (excluding MCDs and CCDs) included in the 1990 U.S. Census. The format is:

- **Columns 1–2** State FIPS Code
- **Columns 4–8** Place FIPS Code
- **Columns 10–75** Place Name
- **Columns 77–78** State Abbreviation
- **Columns 80–88** Total 1990 Population
- **Columns 90–98** Number of 1990 Housing Units
- **Columns 100–109** Land Area
- **Columns 111–120** Water Area
- **Columns 122–130** Latitude
- **Columns 132–141** Longitude

Note that columns 10 through 75 contain the place name, being either a city, town, borough, village, or CDP. Also, columns 100–109 and 111–120 (Land Area and Water Area) are measured in thousandths of a square kilometer. Columns 122–130 and 132–141 (Latitude and Longitude) are measured in millionths of a degree (10^6 units = 1 deg). Latitude begins with either a plus sign (+) or a minus sign (-), indicating North or South; longitude begins with either a plus sign (+) or a minus sign (-), indicating East or West. An excerpt from places.txt follows:

```
01 09400 Brighton city
AL      4518      1735 0000003627 0000000000 +33438850 -086945474
01 09424 Brilliant town
AL       751       366 0000007825 0000000000 +34016723 -087775810
```

The *zips.txt* file contains all 1990 ZIP Codes by state. The format is comma-separated values:

- **Field 1** State FIPS Code
- **Field 2** 5-digit ZIP Code
- **Field 3** State Abbreviation
- **Field 4** ZIP Code Name

- **Field 5** Longitude (decimal degrees)
- **Field 6** Latitude (decimal degrees)
- **Field 7** 1990 100 percent Population
- **Field 8** Allocation Factor (decimal portion of state within ZIP Code)

Note that field 5 (Longitude) is considered a West measurement by default—no minus sign is required. Field 6 (Latitude) is considered a North measurement by default—no plus sign is required. An excerpt from zips.txt follows:

```
"01","35601","AL","DECATUR",86.98868,34.589599,36696,0.009082
"01","35759","AL","MERIDIANVILLE",86.578879,34.861779,2597,0.000643
```

Note that the latitude and longitude for each place was calculated not with respect to its visual center but rather with respect to its legal boundaries.

WARNING

Latitude and longitude measurements are not as accurate as the precision of their values implies. The extra precision is useful only for processing purposes to guarantee numeric separation of features between which is minimal spacing.

Accessing and processing these coordinate files is most easily done on a server using your choice of language. The zips.txt file is used to convert a ZIP Code to its corresponding latitude/longitude; the other files (counties.txt, mcds.txt, and places.txt) are used to obtain additional qualifying data. Undoubtedly, zips.txt is the most significant file because it is used to obtain latitude/longitude data needed for the "Closest Address" algorithm (see the upcoming sections). But counties.txt, mcds.txt, and places.txt can be used to model the new Palm OS 4.0 %LOCATION variable (see "Using Enhanced %LOCATION Information in Palm OS 4.0" later in this chapter). For example, the following thread through the coordinate files can be followed to achieve some of the results provided by %LOCATION:

- Use zips.txt and ZIP Code to look up a state's FIPS code, state abbreviation, and latitude/longitude. This information resembles that obtained via the **L**, **l**, and **G/R** codes for %LOCATION (that is, **%location:L.**, **%location:l.**, and **%location:g#r.**).

NOTE

%ZIPCODE itself provides the information obtained via the **z** code for %LOCATION (for example, **%location:z.**).

- Use mcds.txt and latitude/longitude (from the previous step) to look up the county subdivision FIPS code and county FIPS code. This information resembles that obtained via the **O** code for %LOCATION (for example, **%location:O.**).
- Use counties.txt, mcds.txt, places.txt, and latitude/longitude to obtain a place/county name. This information resembles that obtained via the **c** and **o** codes for %LOCATION (for example, **%location:c.** and **%location:o.**).

NOTE

Using latitude/longitude data to look up additional information in counties.txt, mcds.txt, and places.txt is more involved than performing simple latitude/longitude numeric comparisons. For example, the latitude/longitude of a ZIP Code will most likely *not exactly match* the latitude/longitude of a corresponding county. The "Closest Address" algorithm defined in the following sections needs to be used.

The only codes associated with %LOCATION that are not mimicked are **y** (Country Name) and **Y** (Country Code). The coordinate files presented herein do not explicitly provide Country Name/Code—these fields are expected to be in the U.S. (The coordinate files are a U.S.-oriented resource.)

NOTE

You can find additional resources containing preprocessed ZIP Code interpretations at http://oseda.missouri.edu/mscdc. Specifically, the following interpretations are available in SAS code as of this writing:

- **ZIP Code to State** http://oseda.missouri.edu/mscdc/sasfmats/Szipstab.sas
- **ZIP Code to County** http://oseda.missouri.edu/mscdc/sasfmats/Szipcnty.sas
- **ZIP Code to Metro Area** http://oseda.missouri.edu/mscdc/sasfmats/Szipmetr.sas
- **ZIP Code Names** http://oseda.missouri.edu/mscdc/sasfmats/Szipnmus.sas
- **ZIP Code to "Many Places"** http://oseda.missouri.edu/mscdc/sasfmats/Szipcods.sas

"Many Places" are represented in the list of geographic codes available for each ZIP Code. See http://oseda.missouri.edu/mscdc/sasfmats/zipcods.usgnotes for more details.

Developing & Deploying…

Obtaining Latitude/Longitude Coordinates from External Devices

You can use the Palm VII device's serial port to interface to alternative positioning devices—most notably Global Positioning System (GPS) and Ultra Wide Band (UWB) receivers. These devices supply latitude/longitude data in a format consistent with the National Marine Electronic Association (NMEA) standards.

The NMEA standard (NMEA 0183) defines an electrical interface and data protocol for communication between marine instrumentation. Under the NMEA 0183 standard, all characters used are printable ASCII text (plus carriage return and line feed). The data is transmitted in the form of "sentences." Each sentence starts with a dollar sign ($), a two letter *talker* ID, a three-letter *sentence* ID, followed by a number of data fields separated by commas, and terminated by an optional checksum and a carriage return/line feed (CR/LF). A sentence may contain up to 82 characters including the $ and CR/LF.

Complete NMEA 0183 documentation can be obtained (for a fee) from: NMEA 0183 Documentation, PO Box 3435, New Bern, NC 28564-3435 USA (Telephone: [919] 638-2626; Fax: [919] 638-4885) E-mail NMEA at: nmea@coastalnet.com, or go to the Web site at www4.coastalnet.com/nmea/default.html.

Determining the Closest Address

In order to employ latitude/longitude data in a closest-address search, an algorithm is needed to define how the search will be conducted. A Closest Address algorithm is needed to specify how latitude/longitude data will be processed in order to provide the best possible results (that is, the closest address to the current, or specified, position).

Five steps are involved in locating the address closest to a reference ZIP Code:

1. If the reference ZIP Code (the ZIP Code indicated by %ZIPCODE) is 00000, stop processing. A "Position Information Unavailable" clipping is a reasonable way to stop gracefully.
2. Search an application-specific address database/file for a direct ZIP Code match. This is illustrated previously in this chapter's "Address Locator Example" section.
3. If a ZIP Code match is found, stop. The application-specific address database/file record containing the address closest to the reference ZIP Code has been found.

WARNING

More than one ZIP Code match exists if the application-specific address database/file contains more than one entry for a given ZIP Code. Proper handling of this situation depends on the needs of the application. Traditional choices include presenting all candidate choices to the user or selecting the first encountered match.

4. Because no direct ZIP Code match was found, look up the latitude/longitude corresponding to the reference ZIP Code (see "Extracting Coordinates" section earlier in this chapter). This latitude/longitude is referred to as the *reference* latitude/longitude.
5. Search the application-specific address database/file for the latitude/longitude closest to the reference latitude/longitude. Process one latitude/longitude at a time:
   - Read a latitude/longitude, observing sign conventions (*N* is positive, *S* is negative; *E* is positive, *W* is negative).

- Find the straight-line distance between this latitude/longitude and the reference latitude/longitude, using the Pythagorean Theorem. Keep in mind that latitude/longitude are angle measurements pertaining to a curved Earth surface. The distance's units are the same as those used for the Earth's radius. (Note that the following equations do not take into account any scaling needed for latitude/longitude. For example, if latitude/longitude are measured in millionths of degree, they need to be divided by one million before applying the following equations.)

dist_y = 2 * earth_radius * sin((latitude – latitude_ref) / 2)

dist_x = 2 * earth_radius * sin((longitude – longitude_ref) / 2)

dist_straight = sqrt(dist_x² + dist_y²)

- Find the curved-line distance between this latitude/longitude and the reference latitude/longitude.

dist_curved = 2 * 2 * pi * earth_radius * arcsin(dist_straight / (2 * earth_radius)) / 360

- If this curved distance is less than the previously calculated curved distance, this latitude/longitude (and corresponding ZIP Code) is closer to the reference latitude/longitude than the previous latitude/longitude.

WARNING

Latitude/longitude provide only a two-dimensional model for distance calculations. The curvature of the Earth is taken into account, but the curved-surface model still represents only two dimensions. Elevation is not taken into account.

Note that the application-specific address database/file is more efficient if it contains both the ZIP Code and corresponding latitude/longitude for each address. This will prevent an on-the-fly mapping of each ZIP Code to its corresponding latitude/longitude. Latitude/longitude data can be incorporated into the application-specific address database/file via the address database/file's preprocessing with zips.txt.

WARNING

ZIP Codes are designed to represent linear postal delivery routes, not fully enclosed polygons. This can adversely affect the accuracy of %ZIP-CODE values and the accuracy of Closest Address algorithms.

Locating the Closest Widget Outlet Example

An implementation of the Closest Address algorithm is covered in this section. The zips.txt file from http://ftp.census.gov/geo/www/gazetteer/places.html is used, along with store_addresses_ll.db, an expanded version of store_addresses.db from the "Address Locator (Example)" section earlier in this chapter. The zips.txt file supports the mapping of ZIP Codes to latitude/longitude coordinates, and store_addresses_ll.db provides an annotated list of store outlets for the Unwired Widgets company. The annotations specify the latitude/longitude coordinates corresponding to each outlet's ZIP Code.

A complete WCA source code listing and server-side script are shown in Figures 9.11 and 9.12. Figures 9.13 and 9.14 show the first ten lines of zips.txt and all of store_addresses_ll.db, respectively. Finally, Figures 9.15 and 9.16 show before and after screen shots of the WCA. The after screen shot was generated by entering a ZIP Code of 35806, for which no Unwired Widgets outlet/store exists (the Closest Address algorithm was invoked).

NOTE

The performance of the Closest Address algorithm can be optimized by using a threshold for acceptable distance-to-an-outlet. The threshold can allow a search to be terminated as soon as an outlet is found that is within the threshold distance of the current/specified position.

Figure 9.11 Closest Widget Outlet Example

```
<html>
<head>
<title>Outlet Locator</title>
<meta name="PalmComputingPlatform" content="true">
</head>
<body>
<center>
<font size="4"><b>Outlet Locator Example</b></font>
<form method="GET"
action="http://cgi.unwiredwidgets.com/cgi-bin/closest_outlet_locator.pl">

    ZIP Code: <input type="text" name="zip_input" value="">
    <br>
    <br>
    (Default Is Current Location)
    <br>
    <br>
    <input type="hidden" name="zip"         value="%zipcode">
    <input type="submit"                    value="Locate Outlet">

</form>
</center>
</body>
</html>
```

Figure 9.12 Closest Widget Outlet Example (closest_outlet_locator.pl)

```
#!/usr/bin/perl

use CGI;

$zip_ref  = "";
$lat_ref  = 0.0;
```

Continued

Figure 9.12 Continued

```
$long_ref = 0.0;

$store_name = "";
$store_addr = "";
$store_city = "";
$store_st   = "";
$store_zip  = "";

&find_closest_store;

sub find_closest_store {

    # parse incoming parameters as either "GET" or "POST"
    $q = new CGI;

    # isolate parameter names
    @name_list = $q->param;

    # extract values
    $zip_input_value = "";
    foreach $name (@name_list) {

        # decode encoding
        $value = $q->param($name);

        # save pertinent data
        if ($name eq "zip_input") {$zip_input_value = $value;}
        if ($name eq "zip")       {$zip_value       = $value;}
    }

    # use the user-supplied ZIP Code, if any;
    # otherwise, use the non-00000 default/current ZIP Code
```

Continued

Figure 9.12 Continued

```
    if    ($zip_input_value ne ""     ) { $zip_ref = $zip_input_value;
}
    elsif ($zip_value       ne "00000") { $zip_ref = $zip_value;
}
    else  { die "ZIP Code value is unavailable (e.g. 00000)."; }

    # open store address database
    open (store_addresses_11, "store_addresses_11.db") or
        die "Couldn't open store_addresses_11.db!";

    # process store address database one record at a time
    while (<store_addresses_11>) {

        # read database record
        readline;

        # process database record
        ($field_0, $field_1, $field_2, $field_3, $field_4,
            $field_5, $field_6) = split /,/;
        $zip_read = substr($field_4, 0, 5); # remove trailing space
        if ($zip_read eq $zip_ref) {

            # keep the matching store address
            $store_name = $field_0;
            $store_addr = $field_1;
            $store_city = $field_2;
            $store_st   = $field_3;
            $store_zip  = $field_4;
        }
    }

    # close store address database
    close (store_addresses_11) or
```

Continued

Figure 9.12 Continued

```
        die "Couldn't close store_addresses_ll.db!";

    # return results header
    print "Content-type: text/html\n\n";
    print "<html>\n";
    print "<head>\n";
    print "<title>Outlet Locator</title>\n";
    print "</head>\n";
    print "<body>\n";
    print "<center>\n";
    print "<font size='4'><b>Outlet Locator Results</b></font>\n";

    # return matching store address
    if ($store_name ne "") {

        # direct ZIP Code match found
        print "<br><br>\n";
        print "Store Address Match\n";
        print "<br><br>\n";
        print $store_name;
        print "\n";
        print "<br>\n";
        print $store_addr;
        print "\n";
        print "<br>\n";
        print $store_city;
        print ", ";
        print $store_st;
        print "  ";
        print $store_zip;
        print "\n";
    }
    else {
```

Continued

Figure 9.12 Continued

```
# no direct ZIP Code match found;
# get reference lat/long for "closest" search
find_lat_long();

# search for the store closest to the reference lat/long
find_closest_lat_long();

# report the closest store to the reference lat/long
if ($store_name ne "") {

    # store within 500 statute miles found
    print "<br><br>\n";
    print "Closest Outlet Found\n";
    print "<br><br>\n";
    print $store_name;
    print "\n";
    print "<br>\n";
    print $store_addr;
    print "\n";
    print "<br>\n";
    print $store_city;
    print ", ";
    print $store_st;
    print "  ";
    print $store_zip;
    print "\n";
}
else {

    # no store within 500 statute miles found
    print "<br><br>\n";
    print "No Store Address Match\n";
```

Continued

Figure 9.12 Continued

```
            print "<br><br>\n";
            print "Within 500 Statute Miles\n";
        }
    }

    # return results footer
    print "</center>\n";
    print "</body>\n";
    print "</html>\n";
}

sub find_lat_long() {

    # open ZIP Code database
    open (zipcodes, "zips.txt") or die "Couldn't open zips.txt!";

    # process ZIP Code database one record at a time
    while (<zipcodes>) {

        # read database record
        readline;

        # process database record (use substr() to remove
        # surrounding delimiters such as quotes)
        ($field_0, $field_1, $field_2, $field_3, $field_4, $field_5,
            $field_6, $field_7) = split /,/;
        if (substr($field_1, 1, 5) eq $zip_ref) {

            # keep the latitude/longitude corresponding to the
            # matching ZIP Code
            $long_ref = $field_4; # dec. degrees, default W, no -
            $lat_ref  = $field_5; # dec. degrees, default is N, no +
        }
```

Continued

Figure 9.12 Continued

```
    }

    # close ZIP Code database
    close (zipcodes) or die "Couldn't close zips.txt!";
}

sub find_closest_lat_long() {

    # open store address database
    open (store_addresses_ll, "store_addresses_ll.db") or
        die "Couldn't open store_addresses_ll.db!";

    # process store address database one record at a time
    # (look for the lat/long closest to the reference lat/long
    $earth_radius = 3900.0;    # est. of earth's radius in statute miles
    $pi           = 3.1415927; # approximate value of PI
    $distance_min = "";
    while (<store_addresses_ll>) {

        # read database record
        readline;

        # process database record
        ($field_0, $field_1, $field_2, $field_3, $field_4,
            $field_5, $field_6) = split /,/;
        $lat  = substr($field_6, 0,
            length($field_6) - 2); # remove trailing spaces
        $long = $field_5;

        # calculate the distance between the current lat/long and
        # the reference lat/long
        # (pass arguments to trigonometric functions in radians)
        $distance_y         = 2.0 * $earth_radius *
```

Continued

Figure 9.12 Continued

```
    sin((($lat  - $lat_ref ) * $pi/180.0) / 2.0);
$distance_x         = 2.0 * $earth_radius *
    sin((($long - $long_ref) * $pi/180.0) / 2.0);
$distance_straight = sqrt($distance_x * $distance_x
    + $distance_y * $distance_y);
#
# only direct distances of less than 500 miles are processed
# (the distance along the earth's surface is actually a bit
# longer); this threshold is arbitrary, but seems reasonable
# from a user's perspective (e.g. only show stores within a
# day's drive)
#
# this threshold also serves to simplify the curved-distance
# calculation, as the "asin" trigonometric function is no longer
# needed; this is due to the fact that for small angles
# (e.g. small lat/long measurements between the two points), the
# sin of the angle equals the angle when measured in radians
#
# the original equation:
#     $distance_curved = 2.0 * 2.0 * pi * earth_radius
#         * asin($distance_straight / (2.0 * earth_radius))
#         / (2.0 * $pi);
#
# the new equation:
#     $distance_curved = 2.0 * 2.0 * pi * earth_radius
#         * $distance_straight / (2.0 * earth_radius)
#         / (2.0 * $pi);
#
# the new equation (simplified):
#     $distance_curved = $distance_straight;
#
if ($distance_straight lt 500.0) {
```

Continued

Figure 9.12 Continued

```
            $distance_curved = $distance_straight;

            # keep information if a smaller distance (e.g. closer
            # store) is found
            if ($distance_min eq "") {

                # keep minimum distance
                $distance_min = $distance_curved;

                # keep the matching store address
                $store_name = $field_0;
                $store_addr = $field_1;
                $store_city = $field_2;
                $store_st   = $field_3;
                $store_zip  = $field_4;
            }
            elsif ($distance_curved lt $distance_min) {

                # keep minimum distance
                $distance_min = $distance_curved;

                # keep the matching store address
                $store_name = $field_0;
                $store_addr = $field_1;
                $store_city = $field_2;
                $store_st   = $field_3;
                $store_zip  = $field_4;
            }
        }
    }

    # close store address database
```

Continued

Figure 9.12 Continued

```
    close (store_addresses_ll) or
        die "Couldn't close store_addresses_ll.db!";
}
```

Figure 9.13 ZIP Code Database: The First 10 Lines

```
zips.txt
"01","35004","AL","ACMAR",86.51557,33.584132,6055,0.001499
"01","35005","AL","ADAMSVILLE",86.959727,33.588437,10616,0.002627
"01","35006","AL","ADGER",87.167455,33.434277,3205,0.000793
"01","35007","AL","KEYSTONE",86.812861,33.236868,14218,0.003519
"01","35010","AL","NEW SITE",85.951086,32.941445,19942,0.004935
"01","35014","AL","ALPINE",86.208934,33.331165,3062,0.000758
"01","35016","AL","ARAB",86.489638,34.328339,13650,0.003378
"01","35019","AL","BAILEYTON",86.621299,34.268298,1781,0.000441
"01","35020","AL","BESSEMER",86.947547,33.409002,40549,0.010035
"01","35023","AL","HUEYTOWN",86.999607,33.414625,39677,0.00982
```

Figure 9.14 Store Address Latitude/Longitude Database (store_addresses_ll.db)

```
store_addresses_ll.db
The Widget Outlet,123 Your Street,Toney,AL,35773,86.699951,34.911644
Widget Emporium,456 Your Street,Springville,AL,35146,86.439407,33.738647
Widgets-R-Us,789 Your Street,Center Point,AL,35235,86.661051,33.618045
Unwired Widget Outlet #1,ABC-1 Your Street,Decatur,AL,35601,86.98868,
    34.589599
Get Unwired,DEF-2 Your Street,Hazel Green,AL,35750,86.593484,34.949627
Unwired Widget Outlet #2,GHI-3 Your Street,Laceys Spring,AL,35754,
    86.612869,34.499647
ABC Widgets,JKL-4 Your Street,Meridianville,AL,35759,86.578879,34.861779
John's Widgets,MNO-5 Your Street,Valhermoso Springs,AL,35775,86.678,
    34.538145
Widgets 123,PQR-6 Your Street,Huntsville,AL,35801,86.567318,
    34.726866
```

Figure 9.15 The Before Screen Shot

Figure 9.16 The After Screen Shot

Using Enhanced %LOCATION Information in Palm OS 4.0

Because position-aware WCAs often need to convert %ZIPCODE to other position qualifiers (State and County, for example), a new Palm-specific variable has been created within Palm OS 4.0. Named %LOCATION, it provides a robust mechanism for obtaining additional qualifiers for the current base station. %LOCATION data is not more accurate than its %ZIPCODE counterpart, but it is certainly more descriptive. The regular-expression syntax of %LOCATION is shown in Figure 9.17.

NOTE

The Palm OS 4.0 version of Clipper is required to use the %LOCATION variable. %LOCATION is interpreted upon form submission or upon a link being followed that specifies the variable.

Figure 9.17 %LOCATION Regular-Expression Syntax

```
%location:<code>(<separator>?<code>)*.
```

The syntax for %LOCATION is the keyword **%location:** followed by a list of one or more *<code>s*. The *<code>s* are delineated by an optional *<separator>* character, and the entire %LOCATION string is terminated by a period (.). The *<separator>* is a single character such as the semicolon (;), colon (:), or pound sign (#). It is used to make the %LOCATION specification easier to read. The *<code>s* are single character values chosen from Table 9.1. Note that %LOCATION can be used in lieu of %ZIPCODE via **%location:z.**.

Table 9.1 Code Values

<code>	Name
c	City Name
G	GPS Longitude/Latitude
l	State Name
L	State Code
o	County Name
O	County Code
R	Raw Location Hexadecimal Data
y	Country Name
Y	Country Code
z	ZIP Code

Note that lower case letters denote names (except in the case of **z**), whereas their uppercase counterparts describe the corresponding unique identifier. Further, the U.S.-specific entities of County and State are used as placeholders for, respectively, the small and large political divisions of countries other than the

U.S. The Country entities are based on *Codes for the Representation of Names of Countries, ISO 3166-1993 (E)*. This document is available from the appropriate national standards body (in the U.S., it's the American National Standards Institute; in the United Kingdom, it's the British Standards Institute). Samples of syntactically correct uses of %LOCATION are as follows. (Be sure not to forget the trailing period (.) in the %LOCATION string.)

```
%location:z;c.
%location:z#c.
%location:c#Y.
```

%LOCATION can be used in a form field or appended to the end of a URL:

```
<input type="hidden" name="loc" value="%location:z;c.">
-OR-
<form method="get"
    action="http://cgi.company.com/cgi-bin/script?var=%location:z;c.">
```

NOTE

Unlike %ZIPCODE, %LOCATION can be used in <INPUT> fields regardless of whether they are *hidden*. For example, a City field within a form could have **value='%location:c.'** to initialize it to the current city. The user could then overwrite this field if they were interested in another city.

Developing & Deploying…

Using Simulated Position Information to Test a %ZIPCODE WCA

Certain models of GPS (for example, Garmin's GPS III) provide a "simulation" mode in which the GPS receiver produces NMEA-compatible latitude/longitude sentences. You can use this simulated data to test and demonstrate your position-specific application's capabilities, even when indoors!

Summary

As shown throughout this chapter, the Palm OS-specific variables %ZIPCODE and %LOCATION provide a mechanism for making your applications position-aware. Because a Palm VII device typically communicates with the nearest BellSouth Mobitex base station, the base station ZIP Code is a reasonable estimate of the Palm VII device's encompassing ZIP Code. By using %ZIPCODE, the general area in which a Palm VII device is located can be determined, keeping in mind that gaps or overlaps between base stations, physical obstacles, ZIP Codes that cross state boundaries, and other considerations limit the location as a coarse estimate. The ZIP Code can be used directly or as an index to additional data such as city or state. This additional data can also be obtained directly via %LOCATION, although Palm OS 4.0 is required. If you choose against levying a Palm OS 4.0 requirement on your users, %ZIPCODE can be used to emulate most %LOCATION capabilities.

In either case, position data is available to perform tasks such as locating a store with a specified ZIP Code or determining which store is closest to a given position. The latter task involves mapping %ZIPCODE information to latitude/longitude measurements. Latitude/longitude measurements provide a robust, global description of position information. Data on city and county locations can be obtained through government Census sources or more up-to-date commercial sources. Because the latitude/longitude of a ZIP Code may not exactly match the latitude/longitude of a corresponding county, the Closest Address algorithm needs to be used to employ the data in a closest-address search. The algorithm defines how latitude/longitude data will be processed in order to provide the closest address to the current, or specified, position. Uses for position-based applications include those reliant upon a user's general location, such as weather and news, and their specific location, such as address lookups for a store.

Solutions Fast Track

Finding a User's Position with the Palm VII

☑ %ZIPCODE provides an approximate measure of a Palm VII's location.

- ☑ %ZIPCODE is the ZIP Code of the current base station with which a Palm VII is communicating. Its value will be 00000 if the base station's ZIP Code has not been recorded.
- ☑ ZIP Codes are not always defined by fully enclosed geometric shapes, and they can cross state, county, and city boundaries.

Address Locator Example

- ☑ A direct comparison of a %ZIPCODE value to a database can be made (with limited success) to locate a close entity.
- ☑ No match is guaranteed when performing a direct comparison of a %ZIPCODE value to a database.
- ☑ Base stations are typically 5 to 10 miles away from the user.

Mapping ZIP Codes to Coordinates

- ☑ Several databases exist for mapping ZIP Codes to latitude/longitude coordinates. A free data source is the U.S. Census Bureau: http://ftp.census.gov/geo/www/gazetteer/places.html. Note the file *zips.txt*.
- ☑ Also from the U.S. Census Bureau—counties.txt, places.txt, and mcds.txt can be used to model operation of the Palm OS 4.0 variable %LOCATION.

Determining the Closest Address

- ☑ Pythagorean-based minimum distance searching is more robust than direct ZIP Code matching for "closest address" determination.
- ☑ More than one ZIP Code match exists if the application-specific address database/file contains more than one entry for a given ZIP Code.
- ☑ A possible %ZIPCODE value of 00000 must be handled by a Closest Address algorithm.

Locating the Closest Widget Outlet Example

- ☑ Latitude/longitude processing can take the earth's curvature, but not surface elevation, into account.
- ☑ Latitude/longitude processing is not necessary if a direct ZIP Code match is found.
- ☑ ZIP Codes of 00000 should be anticipated.

Using Enhanced %LOCATION Information in Palm OS 4.0

- ☑ Palm OS 4.0 is required for the %LOCATION variable to be interpreted.
- ☑ %LOCATION can be used to obtain a variety of position qualifiers, including: City Name, GPS Longitude/Latitude, State Name, State Code, County Name, County Code, Raw Location, Hexadecimal Data, Country Name, Country Code, and ZIP Code.
- ☑ The U.S.-specific entities of county and state are used as placeholders for, respectively, the small and large political division of countries other than the U.S.
- ☑ Country entities are based on *Codes for the Representation of Names of Countries, ISO 3166-1993 (E)*. This document is available from the appropriate national standards body. In the U.S., it's the American National Standards Institute; in the United Kingdom, it's the British Standards Institute.

Frequently Asked Questions

The following Frequently Asked Questions, answered by the authors of this book, are designed to both measure your understanding of the concepts presented in this chapter and to assist you with real-life implementation of these concepts. To have your questions about this chapter answered by the author, browse to **www.syngress.com/solutions** and click on the **"Ask the Author"** form.

Q: Why would %LOCATION ever be used if %ZIPCODE can emulate it, especially given that %LOCATION requires the use of Palm OS 4.0?

A: The %LOCATION variable is easier to use than %ZIPCODE, and %LOCATION can be used to initialize text fields. Also, over time, Palm OS 4.0 will become more commonplace.

Q: Will %ZIPCODE be deprecated, now that %LOCATION is available?

A: Given that Palm OS 4.0 is required for %LOCATION, and given the volume of Palm OS 3.*x* devices in the field, %ZIPCODE will most likely enjoy a long life.

Q: Where is a good starting point for additional information?

A: Palm, Inc.'s Web Clipping Development pages, at www.palmos.com/dev/tech/webclipping.

Chapter 10

Integrating Web Clipping with Palm OS Applications

Solutions in this chapter:

- Launching and Sublaunching Applications
- Calling Clipper from Palm OS Applications
- Calling iMessenger from Palm OS Applications
- Unwired Widgets Application About Box Example
- Calling Palm OS Applications from Web Clipping Applications
- Unwired Widgets Sales Chart Example
- Applying iKnapsack to Add PIM Data
- Adding PIM Data for Unwired Widgets Example

☑ Summary

☑ Solutions Fast Track

☑ Frequently Asked Questions

Introduction

One of the revolutions in computing in the last decade is the rise of component-based programming. Many programmers find themselves using off-the-shelf components to perform major tasks within their programs. Rather than having everyone write their own mail clients, Web browsers, help systems, or word processors, modern software systems use existing applications through interfaces that allow them to be linked together.

On Windows systems, dynamic link libraries (DLLs) are used to allow programs to share libraries. These libraries provide functions that are common to multiple programs. A good example is the user32.dll, one of the Windows system DLLs. This library provides access to functions that affect the user interface on Windows, such as routines to show dialog boxes, to change menus, or to control the mouse pointer. Rather than having each programmer build his own method of performing these tasks, the designers of Windows created common code and put it into this DLL—now all Windows programs use this. Mac OS and Unix systems also use this concept of a shared library but with different implementations.

Shared libraries are useful tools, but they have some problems. One problem is that to use a shared library, you have to understand exactly how to load it into memory, find the function to call, set up the parameters correctly, and handle the return value. To solve these issues, desktop systems tend to use rather complicated methods. On Windows, the Component Object Model (COM) exists as a huge specification for using the services of libraries and other applications. The Common Object Request Broker Architecture (CORBA) fills a similar need for non-Microsoft systems. These technologies let applications do things as simple as calling a function or as complex as putting an instance of a Web browser into an application's main window.

On Palm OS, we have a much simpler mechanism: *application launching*. Both Clipper and iMessenger, the two Web applications shipped with the original Palm VII, have interfaces that allow them to be launched from other programs. For Clipper, this is a context switch, one that requires the termination of your current program and the starting of Clipper with arguments that point it to its destination. For iMessenger, the launch acts like a subroutine call for putting mail into the iMessenger outbox to be sent when the user checks her e-mail.

Clipper has another back door to extend its functionality: It allows Web page authors to provide links that invoke other applications on the device. Its method uses two special URL schemes that allow Clipper to use other programs as elaborate subroutines.

This chapter guides you through several useful tasks. First, it introduces the task of calling Clipper from your Palm OS applications for looking at local Web clipping files or for browsing a remote Web site. It then illustrates sending mail by using calls to iMessenger, which can be very useful for situations where you want user feedback. It then reverses the situation by introducing *palm* and *palmcall* URLs that are used by Clipper and other Palm Web browsers to launch plug-in programs. Finally, the chapter closes by looking at iKnapsack, a popular open-source plug-in for Clipper that allows Web pages to add information to the Palm OS applications, such as the date book and address book.

Launching and Sublaunching Applications

One concept used throughout the chapter is the idea of launching one application from another. Two Application Programming Interface (API) calls are used to launch other programs on the Palm OS device:

- **SysUIAppSwitch**
- **SysAppLaunch**

Using SysUIAppSwitch to Launch a New Program

The first call, **SysUIAppSwitch**, is used when you want to end your current program and start another. In the Palm operating system, a variable holds information about the program to run when the current program exits. The prototype (from the Palm OS 3.5 Software Development Kit [SDK]) for this API call is (the line is broken only due to page width constraints):

```
Err SysUIAppSwitch(UInt16 cardNo, LocalID dbID, UInt16 cmd,
    MemPtr cmdPBP)
```

The first two parameters, *cardNo* and *dbID*, identify which application database is to be launched. The *cmd* parameter specifies the launch code to be passed to the new program, and *cmdPBP* is a pointer to a block of memory—called the parameter block—that has information needed by the new program. This block of memory should be allocated using **MemPtrNew**, and it should have its ownership assigned to the system with **MemPtrSetOwner**. This block of memory will be freed by the system when the new application ends.

When an application starts, the system stores a pointer to the last application that ran into this variable. When an application ends, this information is used to start the next application. **SysUIAppSwitch** modifies this variable to point to another program and then posts an *appStopEvent* method to the event queue to cause the current program to end. The *appStopEvent* is received by your application's main event loop.

If you called **SysUIAppSwitch** twice in a row, you would get an unexpected result—your application would end, but you would switch to the second program mentioned. This is because Palm OS keeps track of only one application in its internal variable. The second call to **SysUIAppSwitch** overwrites that variable with the new information, and it also frees any memory for the parameter block from the first call.

Internally, Palm OS uses this call to handle switching applications when you hit one of the hard buttons. It looks in the system preferences to find out which application is mapped to that button, and if it isn't the running program, it calls **SysUIAppSwitch** to switch to the mapped program.

Using SysAppLaunch to Call into Another Program

The second call, **SysAppLaunch**, leaves your current program suspended while another program is opened temporarily to handle a request. This is called a *sub-launch* by the Palm OS documentation, because the caller uses the program as a subroutine. Its prototype is as follows:

```
Err SysAppLaunch(UInt16 cardNo, LocalID dbID, UInt16 launchFlags,
    UInt16 cmd, MemPtr cmdPBP, UInt32 *resultP)
```

The *cardNo*, *dbID*, *cmd*, and *cmdPBP* parameters are the same as in **SysUIAppSwitch**, with the exception that the parameter block should remain owned by the caller and should be freed by the caller after the **SysAppLaunch** function returns. The *launchFlags* parameter should be 0; when this call is used by the system in special circumstances, this parameter is used, but normally the system sets flags correctly for the launched program. The last parameter, *resultP*, holds a pointer to a variable for the return value of the sublaunched program. Whatever value is returned from the sublaunched program's **PilotMain** function will be placed into this variable.

The new program is launched without some of the privileges of a normally launched program. First, the program does not have access to global variables. The program usually accesses global variables as an offset from the MC68000 register A5. For speed purposes, Palm OS doesn't allocate a global section for sub-launched programs, and it sets A5 to point to invalid memory to let you detect global usage. This affects some nonobvious uses of global variables—for example, the virtual table of a C++ class is stored in the global variable pool, so you can't use virtual class methods when your program is sublaunched. The second limitation is the amount of program stack you have available. Rather than creating a new stack, the sublaunched program inherits the stack of the caller. This means that you have even less room than normal for local variables; you also cannot make deep calls to other functions, as each call allocates more of the stack for local variables and return addresses.

Launching Nonapplication Databases

With Palm OS 3.2, Palm introduced a scheme where databases other than applications could also be launched. This was added to support Clipper and Palm Query Applications (PQAs), where the Clipper program remains hidden, but all of the associated Web clipping databases are viewable in the launcher. In this scheme, launchable databases are tagged with a special attribute that tells the launcher that it should include these in the list of applications. When the database is selected, rather than use that database's information, the program finds the associated application, which has type *'appl'* and the same creator code as the database.

It then uses **SysUIAppSwitch** to switch to that program, giving it the launch code *sysAppLaunchCmdOpenDB* and passing to it a parameter block that contains the card number and ID of the launchable database.

Developing & Deploying...

Typical Palm OS Application Structure

Most Palm OS applications follow a standard application flow, based on the original samples used at Palm, Inc. to develop the core applications. The program has a main function that is called by the system when the application starts. This main function calls several other user-supplied functions to perform specific tasks:

- **RomVersionCompatible** Verify that the Palm OS version is recent enough to support the application.

Continued

- **AppStart** Perform startup tasks for the application.
- **AppEventLoop** Run the main event loop until an *appStopEvent* is seen.
- **AppStop** Clean up after the application.

The main function usually performs only **AppStart**, **AppEventLoop**, and **AppStop** after verifying that the application was started with a valid launch code. The usual code used to run an application is *sysAppLaunchCmdNormalLaunch*, which indicates that it is a normal launch. In this chapter, our applications will often respond to other launch codes that direct the launched application to perform specific actions on behalf of the calling application.

Calling Clipper from Palm OS Applications

Launching a Web clipping application from inside your Palm OS application can be amazingly useful. At its simplest, it makes it easy to support enhanced About boxes where users can quickly find out about other programs you've written. It can launch a technical support form for beta testers to submit bugs. You can even use a local PQA file to provide hypertext help systems for your application.

The code in this section is provided in the UWAbout box example included on the CD that accompanies this book; we look at portions of it to illuminate the discussion and explain why we coded it this way. Figure 10.1 is taken from that example code, and the concepts behind it are explained in the next paragraph.

The function defined in Figure 10.1 is called **GoToURL**. It is designed to launch Clipper, pointing it to the URL passed as its sole parameter. Because this code uses the **SysUIAppSwitch** call, it returns immediately, with the application then going through its normal shutdown sequence before Clipper starts to handle the request. After the code listing, we examine the code in detail by looking at why we did each action and what side effects the calls have on the system.

Figure 10.1 GoToURL (UWAbout Example)

```
static Err GoToURL(const char *origURL)
{
    DmSearchStateType searchState;
    UInt16 cardNo;
```

Continued

Figure 10.1 Continued

```
    LocalID dbID;
    Err err;
    Char *url;

    // check for the Clipper application by searching for its
    // program database
    err = DmGetNextDatabaseByTypeCreator(
        true, &searchState, sysFileTApplication, sysFileCClipper,
        true, &cardNo, &dbID);

    // allocate space for the new string and reassign its owner
    url = (Char *) MemPtrNew(StrLen(origURL) + 1);
    if (!url)
    {
        return sysErrNoFreeRAM;
    }
    StrCopy(url, origURL);
    MemPtrSetOwner(url, 0);

    // tell the system that we want to switch to Clipper
    err = SysUIAppSwitch(cardNo, dbID, sysAppLaunchCmdGoToURL, url);
    if (err != errNone)
    {
        MemPtrFree(url);
    }

    return err;
}
```

Determining if Clipper Can Be Called

Before launching Clipper to handle a URL, you should check for its existence. This guards against errors and also lets your code work on devices without

Clipper. In many cases, calling Clipper from your program is an extra feature that can be disabled if the Web clipping interface is not available.

The code in Figure 10.1 starts by declaring the local variables for the function, and then it calls the **DmGetNextDatabaseByTypeCreator** system API to look for an application with the creator code of Clipper.

Because Palm OS applications are just special databases, you can check for the presence of Clipper by checking for the existence of its database. Palm OS applications all have the database type *'appl'*, along with a creator code that matches the creator code of the application. The Palm OS SDK header file <SystemResources.h> provides macros for the creator codes of the built-in applications, and from that we find the macro *sysFileCClipper* is defined as *'clpr'*, the creator code of the Clipper application.

The first parameter is true, to indicate that this is a new search. The second parameter is a pointer to a *DmSearchStateType* structure that will be modified by the search so that we could continue the search later. Because we're looking only for the first result, this variable will be ignored after the call. The next two parameters are the database type and creator. The type is *'appl'*, but we are using a system constant, *sysFileTApplication*, rather than directly specifying the constant value, because using the constant provides better documentation. The fifth parameter is true, to tell the call that we're interested only in the latest version of Clipper. Usually, you can only have one version of a database on a device at a time; however, if your database is in the system ROM, and a copy exists in RAM, this flag protects you from getting the older version. The last two parameters are for output only. On a successful search, these will tell you the card number and database ID needed to get to the program. We have to save these output values so that we can later use them in our call to **SysUIAppSwitch**.

Success or failure is indicated by the return value, which we store in *err*. If this is *errNone*, which has the value 0, then we had a successful match. A failure to find Clipper will return *dmErrCantFind*. These error codes are defined in ErrorBase.h and DataMgr.h, respectively.

Preparing the URL Buffer

When launched from another program, Clipper understands the same kind of URLs that it understands when parsing a PQA file. The supported schemes include *http*, *https*, *file*, *mailto*, *palm*, and *palmcall*, although the last three—although useful within a Web clipping application—are not very useful when directly invoking Clipper from another application. Calling into another application using

Clipper as an intermediary doesn't make a lot of sense, and using a *mailto* URL to launch iMessenger gives you less control than launching iMessenger directly, a task covered later in this chapter.

After you have a URL, you need to place it into a buffer that will be accessible to both your program and Clipper. The way to do this is to allocate a block of memory, change its ownership to the system, then use it as the parameter block for Clipper. In the **GoToURL** function, we are getting the URL passed to us as the *origURL* parameter to the function.

When Palm OS programs are launched, they have a parameter block structure assigned to them that may contain important information about why the program was launched. In the normal case of a launch from the Applications Launcher, this parameter block is empty. For cases like our launching of Clipper to go to a specific location, the parameter block is used to give the launched program its starting instructions.

This code assumes that your URL is already inside a character string indicated by *origURL*. The code determines the length of the string using **StrLen**, adds a byte to hold the null terminator at the end of the C string, then allocates a new memory buffer using **MemPtrNew**. If the allocation fails, we return *sysErrNoFreeRAM*, a system error code indicating that no memory is available. If it succeeds, we copy the old string to the new buffer, and then we change the ownership of the buffer from our application to the system using the **MemPtrSetOwner** call. As we noted in our initial discussion of **SysUIAppSwitch**, memory that is passed to a program launched using this API has to be reassigned to the system; if it were not, the memory block would be freed when the current program ended, and the new program would then be accessing invalid memory.

Launching Clipper to Handle Our URL

The call to **SysUIAppSwitch** uses the card number and database ID we found through the earlier call to **DmGetNextDatabaseByTypeCreator**. The launch code is *sysAppLaunchCmdGoToURL*, a special code reserved in Palm OS to send a URL to a program for processing. The final parameter is the buffer in which we've copied the URL for Clipper to process. We check for errors, but the Palm documentation doesn't define any error conditions.

This code has the potential for a memory leak if things aren't handled correctly. If we allocated this memory first, then checked for Clipper, we could return from our function without freeing this buffer. The buffer is only freed by the system if a **SysUIAppSwitch** call is successful. If it fails for some reason, then we should clean up the buffer ourselves using a call to **MemPtrFree**.

One thing that may confuse you if you're debugging your code is that your function to launch Clipper doesn't end your program. Unlike MS-DOS, where you launch another program and immediately lose control, the Palm OS tries to shut things down in a more orderly fashion.

The call to **SysUIAppLaunch** doesn't actually launch the new application. Instead, it sets up flags inside the Palm OS that tell the system that a new program should start. It also posts an *appStopEvent* to the system event queue. Sometime after you requested the launch, your program will re-enter the event loop, usually in your program's **AppEventLoop** function. After processing any events that were already in the queue, you will get the *appStopEvent*, which will signal that you should shut everything down and close any active forms. If this call happened while a dialog box was active, the *appStopEvent* will signal the dialog box handler to close the form and then repost the event for your application to receive.

Usually you won't need to do anything special here. The closing of your program and starting of Clipper isn't any different from a switch between your program and any of the standard applications. However, if you're using Clipper for a special purpose where you'll need to restore the user interface upon returning from your Web site, you'll need to take special measures to save off your program state so that when you get relaunched, you can re-create the same user situation.

After your program exits, the system starts Clipper, and it attempts to fetch your URL. If an error occurs, the user will be notified with a dialog box, but she will be left in a state with a blank page. In the normal case where Clipper is able to open the page, the user will now be looking at the URL data and can return to your application by hitting the back arrow.

Returning from Clipper

Palm OS is a single-tasking operating system, at least at the user level. Only one program has control of the system at a time, which means that if we're launching Clipper to handle Web browsing from our program, our code is going to lose control of the system until Clipper finishes.

When a user is using Clipper to view a Web clipping application, you have several ways to exit to another program. The most common method is to directly jump to another program by hitting one of the four application keys at the bottom of the Palm OS device. You also can do this by tapping the Home icon, which switches to the Applications Launcher. One not-so-obvious method to exit Clipper is through the **Back** button; the return arrow at the top of the Clipper user interface can cause Clipper to stop running if you happen to be at the beginning of the Clipper history. Normally, if you've run a Web clipping application from the Applications Launcher, hitting Back will return you to the launcher. However, if another program has launched Clipper, hitting the **Back** button will relaunch the original program.

For some programs, this behavior may work just fine. If you've launched Clipper to handle a button in an About box, then relaunching your application should return the user to the normal user interface. However, if you're using Clipper for a task such as providing online help, then you may need to store more information about the state of the program, and when you're relaunched, load that information out of storage and use it to restore your program to the same location.

One problem you will encounter here is that there is no good way to tell if your application is getting launched after returning from Clipper or being launched from the Applications Launcher. In both cases, you get a *sysAppLaunchCmdNormalLaunch* sent to your **PilotMain** function. It's perfectly possible for a user to run your application, use it to launch Clipper, switch out of Clipper to another application such as the Memo Pad, go back to the Applications Launcher, then rerun your program. You are not able to tell that situation from one where the user used your program to launch Clipper and then hit the **Back** button to exit Clipper.

Your best bet to handle this situation is to just use good Palm OS programming guidelines and make your program save its state properly whenever it exits. If your applications can be designed around a single form, then you can simply save extra information in the system's unsaved preferences that can be used to restore the user's place upon relaunch. For a more complex program that uses multiple forms, you will need to decide if returning to the main form is an acceptable outcome, or if it makes sense to preserve the state, even if it means that relaunching your application puts the user in an unexpected state.

Developing & Deploying…

Why Don't You See Clipper in the Launcher?

Even though Clipper is a Palm OS application, why don't you see it listed as one of the many applications in the Applications Launcher? All Palm OS databases have a set of flags that give information to the system about the nature of the database. One of these flags is *dmHdrAttrHidden*, which is defined by the <DataMgr.h> header. This flag cannot be set using the standard Palm OS build tools, but it is possible to alter it directly using a hex editor or through the Data Manager calls on the Palm OS device. This flag can be specified in CodeWarrior for Palm OS by checking the **Set Hidden Bit** checkbox in the PalmRez Post Linker preference panel (see Figure 10.2). The hidden flag is ignored on Palm OS versions before 3.2 (it was introduced so that the Clipper program would not show up in the Launcher).

Figure 10.2 Altering the dmHdrAtrHidden Flag

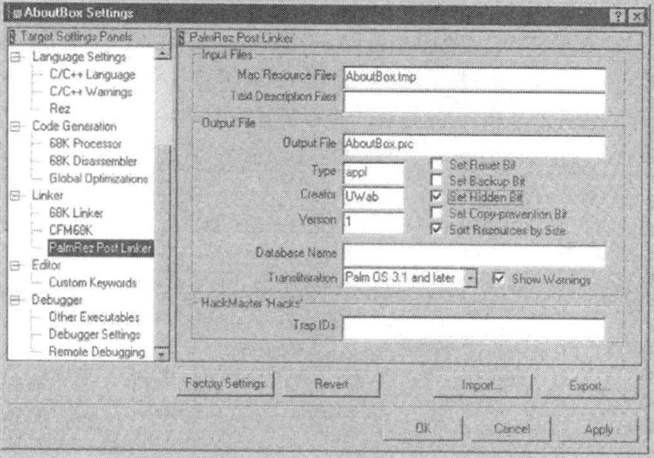

Calling iMessenger from Palm OS Applications

Calling iMessenger is more difficult than calling Clipper. The reason for this difficulty is that you need to consider more parameters when launching an e-mail editor than when calling a Web browser. For Clipper, you need to prepare only a buffer with your URL. To launch iMessenger, you need to decide which e-mail headers you want to specify, prepare a data structure with your fields, then launch iMessenger to handle editing the mail and placing it in the Outbox to be sent on to Palm.Net.

The code from Figure 10.3 is also part of our example program. A button on the form lets the user send an e-mail to Unwired Widgets' tech support. To perform this action, we will set up a template mail in the Outbox for iMessenger that the user will send at a later time.

Figure 10.3 SendTechSupportMail

```
static Err SendTechSupportMail()
{
    DmSearchStateType searchState;
    UInt16 cardNo;
    LocalID dbID;
    Err err;
    MsgAddRecordParamsType message;
    UInt32 result;
    MemHandle subject, from, to, replyTo, body;

    err = DmGetNextDatabaseByTypeCreator(
        true, &searchState, sysFileTApplication, sysFileCMessaging,
        true, &cardNo, &dbID);

    message.category = MsgOutboxCategory;
    message.edit = true;
    message.signature = false;
```

Continued

Figure 10.3 Continued

```
    subject = DuplicateToHandle("Technical Support Query");
    message.subject = MemHandleLock(subject);

    from = DuplicateToHandle("");
    message.from = MemHandleLock(from);

    to = DuplicateToHandle("techsupport@unwiredwidgets.com");
    message.to = MemHandleLock(to);

    replyTo = DuplicateToHandle("");
    message.replyTo = MemHandleLock(replyTo);

    body = DuplicateToHandle("Enter your questions for Tech Support");
    message.body = MemHandleLock(body);

    err = SysAppLaunch(
        cardNo, dbID, 0, sysAppLaunchCmdAddRecord, &message, &result);

    // Free the memory (unlock not needed)
    MemHandleFree(subject);
    MemHandleFree(from);
    MemHandleFree(to);
    MemHandleFree(replyTo);
    MemHandleFree(body);

    return err;
}
```

To explain this code, in the following sections we're going to go through each part—line by line—looking at what happens and why it was written that way. iMessenger is not a perfect program, and calling it by this method can be a bit awkward, which is why we cover it in detail.

Determining if iMessenger Can Be Called

Unlike Clipper, iMessenger is a Palm VII/VIIx-specific program. It is hard-coded to the user's Palm.Net e-mail account, and it uses a special Mobitex protocol to talk to Palm's mail servers. This makes it more responsive than other INetLib applications, but it also prevents it from being ported to non-Mobitex hardware. Because of this, you may find supporting iMessenger to be limiting to your application; however, if you're building a system specifically for the VII and VIIx, iMessenger is an effective method to get mobile e-mail support with a seamless interface.

The way to determine if iMessenger can be called is identical to checking for Clipper before doing a Web clipping request. You must check for the application database; iMessenger will only be loaded onto devices that support it. The creator code for iMessenger is *sysFileCMessaging*, which maps to *'msgs'*. The code at the beginning of Figure 10.3 uses this **DmGetNextDatabaseByTypeCreator** to find the iMessenger program.

Specifying a New E-Mail Message

When you launch iMessenger, you have a wide range of options for specifying the content of the mail message. iMessenger expects to receive the specification for the mail in a *MsgAddRecordParamsType* structure, as defined in the header file <AppLaunchCmd.h>. This structure is reproduced in the following code and has several fields of interest:

```
typedef struct {
    UInt16     category;
    Boolean    edit;
    Boolean    signature;
    Char *     subject;
    Char *     from;
    Char *     to;
    Char *     replyTo;
    Char *     body;
} MsgAddRecordParamsType;
```

The first field, *category*, is a UInt16 that specifies into which folder the new message should go. The valid choices are listed in Table 10.1.

Table 10.1 The *Category* Field

Macro	Value	Description
MsgInboxCategory	0	New messages from Palm.Net
MsgOutboxCategory	1	Messages to be sent on next transmission
MsgDeletedCategory	2	Messages that the user has deleted
MsgFiledCategory	3	Messages that have been read and moved out of the Inbox
MsgDraftCategory	4	Messages being edited, but not ready to be sent

Usually, you will want to use *MsgOutboxCategory* as the destination for new mail messages. Putting a message here will cause it to be sent either immediately or the next time the user checks for mail.

The second field is a Boolean value, *edit*. If this is true, the user gets a chance to edit the message before it is placed in the Outbox. If it is false, the message will be put into iMessenger's Outbox with no user intervention. iMessenger ignores this edit value if you specified one of the other folders.

The field *signature* lets you choose if the user's signature, as set in the iMessenger preferences, is appended to the message. This can be either true or false.

The next fields are all strings that affect the actual message. The *subject* field corresponds to the "Subject:" line of the e-mail. This can either be a string or the value NULL, which gets translated into an empty subject. The next field, *from*, is ignored by iMessenger. You can't use it to change the sender's address, because Palm.Net's gateway always sets it to username@palm.net. For safety, you should just pass an empty string.

The next three fields are required. The field *to* specifies the target e-mail address. You can have multiple targets by separating the addresses by commas. The field *replyTo* gives an address to which replies are sent. Although a string is required, you can pass an empty string to have replies go to the user's Palm.Net account. Finally, the *body* field holds the text of the message. If you're specifying a message for the user to edit, the initial text in the edit window will come from this string.

If you're concerned about memory allocations and ownership for the *MsgAddRecordParamsType* structure, you should rest easy. There are no ownership issues, unlike when we called Clipper. The difference is that iMessenger is sub-launched for the purpose of adding a message, whereas Clipper was invoked through a full application switch. For the memory to survive the ending of our program and the starting of Clipper, it had to be owned by the system. In the case of calling iMessenger, our program never quits, so all memory allocated by our code is still available.

One caveat in setting this structure is that iMessenger—at least in versions on Palm OS 3.2 and 3.5—seems to have a bug with how it treats these strings. In the case where you put a message in the Outbox and edit the message, you must put the strings into memory handles before passing them to iMessenger. In our example, we use a small helper function called **DuplicateToHandle** to do this. The problem is that iMessenger is directly populating the fields using the pointers passed, probably through a call to **FldSetTextPtr**. If you pass a string that isn't ultimately a pointer to a memory that was allocated in a handle, then when the code in the Palm OS user interface manager tries to treat the pointer like a locked *MemHandle*, things can go very wrong.

While we are passing the pointers in the structure as pointers to *Char*, we need to save the memory handles until iMessenger returns. The field handling code used in iMessenger doesn't free the handles, but it could unlock, resize, and relock them while the user is editing the values. If we keep the pointers, they may no longer be associated with the handles upon the return, but the original handle values will still be valid.

Sublaunching iMessenger to Edit and Send E-Mail

Sublaunching applications on the Palm is done through the **SysAppLaunch** API call. A sublaunched application is a bit restricted versus an application that has been launched by normal means. We already discussed some of these limitations at the beginning of the chapter, and we will talk more about them when we talk about running helper applications from Clipper. As a refresher, here is the prototype for **SysAppLaunch**:

```
Err SysAppLaunch(UInt16 cardNo, LocalID dbID, UInt16 launchFlags,
    UInt16 cmd, MemPtr cmdPBP, UInt32 *resultP)
```

The first two parameters to the call to **SysAppLaunch** in Figure 10.3 are *cardNo* and *dbID*; these identify the card number and database ID of the application to be sublaunched. We found these earlier when we did the database search to make sure that Clipper was installed on the system.

The next parameter is *launchFlags*, a UInt32. We use 0 for this value; the system will add any flags needed to tell iMessenger that it is being sublaunched, and global variables are not available.

The next two parameters are *cmd* and *cmdPBP*, which serve the same purpose as they do in **SysUIAppSwitch**; they indicate what command to execute, and they provide a parameter block. The command we use to add a new e-mail to iMessenger is the standard launch code *sysAppLaunchCmdAddRecord*. Both iMessenger and Palm's Mail application support this launch code to add a new record to their database; however, Mail uses a different format for the parameter block, because it requires different fields in its message database.

As explained earlier, an application launched by **SysAppLaunch** doesn't need a memory block owned by the system of its *cmdPBP* parameter. However, this also means that if you've dynamically allocated memory for the parameter block, then you need to free the memory upon return. Here, we provide the address of the local variable message, a *MsgAddRecordParamsType* structure that is on the program stack.

The final parameter, *resultP*, is the return value of the sublaunched application. This value is stored into the UInt32 variable whose address was passed to **SysAppLaunch**. For iMessenger, the result code is always 0, so we can ignore this value after our call.

Returning from iMessenger

Unlike Clipper, when we get control back from the **SysAppLaunch** call, iMessenger will have already run and completed. This means that the return code, which we stored in *err*, could actually have a valid error value. Usually, it will be *errNone* (0), but other possibilities include *sysErrParamErr*, which indicates a problem with your parameter block; *sysErrNotEnoughSpace*, which is returned when there isn't enough free memory to launch the program; and *sysErrOutOfOwnerIDs*, which shouldn't happen with iMessenger—it usually occurs only with deeply nested sublaunching. Because we've allocated handles to memory, we need to deallocate them now. This is done through a series of **MemHandleFree** calls. You do not need to explicitly unlock a handle that is being freed, so we don't need the **MemHandleUnlock** calls; calling that API may even be dangerous, because we don't know what state the handles have been left by the field code. Finally, we just return any error values back to the caller.

Unwired Widgets Application About Box Example

As an example, we've built a quick test program that displays a dialog box with two button choices. This program uses the test framework described in the sidebar "Building a Quick Test Framework," where a dialog box runs the entire program event loop logic. This dialog box is shown in Figure 10.4. This example is also included on the accompanying CD in the project UWAbout which was mentioned earlier in this chapter.

Figure 10.4 "About Unwired Widgets" Main Form

This dialog box has two active buttons. The first button is labeled Visit the Website, and it invokes our GoToURL code, pointing it to the Unwired Widgets Palm-friendly Web site at www.unwiredwidgets.com/about/. The second button, Send Mail to Support, invokes iMessenger using our **SendTechSupportMail** function. The code in that function puts a new message into the Outbox, giving the user a chance to edit the text. We've filled the message with text asking the user to replace it with his actual question for Unwired Widgets tech support. The code to handle the events of this About box is the function **AboutBoxHandleEvent**, shown in Figure 10.5.

Figure 10.5 AboutBoxHandleEvent

```
static Boolean AboutBoxEventHandler(EventType *event)
{
    if (event->eType == ctlSelectEvent)
```

Continued

Figure 10.5 Continued

```
    {
        switch (event->data.ctlSelect.controlID)
        {
        case MainVisitWebsiteButton:
            GoToURL("http://www.unwiredwidgets.com/about/");
            return true;

        case MainSendMailButton:
            SendTechSupportMail();
            return true;
        }
    }

    return false;
}
```

In the original version of this dialog box, I had an **OK** button that dismissed the dialog box using the normal mechanism. This ended up being a bad idea because of how Palm OS handles programs that exit on their own. If an application exits without another application being queued up, Palm OS launches the last application that was run. In my design, this seemed like an acceptable behavior, because this program would be run from the Launcher. The problem showed up with the **GoToURL** function, which causes an application switch to Clipper to handle bringing up the Web site. Exiting from Clipper caused the About Box program to relaunch, but now, if the user hit the **OK** button to exit, Clipper would be relaunched instead of the Palm OS launcher. Apparently, Palm OS remembers only the last application you ran; it doesn't save a stack of applications where you can keep returning to the previous one across multiple launches. By removing the **OK** button, the only way to exit from the dialog box is by using the Home button to go to the launcher or by hitting one of the hard buttons that launch the PIM applications. These all cause the dialog box to close but change the previous application pointer in the OS so that the next program launched is the one that maps to the button.

Developing & Deploying...

Building a Quick Test Framework

The example programs in this chapter don't follow the standard Palm OS program structure that most code seems to take. A standard Palm OS program goes through three phases in its lifetime, all called sequentially from PilotMain. See the earlier sidebar "Typical Palm OS Application Structure" for details.

For small, quick programs that can be handled all from a single dialog box, a big framework like this is overkill. Fortunately, Palm OS has a routine that performs all of phase two, the event loop, for you. It's called **FrmDoDialog**, and it's usually just used to bring up a modal form for a short time in response to some button press or command. However, **FrmDoDialog** actually performs several roles. First, it draws the form if it's not already visible, then it goes into its own event loop where it does everything that your **AppEventLoop** routine would normally do. If you've set up an event handler for your dialog box, it will get the first look at events.

There are two special behaviors of **FrmDoDialog** that will help you use it. First, if you don't handle the **ctlSelectEvent** for a button on your form, the **FrmDoDialog** event loop will handle it and terminate, returning the button's ID to the routine's caller. This is also the only way to close a dialog box without ending your application.

The second important behavior involves **appStopEvents**. These get sent when you switch to another program; hitting one of the hard buttons at the bottom of your Palm OS device or tapping the application silkscreen are ways to generate this event. The **FrmDoDialog** handler sees this event, reposts the **appStopEvent**, and returns to the caller, indicating that the default button was pressed.

Calling Palm OS Applications from Web Clipping Applications

The previous chapters of the book have discussed at length Clipper's limitations with regards to displaying Web pages and interacting with Web sites. Most of these are design trade-offs that Palm's engineering staff made to fit the Web experience onto the low-memory Palm VII platform and the low-speed Mobitex data network. One very smart decision they made in designing Clipper was adding the capability for it to make calls into other Palm OS applications. This capability to extend Clipper makes the Web clipping concept much more powerful, letting it serve as a network and user interface "glue" between Web sites and programs on the device.

Palm, Inc. designed two methods to call into other applications from Clipper. These take the form of special URL schemes that Clipper interprets as requests to launch other programs when used for a hypertext link or form target. These schemes are *palm* and *palmcall*, which differ in how they launch the helper application. A *palm* URL does a complete application switch away from Clipper, whereas a *palmcall* loads the new application as a subroutine, returning to Clipper after execution.

In the text, I often refer to the applications that can be called by Clipper as *plug-ins*. This usage comes from the Macintosh where it has become a noun that describes any chunk of computer code that gets loaded and executed by another program. Adobe Photoshop uses plug-ins to implement user-written filters; Metrowerks CodeWarrior uses them to implement compilers and linkers. Because these helper programs are not usually called on their own but instead are called by Clipper, they fit into the plug-in paradigm.

Clipper isn't the only Web browser on the Palm to support these kinds of add-on applications. At the time this book was being written, there was support for the *palm* and *palmcall* schemes in the following:

- **Pendragon Browser** From Pendragon Software Corporation, at www.pendragon-software.com.
- **Browse-It** From Pumatech, part of its Intellisync suite of tools at www.intellisync.com.
- **SureWave Browser** From JP Mobile (www.jpmobile.com); a PQA browser that works on any Palm OS 3.1 or later device, allowing Web clipping applications to be deployed on older Palm OS devices that can't run Clipper.
- **Blazer** A Web browser from Handspring at http://blazer.handspring.com.

Several plug-ins are available online that support this interface and provide useful functions. You may want to experiment with these to get a feel for their use before building your own plug-ins. Online plug-ins include the following:

- **HiBrowz** A file download tool that is part of the open source ZBoxZ suite of applications available at http://palmboxer.sourceforge.com. This suite includes mechanisms for using the Palm OS device as a file transport mechanism and for manipulating standard graphics and text formats.
- **ePQA** A tool for filling in Clipper forms from the address book database and also for verifying credit card numbers, from Stevens Creek Software at www.stevenscreek.com. This plug-in also lets you interface with the Stevens Creek order entry system, Take an Order, for doing more complex field sales with a catalog of products on the device.
- **iKnapsack** A standalone application and Clipper plug-in router that comes bundled with plug-ins for adding data to the device applications and for dispatching e-mail. Using this plug-in is discussed in detail later in this chapter. It is available from www.tow.com/software/palm.shtml.

Launching Applications Using *palm* URLs

The *palm* URL scheme launches an application, replacing Clipper as the active application. Internally, Clipper uses the **SysUIAppSwitch** call to post an *appStopEvent* to it and tell Palm OS to launch your application. Its code is similar to the **GoToURL** function shown earlier in the chapter. It makes a copy of the URL used to launch your program, sets its ownership to the system, then tells the system to launch your application later using the *sysAppLaunchCmdURLParams* launch code.

Activating Helper Applications Using *palmcall* URLs

The *palmcall* URL scheme loads the specified application, leaving Clipper running and waiting for the called application to return control. This is done through an internal **SysAppLaunch** call, similar to how we sublaunched iMessenger earlier. Clipper uses RAM from both the system heap and from the stack, so your helper application won't have as much of either available as it would if it were launched directly from the system. Clipper also uses a *sysAppLaunchCmdURLParams* launch code to start the helper application, so applications that want to handle *palm* and *palmcall* URLs in different manners will need to inspect the passed URL to determine the proper behavior.

Passing a Parameter Block

When a Palm OS application is launched from Clipper, it gets passed a launch code and a parameter block. For normal launches, this parameter block is ignored, because it doesn't contain any useful information. For launches caused by Clipper, this block contains a null-terminated string with the URL used to launch the application. This is the complete URL, so it will always have one of the following forms:

```
palm:<creator>.<type>?text

palmcall: <creator>.<type>?text
```

The *palm* or *palmcall* part of the query string just indicates what method was used to invoke the application. *Creator* is replaced by the four-byte creator code, and *type* is replaced by the four-byte database type, which is usually *'appl'*, the standard type for Palm OS applications. These are actually representations of 32-bit values, where each character is 8 bits of the number. In theory, these characters can be anything, but in practice they are limited to printable ASCII characters. Creator codes for plug-ins (and other Palm OS applications) must be registered with Palm, Inc. at its developer Web site at www.palmos.com; registration isn't needed for internal applications, but it should be done for any applications that get distributed to be sure that your databases and resources will not conflict with other resources and databases on the device. In general, you don't need to parse out this information, because it can already be known to the application through inspecting the launch code or checking the current application's database.

The *text* part of the prototype string can be whatever you want, with a few slight caveats. First, any characters that are dangerous in HTML should be escaped using %HH codes. For example, if you wanted to include text that used a percent sign (as is done in our example), you need to escape the percent as **%25**, because 0x25 is the hexadecimal representation of ASCII code 37, the percent sign. This escaping is useful for representing quotation marks, line feeds, and binary data. Second, although you could write **%00** to encode ASCII 0, the application can't tell the difference between an encoded zero character and the character that encodes the end of the query string. Table 10.2 shows some character codes that must be encoded when represented in a URL string. This encoding is explained in more detail in RFC 2396, "Uniform Resource Identifiers (URI): Generic Syntax."

Table 10.2 Dangerous Characters in URLs

Character	Description	Hex Code
'	Apostrophe	%27
"	Quotation mark	%22
%	Percent sign	%25
LF	Line feed	%0A
SP	Space	%20

Specifying Parameters Using Forms

Clipper supports a technique for making the interaction between itself and plug-ins more interactive. In addition to using *palm* and *palmcall* URLs in static links based on the HTML anchor tag, you also can make the URL a target of an HTML form element. If you do this, your application will be called with a query string identical to what would be requested of a HTTP server using a GET operation. To do this, you specify your *palm* or *palmcall* URL as the target of the form, omitting anything after the creator code and database type.

Your query string, in this situation, would look like a series of names and value pairs, separated by ampersands. For example, if you had this HTML code on your page:

```
<form target="palmcall:UWhw.appl" method="get">
<h1>Hawaii Customs</h1>
<p>
<input type="RADIO" name="type" value="Hello">Hello<br>
<input type="RADIO" name="type" value="Goodbye">Goodbye<br>
<input type="TEXT" name="person" maxlength="20"><br>
<input type="HIDDEN" name="word" value="Aloha">
<input type="SUBMIT"></p>
</form>
```

If you picked the Hello button, entered **Cyndi** into the empty text field, and then hit the **Submit** button, Clipper would format this as:

```
palmcall:UWhw.appl? type=hello&person=Cyndi&word=Aloha
```

All of the parameters are passed as if they had been posted to a Web site. If you left the person's name blank, Clipper would use the URL:

```
palmcall:UWhw.appl?type=hello&person&word=Aloha
```

This is a bug in Clipper versions before Palm OS 4.0. When they have empty fields in a form, the value gets posted with only the name but no equals sign. In Palm OS 4.0 and later, Clipper should post the URL string as:

```
palmcall:UWhw.appl?type=hello&person=&word=Aloha
```

This problem broke form processing with some Web packages that always expected both names and values.

Debugging...

Clipper Plug-Ins

Debugging a plug-in for Clipper is fairly easy using CodeWarrior's debugger. You debug the plug-in the same way you debug other applications. From CodeWarrior, you download the plug-in to the device or emulator and then start the program. Unlike most programs, your code will likely immediately exit because it does nothing for a normal Palm OS launch code. However, the CodeWarrior debugger remains attached to your program after it exits. You can then launch your test PQA and invoke your program; if the code hits a breakpoint, the debugger will become active.

One technique for debugging your plug-in more quickly is to add code for normal launches that relaunches the plug-in with the launch code to simulate a launch from Clipper. This works great because your plug-in gets executed as soon as it is downloaded to the device, so you don't have to go through extra steps to get into checking your code. This technique is shown in the Sales Chart example in the next section.

Unwired Widgets Sales Chart Example

To show how *palmcall* URLs can be used to make PQA content more interesting, our example uses a helper application to draw a bar chart representing sales of widgets. Although this could be done using a graphic downloaded from the remote server, just sending the raw data results in faster download times and fewer bytes of data for which the user has to pay. Because the Palm VII and VIIx devices use the slow and expensive Mobitex network, this can give your application a significant advantage. The example code was built with CodeWarrior for Palm OS R7 and is in the project UWBarChart.mcp, included on the CD.

Designing the Query String

An application called from Clipper is passed the entire text of the URL used to invoke the query string. As explained earlier, this text will look like *palmcall:crtr.appl?query*. The leading part of this string isn't very interesting after the query has been successfully routed to our application, so in practice, we're only concerned with the text that follows the question mark.

You can go two ways in deciding what form the text after the question mark takes. If you go with a compact encoding, your PQA files will be smaller, and pages served from the Web server will load faster. If you use something resembling URL encoding, you may be able to use the technique described earlier in "Specifying Parameters Using Forms" to make your *palmcall*-invoked applications more interactive.

For this example, we are building a widget that will display three horizontal bars, each with a label. We are going to pick a compact encoding that will be easy for us to parse. The query string will be a list of comma-separated values, with this order:

- Bar chart title
- Minimum value for setting the horizontal range
- Maximum value for setting the horizontal range
- First label
- Second label
- Third label
- First value
- Second value
- Third value

For simplicity, we will only allow positive integer values. This makes sense for a simple bar chart, because displaying a negative value would require drawing the bars backwards. An example of this query string would be a chart showing sales of red, blue, and green widgets:

```
Widget Sales,0,100,Red,Blue,Green,40,80,10
```

For this example, we have registered the creator code *'UWbc'*, the Unwired Widgets Bar Chart. So, to call this using the previous query string, your code would look like this:

```
<A HREF="palmcall:UWbc.appl?Widget Sales,0,100,Red,Blue,Green,40,80,10>
    Show Bar Chart</A>
```

Building a Test PQA

Because we're mainly interested in testing the bar chart widget, the Web clipping application we build for testing will be simple. We start with a header, then immediately add a series of links. Each link will invoke the bar chart display helper with different parameters. We need to test the widget with both good and bad data. Because our application interfaces with files beyond our control, it is important to verify that it can be used (and misused) without endangering other programs and data on the device. The HTML source for our test is included in Figure 10.6. A screen shot of the form, as seen in Clipper, is shown in Figure 10.7. We're using the Palm-specific *button* attribute for the anchors so that they will appear as buttons in Clipper.

Figure 10.6 UWBarChart.html

```
<HTML>
<HEAD>
<TITLE>Bar Chart Test</TITLE>
</HEAD>
<BODY>
<H1>Bar Chart Test</H1>
<P><A BUTTON
HREF="palmcall:UWbc.appl?Test 1,10,80,blue,red,green,60,30,25">
Graph 1: 60/30/25</A></P>
<P><A BUTTON
HREF="palmcall:UWbc.appl?Test 2,100,800,blue,red,green,600,300,250">
Graph 2: 600/300/250</A></P>
<P><A BUTTON
```

Continued

Figure 10.6 Continued

```
HREF="palmcall:UWbc.appl?Test 3,10,80,blue,red,green,78,79,80">
Graph 3: 78,79,80</A></P>
<P><A BUTTON
HREF="palmcall:UWbc.appl?Test 4,10,80,blue,red,green,10,11,12">
Graph 4: 10/11/12</A></P>
<P><A BUTTON
HREF="palmcall:UWbc.appl?Test 5,10,80">
Graph 5: Too Few Parameters</A></P>
<P><A BUTTON
HREF="palmcall:UWbc.appl?Test 6,ten,eighty,blue,red,green,60,30,25,40">
Graph 6: Too Many Parameters</A></P>
<P><A BUTTON
HREF="palmcall:UWbc.appl?Test 7,ten,eighty,blue,red,
    green,sixty,thrity,twentyfive">
Graph 7: Non Numeric Values</A></P>
<P><A BUTTON
HREF="palmcall:UWbc.appl?Test 8,10,80,blue,red,green,5,20,115">
Graph 8: Out of Range Values</A></P>
<P><A BUTTON
HREF="palmcall:UWbc.appl?Test 8,-50,50,blue,red,green,-30,0,30">
Graph 9: Negative Values</A></P>
</BODY>
</HTML>
```

Parsing the Query String

Because we get the entire URL passed to our helper application as a single string, we have to take it apart into pieces that we can use for our display. This is known as *parsing the string*. In the query string, we have two kinds of data types: string and integers. To pull out these values, we have two functions, **ParseLabel** and **ParseNumber**. Each function takes a pointer to the pointer we're using to keep track of the current character we're reading. We use a double pointer so that when we return from the parsing function, the pointer will have the value of the next character to read. These two helper functions are combined in the function **ProcessParameters** to completely decode the string.

Figure 10.7 Bar Chart Test PQA

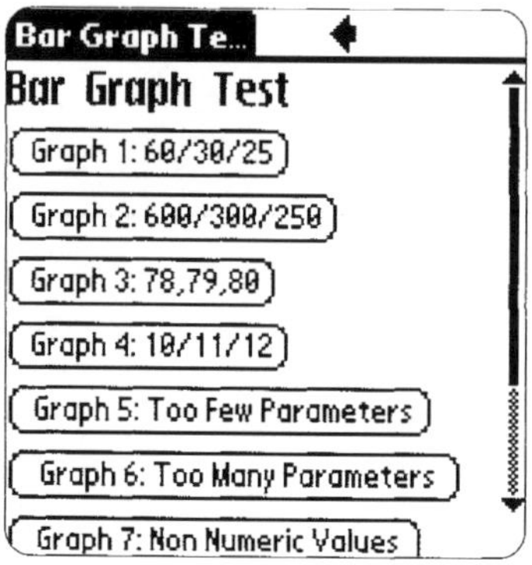

Pulling Numbers from the Parameter List

In our example, the **ParseNumber** routine (Figure 10.8) extracts a number from the current string, expecting a number to begin at the start of the string. It puts the number, if found, into the variable to which the second parameter points.

Figure 10.8 ParseNumber

```
static Boolean ParseNumber(Char **string, Int32 *number)
{
    Char *newStringStart;

    /* if we're passed a NULL pointer, abort */
    if (*string == NULL)
    {
        return false;
    }

    /* check to see if the leading character is a number */
    if (!TxtCharIsDigit((*string)[0]))
    {
        return false;
    }

    /* convert the string into a number */
```

Continued

Figure 10.8 Continued

```
    *number = StrAToI(*string);

    /* find the start of the next field */
    newStringStart = StrChr(*string, ',');
    if (newStringStart)
    {
        *string = newStringStart + 1;
    }
    else
    {
        *string = NULL;
    }

    return true;
}
```

To understand this, we first look at the function prototype. **ParseNumber** returns a Boolean value: true or false. A true result indicates that we successfully pulled a number out of the string and put it into the parameter *number*. A false result means that we need to stop parsing the query string, because we expected a number and got nothing. The code detects the start of the number by calling **TxtCharIsDigit**, the Palm OS version of ANSI C's **isdigit** call that was introduced with Palm OS 3.2. If we don't have something that starts with a digit, then the later call to **StrAToI** to turn the string into a number will silently fail. After we've grabbed our number, we search for the comma that separates this parameter from the next, and if we find it, we advance the character pointer.

Extracting Strings from the Parameter List

ParseLabel (Figure 10.9) has a similar structure to **ParseNumber**; it takes the string from the start of its first parameter, allocates memory for it with a **MemPtrNew** call, and returns it in the variable pointed to by the second parameter.

Figure 10.9 ParseLabel

```
static Boolean ParseLabel(Char **string, Char **label)
{
    Char *stringEnd;
    UInt16 length;

    /* if we're passed a NULL pointer, abort */
    if (*string == NULL)
    {
        return false;
    }

    /* find the end of the string */
    stringEnd = StrChr(*string, ',');

    if (stringEnd)
    {
        /* if we find a comma, copy up to the comma into the new string */
        length = stringEnd - *string;
    }
    else
    {
        /* else, copy from end of string to label */
        length = StrLen(*string);
    }

    *label = MemPtrNew(length + 1);
    if (*label)
    {
        MemMove(*label, *string, length);
        (*label)[length] = 0;
    }
```

Continued

Figure 10.9 Continued

```
    /* advance string to the next field */
    *string += length;
    if ((*string)[0] == ',')
    {
        (*string)++;
    }
    else
    {
        *string = NULL;
    }

    return true;
}
```

ParseLabel has an easier time than **ParseNumber** because label strings can be anything, whereas numbers have a more defined format. The only validity check we have here is to prevent us from trying to pull a string out of an empty parameter list. We're using an interesting construct for parsing out the string. As long as we have more input (even if it is just the end-of-string NULL character), the pointer in the string has a valid value. After we parse the last item in the list, we set the pointer to NULL. If this is the last item, then we won't have any trouble, because we aren't going to use the pointer again. But if we try to parse anything else off that pointer, it will be caught by the initial logic in the two parse functions, and we know that we have an error.

Parsing the Parameter List as a Whole

Our example code in Figure 10.10 uses these two parsing functions to turn the parameters into variables that will be used by the bar chart display code.

Figure 10.10 ProcessParameters

```
static Boolean ProcessParameters(
    MemPtr cmdPBP,
    BarChartParameters *chart)
{
```

Continued

Figure 10.10 Continued

```
Char *cmd = (Char *)cmdPBP;
Int16 i;
Boolean success = true;

/* clear the chart structure */
MemSet(chart, sizeof(BarChartParameters), 0);

/* scan for the '?' that starts the parameter list */
cmd = StrChr(cmd, '?');
if (cmd == NULL)
{
    return false;
}

/* skip the question mark */
cmd += 1;

/* read the title */
success = success && ParseLabel(&cmd, &chart->title);

/* read the mimimum value */
success = success && ParseNumber(&cmd, &chart->min_range);
success = success && ParseNumber(&cmd, &chart->max_range);

/* read the three labels */
for (i = 0; i < 3; ++i)
{
    success = success && ParseLabel(&cmd, &chart->label[i]);
}

/* read the three values */
for (i = 0; i < 3; ++i)
{
```

Continued

Figure 10.10 Continued

```
        success = success && ParseNumber(&cmd, &chart->value[i]);
    }

    return success;
}
```

The end result of the **ProcessParameters** function is a filled *BarChartParameters* structure. Like the two parsing functions, we indicate success via a true or false return value, with the structure being legitimate only if our **ProcessParameters** call returns true. This *BarChartParameters* structure will later be freed by a call to **FreeChart**, so we need to make that sure there is no garbage in the structure, even if it isn't filled; that is why we have the call to **MemSet** to fill it with zeros.

Because the URL string we were passed by Clipper starts with *palmcall:UWbc.appl?*, we skip ahead to the character after the first question mark to start pulling out parameter values. If you expect your creator ID to have an embedded question mark, then you should use alternate code here. After we've found the position for the start of the parameter list, we start a series of calls to the parsing functions for each of our parameters. Here, we use the shortcut operators in the C language to make it easier to call the various functions. The *&&* operator (logical **AND**) first evaluates the left side of the expression, and then if that value is true, it evaluates the right side. As long as *success* remains true, we continue to call the **ParseNumber** and **ParseLabel** functions. However, as soon as one of those fails, *success* gets assigned false, and the further logical expressions will see only the false value in *success* and never execute any of the further parsing calls. Using this form simplifies the code significantly versus what would happen if we used **if** statements to control the program flow.

The code that calls **ProcessParameters** in **PilotMain** uses its return value to either bring up the dialog box that shows the chart or display an error message. To display the error, we use the standard **FrmAlert** call with an alert we've defined to tell the user that the parameters were wrong, as shown in Figure 10.11.

Figure 10.11 Bad URL Alert

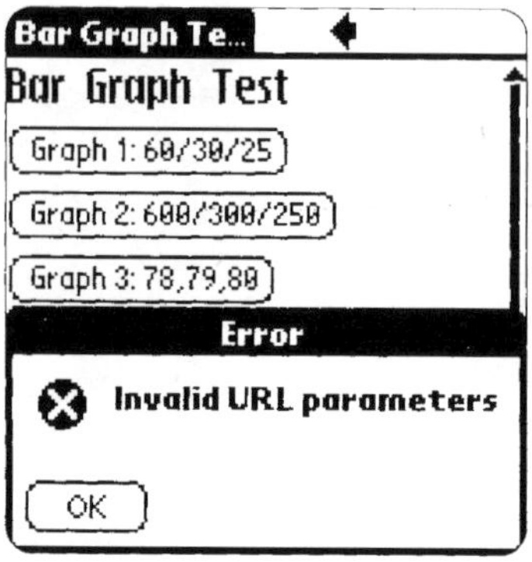

Drawing the Bar Chart

The code to draw the chart is fairly simple. We've put the actual drawing code into a function called **DrawBarChart** (Figure 10.12). This function takes two parameters: a pointer to the form that holds the chart and an index for the form gadget that forms the boundaries for the chart. We actually store the pointer to the *BarChartParameters* structure in the gadget's data pointer. This lets us get to this data without using global variables when we redraw the form from a **frmUpdateEvent**. Because the sublaunch by Clipper leaves our code without global variables, this is quite convenient.

Figure 10.12 DrawBarChart

```
static void DrawBarChart(
    FormType *frm,
    UInt16 gadgetID)
{
    BarChartParameters *chart;
    RectangleType bounds, bar;
    UInt16 gadgetIndex;
    Int16 i, yOffset;
    Int32 range, drawnWidth;
    Char buffer[12];
    CustomPatternType origPattern, newPattern;
    FontID origFont;
```

Continued

Figure 10.12 Continued

```
// save draw system state to restore when we're done
WinGetPattern(&origPattern);
origFont = FntGetFont();

// set the font to Normal
FntSetFont(stdFont);

// set the new fill pattern for diagonal lines
newPattern[0] = newPattern[4] = 0x11;
newPattern[1] = newPattern[5] = 0x22;
newPattern[2] = newPattern[6] = 0x44;
newPattern[3] = newPattern[7] = 0x88;
WinSetPattern(&newPattern);

// get the index of the gadget for future use
gadgetIndex = FrmGetObjectIndex(frm, gadgetID);

// retrieve the data pointer from the gadget
chart = FrmGetGadgetData(frm, gadgetIndex);

// get the dimensions of the gadget
FrmGetObjectBounds(frm, gadgetIndex, &bounds);

// each pixel represents (range / width)
// to convert a value, we do (value - min) / (range / width)
// which converts into (relval * width) / range
// we do the multiply first to avoid losing precision

// we determine the pixel width of each bar by
// 1) subtracting the minimum value
// 2)
range = chart->max_range - chart->min_range;
```

Continued

Figure 10.12 Continued

```
// our layout:
// the widget has width 150, of which we use 135 for the bar chart,
// saving the final 12 pixels for the value, if needed.
// each bar has 12 pixels of vertical space for the caption, then
// 1 pixel of separation, then 16 pixels for the vertical bar
// height, then another 2 pixels of separation, giving a total
// height of (12 + 1 + 16) * 3 + (2 * 2) == (29 * 3) + 4 ==
// 87 + 4 == 91

for (
    i = 0, yOffset = 0;
    i < 3;
    ++i, yOffset += (12 + 1 + 16 + 2))
{
    // draw the text label
    WinDrawChars(
        chart->label[i],
        StrLen(chart->label[i]),
        bounds.topLeft.x,
        bounds.topLeft.y + yOffset);

    // determine the bar's length
    drawnWidth = chart->value[i] - chart->min_range;
    drawnWidth *= (bounds.extent.x - 15);
    drawnWidth /= range;

    // draw the bar
    bar.topLeft.x = bounds.topLeft.x + 1;
    bar.topLeft.y = bounds.topLeft.y + yOffset + 14;
    bar.extent.x = max(drawnWidth - 2, 0);
    bar.extent.y = 14;
    WinFillRectangle(&bar, 0);
```

Continued

Figure 10.12 Continued

```
        WinDrawRectangleFrame(rectangleFrame, &bar);

        // draw the label after the bar
        StrIToA(buffer, chart->value[i]);
        WinDrawChars(
            buffer,
            StrLen(buffer),
            bar.topLeft.x + drawnWidth + 2,
            bar.topLeft.y + 1);
    }

    // restore windows drawing values
    WinSetPattern(&origPattern);
    FntSetFont(origFont);
}
```

The actual drawing consists of drawing the text of the bar labels, drawing a filled rectangle for each bar, drawing a rectangular frame to give a solid border around the bar, and finally, drawing the value after the bar. The code figures the bounds of each rectangle by performing a scaled multiply and divide to turn the value of the bar into a pixel coordinate. In general, with integer math, if you need to do both a multiply and divide, you should first do the multiply that scales up your number and then perform the divide. Otherwise, you could lose significant digits due to round-off error. One example of this code in use is shown in Figure 10.13, which shows how the bar chart appears on the screen in our test code.

We have calls to the code to draw the chart in two places in the program. The first is in the setup for the dialog box; our code initializes the form, draws the form, draws the bar chart, and then jumps into the dialog box handling code. The second place where the chart can be drawn is in the event handler for *frmUpdateEvent*; normally, you don't need an event handler for a dialog box, but because we've added custom drawing code, we need to be able to redraw when the system tells us. Usually, you won't ever see an update event; these are only sent on a real device when a window gets displayed on top of your window, and there isn't enough free memory to make a copy of the screen under the new window. On debug versions of Palm OS, this event gets sent more often to help programmers find bugs in the redraw logic of their code. However, for dialog boxes, there are very few opportunities for the system to pop up a window. You're better off being safe, however, especially with Palm OS 4.0 and its attention manager providing new ways for the system to interrupt your display code, so we've implemented the update logic through the **ChartEventHandler** function.

Figure 10.13 Bar Chart Dialog Box

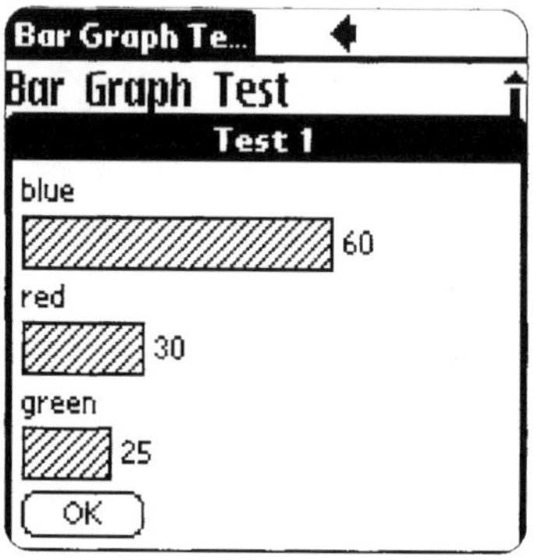

Cleaning Up Before Returning to Clipper

After the user dismisses the dialog box by hitting the **OK** button, we still have a *BarChartParameters* structure that has memory allocated. To clean up that allocation, our **PilotMain** calls the **FreeChart** function, as shown in Figure 10.14. We rely on the **ProcessParameters** function to have initialized any unused pointers to NULL, because if a pointer doesn't have NULL, this code assumes that it points to memory that was allocated by **MemPtrNew**.

Figure 10.14 FreeChart

```
static void FreeChart(BarChartParameters *chart)
{
   Int16 i;

   if (chart->title)
   {
      MemPtrFree(chart->title);
      chart->title = NULL;
```

Continued

Figure 10.14 Continued

```
    }

    for (i = 0; i < 3; i++)
    {
        if (chart->label[i] != NULL)
        {
            MemPtrFree(chart->label[i]);
            chart->label[i] = NULL;
        }
    }
}
```

Testing the Plug-In without Clipper

In development, you may find it useful to have a shortcut to quickly test your plug-in. In our sample code, we have the function **URLLaunchSelf** (shown as Figure 10.15) to help with this. Having to install a test PQA, launch it, and then click on a link to start your plug-in can really slow down the debugging process, especially if you're trying to reproduce a problem such as a sporadic memory leak. You can use the fact that your plug-in for Clipper is also a Palm OS application that can respond to the standard launch codes.

The key concept for this is that an application can sublaunch itself. The application just has to get its own database info, then use that in a call to **SysAppLaunch**, mimicking the parameters that Clipper would pass to it when it was called from a URL.

Figure 10.15 URLLaunchSelf

```
static UInt32 URLLaunchSelf(const Char *query)
{
    UInt16 cardNo;
    LocalID dbID;
    Char *newQuery;
    UInt32 result, creator, dbType;
```

Continued

Figure 10.15 Continued

```
// get the current application
SysCurAppDatabase(&cardNo, &dbID);

// get the creator and type of the application
DmDatabaseInfo(
    cardNo, dbID,
    NULL, NULL, NULL, NULL, NULL, NULL, NULL, NULL, NULL,
    &dbType, &creator);

// construct the new query string
// "palmcall:xxxx.xxxx?" + query + terminator
newQuery = MemPtrNew(20 + StrLen(query));

if (newQuery == NULL)
{
    return sysErrNoFreeRAM;
}

StrPrintF(
    newQuery,
    "palmcall:%c%c%c%c.%c%c%c%c?%s",
    // the four byte code for the creator
    creator >> 24,
    creator >> 16,
    creator >> 8,
    creator,
    // the four byte code for the type (usually appl)
    dbType >> 24,
    dbType >> 16,
    dbType >> 8,
    dbType,
    // the query string
    query);
```

Continued

Figure 10.15 Continued

```
    // sublaunch ourself to do the URL request, as if Clipper had
    // launched us
    SysAppLaunch(
        cardNo,
        dbID,
        0,
        sysAppLaunchCmdURLParams,
        newQuery,
        &result);

    // free the memory allocated for the test launch
    MemPtrFree(newQuery);

    return result;
}
```

This code is fairly generic and can be reused in any plug-in that handles the *palmcall* URL scheme. We start by allocating memory on the heap for the URL string, which is formatted into memory using a call to **StrPrintF**. We re-create the four-byte creator and type codes by individually outputting each character of the code. The shift operators isolate each byte of the code in an endian-independent manner, which means that this code does not have to be tweaked to operate on little-endian ARM-based Palm OS devices, after they arrive on the market.

After we create the query string, we sublaunch our application, using the same launch code that Clipper uses for *palmcall* URLs. Eventually, we return from this sublaunch, so we clean up the memory we allocated and return to the caller.

This method isn't a perfect simulation of a Clipper launch. The biggest problem is that because our application is launching itself, the sublaunch will have access to global variables, because it's been launched by itself. If you've built your code to completely ignore globals, you shouldn't have a problem. The other difference is in the amount of memory and stack you have available. Your resources won't be as constrained when using this relaunch as they are when your code is launched from Clipper or another browser.

If you think that these issues will affect your testing, you can always relaunch yourself in a standard context by using the **GoToURL** code from earlier in this chapter to launch Clipper, passing it your *palmcall* URL, so that it goes and immediately relaunches your application.

Applying iKnapsack to Add PIM Data

One popular third-party program that can be used in Web clipping applications is iKnapsack, a free package developed by Adam Tow. This is available from Adam's Web site at www.tow.com/software/palm.shtml. The version that is current at the date of publication is included with this book on the CD. When combined with the companion Add Palm Data plug-in, it enables Web clipping applications to easily add new Address Book, Calendar, To Do List, Expense, and Memo pad entries for the built-in applications. It is available under an open source license, making it easy to distribute with your Web clipping applications.

iKnapsack can also be used from within Palm OS applications to simplify many of the operations explained earlier in the chapter. It supports a launch code that invokes your default mail program to create a new mail message.

Understanding iKnapsack's Architecture

The iKnapsack program acts as a clearinghouse for Web requests and plug-ins to handle those requests. When run on its own, it lets you do a few useful tasks, such as jumping directly to an entered URL using the default Web browser or launching the default e-mail program. It also lets you manage your installed Web clipping applications by showing them and their sizes in a numbered list, with commands for launching the WCA, deleting it from memory, and beaming it to another device. iKnapsack also provides an interface for viewing and managing its plug-ins. In many ways, iKnapsack servers as a Palm analogue to the Macintosh's Internet Config software as an add-on to the operating system for handling details of accessing the Internet.

Using the iKnapsack User Interface

iKnapsack shows up in the Palm OS launcher and can be launched as a normal application. The initial screen for iKnapsack (Figure 10.16) shows the four main actions that you can perform.

The **Connect To** button brings up a form where you can enter a URL, and Clipper will be invoked to view that site. Actually, if you've picked a program other than Clipper to handle the URL, it will be invoked instead, which is useful for people using one of the other browsers. The dialog box will automatically prepend *http://* to your request if you do not specify a URL scheme. I find myself using this feature fairly frequently on my Palm VII to launch sites such as the Google minibrowser search engine (at http://wap.google.com) for which I haven't built a WCA.

Figure 10.16 iKnapsack Initial Screen

The **Email** button launches your default e-mail program. On the Palm VII, this will be set to iMessenger the first time you use iKnapsack. This is useful for testing your settings for an e-mail client, and it also shows how other Palm OS applications can use iKnapsack to route mail requests to the application the user has selected.

Setting Your Default Programs

The Options/Preferences menu choice brings up a dialog box (Figure 10.17) that lets you pick which Palm programs are used for e-mail, Web browsing, and viewing Web clipping applications.

Figure 10.17 shows the default applications that iKnapsack picks when first installed on a Palm VII or Palm VIIx device. The e-mail client is iMessenger; both Web browsing and viewing of PQAs are handled by Clipper. When you tap the pop-up list, it lets you pick from any application installed on the device—but you have to be careful, because picking an application that doesn't support the required launch codes will cause that functionality to malfunction. Picking your Solitaire game to handle e-mail won't make it a mail client, and many programs that handle e-mail or Web browsing don't take the right launch codes to be called by iKnapsack.

Figure 10.17 iKnapsack Preferences

Web browsing is separated from Web clipping so that iKnapsack can use a different program to visit a URL. You might use this if you're using a device with Cellular Digital Packet Data (CDPD) service such as OmniSky, where you have both Web clipping and Transmission Control Protocol/Internet Protocol (TCP/IP) available, and you want to use a browser with more features most of the time.

Managing the iKnapsack Plug-Ins

Clicking the **Plug-ins** button on the main screen brings you to the plug-in management screen, shown in Figure 10.18. This shows a list of all the plug-ins for iKnapsack that are installed on the device, and it lets you configure them, bring up information on using them, and delete them.

Figure 10.18 iKnapsack Plug-In List

Hitting the **Done** button returns to the main screen. Tapping a name on the list will highlight it and enable the action buttons. If you hit the **Info** button, a dialog box appears giving more information about the plug-in. For example, bringing up the **Info** screen for the **Add Palm Data** plug-in is shown in Figure 10.19.

Figure 10.19 Add Palm Data Information Dialog Box

The convention for these Info screens is to provide a general description upon hitting **Info** and to provide usage information for people writing Web pages that use that plug-in in the Tips dialog box that appears if you tap the "**i**" button in the upper-right corner of the Info dialog box. For **Add Palm Data**, the first page of the usage info is shown in Figure 10.20.

Figure 10.20 Add Palm Data Usage

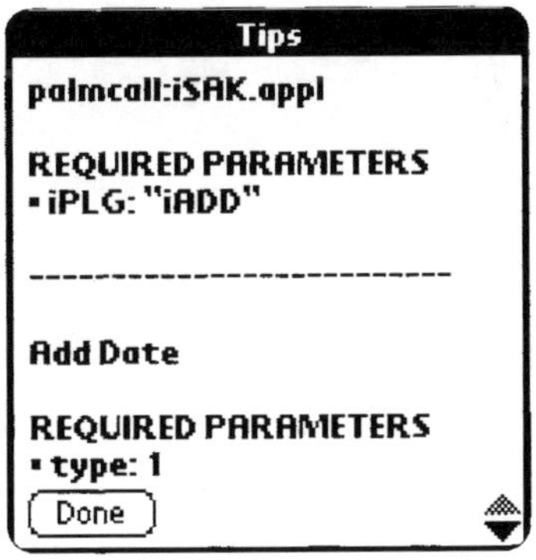

To delete plug-ins, you select the plug-in from the list and choose **Delete Plug-in** from the Plug-in menu. You also can beam plug-ins, either individually or as a complete set, to other iKnapsack users by using a menu choice. This beaming is done as standard Palm OS databases, so the device you beam to doesn't need a copy of the iKnapsack software (although without iKnapsack, the user would have a tough time actually using the plug-ins).

Managing Your Web Clipping Applications

Hitting the **Web Clipping Apps** button from the iKnapsack main page brings up a list of Web clipping applications. An example of this is shown in Figure 10.21. From this list, you can launch the Web clipping viewer on a particular application; launch it with no application specified, which leaves Clipper showing a blank screen with a **Back** button; delete a Web clipping application; or beam one to another Palm OS device (again done as a standard Palm OS database, so iKnapsack isn't needed on the remote device).

Figure 10.21 Web Clipping App List

The **Open** action button opens the selected item in the list; the other actions are available from the Web clipping menu. This form doesn't provide any capabilities that aren't already present in the Launcher, but it does aggregate almost everything you can do with the WCAs into an interface that is quicker to use than the Palm OS Launcher. The only feature it is missing is the capability to put Web clipping applications into categories, which is understandable because the Launcher's category data is stored separately from the applications.

Using the Add Palm Data Plug-In

You use iKnapsack as you would call a Clipper plug-in that you wrote yourself. It works either from a <A> hypertext link or from a <FORM> submission.

Because iKnapsack works as a router to direct *palmcalls* to its plug-ins, you also need to know the plug-in's creator code. The creator code for iKnapsack is 'iSAK'. For the **Add Palm Data** plug-in, it is 'iADD'. A *palmcall* to a plug-in invokes the iKnapsack program but adds a leading parameter that indicates which plug-in ultimately gets the call. All of our calls in this section will take this form:

```
<a href="palmcall:iSAK.appl?iPLG=iADD&type=<n>&<other parameters>">
```

This starts with the familiar *palmcall* invocation, followed by the specification of iKnapsack, which is a standard Palm OS application of type *'appl'*. The creator code of the plug-in is 'iADD' so it gets specified first, then we have the plug-in–specific parameters. For the **Add Palm Data** plug-in, the first parameter is always the type. This is a second layer of routing that picks the operation that we're doing. The possible types are listed in Table 10.3. The parameters that follow the type specifier as *<other parameters>* are specific to each operation.

Table 10.3 Add Palm Data's Type Parameters

Type Number	Description
1	Add date book entry
2	Add address book entry
3	Add to do list entry
4	Add memo pad entry
5	Add expense record

The initial release of iKnapsack and its plug-ins had each of these as a separate plug-in for the program. This was changed for the 1.2 release to consolidate the code into one Palm resource (PRC) file to make installation of the iKnapsack system easier and to allow the various add data calls to share common code. Because of this aggregation, you have to go through three layers of specifying what to do (palmcall, plug-in name, operation type) rather than just the one (palmcall) that you would use for a custom system.

Adding a Date Book Entry

This plug-in operation lets you add entries directly into the database used by the Palm Date Book application. The parameters for additions to the date book are shown in Table 10.4.

Table 10.4 Add Date Book Entry Parameters

Field Name	Description	Values	Default
type	Operation type	1 = add Date Book entry	No default
desc	Description of the event	ASCII text	No default
date	Date the event takes place	YYYY-MM-DD, all numeric, e.g., 2001-06-15	No default
text	Text for the event note	ASCII text	(Empty string)
start	Start time	Time in 24 hour HH:MM format, e.g., 09:45, 17:20	Leave empty only if *notime* is 1
end	End time	Time in 24 hour HH:MM format, e.g., 09:45, 17:20	Leave empty only if *notime* is 1
notime	Specifies that the event has no specific time	1 = event has no specific time	0
alarm	Indicates if an alarm should be set	1 = event has alarm	0
adv	Units of time to sound alarm in advance	Positive number or 0	0
advunit	What units to use for the "adv" field	0 = Days, 1 = Hours, 2 = Minutes	0

Because the Palm Date Book has no concept of time zones, the times you specify are considered to be in the local time of the device. Also, based on the limitations of the Palm Date Book database, you can't easily specify an event that spans midnight, because each event has only one date field.

The time values should be limited to increments of five minutes, again by the design of Palm's database. You can specify other times, but you could cause problems with Date Book's display logic. There also is no mechanism for interfacing with the repeat function the Date Book has, so setting up multiple events will require multiple invocations of this plug-in. No default time exists; if you don't specify the *notime* parameter, and you leave off the start or end times, you will get random times assigned to your event, based on whatever happened to be in memory when the plug-in was called.

WARNING

Using this plug-in, getting corrupt data into the Date Book database is easy. Be careful that you don't specify an end time that occurs before a start time, and that your other value strings are all correct.

Although this plug-in could be used with a form to specify some or all of the values, we don't recommend this usage due to the problems with validating data. In playing with it to learn more about its behavior, we set up a form that let us directly specify each value from a text input field. By using invalid formats, setting the end time before the start time, and using ridiculous values, we were able to get the date book database thoroughly corrupted. Fortunately, it only took a reload of the emulator session to fix those problems; the lesson is to test in the emulator before you test on a real Palm OS device that holds important data.

The syntax for calling this plug-in is as follows:

```
<a href="palmcall:iSAK.appl?iPLG=iADD&type=1&desc=...&date=...&text=...&
    start=...&end=...&notime=...&alarm=...&adv=...&advunit=...">Anchor text</a>
```

Of course, in the real HTML, you wouldn't break up the parameter string with a line feed, it would all be on a continuous line of text. You also can implement it as a form submission, with the following syntax:

```
<form action="GET" action=" palmcall:iSAK.appl?iPLG=iADD&type=1">
<input type="HIDDEN" name="desc" value="...">
<input type="HIDDEN" name="date" value="...">
<input type="HIDDEN" name="text" value="...">
<input type="HIDDEN" name="start" value="...">
<input type="HIDDEN" name="end" value="...">
<input type="HIDDEN" name="notime" value="...">
<input type="HIDDEN" name="alarm" value="...">
<input type="HIDDEN" name="adv" value="...">
```

```
<input type="HIDDEN" name="advunit" value="...">
<input type="SUBMIT">
</form>
```

The slight disadvantage of using a form is that you must use a **Submit** button, whereas with a hypertext link, you can pick either underlined text or a button.

WARNING

If you're testing this Date Book code on a fresh emulator session or a totally clean device, you may get a failure when adding a Date Book entry. This is because the plug-in requires that a Date Book database exist on the device, but the database doesn't get created until the first time the user enters the Date Book application. In practice, almost any Palm OS device user will have run the Date Book at least once before installing iKnapsack and its plug-ins, so this error should almost never appear.

Adding an Address Book Entry

Putting a new entry into the Address Book has fewer potential problems than adding to the Date Book. Entries in the Address Book aren't linked, and no relationship exists between the data items in a record, so you don't have to worry about bad Address Book entries affecting other entries.

The parameters for the "Add to Address Book" operation are shown in Table 10.5.

Table 10.5 Add Address Book Entry Parameters

Field Name	Description	Values	Default
Type	Operator type	2 = add Address Book entry	None
First	First name	ASCII string	Empty
Last	Last name	ASCII string	Empty
Comp	Company	ASCII string	Empty
Title	Job Title	ASCII string	Empty

Continued

Table 10.5 Continued

Field Name	Description	Values	Default
Work	Work phone number	ASCII string	Empty
Home	Home phone number	ASCII string	Empty
Fax	Fax phone number	ASCII string	Empty
Other	Other phone number	ASCII string	Empty
e-mail	E-mail address	ASCII string	Empty
Addr	Street address	ASCII string	Empty
City	City	ASCII string	Empty
State	State	ASCII string	Empty
Zip	ZIP code (or Postal Code)	ASCII string	Empty
Country	Country	ASCII string	Empty
cust1	First custom data field	ASCII string	Empty
cust2	Second custom data field	ASCII string	Empty
cust3	Third custom data field	ASCII string	Empty
cust4	Fourth custom data field	ASCII string	Empty
Text	Additional text note	ASCII string	Empty

All parameters are ASCII strings, and each field is limited to 4K of data, although we'd expect the parameter string for the URL to have a much shorter limitation. You can't specify the category for the entry; all new Address Book entries through this method will be placed in the "Unfiled" category. Fields that are not specified in the parameter list will be left empty. All records need at least a first name, last name, or company name record; if they are lacking these, they will be filed under "-Unnamed-" in the Address Book.

Adding a To Do List Entry

Adding items to the To Do List follows the same pattern as the other plug-ins. Its parameters are shown in Table 10.6.

Text is always required. Not having an entry for *text* could leave your To Do List in arrays. The date can be anytime; setting a due date before the current date will make entries show up with exclamation points next to the date to show that they are overdue. Like the other iKnapsack plug-ins, the category of the To Do item cannot be specified and is set to "Unfiled." Also, any items added are marked as incomplete. You can't use this plug-in for "to done" entries.

Table 10.6 Add To Do List Entry Parameters

Field Name	Description	Values	Default
Type	Operator type	3 = add To Do List entry	None
Priority	Priority for the item	Number from 1 to 5	1
Date	Due date	Date in YYYY-MM-DD format, e.g., 2001-06-03	No due date
Text	Description of the item	ASCII string	None

Adding a Memo Pad Entry

Memo pads are the simplest format to specify with the Add Palm Data plug-in, because they have only one parameter for *text*, which is described in Table 10.7.

Table 10.7 Add Memo Pad Entry Parameters

Field Name	Description	Values	Default
type	Operator type	4 = add memo pad entry	None
text	Memo pad text	ASCII string	None

When Memo Pad entries are shown in the Memo viewer, the first line of the Memo is used as the title, so you should keep that convention when adding your own entries. As a reminder, to add line feeds into the text, you need to specify **%0A**. Plain line feeds or carriage returns in the parameter are ignored, so if you aren't careful, you could end up with a Memo with a very long first line.

Adding an Expense Entry

Not all Palm OS devices have the Expense program. It was added with the PalmPilot Personal as an installable program, and put in the ROM on the PalmPilot Professional. It is present on most of the newer Palm OS devices, with the exception of the Palm m100 and m105, where it was removed to make space for the Note Pad program, and the Palm VII and VIIx, where it was removed to make space for iNetLib and Clipper. It can be installed as an after-market program on all of these devices. This plug-in lets you add expense entries; this may be useful if you wanted to set up a small PQA that acted as expense macros for commonly purchased items. The parameters for the Add Expense Entry plug-in are shown in Table 10.8.

Table 10.8 Add To Do List Entry Parameters

Field Name	Description	Values	Default
type	Operator type	5 = add expense record	None
date	Date of the expense	YYYY-MM-DD format	None
amt	Amount of expense	Number (US Dollars)	None
vend	Vendor name		Empty
text	Extra text		Empty
city	Location of expense		Empty
attendees	Who was involved		Empty
pay	Payment Method	Number from 0 to 7 (see Table 10.9)	7 (Unfiled)
typ	Expense type	Number from 0 to 27 (see Table 10.10)	17 (Other)

Required fields are the date and amount. Beyond that, everything is optional. Two of the parameters require some additional explanation. The payment method parameter defaults to "Unfiled" and is used to pick how the item was paid. Its choices are shown in Table 10.9; whether you use this depends on how you track expenses. Because this field isn't definable by the user, we've not found it to be too useful—there is no way to specify a Discover or Diner's Club card other than the nonspecific "Credit Card" choice.

Table 10.9 Expense Payment Methods for *pay* Parameter

Number	Method
0	American Express
1	Cash
2	Check
3	Credit Card
4	MasterCard
5	Prepaid
6	Visa
7	Unfiled (Default)

The *typ* parameter is a bit controversial. In its first version, before the plug-ins were combined into a single "Add Palm Data" program, this was called *type*, but it clashed with the *type* parameter, which is used to pick the operation under the new scheme. Also, like the payment field, you can't define what the types are, which means you have to shoehorn expenses into these fields, which seem to be closely aligned with one kind of business traveler, while neglecting day-to-day expenses, such as cell phones and computer books. The possible values, and the type to which they map, are shown in Table 10.10.

Table 10.10 Expense Types for *typ* Parameter

Number	Expense Type
0	Airfare
1	Breakfast
2	Bus
3	Business Meals
4	Car Rental
5	Dinner
6	Entertainment
7	Fax
8	Gas
9	Gifts
10	Hotel
11	Incidentals
12	Laundry
13	Limousine
14	Lodging
15	Lunch
16	Mileage
17	Other (Default)
18	Parking
19	Postage
20	Snack
21	Subway
22	Supplies
23	Taxi

Continued

Table 10.10 Continued

Number	Expense Type
24	Telephone
25	Tips
26	Tolls
27	Train

Adding PIM Data for Unwired Widgets Example

As an example to show you how to use the iKnapsack plug-ins, we've developed a small Web clipping application for the Unwired Widgets catalog. Using it, you can add the headquarters to your address book, make a date for the next shareholders meeting, remember to book the flight for the meeting, save the board of directors ballot to the Memo pad, and record the parking for the meeting on your next expense statement.

Obviously, you wouldn't normally put all of these functions onto one page, but humor us for the example. In a normal context, you could show a calendar with dates as hyperlinks to add appointments. You might have a corporate address book where a search for a name returned the information along with a button that would add that person to the address book. You could also possibly use these to make device macros to add templates for the various applications. Our example HTML file is shown in Figure 10.22.

Figure 10.22 Adding PIM Data Example HTML Code

```
<html>
<head>
<title>UW Corporate Info</title>
</head>
<body>

<h1>Unwired Widgets</h1>
<h2>Corporate Information</h2>
```

Continued

Figure 10.22 Continued

```
<p>The UW shareholders meeting is coming up this June, and we have
all the information you need to update your Palm PDA to prepare for
it, if you have the iKnapsack plug-in from Foundation Systems.</p>

<ul>

<li><a href="palmcall:iSAK.appl?iPLG=iADD&type=2&comp=Unwired
Widgets (Headquarters)&work=888-555-0123&email=hq@unwiredwidgets.com&
addr=123 Main Street&city=Austin&state=TX&zip=78704">Add the corporate
address to your Palm's address book</a></li>

<li><a href="palmcall:iSAK.appl?iPLG=iADD&type=1&date=2001-06-18&
start=14:30&end=17:30&desc=Unwired Widgets Shareholders' Meeting">Add
the shareholders meeting to your date book</a></li>

<li><a href="palmcall:iSAK.appl?iPLG=iADD&type=3&priority=1&
desc=Buy airline tickets to go to Unwired Widgets shareholder's
meeting">Add to-do entry to remind you to book your
flight</a></li>

<li><a href="palmcall:iSAK.appl?iPLG=iADD&type=4&text=
Unwired Widgets Board Candidates%0A%0AWest
Region: Stanley Smith, Christina Marrs, Willam
Ammo%0ANortheast Region: Gordon Gano, Brian Ritchie, Guy
Hoffman%0ASouth Region: Chris Stamey, Peter
Holsapple%0APacific Region: Angie Hart, Simon Austin">Add
the Board of Director Candidates to your memo pad</a></li>

<li><a href="palmcall:iSAK.appl?iPLG=iADD&type=5&
date=2001-06-18&amt=8.00&city=Austin, TX&typ=18">Add parking costs for
the meeting to your expense records</a></li>
```

Continued

Figure 10.22 Continued

```
</body>
</html>
```

Figure 10.23 shows this HTML file as it appears in Clipper. Because the view is longer than one screen, we've split it into two screen shots.

Figure 10.23 The Example as Rendered by Clipper

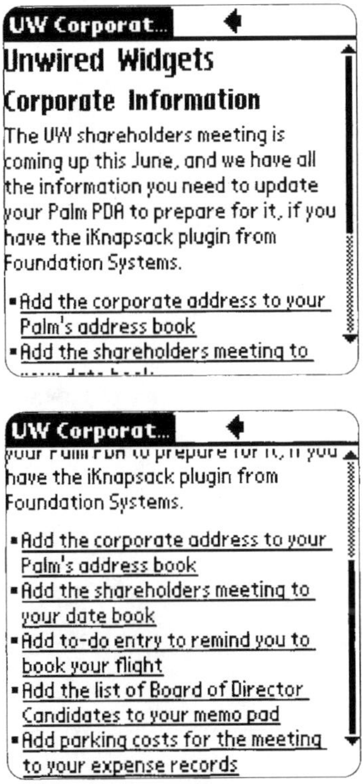

Figures 10.24 through 10.28 show the entries that have been added to the different Palm OS applications by clicking on the links within the example HTML file. These screen shots are taken from the standard Palm OS applications after each link in the Web clipping file was followed.

Figure 10.24 Data Added to the PIM Applications

Figure 10.25 Address Added to the PIM Applications

Figure 10.26 To Do Added to the PIM Applications

Figure 10.27 Memo Added to the PIM Applications

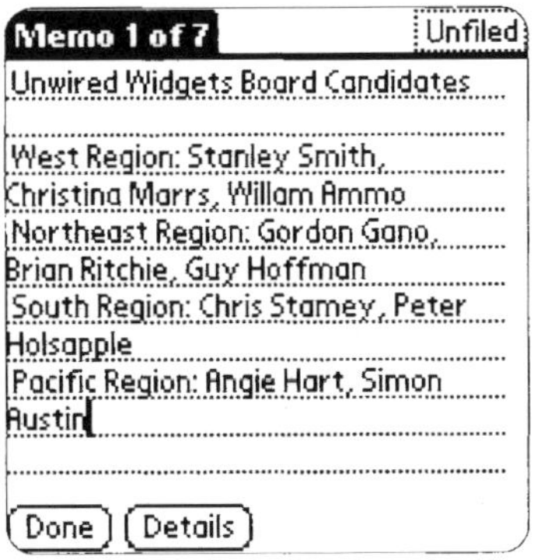

Figure 10.28 Expense Added to the PIM Applications

Summary

This chapter has explained many of the ways you can combine Web clipping with other Palm OS applications. This is a very useful technique, and proper use can reduce your development time and give you a higher quality application. At its simplest, your applications can just use Clipper and its companion, iMessenger, to provide Web browsing and e-mail functionality for standard Palm OS applications. More creative applications can be constructed by using Clipper as the base user interface for your application, with it calling into plug-ins that you create to enhance the user experience. In some cases, you don't need to write the plug-ins yourself. Software such as iKnapsack exists that provides useful functions already, and making effective use of these can be a big win.

Solutions Fast Track

Launching and Sublaunching Applications

☑ Two Application Programming Interface (API) calls are used to launch other programs on the Palm OS device: **SysUIAppSwitch** and **SysAppLaunch**.

☑ **SysUIAppSwitch** is used when you want to end your current program and start another. Palm OS uses this call to handle switching applications when you hit one of the hard buttons. It looks in the system preferences to find out which application is mapped to that button, and if it isn't the running program, it calls **SysUIAppSwitch** to switch to the mapped program.

☑ **SysAppLaunch** leaves your current program suspended while another program is opened temporarily to handle a request. This is called a *sub-launch* by the Palm OS documentation, because the caller uses the program as a subroutine.

Calling Clipper from Palm OS Applications

☑ Check for the existence of Clipper before calling it and assign memory that holds the URL string to the system.

☑ Have an orderly shutdown of your program after setting up the Clipper launch.

- ☑ Use Clipper as an easy way to Web-enable Palm OS applications.

Calling iMessenger from Palm OS Applications

- ☑ Use iMessenger to add e-mail interactivity to your programs.
- ☑ Messages are just placed in the iMessenger Outbox, they don't get sent immediately.
- ☑ Take extra precaution with memory if you are allowing the user to immediately edit the e-mail.

Unwired Widgets Application About Box Example

- ☑ This example shows how to use Clipper and iMessenger in a realistic program.
- ☑ Using a dialog box as a testbed is a quick method to try out new code without building a huge application.

Calling Palm OS Applications from Web Clipping Applications

- ☑ Plug-ins for Clipper allow Web pages to interact with other programs on the device.
- ☑ Plug-ins are also useful for complex user interfaces and for rendering data in an efficient manner.

Unwired Widgets Sales Chart Example

- ☑ A plug-in for Clipper is used to draw a bar chart based on textual data.
- ☑ This code shows one technique for parsing parameters to a Clipper plug-in.

Using iKnapsack to Add PIM Data

- ☑ iKnapsack provides an interface for users to manipulate Clipper and its plug-ins.
- ☑ The Add Palm Data plug-in allows Web clipping applications to add data to the applications that come standard on the device.

- ☑ When using this plug-in, be very careful with the parameters, or you could find the Palm's databases corrupted.

Adding PIM Data for Unwired Widgets Example

- ☑ The Add Data Plug-in for iKnapsack is an effective tool when combined with Clipper to save data about an important event.
- ☑ The plug-in can also be used to create templates for frequently added data on the device.

Frequently Asked Questions

The following Frequently Asked Questions, answered by the authors of this book, are designed to both measure your understanding of the concepts presented in this chapter and to assist you with real-life implementation of these concepts. To have your questions about this chapter answered by the author, browse to **www.syngress.com/solutions** and click on the **"Ask the Author"** form.

Q: On what devices can I use iMessenger?

A: iMessenger is provided only on the Palm VII and Palm VIIx handhelds. Although it uses INetLib, it uses special calls in the library that do not work on other devices with INetLib. It also relies on the user account established with Palm.Net to store e-mail; users of non-VII devices do not have Palm.Net accounts, so they would not have e-mail access.

Q: Why do I get an *Owner App Not Found* error when I try to test my PQA?

A: This occurs when you install a Web clipping application on a device that doesn't have Clipper. You must have a Palm VII, a Palm VIIx, or any device with the Mobile Internet Kit installed to use these files. Most new devices with network connectivity provide INetLib and Clipper.

Q: Why does my Clipper plug-in crash with a *Bus Error*?

A: The usual reason is that your code is using global variables. These aren't available when your application has been called using the *palmcall* URL scheme.

Q: Why does my Clipper plug-in crash on the Palm OS Emulator with a stack error?

A: When your application is called from a *palmcall* URL, it has to share stack space with the Clipper program already running. Because of this, you don't have as much room as normal for local variables.

Q: After calling Clipper to view a URL, the user hit the Back arrow, and my original program restarted. Is this normal?

A: Yes. Launching Clipper involves switching applications, which ends your application. When it gets run after Clipper completes, it acts like it had just been launched. You should try to save context yourself and restore that upon being rerun.

Q: After using the iKnapsack plug-in, I'm having problems using the Date Book. What's wrong?

A: If you have malformed data in the parameter list for the Add Palm Data plug-in, it is easy to corrupt the internal databases on the Palm. Leaving off parameters or giving bad data can cause user interface glitches or loss of data. Check your HTML code for anything you may have missed.

Chapter 11

Using the Internet Library in Palm OS Applications

Solutions in this chapter:

- A Hello World Program
- Finding and Initializing Internet Library
- Creating an INetLib Connection
- Moving to an Event-Driven Model
- URLFetch: An Improvement on Hello World
- Accessing a Server-Side Application
- Receiving Responses from the Server
- Authenticating the User and Device
- Providing Configuration Aliases
- Optimizing Transport
- An Unwired Widgets Mail Reader Example
- Securing Data
- Testing for Proxy Issues and Known Bugs

☑ Summary

☑ Solutions Fast Track

☑ Frequently Asked Questions

Introduction

Chapters 1 through 9 covered Web applications based on the Clipper. Chapter 10 described integration of Clipper with native Palm OS applications. This chapter goes one step further by developing a native Palm OS application that replaces the browser-based user interface. By replacing the client side with a native application, your Web application can use all Palm OS features.

Developing a native application to access your Web site is a difficult task. You find that you may have to implement much of the functionality of Web clipping to get even a basic application working. However, the rewards can be great. One of the basic advantages of having a standalone application is that your data is available offline. Your application can accept new data from the user and display and analyze existing data. Later on, it can connect to the server synchronizing changes in a batch mode. Moreover, because you control the protocol spoken between the server and the application, you can squeeze as many bytes out of the protocol as needed.

Because native applications have full control of the device, you can implement databases and unique user interface methods. A native application can be smarter, anticipating the user's requests and providing a smoother workflow. This chapter gives you much of the background you need to implement the network parts of a native Palm OS application and teaches you how to make Palm's Internet Library work for you.

Choosing Your Language

Most of the native applications for Palm OS are written in either C or C++; we discuss C in this book. You may choose to implement your program in other languages, of course, which could include Java and Visual Basic. Languages other than C/C++ usually fall behind in the support for the latest SDKs. For example, at the time of this writing, the Visual Basic virtual machine (VM) from AppForge does not support any networking API, though they have promised it for the next release. In Java alone, you have choices ranging from Waba to KJava. KJava is the most popular Java. It confirms to Sun's Java 2 Micro Edition (J2ME) specs and the slowest of all the Java VMs. Waba, on the other hand, uses Java syntax but stays away from the Java name. This gives them enough freedom to implement non-portable constructs or features, if necessary. Fortunately, at the time of this writing, Waba programs are still portable across Windows CE devices as well as desktops and desktop browsers (as applets). The Waba group is also working on integration with Jump (a Java-to-68K assembly translator). After this is done, Waba may become one of the fastest VMs on the market. IBM's VisualAge Micro Edition (VAME)/J9 is positioned somewhere in between. You can access all native functions, but the program is not portable outside Palm OS. As of this writing, this may be your only option to write relatively fast programs and still be able to access the latest API. If you are not addicted to Java, you may want to consider C/C++. Your program will be faster, and deployment will be easier.

For clarity, this chapter's examples are written in C, not C++. Although C++ is a fine choice for real-world applications, its use is more complex than needed to illustrate the use of the Internet Library. Because C++ is a superset of the C language, you should be able to use the code provided here with minimal changes in a C++-based application.

History of INetLib and NetLib

Palm OS versions 2.0 and higher provide a Transmission Control Protocol/Internet Protocol (TCP/IP) stack to the applications. Applications use a Palm OS shared library to connect, read, and write data to hosts on the network. The interface is based on the sockets API in Berkeley Unix, which has become a de facto industry standard. This network library, called *NetLib,* has both a Palm-native API and a wrapper library that has a UNIX-like interface.

When Palm VII was first released at the Palm Source Conference in 1999, everyone was excited about the first wireless-ready device. However, the first release of Palm VII came with two surprises:

- The built-in browser could never use NetLib (the regular wireline connection or Minstrel modem) to fetch URLs.
- Though the radio proved to be a very reliable wireless channel, applications could only do HTTP transactions over the radio. INetLib was not designed to work with existing NetLib.

The second problem was quite reasonable, considering that the radio works over Cingular Wireless's Mobitex wireless network. The network is just not capable of providing the bandwidth needed for a TCP/IP connection. Developers could not see any technical reason why Clipper could not work over a modem. So naturally, a couple of unofficial patches were available that "fixed" this problem. The 3.5 release of Palm OS has taken out this restriction. Now INetLib can use NetLib over regular modems or with the radio interface. Although INetLib header files describe other protocols such FTP, INetLib supports only

HTTP protocol as of Palm OS version 4.0. Some elements of an earlier INetLib design are left in the header files, so users should refer to the Palm OS device documentation and examples to see what is possible.

Why Use HTTP?

For developers not familiar with Web application development, using HTTP for non-HTML applications may sound strange. It may seem much easier to just have a server application waiting on a particular port instead of adding the burden of a Web server, the HTTP protocol, and the resulting inefficiency. Before you label HTTP as inefficient, however, you may want to consider the following points:

- Placing an application inside a Web framework makes its development easier. Because the application is isolated from the socket interface, a crash in one instance of the application will not affect the Web server or other instances of the service. Load balancing issues are automatically resolved when you use a Web server.
- Limiting yourself to HTTP transactions will make your solution work over Palm VII radio as well as regular channels (wireline channels and external wireless modems). Increasingly, wireless devices (such as Wireless Application Protocol [WAP] phones, Research in Motion [RIM] devices, Motorola PageWriter, and the Glenayre AccessLink pager) provide messaging-based transport, which can easily be adapted to access HTTP-based services. In the future, you will be able to support these devices if your server application limits itself to HTTP-based transactions.
- Most firewalls are either set up to allow HTTP traffic (port 80) or have some mechanism to tunnel the HTTP traffic and route them to the internal server.
- Newer Internet standards like Extensible Markup Language-Remote Procedure Call (XML-RPC) and Simple Object Access Protocol (SOAP) use HTTP as their underlying transport. Even the much-publicized Microsoft .NET Web services use HTTP, XML, and SOAP. Chances are, at this stage, you may not be using these technologies. However, when you do have to move your server to these newer frameworks, you can avoid redesigning the client.

Palm VII was released with a built-in browser and new library that provides HTTP-based transactions. INetLib wasn't magical—it was just a library to fetch arbitrary URLs from the Internet. However, it was the first time an HTTP library was available for Palm OS. The convenience of the built-in antenna more than compensated for INetLib's initial limitations. Underneath, INetLib used a very efficient User Datagram Protocol (UDP)-based interface over the radio. With INetLib versions 3.5 and above, it is usable even over the wireline channel.

A typical networked application opens a socket connection to a host on the Internet, exchanging arbitrary data back and forth between the handheld and the server. INetLib-based applications instead reduce the transaction to one or more URL requests.

A Hello World Program

Sticking to the age-old tradition, we will start with a program that will fetch a "hello.txt" file from a Web server. The source code for the program (see Figure 11.1) is available on the CD that accompanies this book. Project files for CodeWarrior and Falch.Net DevStudio are also provided on the CD. If you prefer using the GNU Compiler Collection (GCC) from a command-line environment, ignore the project files and directly compile the Hello_World.c file instead. Create a file named "hello.txt" in your Web directory and update the URL given in the source code, then make sure that the URL is correct using a desktop browser like Internet Explorer. If you prefer to use the precompiled Palm resource (PRC) file given, you may do so, provided that the URL given in the listing is accessible from your desktop.

Figure 11.1 A C Program to Fetch a URL Using a GET Request

```
#include <PalmOS.h>
#include <INetMgr.h>
#include <CTP.h>

#include "Hello_World_res.h"

#define MAX_RESPONSE_SIZE   4096
#define HandleError(err) ErrFatalDisplayIf(err != 0, "Error!")

// Replace this line with the URL of your hello.htm file
```

Continued

Figure 11.1 Continued

```
#define SERVER_URL "http://www.unwiredwidgets.com/hello.txt"

INetConfigNameType cfgName  = { inetCfgNameCTPDefault };

UInt32 PilotMain(UInt16 cmd, void *cmdPBP, UInt16 launchFlags)
{
    Err          error;
    UInt16       cfgIndex, libRefNum;     // Reference # INet lib.
    MemHandle    inetHan, inetSockH;
    Char         *responsePtr;
    UInt32       totalBytes, bytesRead, reqestedBytes, offset = 0;
    UInt32       downloadSize = MAX_RESPONSE_SIZE;
    UInt32       algorithm = ctpConvNone; /* no conversion */

    if (cmd == sysAppLaunchCmdNormalLaunch)
    {
        /* find INetLib - a Palm OS shared library */
        error = SysLibFind("INet.lib", &libRefNum);
        HandleError(error);

        /* allocate memory to hold the file retrieved */
        responsePtr = MemPtrNew(MAX_RESPONSE_SIZE);
        HandleError(responsePtr == NULL);

        /* choose whether to use wireline connection or wireless */
        error = INetLibConfigIndexFromName(libRefNum, &cfgName,
                    &cfgIndex);
        HandleError(error);

        /* open the library */
        error = INetLibOpen(libRefNum, cfgIndex, 0, NULL, 0,
&inetHan);
        HandleError(error);
```

Continued

Figure 11.1 Continued

```
/* Set the default settings for buffer size and conversion
 * algorithm to be used */
error = INetLibSettingSet(libRefNum, inetHan,
    inetSettingMaxRspSize, (UInt8*)&downloadSize,
    sizeof(downloadSize));
HandleError(error);
error = INetLibSettingSet(libRefNum, inetHan,
        inetSettingConvAlgorithm, (UInt8*)&algorithm,
        sizeof(algorithm));
HandleError(error);

/* start the fetch of URL. This command merely "starts" the
 * the communication, you should read the result explicitly
 * from the socket by making another call.
 */
error = INetLibURLOpen(libRefNum, inetHan,
            (UInt8 *)SERVER_URL, NULL, &inetSockH, -1, 0);
HandleError(error);
reqestedBytes = 4096;
totalBytes = bytesRead = 0;
do
{
    /* read something from the socket - blocking call */
    error = INetLibSockRead(libRefNum, inetSockH,
                responsePtr + totalBytes,
                reqestedBytes - totalBytes,
                &bytesRead, 20 * SysTicksPerSecond());

    /* update our pointers for the next write */
    offset += bytesRead;
    totalBytes += bytesRead;
```

Continued

Figure 11.1 Continued

```
        } while (
                        (bytesRead != 0) && /* until the peer is done */
                        !error &&           /* or until the first error
*/
                        /* or we downloaded too much already */
                        (totalBytes < MAX_RESPONSE_SIZE)
                    );

        if (totalBytes > 0) /* got something? */
        {
            responsePtr[totalBytes] = 0;
            FrmCustomAlert(ServerResponse, responsePtr, NULL, NULL);
        }
        else
            FrmCustomAlert(ConnectionError,
                "No response from server", NULL, NULL);
        /* final cleanup code */
        MemPtrFree(responsePtr);
        INetLibSockClose(libRefNum, inetSockH);
        INetLibClose(libRefNum, inetHan);
    }

    return 0;
}
```

This may be one of the biggest Hello World programs you have ever seen, but many Palm OS programs are much larger. This program has been stripped to the essential steps needed to fetch a URL from the Internet.

Developing & Deploying...

Setting Up Your Development Environment

If you choose C/C++ as your preferred language, you have two choices for your development environment:

- **PRC-Tools** Based on GCC, the open source GNU compiler, with your choice of integrated development environment (IDE).
- **CodeWarrior for Palm OS Platform** From Metrowerks and Palm, Inc. available on the companion CD.

Although PRC-Tools does not come packaged with an IDE, you can use any IDE that works with GNU compilers. Two popular choices tailored specifically for Palm OS programming are Falch.net Studio and PilotMAG.

The Metrowerks CodeWarrior IDE, on the other hand, is a completely integrated environment with compiler, editor, and debugger built in. It also includes a resource editor called Constructor and a resource compiler. Constructor for Palm OS—now owned, maintained, and supported by Palm, Inc.—lets you design your user interface in a graphical environment.

Both PRC-Tools and CodeWarrior use the Palm OS software development kit (SDK), distributed by Palm, Inc. Hence, any code developed using one environment is portable to the other. However, resources created in Constructor are stored in MacOS resource format. Some IDEs, such as Falch.net Studio, provide an import tool to convert Constructor-based resources to the text format used by the Pilot Resource Compiler (PilRC). After the resources are available in PilRC format, you may use it with CodeWarrior by adding a special PilRC plug-in to the IDE. We have used this setup for the examples in this chapter to keep the code compatible between PRC-Tools and CodeWarrior.

For more information on setting up these development environments, see www.palmos.com/dev/gettingstarted.html. CodeWarrior includes project stationery that provide a skeleton for your project, while the Falch.net IDE includes similar wizards that work with PRC-Tools.

Running the Hello World Program

You must have the Palm OS Emulator (POSE) running with a Palm OS ROM v3.2 or above. Please refer to Chapter 2 for instructions on how to download and set up POSE. If you plan to use LZ77 compression, explained later in this book, make sure that you have LZ77Mgr compression library, which is part of Palm OS 4.0. If you are using Palm OS 3.5, you may download the LZ77Mgr library as part of the INetLow example from www.palmos.com. Installing a PRC file is identical to the steps for installing a Palm Query Application (PQA) file—you can drag and drop the PRC file into POSE or choose the **Install Application/ Database** option from the POSE context-menu. Tap on the application icon and you will see the contents of the text file displayed on the screen after a few seconds, as shown in Figure 11.2. Because our application does not have a full-screen form, the rest of the screen will be blank.

Figure 11.2 Hello World Application

In some cases, your application may instead display an error message. Possible error situations include the following:

- Your device does not have INetLib library.
- The URL in Hello_World.c is invalid.
- Palm.Net proxy is unable to reach your server.
- The URL is correct, but your Web server had an internal error.
- The particular INetLib configuration requested is not valid.

Unfortunately, our application does not handle these errors separately. If INetLib is missing, it will produce a fatal error message and reset the device. In all other cases, our application merely displays "No response from server," as shown in Figure 11.3. As we advance through this chapter, we will discuss ways to detect and handle these error conditions.

Figure 11.3 Error Message from the Hello World Application

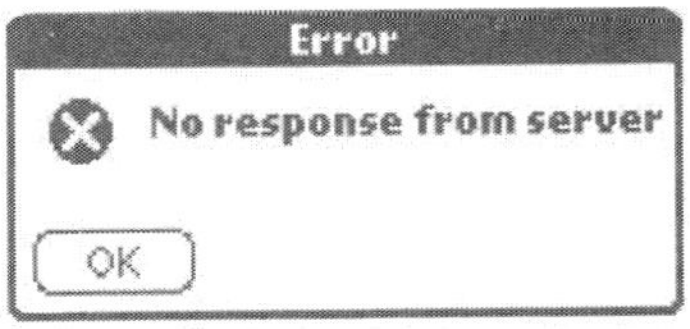

Debugging...

Proxy Settings

If you are running this Hello World program on a device that has never been used for Web clipping, make sure that you have set up the proxy server address correctly. Any changes to a proxy server address will be published on www.palmos.com and on Web Clipping Announcements Forum. If you experience problems accessing the proxy server from your native application, test at least a few of the well-known PQAs on the same device before you decide to debug your application.

Anatomy of the Hello World Program

This section gives a short description of the Hello World program given in Figure 11.1. Detailed explanations of each of the functions are given in the sections that follow. The entry point is **PilotMain()**, just like **main()** in desktop C programs. When the user taps on the icon on the screen, Palm OS will launch our application by calling **PilotMain()**. Notice that three arguments are passed to the program: a *command number*, a *parameter string*, and *launch flags*. Most of our code is inside an *if-block*, which executes only when the application receives a "normal" launch command. In this chapter, we will only be concerned with the "normal" launch code. All of our code will either be inside this if-block or as functions that are called from inside this block. Other launch codes are related to desktop synchronization, the "find" utility, and so forth; launch codes other than *sysAppLaunchCmdNormalLaunch* are merely ignored by this program.

The INetLib library is provided as a Palm OS shared library. Certain steps need to be taken to use any standard Palm OS library. First, we must find the library using the system call **SysLibFind**. **SysLibFind** takes the name of the library as its argument and returns a reference number to the library via one of the parameters. This reference number must be passed back to all subsequent calls to the library. The reference number is actually an index to a table, which helps Palm OS identify the right place to redirect your call.

```
error = SysLibFind("INet.lib", &libRefNum);
```

Debugging...

Handling Fatal Errors

In the Hello World example, errors are handled by *fatal alerts*, which will alert the user and then reset the system. You may see these kind of fatal alerts used in examples throughout this book as well as in other Palm OS examples elsewhere. A real-world example must produce a warning to the user and bail out of the program gracefully. Even though "resetting" the system may sound strange, this is a common trick in Palm OS programming, particularly when handling unusual circumstances. A missing library is one such case. Resetting the device is not as slow as a desktop "reboot" and it will make sure that all resources are properly released. This is particularly useful when developing prototype or proof-of-concept applications. Alert methods other than **ErrFatalDisplayIf** usually require additional user interface resources attached to the program. Hence, this method is also used in libraries and many internal routines of Palm OS where such resources are not available.

Fatal alerts also serve as breakpoints while debugging an application. If an application running under POSE issues a fatal alert, POSE traps the alert and gives three options to the developer: continue, break into the debugger, or reset. Once you break into the debugger, it would be identical to a regular breakpoint. The **continue** option is very handy and it makes a fatal alert just as common as printf in a desktop console application or MsgBox in a Visual Basic application. Note that the continue option is available only on POSE. This option would be too dangerous on a real device. Hence, the real device always resets the device upon fatal alert.

The next set of calls allocates memory to hold the response received from the server. **MemPtrNew** is identical to the C standard library's Multicast Address Allocation (malloc). **INetLibConfigIndexFromName** is used to choose a configuration: wireless or wireline. The wireless configuration will use the radio, whereas the wireline configuration will use either a regular clip-on modem or a wireless modem like Minstrel. The next call to **INetLibSettingSet** is passed certain parameters that will force the library not to use any compression. If we had not given that parameter, the Palm.Net server would have converted the response in a form suitable for HTML browsing using Clipper.

The real work of fetching the URL is done by the **INetLibURLOpen** call. It will initiate a GET request for the URL and return from the function. However, it will not wait until the HTTP transaction is over. Naturally, the data is also not returned by this function. The application is expected to call **INetLibSockRead** to fetch the server response. Soon after **INetLibURLOpen** is called, we enter a loop with **INetLibSockRead**. **INetLibSockRead** will block until the data is available. We continue to read data, a piece at a time, until **INetLibSockRead** returns zero for the data length. This indicates that no further data exists. After the data is fetched, it is displayed to the user via an alert. After we are done, we close the INetLib session by closing the associated socket and also closing the library. You may have already noticed that the program is badly structured, does not handle errors properly, and does not even let the user cancel the transaction. However, it describes the basic steps required for an INetLib session. As we proceed, we develop a complete native application to access the Unwired Widgets Web site.

NOTE

OmniSky users may see text appended to the end of the server response when fetching HTML files. The OmniSky servers add this unexpected text which normally appears as "help" and "home" links at the bottom of the page in PQAs. More details are given in the "Testing for Proxy Issues and Known Bugs" section, under "OmniSky Servers," later in this chapter.

Finding and Initializing Internet Library

The Hello World example in Figure 11.1 makes many assumptions about the operating environment. Until recently, Internet Library was available only on version 3.2 or above of Palm OS on Palm VII devices (INetLib was also supported on devices enabled with OmniSky's service). With the recent releases of Palm OS

(3.5 and 4.0), this library is an optional component and can be added to any device. Moreover, with many different hardware vendors, keeping track of devices that support Internet Library is impossible. This is not an issue with Web clipping applications, because your application will never be invoked or used if the Internet library is not available. However, because our application is distributed as a standalone PRC file, we must verify that we are running on a compatible device. A device that runs a Web clipping application will be capable of running your application, because they use the same library.

Checking for the Internet Feature

Palm OS documentation describes a method to check if Internet Library is installed. Applications can access a *feature* to verify if the Internet Library is installed. Although the Palm OS documentation and the sample provided on Palm's Web site suggests checking this feature, there is no documentation anywhere on why this is required. Your application will detect the problem when you try to open the library using **SysLibFind** (explained in the next section). Therefore, in our opinion, this step is not necessary. Moreover, there are certain devices in which this feature is not set until the first invocation of Clipper. We normally check features to find out whether a certain system call is available. This is because system calls are implemented using *direct traps,* special instructions that invoke behavior in the operating system, and there is no way to determine if a trap is implemented or not. However, that is not the case with INetLib, which is a shared library. Shared libraries use an *indirect trap* mechanism that requires the reference number argument obtained from **SysLibFind**. If you insist on checking this feature (and sticking to the documentation), the following code will do the trick. None of the examples in this book check for this feature.

```
value = 0;
error = FtrGet(INetLibFtrCreator, inetFtrNumVersion, &value);
if (error || !value) { /* INetLib is not installed */ }
else { /* call SysLibFind(), and then use library */ }
```

Developing & Deploying...

Using Features

Features are similar in certain ways to registry entries in Windows. Palm OS provides a mechanism to GET and SET features based on a *creator ID* and a *feature number*. The creator ID parameter identifies the developer and helps avoid conflicts between features used by different applications. The feature number argument is used as an index to an array of features used by the same application. After a feature is set, it remains "set" until it is unregistered or the device is reset. This functionality is similar to the Windows Registry but without the hierarchy or complex data.

Whenever an application needs to flag something to other Palm OS applications, it uses features to do so. This is especially used in situations where you cannot pass the data via the normal channels (stack, global variable, and so on). In the case of the example in this section, Internet Library sets this flag to announce to the rest of the world that it exists.

Finding the Internet Library

The Internet Library is provided as a shared library. Before they are used, Palm OS shared libraries must be loaded using **SysLibLoad**. This API will open the library resource database, locate the entry points to the library functions, and lock the library in memory. The entry points to library functions are stored in a dispatch table. Each Palm OS library that is open will have its own dispatch table. Palm OS also provides a function named **SysLibFind** that returns a library "reference number" to the caller. This reference number will uniquely identify the library (and hence its dispatch table) among all other libraries that are open. Moreover, library functions are accessed via a system trap interface that takes this reference number as its first argument. Users (programmers) will never have to worry about how traps are called, but you can always look at the Palm OS header files or the Palm OS Knowledge Base to get more insights. The following code locates INet.lib and retrieves its reference number:

```
UInt16  libRefNum = 0;
error = SysLibFind("INet.lib", &libRefNum);
```

NOTE

The reference number returned by **SysLibFind** has always been a problem to library designers as well as users. Unlike shared library mechanisms on Windows and Unix, the mechanics of a shared library are not transparent to the user. The library reference number is required in all subsequent calls and will have to be maintained as a global variable, a static variable, a Palm OS feature, or something similar.

Initializing the Internet Library

With the Palm OS 3.5 release of INetLib, the library can be used to fetch data over a regular modem or any other TCP/IP network connection.

Palm OS 4.0 provides a setting under the Preferences panel for the user to select his default connection. You can either use that setting or provide your own user interface to make this selection. The user will then have the choice to use the application over the radio, a wireless modem such as Minstrel, or the clip-on modem at any time. Your application can also restrict usage over any particular channel by requesting Internet Library to use one or the other.

Choosing a Configuration

A configuration is a specific set of values for several of the Internet library settings. **INetLibOpen** API function takes a configuration index value that points to one of the predefined configurations. A configuration defines the channel to be used. **INetLibConfigIndexFromName** can be used to find the index by providing a name for the configuration. Table 11.1 summarizes the default configurations available.

Table 11.1 Default INetLib Configurations

Alias	String Value	Description
InetCfgNameDefault	*.Default*	Generic configuration with no proxy. Uses Network panel settings.
InetCfgNameDefWireline	*.DefWireline*	Generic configuration with no proxy. Uses Network panel settings.

Continued

Table 11.1 Continued

Alias	String Value	Description
InetCfgNameDefWireless	*.DefWireless*	Generic configuration with no proxy. Uses Network panel settings.
InetCfgNameCTPDefault	*.CTPDefault*	Points to *.CTPWireless* on Palm VII and *.CTPWireline* on others.
InetCfgNameCTPWireline	*.CTPWireline*	Points to a wireline configuration that uses the Palm Web clipping proxy server.
InetCfgNameCTPWireless	*.CTPWireless*	Points to a wireless configuration that uses the Palm VII radio and the Palm Web clipping proxy server.

Your application can use any of these configurations. If your application is running on a device previous to version 4.0, you may provide an interface to the user to make this selection. Otherwise you may want to choose just one of the interfaces. Examples in this chapter do not try to provide such a user interface, but we have provided a "ConfigBrowser" example under the section "Providing Configuration Aliases."You may refer to that example for sample code.You can also install and run the program to view configurations available on your device. A ready-to-run copy of the compiled PRC will be available on the CD that accompanies this book. For now, ignore other details provided by the ConfigBrowser program.

In Table 11.1, we listed what was available to you according to Palm OS documentation—but in reality, only three of these configurations are currently really useful: **inetCfgNameCTPWireless**, **inetCfgNameCTPWireline**, and **inetCfgNameCTPDefault**, which points to one of the other two. Other configurations try to connect to the server directly without the proxy but still expect the other side to do a proxy's job.The result is that you will get HTTP headers included in the reply even if you request INetLib not to include headers. In those modes, INetLib is not very useful because it does not do anything other than connect to port 80. Even if you manage to parse the headers out and extract the data, it is probably not a reliable method because the Palm OS documentation does not give any information about such behavior.These options are probably meant for other vendors to substitute Palm.Net with their own proxies.This is the behavior of INetLib as of Palm OS version 4.0, and it may change in future releases.

Creating an INetLib Connection

After you decide on the configuration you want to use, you must open the Internet Library using the **INetLibOpen** call. **INetLibOpen** takes many arguments, one of which is the configuration index you chose in the previous section. In addition, you can also specify whether you would like to make use of the cache or not. For standalone applications, using cache may not be appropriate, but then again, it depends on your application. After the INetLib is opened, you have the option to fine-tune the connection parameters before you actually initiate an HTTP transaction.

Choosing a Conversion Algorithm

Conversion algorithms determine the translation done on the data by the proxy server. The Internet Library provides four choices. The choices are indicated by the enumeration constants *ctpConvCML*, *ctpConvCML8Bit*, *ctpConvNoneLZ77*, and *ctpConvNone*. If your application must run on an existing Palm VII device with the existing proxy, you essentially get only one of the options: *ctpConvNone*. This instructs the server not to make any conversions. You can also use the *ctpConvCML* if you are ready to program a decoder for CML, Palm's proprietary format. The following sections explain each conversion algorithm.

Five-Bit CML Conversion (*ctpConvCML*)

The 5-bit CML conversion is the method used by Clipper and is probably useful only for Clipper. The conversion algorithm is optimized for a typical HTML page of English text. All characters are encoded using a 5-bit scheme. So naturally, the scheme can only accommodate 32 different values. The first six values (0 through 5) are used for escape sequences and control characters, and the remaining 26 are used for the 26 lowercase characters. Any ASCII value that does not belong to this group would be represented by an escape pattern: *cmlCharEsc* (2), followed by the 8-bit value. Because most of the characters occupy only 5 bits, they are bit-packed together—approximately 8 CML-encoded characters can fit in 5 bytes. You can find more information on CML encoding from Palm File Format Spec.pdf, part of Palm OS SDK 4.0 documentation, which is available for download from www.palmos.com/dev/tech/docs. Although both PQA files as well as server response use CML format, Palm OS documentation does not describe the exact over-the-air format, which may include additional headers.

One disadvantage to using this conversion method is that a CML decoder must be developed, because the one used by Clipper is part of Clipper's code and unavailable to applications. This would also involve some reverse engineering and is certainly not worth the effort. Also, your data may not fit within the range of characters for which CML is optimal.

Eight-Bit CML Conversion (*ctpConvCML8Bit*)

The 8-bit CML conversion will be identical to *ctpConvCML*, except that the bit packing is left out. Because 5-bit encoded characters are difficult to decipher, you may use this option for debugging your application. Again, this is only useful if you have your own CML decoder.

LZ77 Compression (*ctpConvNoneLZ77*)

The new Palm.Net proxy supports LZ77 compression. When used, the Palm.Net proxy will compress data going to the device using the 1977 Lempel-Ziv (LZ) algorithm. The application on the device can make use of "Lz77.lib" to decompress the response. This library is provided as a standard part of Web clipping with Palm OS 4.0 and can be downloaded separately for Palm OS 3.5 devices. It is included as LZ77lib.prc file in the INetLow sample, part of 4.0 SDK. It is also available in the Palm OS 3.5 version of InetLow, which is available from Knowledge Base. Though we never have to worry about LZ77 on the server side, many LZ77 implementations (and variants) are available for desktops—including "deflation" which is used in zlib compression library, gzip, and others.

NOTE

LZ77 is available only with the new version of the Palm.Net proxy server, codenamed Elaine. Unfortunately, there is no way to determine the version of the proxy programmatically. At the time of this writing, content-dev2.palm.net is the new proxy and content-dev.palm.net is the old one. Incompatibilities exist between the new and old servers, as explained later in this chapter in Table 11.2. Installing LZ77Lib.prc on your device gives your handheld the ability to support LZ77 compression, but to support LZ77, both the client and server must support the compression scheme.

If you have been planning to optimize your server output by using a proprietary 8-bit format, you may want to consider this option. You are probably better off leaving the server output as the inefficient 7-bit format and have the Palm servers do the compression for you. Problems with debugging the binary response itself may justify the use of plain-text response from the server. See the section "Optimizing Transport" later in this chapter for a more detailed discussion.

No Conversion (*ctpConvNone*)

You will usually use the *ctpConvNone* conversion setting if LZ77 is not available. This tells the Palm.Net proxy that you want your data passed from your server without changes.

Setting Conversion Algorithms for the Connection

The conversion method is set using **INetLibSettingSet**, which is a generic API to set all INetLib settings. All calls to **INetLibSettingSet** take a parameter identifier (*inetSettingConvAlgorithm*, in this case), the parameter, and its length. The API copies the passed bytes to INetLib's internal data structures. Because different settings have different sizes, **INetLibSettingSet** cannot determine the number of bytes to copy on its own, so the caller is expected to pass along the size of the setting. For example, the setting *inetSettingRadioID* (a 64-bit value) occupies 8 bytes, while **inetSettingConvAlgorithm** occupies only 4 bytes. The last parameter provides the number of bytes to copy.

```
UInt32 convAlgorithm = ctpConvNoneLZ77;
error = INetLibSettingSet(libRefNum, inetHan,
            inetSettingConvAlgorithm, (UInt8*)&convAlgorithm,
sizeof(convAlgorithm));
```

Debugging...

Header File Inconsistencies

If you are working with Palm OS 3.5 SDK as well as Palm OS 4.0 SDK, you may notice some inconsistencies in the enumeration names of CTP constants. CTP.h, which is included as part of 3.5 SDK, defines *CTPConvEnum* as follows (comments have been trimmed to fit the page):

```
typedef enum {
ctpConvCML = 0, // CML
```

Continued

```
    ctpConvCML8Bit = 1, // CML in 8-bit debug form
    ctpConvCMLLZ77 = 2, // CML with LZSS
    ctpConvNone = 3     // Return in native Web format.
} CTPConvEnum;
```

While CTP.h in 4.0 SDK defines CTPConvEnum as:

```
typedef enum {
    ctpConvCML = 0,         // CML
    ctpConvCML8Bit,         // CML in 8-bit debug form
    ctpConvNoneLZ77, // Raw data with LZ77 (No primer)
    ctpConvNone, // Return in native Web format.
    ctpConvBest, // Best compression between .....
    ctpConvCMLLZ77Primer1 // Lz77 Primer#1 (English Clipper)
} CTPConvEnum;
```

When 3.5 SDK was released, LZ77 was never implemented, and you probably would not have used any of the values shown in bold. However, if you are porting any recent code written using 3.5 SDK to 4.0 SDK, you should not be surprised when the compiler complains about an undefined variable *ctpConvCMLLZ77*. Simply replace it with *ctpConvNoneLZ77*. Also, make sure you do not confuse *CTPConvEnum* with *INetCompressionTypeEnum*. Although the lists look similar, they are not identical in their values:

```
typedef enum {
    inetCompressionTypeNone = 0,
    inetCompressionTypeBitPacked,
    inetCompressionTypeLZ77,
    inetCompressionTypeBest,
    inetCompressionTypeLZ77Primer1
} INetCompressionTypeEnum;
```

Maximum Response Size

Another commonly used INetLib setting is *inetSettingMaxRspSize*. It species the maximum number of bytes the application expects to receive as response from the server. The server may send more data, and the proxy will discard anything that exceeds this limit. The proxy will not make sure that the truncated data is a well-formed document. This means that your response parser must be tolerant enough to handle truncated data.

You should set this parameter to a value high enough to accommodate any large response you expect to receive from the server. Tests have shown that you cannot set this value above 32K. Although the server truncates larger responses, the truncation is arbitrary and may not occur exactly at the limit specified. Moreover, if you use LZ77 compression, the parameter specifies the number of compressed bytes transmitted. LZ77 decompression could expand the data easily up to five or six times the compressed size. Because you are controlling both sides of the application, make your server-side script fragment data into smaller chunks. The *inetSettingMaxRspSize* parameter is set by the following call:

```
UInt32 maxSize = 4096;

error = INetLibSettingSet(libRefNum, inetHan, inetSettingMaxRspSize,
(UInt8*)&maxSize, sizeof(maxSize));
```

Moving to an Event-Driven Model

Before we explore any more complex examples, we must learn how to make our program event-driven. Tight loops like the one mentioned in Figure 11.1 tie up the user interface and even consume more battery power by keeping the CPU busy. We are blocking every other Palm OS function while waiting for the response from the server. Moreover, the user is forced to spend his time staring at the screen. Although Palm OS does not support multithreaded programming for users, some system libraries such as INetLib, NetLib, and the Serial Library execute in their own threads. This means that users of INetLib don't have to wait for data to arrive using a blocking call such as **INetLibSockRead**. Instead, the Palm OS event mechanism will notify us when the data is available in the socket. The following paragraph briefly explains how the notification works.

A Quick Introduction to the Palm OS Event Model

Palm OS maintains a queue of events that applications and libraries can use to exchange data. For example, when the user taps on the screen, the interrupt handler will identify the x and y coordinates and deliver the tap as an *event* to the queue. A native application can retrieve this event by calling a Palm OS function

EvtGetEvent. If any events are available in the queue, **EvtGetEvent** will return immediately with the event. Otherwise, it will block until an event is available or until a timeout period expires. Please note that a *tap* consists of a *penDownEvent* followed by a *penUpEvent*. For the sake of simplicity, we just consider it as one event. A basic event loop is as follows:

```
do {
        EvtGetEvent(&event, evtWaitForever);
        /* process events */
} while (event.eType != appStopEvent)
```

EvtGetEvent normally returns only events directly related to hardware: penDown and penUp events. **EvtGetEvent** cannot notify you that a certain button was pressed, because the operating system has no idea where you have drawn the button. Because most of the user interface is managed by the Form manager routines, we need to pass these pen events to the Form manager and then let it decide if the tap was really on top of a button or not. Similarly, the operating system needs to handle many events—for example, powering down the display when the **Power** button is pressed. So a well-behaved application must pass the events down to three other operating system functions: **SysHandleEvent**, **MenuHandleEvent**, and **FrmDispatchEvent**. The last call serves to route events to your form's event handler function and then to the system if your code doesn't handle them. The updated event loop is as follows:

```
do
{
    EvtGetEvent(&event, evtWaitForever);

    // Handle event
    if (!SysHandleEvent(&event))
     if (!MenuHandleEvent(0, &event, &error))
        if (!ApplicationHandleEvent(&event))
           FrmDispatchEvent(&event);

} while (event.eType != appStopEvent);
```

You might have noticed that your application gives control to **SysHandleEvent** only if it decides to do so. This way, Palm OS gives lot more control to the application. For example, your application can decide whether it should let the user "power down" the device or not. Of course, that would be a "rude" thing to do and your application will not be certified, but you get the picture.

Apart from hardware interrupt handlers, libraries and applications can use the event manager to pass data around. Some of these libraries are intelligent enough to hook into **EvtGetEvent** by patching the system trap used for the call. This means that the programmer need not do anything special to get those events, because they get returned in the usual manner. Unfortunately, for whatever reason that Palm may have, INetLib requires the caller to use a special substitute for **EvtGetEvent**, called **INetLibGetEvent**. This call does everything that **EvtGetEvent** does and more—the "more" being the job of returning INetLib events.

INetEventType and **EventType** structs are identical in size and any one may be used in place of the other. Throughout the example code, you will see event pointers type casted from one to the other. It is perfectly safe to do so, and we do it only to get access to certain values inside the event struct.

```
do
{
    INetLibGetEvent(inetRefNum, inetHan,
        (INetEventType*)&event, evtWaitForever);

            // Handle event
            if (!SysHandleEvent(&event))
     if (!MenuHandleEvent(0, &event, &error))
         if (!ApplicationHandleEvent(&event))
             FrmDispatchEvent(&event);

} while (event.eType != appStopEvent);
```

INetLib Events

INetLib uses two events to communicate its status to caller applications: *inetSockStatusChangeEvent* and *inetSockReadyEvent*. As you may have guessed from the name, *inetSockStatusChangeEvent* is issued whenever a change occurs in the status of INetLib or your request. *inetSockReadyEvent* is issued when data is available for read via **INetLibSockRead**. The event data structures associated with these events contain more details on status change. The event structure will contain one of the following structs depending on the event:

```
struct  {
   MemHandle   sockH;
   UInt32      context;
   Boolean     inputReady;
   Boolean     outputReady;
} inetSockReady;

struct  {
   MemHandle    sockH;
   UInt32       context;
   UInt16       status;
   Err          sockErr;
} inetSockStatusChange;
```

INetEventType, like *EventType*, is declared as a union of C structures, and it is up to us to interpret it as either an *inetSockStatusChange* struct or an *inetSockReady* struct. We do that based on the event type.

When an application receives an *inetSockStatusChange* event, the *data.inetSockStatusChange.status* field will contain the status change. A list of status changes is given in INetLibEvent.h and is self-explanatory. Our sample application uses all of these events, so you can look at the source code for more information. If your application is not interested in providing a "progress" indicator, you can completely ignore *inetSockStatusChange* events, because the *inetSockReady* event signals you when the server response has finally reached the device.

URLFetch: An Improvement on Hello World

Although we can add the event mechanism just described to our Hello World application, we will instead create a new application. We will also add a basic Palm OS application framework to this sample. The sample will have the following features:

- It will have a text field to accept the URL input rather than a hard-coded URL value.

- It will have a database that will collect server response. This will also enable us to display responses that are more than one page.
- It will include an event-driven application that will enable us to cancel an existing request or initiate a new request.
- It will use different INetLib configurations.
- It will have better error handling.

Understanding the URLFetch Example

We have used two freeware tools to auto-generate documentation for URLFetch. The first tool, CCDOC, a freeware application written by Joe Linoff, generates javadoc-style documentation for the functions. The second tool, LXR, part of the Linux Cross Reference Project, generates a HTML cross-referenced version of source code.

We now go through a few important Palm OS concepts introduced in the URLFetch example. The descriptions are very brief, and we assume that you are familiar with C programming on another platform. Otherwise, you may want to refer to one of the books dedicated to Palm OS programming in C.

Palm OS Device Databases

Unlike desktop databases, Palm OS device databases are very limited in functionality. A database contains a sequence of records, where each record can store any chunk of data from 1 to 64K. The database library has no knowledge of what is inside each record. The Database Manager provides an API to create records, delete records, and write arbitrary chunks of data inside a record. Because the database resides in the Palm device's RAM, no specific function exists to read a record; we can open a record and directly access its contents via a pointer.

User Interface: Lists and Fields

The List Manager provides a very simple API to create and display lists. We can use the PilRC resource editor to specify the location and size of the list.

```
LIST "" ResponseListRsps AT (2 16 156 117) VISIBLEITEMS 9
```

After the form is loaded, we use **LstSetListChoices** to set the number of entries. We do not pass any data to the List Manager, but instead opt to have a callback function called to draw each entry. Usually, List Manager expects the caller to pass all the display data as an array of strings. In this example, we take the burden of drawing the list ourselves. This gives us the convenience to read records one by one and avoid making duplicate copies of data, which saves memory. The callback function reads the record and draws one row of data within the bounds specified by the caller, the List Manager.

The application switches to "ViewResponse" form when the user taps on any item. We use a text field to display the contents of the record on to the screen. Because this is a noneditable text field, its usage is very simple.

```
FldSetTextPtr(fldPtr, recPtr);
     // Where fldPtr points to the field structure and recPtr points
     // the record which is opened and locked.
```

Browsing the Documentation

You can browse the documentation by opening ccodc.index.html in the Hello_World directory. The links to source files within the documentation point to the Unwired Widgets Web site. We have made the source available on a cross-reference tool called LXR. LXR enables us to link identifiers and functions to their definitions and references. Moreover, as we proceed into the URLFetch example, you will be able to compare different versions of the URLFetch example and see what has changed. If you already have a code browser such as SourceInsight, you can directly browse the local CD copy.

Accessing a Server-Side Application

The previous example fetched a file from the Internet. If we need to access a server-side application instead of a file, the client does not need any changes. As far as the client is concerned, the data is retrieved by a GET request, and any application that can respond to a GET request can provide data to this client.

How Server-Side Applications Differ from Web Clipping

Server applications that used Clipper for display used HTML or plain text as their output format. Using HTML was the easiest way to display the data on a Palm OS device. However, unlike Clipper, your native applications are more interested in the real data rather than its presentation. Displays are now managed by your own code using the native Palm OS user interface. If we use our custom application to access the Web pages developed in Chapters 5 through 8, we will find that we will need to parse HTML data, and then extract the data from it. This is a very tedious and unreliable method. Because we control both sides of the application, it makes sense to provide raw data to the client.

Data can be sent to a client in any format negotiated by both client and server. The easiest solution is to send a serialized form of server-side data structure to the client. For example, the server application may send the order information as a comma-separated stream of items. A more elegant solution is to use a standard data-exchange format like XML. XML is very similar to HTML, except that tags are used to create a hierarchy of data rather than to display elements (you can find more information on XML from www.w3.org/XML). The complexity of the data format chosen directly determines the complexity of your client-side code. If you choose XML as your data format, you would also need an XML parser on the client. Even though this adds a significant amount of code to your application, it would improve the manageability of your code. If you prefer efficiency to manageability, you can also use your own proprietary format that uses 8-bit data. See the section on "Optimizing Transport" later in this chapter for a more detailed discussion.

Using POST Operations

Issuing a POST request is little more complicated than GET. We were using **INetLibURLOpen**, which is actually a wrapper around a couple of other INetLib functions that do the real work. We have to abandon **INetLibURLOpen** for two reasons: **INetLibURLOpen** does not support POST operations, and it does not give you complete control of the socket settings. The following section describes the steps involved to perform more complex HTTP transactions using INetLib.

Opening the Socket

INetLib allows us to make four parallel connections at the same time. It uses a *socket* to identify each connection. A socket is an entity that defines the end points of a communication. In a desktop operating system, a socket includes the IP address, port number, and protocol used for either ends of a communication pipe. The port number lets the operating system route the incoming packets to the appropriate application, and the socket data structure allows the application to distinguish the packet among all the connections it has made. INetLib sockets differ from standard BSD sockets; both allow sending and receiving data over the network, but INetLib is limited to connecting out from the device to a server, while standard sockets also allow the system to wait for an incoming connection.

INetLibSockOpen creates a new socket and returns a handle for use in all subsequent INetLib calls. It is declared as:

```
Err INetLibSockOpen(UInt16 libRefNum, MemHandle inetH, UInt16 scheme,
    MemHandle *sockHP);
```

The arguments *libRefNum* and *inetH* are the usual arguments as given to all of the INetLib calls. The *scheme* argument must be one of the values in the enumeration *INetSchemeEnum*.

Even though it might seem that INetLib supports all these protocols, the scheme argument is ignored by INetLib at least until the 4.0 DR4 release. However, this does not give us the freedom to pass anything we want—we should still stick with the documentation. Also note that the MemHandle is *returned to the caller.* This means that we need not allocate any buffer for the socket, except to store the MemHandle itself. You must declare a MemHandle object and pass its address to the function. Upon return, if the error value is not set, this handle points to the socket created.

INetLibSockOpen does not initiate any communication. It just creates and prepares a socket for the real communication later.

Associating the Socket with an HTTP Request

INetLibSockHTTPReqCreate creates an HTTP request and associates it with a socket. It is declared as:

```
Err INetLibSockHTTPReqCreate (UInt16 libRefnum, MemHandle sockH,
    UInt8 * verbP, UInt8 * resNameP, UInt8 * refererP);
```

LibRefNum and *inetH* are the usual arguments to all INetLib calls as described before. The *verbP* argument should denote whether the request is a GET or POST. They are denoted by strings "GET" and "POST" respectively. As of Palm OS 4.0, the argument is ignored by INetLib. Later, when you call **INetLibSockHTTPReqSend**, (described later), INetLib sets the operation as POST or GET depending on whether the data argument is empty or not. There is probably a good reason for Palm OS to ignore the argument (a more detailed explanation is given in the next section). *ResNameP* should contain the complete URI of the resource. This includes the "http://" or "https://" scheme prefix, the hostname, and the path. Rather than use the scheme argument to

INetLibSockOpen, INetLib checks the first few characters of the *resNameP* to identify the scheme.

WARNING

If you forget to include "https://" as part of the *resNameP*, you may find that your HTTPS transaction was degraded to HTTP even if you specified the *inetSchemeHTTPS* argument to **INetLibSockOpen()**. Unfortunately, INetLib does not warn you about this mistake.

Preparing HTTP Data

Most HTTP transactions involve passing name and value pairs as part of the request. Any data passed from a client to a Web server must be sent as part of the request body or as part of the URL in the request header. However you choose to send it, the data must be encoded using either **application/x-www-form-urlencoded** or **multipart/form-data**. The encoding is done so that the receiving side can decode and extract the name–value pairs without data corruption. You can also send data as part of the URL path. Web servers such as Apache support addressing a URL of the form "http://x.y.com/a/b.pl" as "http://x.y.com/a/b.pl/c/d/e/f/g", where any amount of text can be appended after the name of the executable. Apache will still invoke b.pl and the complete URL will be available to the Common Gateway Interface (CGI) program as a *path_info* environment variable. This is a very nice trick for sending data to a CGI program without changing GET or POST data. Browsers always retain this portion of text even while following links helping us maintain "sessions". Some systems, such as Microsoft Internet Information Server (IIS), use cookies to maintain sessions, which are easily supported on the Palm OS device. See Chapter 8 for more details.

The **multipart/form-data** content type is used for uploading files from Web browsers. The usual type used is **application/x-www-form-urlencoded**, which is the default content type. Forms submitted with this content type must be encoded as follows:

- Control names and values are escaped. Space characters are replaced by a plus sign (+), and nonalphanumeric characters are replaced by %HH, that is, a percent sign and two hexadecimal digits representing the ASCII code of the character. Line breaks are represented as "CR LF" pairs (for example, %0D%0A). Spaces can also be encoded as %20, the hexadecimal form of ASCII 32, the space.

- The control names/values are listed in the order they appear in the document. The name is separated from the value by an equals sign (=), and name/value pairs are separated from each other by an ampersand (&).

Developing & Deploying...

MIME Types

Multipurpose Internet Mail Extensions (MIME) was proposed in 1992 to handle multipart textual and nontextual content in Internet mail messages. As early as 1985 (Request for Comments [RFC] 904), and 1988 (RFC 1049), researchers started defining methods to encode nontextual information passed around in mail messages. The newest MIME standard is RFC 2045. Initially, this standard was intended only for mail messages. Later on, MIME types were used even in HTTP as the Content-Type header, and it has now become the Internet standard for representing nontextual data.

In the case of HTTP POST, the method used by the client for encoding the data must be specified in the header. Otherwise, the receiving side would not know how to decode it. The default encoding for a HTTP POST request is "application/x-www-form-urlencoded". The x- prefix denotes that it is a private encoding used by mutual agreement between the peers (the browser and the server). The only other MIME type allowed for HTTP POST is multipart/form-data, which is primarily meant for file upload.

MIME types are also used by the Web server to denote the encoding used in the server response. If a CGI script generates the content, it is the duty of the script to specify the proper Content-Type header. In the case of static content, the Web server refers to the MIME types configuration (the Apache Web server keeps these settings in a text file called mime.types). The official list of registered media types is available at ftp://ftp.isi.edu/in-notes/iana/assignments/media-types/. Remember that you will not find "application/x-www-form-urlencoded" there because it is not a media type, and it is a private MIME type used by HTTP.

URL encoding is done for both field names and values. URL-encoded values are formatted into the POST/GET data in the format *var1=value1&var2=value2*, where *var1*, *var2*, and so on are the URL-encoded field names, and where *value1*, *value2*, and so on are URL-encoded values. Note that the delimiter "&" is not URL-encoded and it is part of the format specification.

URL-encoded text can then be used in either GET or POST. GET requests will include the data as part of the URL, whereas POST requests include the data in the request body. Even though the RFC allows us to keep most nonalphanumeric characters unencoded, we will encode everything that is not alphanumeric. This is allowed by the RFC, and there have been issues with the Palm.Net proxy changing reserved characters, so we are just playing safe. The method **URLEncode** shown in Figure 11.4 URL-encodes a string named *data* and writes the result on to the *encStr* buffer. You can also calculate the length of buffer required by calling **URLStrLen**.

Figure 11.4 URL Encoding for GET Data (Query String) as well as POST Data

```
#define ENCODING_REQUIRED(x) \
    (((x < '0') || (x > '9')) && ((x < 'a') || (x > 'z')) && \
     ((x < 'A') || (x > 'Z')))
/**
 * URL Encoding for POST and GET variables. Encodes everything
 * except digits and letters (alphanumeric characters).
 */
UInt16 URLEncode(Char *data, Char *encStr, UInt16 dataLen)
{
    UInt16 i, len;
    Char * hexStr = "0123456789ABCDEF";

    /* All characters except 0-9, a-z, A-Z are escaped */
    for (len = 0, i = 0; i < dataLen; i++, len++)
    {
        if (ENCODING_REQUIRED(data[i]))
        {
            encStr[len] = '%';
            encStr[++len] =
                hexStr[(data[i] >> 4) & 0x0F];
```

Continued

Figure 11.4 Continued

```
                encStr[++len] =
                    hexStr[data[i] & 0x0F];
            }
            else encStr[len] = data[i];
        }

        encStr[len] = 0;

        return len;

}

/**
 * Calculates the length of resulting string if the data were
 * to be URL-encoded. This can be used to precalculate the
 * length of buffer required
 */
UInt16 URLStrLen(Char *data, UInt16 dataLen)
{
    UInt16 i, len;

    /* All characters except 0-9, a-z, A-Z are escaped */
    for (len = 0, i = 0; i < dataLen; i++, len++)
    {
        if (ENCODING_REQUIRED(data[i])) len+= 2;
    }
    return len;
}
```

Sending Request Data

After you are done preparing the HTTP request, **INetLibSockHTTPReqSend** can be used to send the request to the proxy. It is declared as:

```
Err INetLibSockHTTPReqSend (UInt16 libRefnum, MemHandle sockH,
    void * writeP, UInt32 writeLen, Int32 timeout);
```

Most parameters are obvious except for *writeP* and *writeLen*. The *writeP* portion is the data portion of the request. That parameter will be used only for POST operation. Even though we have explicitly stated the request method using the *verbP* parameter to **INetLibSockHTTPReqCreate**, INetLib determines whether to use a GET or POST by looking at the *writeP* argument.

Choosing between GET and POST

You must have noticed that we used GET in the first and second examples, and POST in others—but how would you decide which is more appropriate? While developing WCA pages, this was an easy decision: Your form submissions used the POST method unless otherwise specified, and every other link used the GET method. When you use INetLib from your own native application, the choice may not be very clear. Even though you can use either one of them, you should keep the differences in mind while designing your application.

Any request sent from an HTTP client to an HTTP server includes a method description followed by the request parameters. Among all the HTTP methods, GET and POST are the most popular. Even though the methods differ in semantics, both of them are quite capable of doing the other's job. Therefore, the developer has the freedom to chose the method that best suits his situation.

The GET method was originally intended to "retrieve" information from the Internet. The method is expected not to have any side effects other than providing the requested HTML, image, or file back to the client. The server may either return a static document or generate one dynamically using a CGI, a Java servlet, or an Active Server Page (ASP) program. If you enter a URL directly into a browser or follow a link on a Web site, you are using a GET request. A GET request URL can optionally include additional data to be submitted to the server, as long as the data is encoded properly and embedded inside the URL. Hence, GET methods can only transmit data that will fit into a URL's allowed size. Moreover, all of the embedded data in the URL are directly visible to end-users.

On the other hand, the POST method is intended to "post" (submit) information to the Internet. A POST method can also return HTML, images, files, or arbitrary data after the submitted data has been processed. Hence, POST usually involves side effects such as changing a database or sending an e-mail. Using the POST method is preferred over GET when you submit large amounts of data because the data is transmitted as part of the request "body" and doesn't have to conform to URL size limitations.

GET and POST have one more small difference between them. Browsers normally do not warn the user if plain-text data is sent over an unencrypted channel for a GET request. They also do not warn about duplicate GET requests (hitting the **Refresh** button on the browser, for example). Caching proxies can also resend information from repeated GETs without accessing the target server.

Newer proxies know how to interpret HTTP headers better (for example, "Etag:" header fields) and differentiate static content from dynamic content. However, POST requests are never cached, and so you are always safe with POST. Except for the differences in conventions and efficiency, Web developers can choose GET or POST depending on the specific situation. GET and POST are identical in their capabilities, although you should always choose whichever one is more appropriate for the situation.

Developing & Deploying...

GET, POST, and Hiding Business Logic

Neither GET nor POST guarantee that your data or your business logic is hidden from the user. Several newsgroup postings suggest that POST is more secure because the form variables are not visible in the URL. This is not true, because a smart user can always look at the HTML source and get information about your form variables. You should not rely on a particular browser's inability to "view source." A programmer can always replace Clipper or your application with a better one.

Using encryption to solve this problem will not work either. Encryption can only be used to hide data from a third party—but not the end user. In fact, unless you change the Palm OS device hardware, there is no way you can prevent a user from understanding the query format. The solution to this problem lies in designing a Web site such that it does not matter if the user understands the query format. Chapter 8 discusses session management using session IDs that covers the same topic. Discussions in Chapter 8 will give you more insights on how to design your site.

Passing Data via GET

If you looked at the **INetLibSockHTTPReqCreate**, it might appear as if Palm OS does not let us send data using GET. Although the API does not do what we expect it to do, we should not blame it for this one. Instead of passing the data as an argument to **INetLibSockHTTPReqSend**, you must append the data to the URL after adding the query symbol "?". GET requests in HTTP don't have bodies, so there is no other place to put our data.

Debugging...

Problems with INetLib Acting Smart

You may have noticed that certain INetLib functions ignore some of their arguments. Even if you specified GET as the request method, INetLib would automatically assume a POST if the *writeP* argument to **INetLibSockHTTPReqSend** is not NULL. When Palm designed the INetLib interface, they must have intended to provide the same interface for GET and POST whereby the programmer could switch between the two just by changing one argument. Providing such an interface is not an easy job. Let us assume that we specified GET as the request method and then gave a *writeP* argument to **INetLibSockHTTPReqSend**. Because a GET request cannot have a request body, they will have to add the URL-encoded name-value pairs as a query string to the URL. Now what if the URL already had a query string? They would have to merge the two and create a new query string. Although this is not difficult, it is messy. Whatever the reason, Palm's programmers chose to change the request method to suit the data rather than reformatting the data.

Also, theoretically, if you are using POST, you can make a request with URL-encoded parameters sent via both the query string as well as the request body. Ideally, INetLib should have respected the request method specified or removed the option from the interface (*verbP* parameter to **INetLibSockHTTPReq**). If the user specifies a GET request and then gives a request body, it should have returned an error instead of assuming that the user wanted to do POST.

A similar issue exists with HTTP and HTTPS schemes. Even though we specify **inetSchemeHTTPS** as the *scheme* argument to **INetLibSockOpen**, it is completely ignored. INetLib instead looks at the first five letters of the *resNameP* argument to **INetLibSockHTTPReq** to determine whether to use security or not. Even if you had specified HTTPS via the scheme argument, your request will be downgraded to HTTP if the string "https://" is missing in the *resNameP*. Ideally, if you follow the documentation, this should never happen—but if your program did have a bug, you would not know about it. Instead of giving an error response to the caller, INetLib assumes that you wanted to do HTTP. If your Web server supports both secure and insecure connections, you may not realize the mistake at all.

URL Encoding and the Palm.Net Proxy

Although Palm.Net's URL encoding is based on RFC 2396, keep in mind that quite a few differences exist. First of all, Palm.Net uses certain "reserved" patterns in the data to encapsulate %DEVICEID and %ZIPCODE information. These patterns are of the form "[d<x>.<y>]" where *x* and *y* are numbers printed in Base 26 (more details in the section later in this chapter, "Authenticating the User and Device"). Whenever Palm.Net finds this pattern in the POST/GET data, they consider it as the radio ID and reformat it to add a "1" or "0" to the beginning of it. It is supposed to show whether Palm.Net was able to authenticate the device or not. Apparently, the Palm OS device does not use any reserved form variables for this purpose. Instead, they go through the entire data and scan for this pattern. Ideally this pattern would never be part of your real data because you are expected to URL encode all of your data, and URL encoding will remove the "[" and "]" characters and escape the proxy's scan. Palm.Net also does some URL encoding on its own. This additional attempt at URL encoding by Palm.Net creates a lot more problems. **INetLibSettingSet** can be used to set the Content-Type of your request to "application/x-www-form-urlencoded". However, that call is not supported on INetLib in PalmOS 3.5 and earlier, and it is even documented as a read-only setting. The key to the problem is whether Palm.Net thinks that the data is URL-encoded or not. This issue becomes more complicated because of some incompatibilities between the new Elaine server and the old Elaine server. In Table 11.2, we describe the issue based on OS version, Proxy version, and INetLib settings.

Table 11.2 URL Encoding

For Palm OS 3.2

	Old Elaine	**New Elaine**
Content-Type: Not Set LZ77 Compression: Not Set	OK.	Results in Double URLEncoding (Data corruption).
Content-Type: application/ x-www-form-urlencoded	N/A because INetLibSettingSet() returns "unimplemented setting" error.	N/A because INetLibSettingSet() returns "unimplemented setting" error.
LZ77 Compression: Requested (You must download Lz77lib.prc - part of INetLow example.)	No response from server. Server does not support LZ77, but does not report any error.	OK.

For Palm OS 3.5

	Old Elaine	**New Elaine**
Content-Type: Not Set LZ77 Compression: Not Set	OK.	Results in Double URLEncoding (Data corruption).
Content-Type: application/ x-www-form-urlencoded	N/A because INetLibSettingSet() crashes with "INetLib.c line 3379 SockSet" error.	N/A because INetLibSettingSet() crashes with "INetLib.c line 3379 SockSet" error.
LZ77 Compression: Requested (You must download Lz77lib.prc - part of INetLow sample.)	Server does not support LZ77. However, you do get an error response back.	OK.

Continued

Table 11.2 Continued

For Palm OS 4.0

	Old Elaine	New Elaine
Content-Type: Not Set LZ77 Compression: Not Set	No response from server.	Results in Double URLEncoding (Data corruption).
Content-Type: application/ x-www-form-urlencoded	No response from server.	OK.
LZ77 Compression: Requested (You must download Lz77lib.prc - part of INetLow sample.)	No response from server.	OK.

Table 11.2 was created using tests done with the "Unwired Widgets Mail Reader" example (explained later in this chapter). Options to set Content-Type and request LZ77 compression are available as checkboxes on the screen.

Receiving Responses from the Server

After the request has been sent to the server, the program can return to its event loop. Because we are now using the event-driven model, INetLib signals us with events after the data is ready. Even intermediate status messages arrive as events.

Waiting for INetLib Events

After you have modified the event loop as specified in the earlier section "Moving to an Event-Driven Model," you do not need to worry about INetLib events. You will get informed if and when any change occurs in the status of INetLib. However, you still need to verify that your event handlers handle the two INetLib events. If you allow the user to switch forms while the transaction is in progress, you must make sure that INetLib events are always handled. You can either require the handler code to be called directly from EventLoop or make the event handlers of each of the forms handle the events appropriately. If you are displaying status messages while handling INetLib events, make sure that they do not try to access form objects that do not exist. The code shown in Figure 11.5 is taken from the UWMail example (discussed later in this chapter).

Figure 11.5 Handling INetLib Events

```
/* code snippet - variables are declared elsewhere */
case inetSockStatusChangeEvent:
case inetSockReadyEvent:
       handled = HandleINetEvents(event);
       break;
/* code snippet */

Boolean HandleINetEvents(EventPtr event)
{
     Boolean handled = false;
     INetEventType *ievent = (INetEventType *) event;

     if (event->eType == inetSockStatusChangeEvent)
     {
          if(ievent->data.inetSockStatusChange.sockErr)
          {
               EndURLFetch();
               ErrAlert(ievent->data.inetSockStatusChange.sockErr);
          }
          else
          {
               ShowStatus(ievent->data.inetSockStatusChange.status);
               if (ievent->data.inetSockStatusChange.status ==
                    inetStatusClosed)
               {
                    EndURLFetch();
               }
          }
          handled = true;
     }
     else if (event->eType == inetSockReadyEvent)
     {
          DownloadResponse(ievent);
```

Continued

Figure 11.5 Continued

```
        handled = true;
    }
    return handled;
}
```

Checking the Socket Status

INetLibSockStatus returns the current status of the socket. If an application does not have an event loop and would instead like to poll INetLib for any status change, this function lets you detect status changes. Running a tight loop with polling is not advisable because it uses more battery power, and it blocks events from being processed by other parts of your code. If your application is spending most of the time in **EvtGetEvent** or **INetLibGetEvent**, you will get a better battery life because the device will be able to go to sleep while not in use.

Reading Data from the Socket

After we receive *inetSockReadyEvent*, you can call **INetLibSockRead**, as long as the socket that is ready is the one your application requested. INetLib supports several simultaneous HTTP connections. Although other applications will not request URLs at the same time, comparing the socket parameter of the event and making sure it matches the request we sent is always a good idea. Figure 11.6 shows the relevant code.

Figure 11.6 Reading Data from the Socket

```
/* code snippet - variables are declared elsewhere */
if (inetSockH &&
        ievent->data.inetSockReady.sockH == inetSockH
        && ievent->data.inetSockReady.inputReady
{
      error = INetLibSockRead(inetRefNum,
            inetSockH, responseBufP,
            reqestedBytes, bytesReadP,
            timeout);
}
```

Handling Connection Errors

Almost all INetLib functions return a *short* that indicates the status of the request. If your application is following an event-driven model, you may also be notified with error values. Every time you get an *inetSockStatusChangeEvent*, you must check the *inetSockStatusChange.sockErr* field of the event structure. You can display a human readable error message by calling **ErrAlert**, but HTTP errors usually have a *reason* text that is different from what is produced by **ErrAlert**.

Interpreting Return Values from Palm OS Routines

Most Palm OS functions return a 2-byte status code. These error values are categorized by the high byte into different error classes. For example, an error value that falls between 0x0200 and 0x02FF belongs to Data Manager Error Class. These classes are listed in Palm's ErrorBase.h header file. Not all errors returned by a function fall into its particular category. While INetLib functions return error numbers from 0x1400 through 0x14FF, they also return some errors from the network library, which fall into the 0x1200 to 0x12FF range. For example, if the Palm VII transmitter battery is too low, INetLib reports the error *netErrNiCdLowBattery*.

After you get the error number, interpreting the error number is easy but slightly error prone. Individual error numbers are listed in the header files using the decimal system. Error class values are themselves listed in hexadecimal. Therefore, you must always remember to convert the "lower byte" back to decimal before you look it up in the header file. Let us assume that you got an error value of 5140 decimal. Converting it to hexadecimal gives you 0x1414. Looking up 0x1400 in ErrorBase.h points you to INetLib error class. We should then open InetMgr.h and look up the suberror 0x14. Because INetMgr.h lists error numbers in decimal, you must look for 20 and not 0x14. If you do not do this conversion, the error may appear to be *inetErrInvalidHostAddr* instead of the correct *inetErrBufToSmall*. The error lookup isn't complicated, but you do not want to get confused and waste time chasing a bug that does not exist.

Handling Server Errors

INetLib provides a great deal of information when the error is at the client or at the proxy. However, after the proxy is able to deliver the request to the server, it does not translate HTTP error responses back to the client in the usual way. If the HTTP request generated a 400 series or 500 series error, we will not get an *inetSockStatusChangeEvent.* We have to repeatedly call **INetLibSockHTTPAttrGet** and check for errors. If we already have a function called at intervals to create an animation, you can include the code in Figure 11.7 to catch server errors.

Figure 11.7 Handling Server Errors

```
/* variables inetError, httpError, httpStatusMsg, inetRefNum,
   inetSockH are all assumed to be declared in a global struct g
*/
/* check for HTTP errors */
if (g.inet.inetError == 0)
// so that we won't clear it accidentally
{
    size = sizeof(g.inet.inetError);
    err = INetLibSockHTTPAttrGet(g.inet.inetRefNum,
        g.inet.inetSockH, inetHTTPAttrResult, 0,
        &g.inet.inetError, &size);
    if (!err && (g.inet.inetError != 0))
    {
        /* get HTTP error code */
        size = sizeof(g.inet.httpError);
        err = INetLibSockHTTPAttrGet(g.inet.inetRefNum,
            g.inet.inetSockH, inetHTTPAttrErrDetail, 0,
            &g.inet.httpError, &size);

        /* get HTTP status message (in text) */
        size = MAX_HTTP_STATUS;
        MemSet(&g.inet.httpStatusMsg[0], MAX_HTTP_STATUS, 0);
            err = INetLibSockHTTPAttrGet(g.inet.inetRefNum,
            g.inet.inetSockH, inetHTTPAttrReason, 0,
            &g.inet.httpStatusMsg[0], &size);
        if (!err) g.inet.httpStatusMsg[size] = 0;

        MemSet(&ievent, sizeof(ievent), 0);
        ievent.eType = inetSockStatusChangeEvent;
```

Continued

Figure 11.7 Continued

```
            ievent.data.inetSockStatusChange.sockErr =
                (UInt16)g.inet.inetError;
            EvtAddEventToQueue((EventType *)&ievent);
        }
    }
```

We will also have to modify appropriate sections in the **HandleINetEvents** routine to make sure that it looks at the variables *inetError* and *httpError*. Figure 11.8 illustrates the modifications to our error-handler code.

Figure 11.8 Displaying Server Errors

```
        /* code snippet */
        if(ievent->data.inetSockStatusChange.sockErr)
        {
            if (g.inet.inetError != 0)
            {
                StrPrintF(g.errBuff,
"HTTP Error %ld.", g.inet.httpError);
                FrmCustomAlert(CustomErrorAlert, g.errBuff,
                    g.inet.httpStatusMsg, NULL);
            }
            else
                ErrAlert(ievent->data.inetSockStatusChange.sockErr);
            EndURLFetch();
            ShowStatus(0);
        }
        /* code snippet */
```

You may have noticed that you have three error values to interpret: *inetHTTPAttrResult*, *inetHTTPAttrDetail*, and *inetHTTPAttrReason*. The real HTTP error code is *inetHTTPAttrDetail*. If your request creates an HTTP error of 404, the value of *inetHTTPAttrDetail* will be 404; *inetHTTPAttrResult* is the same error code converted to a value in *inetErrorClass*; *inetHTTPAttrReason* is a textual representation of the error code. Most Web servers return both a numerical value and a page explaining the error. INetLib does not deliver the text, but the text in *inetHTTPAttrReason* should explain the error sufficiently. If you need the exact text from your Web server, you must turn on HTTP headers using the *inetHTTPAttrIncHTTP* setting, but then you have to remember to parse the headers for normal responses as well.

If you are displaying an error message to the user, you should choose *inetHTTPAttrReason* rather than doing **ErrAlert** or **SysErrString** on *inetHTTPAttrResult*. The second one produces a string better-suited for Clipper, as you can see in Figures 11.9 and 11.10.

Figure 11.9 Values of *inetHTTPAttrDetail* and *inetHTTPAttrReason* Used Together

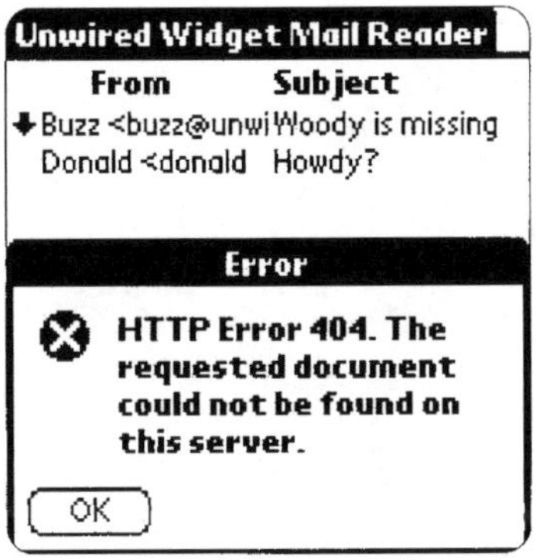

Figure 11.10 Value of *inetHTTPAttrResult* Converted to Text Using ErrAlert() or SysErrString()

Debugging...

Debugging Your Application

Your development environment determines how you debug your application. We have divided the debugging problems into three categories. However, in most cases you may have to explore all three of these because you will not usually know the exact location of your problem.

- **Debugging the client** Both CodeWarrior and the GNU Debugger (GDB) provide source level debugging on your applications. Your application can run as usual on the emulator while you step through code line by line. This being a network application, you have to remember that the proxy and the Web server may time out while you are debugging the application. Hence, you may want to relax the timeout values in the client and server (session timeouts, if any) while you are debugging.
  - **CodeWarrior Settings** You must choose the **Enable debugger** option from the **Project** menu before you can debug an application. In the project view, you should also see a dot in the "bug" column next to each source file you want to debug. You can toggle the dot by clicking in that area. You can also set additional debug options under "68K Linker" in the project settings window.
  - **PRC-Tools** Make sure m68k-palmos-gcc is invoked with -g option. Taking out -O option from the command line may also help. Optimization rearranges, removes, or inserts code. Optimized code is hard to debug because source lines may not match with the actual code.
  - **Falch.net IDE** The IDE tries to imitate Visual Studio and provides Debug and Release configurations. You can switch to either one of them by choosing the **Set Active Configuration** option from the **Project** menu.

In CodeWarrior as well as Falch.net, you can set and remove breakpoints by clicking on the left margin of the line or by pressing the **F9** key. Repeated clicks or F9 toggles the breakpoint. Falch.net IDE uses buttons similar to Visual Studio, whereas CodeWarrior uses their own conventions. The icons are self-explanatory, so you should not have trouble

Continued

with them. Earlier versions of CodeWarrior used icons that looked like the buttons of a CD player. However, icons in the new versions imitate those used in Visual Studio. Developers who use pure gdb can use the usual gdb commands **break at <line>** or **break in <func-name>** to set breakpoints.

- **Debugging the server** If you do not get any response from the server, or you get internal errors in the server, you should switch to a desktop browser. A desktop is a much better environment than the handheld for debugging applications. When you first detect that the server is not sending any response, you should turn on the INetLib option to include headers. The first line of the header contains the HTTP status code. You will know the error is at the server when you get a 400- or 500-series HTTP error.
  - **Examine the server log** If it is an internal error, the server log will have the details. Servers such as Apache log the errors to a text file according to the configuration (usually in /var/log or /usr/local/apache/log).
  - **Headers printed by the application** The application must always print at least a Content-Type header line or the server will generate an error. The exception to this rule is for scripts tagged as No Parse Header (NPH). For more information, look at CGI documentation.
  - **A missing or inaccessible file** This can easily be detected by using a desktop browser. You should make sure that your files are on the Web server and that any scripts have the proper file extension or are correctly marked as executable. Moreover, you must make sure that the Web server has appropriate credentials to access the file.
- **Debugging the transport** This is the most difficult thing to debug. However, you may need to in most cases, unless you suspect a bug in INetLib. In most cases, debugging the client or server can locate the problem. If the server works with a desktop browser and your application can access other URLs, there may be something special with your particular request. In that case, it is worth digging into the transport.

Tcpdump is one piece of software available on Linux (and Unix) boxes that might come in handy when you debug transport. Run your application in the emulator and request **tcpdump** (Unix commands are

Continued

case-sensitive) to dump packets that travel between certain IP addresses. Later you can examine the file to see what went wrong. If you need to see what the proxy sent to your Web server without running Tcpdump, you can run the following Perl script given. You can use the Tcpserver program from Dan Bernstein (Qmail author) to turn any Perl script into a server. The script produces an output suitable for Unwired Widgets Mail Reader:

```
#!/usr/bin/perl

open MYFILE, ">/tmp/dumpMe.log";

print MYFILE while(<>);

print "Content-Type: text/html\r\n\r\n-ERR Request has been
logged.";
```

Authenticating the User and Device

Many of your WCA applications use device IDs, URL rewriting, or cookies to maintain sessions or to authenticate the user. For native applications, you may or may not need this depending on your design. If your application synchronizes with the server once every few hours and takes just a few seconds to do it, supporting sessions does not make sense. You might as well include the logon credentials every time you synchronize with the server. Because your application keeps the user ID and password in a database or memory, we are also not bothering the user. However, if you plan to reuse server-side code for both native Palm OS clients and desktop Web browsers, you may find that the Palm OS application has to deal with the same backend code that expects to receive cookies or device IDs.

Overview of Cookies, Sessions, and User Authentication

HTTP is a *stateless* protocol, which means that requests to the server are all treated as independent transactions. For example, you may have a link to download a file from your Web, which leads the user to a license agreement, and eventually from that page to the final download page. You have no way to prevent the user from bypassing your license agreement—provided that the user knows the URL. This stateless nature is very powerful, and it allows for simple HTTP server implementations but does complicate designing applications that have state associated with the user. We are not completely helpless, however. If there is a way to uniquely identify a client browser every time, we can solve the stateless issue by maintaining the client's state on the server. The obvious idea of using the originating IP address to identify the user will not work, because the client could be behind a proxy along with hundreds of other users, all sharing the same IP address. Another solution would be to require the client to send a username and password with every request. After we authenticate the username and password, we know that the request came from a particular user. Unfortunately, this is a costly operation, for two reasons:

- The username and password are sensitive and confidential information. Moreover, the browser needs to remember this information even after the browser window is closed. This would mean that the browser would have to write this information to a file (for a desktop browser) or database record (for a Palm OS browser). Usernames and passwords should never be saved on nonvolatile memory because this defeats the whole purpose of having a username and password. Unfortunately, new versions of Microsoft Internet Explorer and Mozilla store usernames and passwords on the hard disk.
- Because the username and password are transmitted with every request, each of those requests has to be encrypted. Secure Sockets Layer (SSL) transactions are CPU-intensive, and most sites keep SSL just for the initial logon screen. After the logon is over, the user is switched to HTTP to save server CPU and bandwidth.

In February 1996, Netscape Communications and AT&T Bell Labs proposed the use of *cookies*. Cookies are a set of (key, value) pairs given to a client browser by the Web site. The browser is expected to return the cookies every time it visits the Web site (or a subsection of the Web site). The (key, value) pairs originally generated by the server are expected to be unique enough to identify the client again upon receiving the cookie the second time. It is up to the server to maintain the uniqueness of the cookie. Netscape's initial draft was later replaced by RFC 2109, and RFC 2965 is a proposed replacement for RFC 2109.

Remember that a cookie should not be used to store the username and password. Instead, it should contain a unique ID that will help the server retrieve the username, password, or an "authenticated" flag from storage that resides on the server. This unique ID is usually referred to as the *session ID*. The session ID value should be unique and long enough that the user cannot guess a valid session ID.

If you are using Microsoft IIS, Java Servlets, or JSP, the programmer does not have to worry about cookies or session IDs directly. The framework provided by these engines automatically uses cookie information to provide a session object to the programmer. Java Servlets also provide a URL rewriting option that stores session data in the URL strings that the client uses to fetch new pages, rather than requiring cookies. The next section looks at how cookies and session IDs are used together.

Using Cookies for Session Management (Palm OS 4.0)

Now we look at how cookies help user authentication. Palm OS versions 4.0 and above support cookies. We take an ASP application running on Microsoft IIS and Perl CGI script running on Apache as examples. The basic steps are explained here—refer to Chapter 8 for complete server-side examples on user authentication. However, the Perl example later in this section is complete, and it shows the use of cookies for something other than session management or user authentication: keeping track of the time of last visit. This should be sufficient for you to understand the client-side code.

Microsoft ASP framework provides a *session object* that is available to every ASP page under the application. When the client does not provide a cookie in the header, it is assumed to be a new session. Soon after creating the session object, the ASP framework will add a cookie to the response header that looks very similar to the header line given below. The following response shown in Figure 11.11 was received from the site search.microsoft.com. If you want to recreate the same example, the commands are also given in the figure.

Figure 11.11 Data Sent from Microsoft IIS/ASP to Client (Elaine Proxy)

```
HTTP/1.1 200 OK
Server: Microsoft-IIS/5.0
Date: Tue, 24 Apr 2001 16:27:56 GMT
Content-Type: text/html
Set-Cookie: ASPSESSIONIDGQGGGLXO=ODCLFDLDACOANLLBJMHLMHHM; path=/
Cache-control: private
```

To recreate the same example, run **telnet** and connect to "search.microsoft .com" port 80. Then type the following commands on the telnet window. (The characters typed may not appear on the screen if you are using Windows. There is one space before and after the first backslash [/]. Remember to press **Enter** twice after typing "HTTP/1.0", which will send one blank line to the server and inform the site that we are done with our HTTP request.)

```
prompt> telnet search.microsoft.com 80
GET / HTTP/1.0          <== user input
                         <== A blank line
```

After the session ID has been added to the response header, the script can retrieve variables from the request and store them as *session variables*. The code in Figure 11.12 illustrates how to store a username and password retrieved from the client in the session object.

Figure 11.12 Server-Side Code Demonstrating the Use of ASP Session Objects

```
Request:
http://www.unwiredwidgets.com/login.asp?userid=george&password=secret1
Login.asp:
'Code snippet
Server["userid"] = Request.QueryString("userid")
Server["password"] = Request.QueryString("password");
'Authenticate the user - code depends on your database and system.
Server["authenticated"] = 1;
```

After the client receives the cookie, Palm OS will store the cookie in a cookie database, sometimes referred to as the *cookie jar.*

Palm OS will send the cookie back to the same server for all subsequent requests that match the same path and domain. ASP framework will retrieve the cookie from the header and locate the Session object in memory completely transparent to the application.

```
Request: http://www.unwiredwidgets.com/GetDocument.asp?docID=2378783
GetDocument.asp:
'Code snippet
If (Server["authenticated"] = 1) then
        ' Send the document back
End If
```

Client-Side Code

INetLib library has two settings related to cookies: *inetSettingEnableCookies* and *inetSettingMaxCookieJarSize*. The following code illustrates their use:

```
/* code snippet from URLFetch example */
Err error;
error = INetLibSettingSet(g.inet.inetRefNum,
                    g.inet.inetHan, inetSettingEnableCookies,
                    &cookiesEnabled, sizeof(cookiesEnabled));
if (!error)
    error = INetLibSettingSet(g.inet.inetRefNum,
                    g.inet.inetHan, inetSettingMaxCookieJarSize,
                    &maxCookieJarSize, sizeof(maxCookieJarSize));
/* code snippet from URLFetch example */
```

Perl/CGI Example

The code in Figure 11.13 demonstrates the use of cookies from Perl. This script sends the current time to the client as a *cookie value*. This cookie value will be returned to the server when the client connects to the server again. The script will display an appropriate message and send a new value to the device, which will replace the earlier cookie on the device. The script, cookie-test.pl is included on the CD that comes with this book. The program uses the Perl module CGI, which should be familiar to all Perl programmers. You can get more information on this package from the command **man CGI** (Unix).

Figure 11.13 cookie-test.pl: A Perl CGI Script Using Cookies to Keep Track of Users

```
#!/usr/bin/perl
use CGI;
$query = new CGI;
$lastVisit = $query->cookie(-name=>'l');
$cookie = $query->cookie(-name=>'l',
                         -value=> time,
                         -expires=>'+1M',
                         -path=> '/',
```

Continued

Figure 11.13 Continued

```
                                 -domain=> '.unwiredwidgets.com');
print $query->header(-cookie=>$cookie);


if (!defined($lastVisit) || ($lastVisit <= 0))
{
   print "You are new to this site. Welcome!\n";
}
else
{
   print "Haven't seen you since ", scalar(localtime($lastVisit)),
        "\n", time - $lastVisit, " seconds is quite a long time!\n";
}
```

Running URLFetch with cookie-test.pl

To run URLFetch with cookie-test.pl, complete the following steps:

1. Retrieve the URLFetch source code from the CD.
2. Enable the code that deals with cookies by uncommenting the "#define ENABLE_COOKIES" line in InetInterface.c (approximate line 57).
3. Rebuild the URLFetch program. Copy cookie-test.pl to the appropriate place in your Web site. The script must have execute permission (Unix), and the directory must have scripting permission (Unix and Windows). Remember to enter the URL to your site instead of the one shown in Figure 11.14. The Perl script should also be modified with the appropriate "domain" value for the cookie.
4. Tap on the **Fetch** button, and the first run will produce the response shown in Figure 11.15 from the server.

A second fetch on the same URL will return the response shown in Figure 11.16 from the server.

Figure 11.14 Demonstration of Cookies—First Visit to the Site: Request URL

Figure 11.15 Demonstration of Cookies—First Visit to the Site: Server Response

Figure 11.16 Demonstration of Cookies—Second Visit to the Site: Server Response

Looking Under the Hood

This section looks at what happens "under the hood" when you use cookies with INetLib. Note that you never have to deal with this data directly. However, it will help you understand how cookies work. When you use URLFetch for the first time, INetLib tries to match the URL with its cookie database and finds no matches. Therefore, it sends the code shown in Figure 11.17 to the server.

Figure 11.17 Request Data Sent from Elaine Proxy to Destination Web Server

```
GET /cgi-bin/cookie-test.pl HTTP/1.0
user-agent: Mozilla/2.0 (compatible; Elaine/2.0)
X-Forwarded-For: 192.168.166.6
Host: www.unwiredwidgets.com
Via: 1.1 wp410usjc (NetCache 4.0R4D11)
Connection: Keep-Alive
```

After the Web server receives the request, it will invoke our CGI script and respond with the data shown in Figure 11.18. (The Set-Cookie line is wrapped to the next line to accommodate for the page size of this book.) Note that the Web server adds everything up to the Set-Cookie line.

Figure 11.18 Response Data Sent from Destination Web Server to Elaine Proxy

```
HTTP/1.1 200 OK
Date: Tue, 24 Apr 2001 19:31:38 GMT
Server: Apache/1.3.9 (Unix)
Set-Cookie: l=988140704; domain=.unwiredwidgets.com; path=/;
    expires=Thu, 24-May-2001 19:31:44 GMT
Connection: close
Content-Type: text/html

You are new to this site. Welcome!
```

The next request to the server will include this cookie shown in Figure 11.19, if the URL path and domain matches.

Figure 11.19 Request Data from Elaine Proxy to Web Server (Second Request)

```
GET /cgi-bin/cookie-test.pl HTTP/1.0
user-agent: Mozilla/2.0 (compatible; Elaine/2.0)
Cookie: 1=988140704
X-Forwarded-For: 192.168.166.6
Host: www.unwiredwidgets.com
Via: 1.1 wp410usjc (NetCache 4.0R4D11)
Connection: Keep-Alive
```

Using the Device ID for Session Management

Using the device ID for session management is not as easy as using cookies. However, it will work on all devices including those running Palm OS versions 3.2 and 3.5. In Palm OS 4.0, cookies are transparently supported by INetLib and Elaine. INetLib will match the given URL with the cookie database and send the cookie along with the header. The device ID, on the other hand, needs to be included in the URL explicitly with every request. The following sections describe how to retrieve the device ID and send it along with the URL request.

Matching the device ID with the session object on the server is the most difficult part for the server-side code. Unlike cookies, which were transparently handled by the framework, the device ID needs to be matched explicitly with the list of all open sessions. (Refer to Chapter 8 for server-side examples of this.) Regardless of how you choose to do it on the server side, the client side remains the same—a device ID will be included in every URL request sent to the server.

Retrieving the Device ID

The device ID uniquely identifies a Palm OS device. The device ID is different from the ROM ID (or the *Flash ID*, as it is sometimes called). The device ID will be available for all devices with INetLib installed, but the ROM ID is available only on devices that have a Flash ROM. We can retrieve the device ID (which is also called the *Radio ID*) by calling **INetLibSettingGet** with *inetSettingRadioID* as the setting argument.

Let us modify our URLFetch example to include the device ID:

```
UInt32  radioID[2];
UInt16  ridLength = 2 * sizeof(UInt32);
```

```
Err      error = 0;

error = INetLibSettingGet(libRefNum, inetH,
                          inetSettingRadioID,
                          radioID,
                          &ridLength);
```

The above example illustrates the use of **INetLibSettingGet** to retrieve the device ID. However, you might have noticed that the device ID looks different than the one you got from the Web Clipping application. The variable %DEVICEID also had a validation prefix. This validation code indicates whether the proxy recognizes the device and whether the user has a real Palm VII device. This code is not sent from the device but is added by the Palm.Net proxy server after it verifies that the request is coming from a Palm VII or VIIx device. However, the device may possibly send data that looks like the output of the server, so you cannot rely on this "validation code." See the sidebar in the next section titled "Security Issues with Device ID" for more details.

Adding Validation Code to Device ID

Palm.Net proxy searches all POST and GET variable names for a string of the form [d<x.y>], where *x* and *y* are 32-bit numbers printed in Base 26. The proxy uses Base 26 instead of Base 10 (decimal) or Base 16 (hexadecimal) only to reduce the number of bytes transmitted.

Why Use Base 26?

The device ID for the Palm VII and VIIx is based on an internal radio ID. This radio ID contains 32-bit numbers, which can have any value from 0 to 2^{32}. However, URL encoding does not allow 8-bit data. Therefore, we have to convert this 32-bit number to text. The most obvious choice would be to print it as a decimal number. However, decimal numbers use only 10 possible digits and will occupy more space to print than hexadecimal numbers, which use 16 possible characters. The higher the base used, the shorter the string. The shortest form—the true binary form of the integer—can be considered as Base 256 form. Palm.Net uses Base 26 and uses all lowercase characters. The scheme does not use uppercase characters, because the CML encoding is optimized for lowercase text.

Base 26 Conversion Algorithm

The function **StrIToB26A** in Figure 11.20 behaves in a similar fashion to the Palm OS function **StrIToA**, except this function prints Base 26 instead, using lowercase characters instead of the decimal system.

Figure 11.20 StrIToBase26A—Decimal to Base 26 Alpha Converter

```
#define base26MaxLength 8


Char* StrIToB26A(UInt32 base10value, Char* base26AlphaStr)
{
     int  index = base26MaxLength - 1;


    /* keep on dividing the value until we get 0
     * storing all reminders in Base 26, starting
     * from the far right.
     */
     base26AlphaStr[index] = 0;
     do
     {
         base26AlphaStr[—index] = (base10value % 26) + 'a';
         base10value = base10value / 26;
     } while (base10value > 0);


     /* move string, if needed,  to the left end */
     if (index > 0)
       MemMove(base26AlphaStr, base26AlphaStr + index,
       (base26MaxLength - index));


     return(base26AlphaStr);
}
```

The index value is decremented (iterated from 7 to 0) because of the way the remainders are calculated. The first value calculated is actually the last digit of the sequence. If the number happens to be less than seven digits when printed, we move the printed value to the beginning of the buffer to remove the unwanted characters. Hence, **GenerateDeviceID** will have the modifications shown in Figure 11.21.

Figure 11.21 Code to Request Validation Code for Device ID

```
...
Char     value01base26AlphaStr[base26MaxLength];
Char     value02base26AlphaStr[base26MaxLength];
...
StrIToB26A(radioID[0], value01base26AlphaStr);
StrIToB26A(radioID[1], value02base26AlphaStr);

StrCopy(deviceID, "[d");
StrCat(deviceID, value02base26AlphaStr);
StrCat(deviceID, ".");
StrCat(deviceID, value01base26AlphaStr);
StrCat(deviceID, "]");
...
```

Debugging...

Security Issues with Device ID

Palm OS does not insist on a specific field name to be used for the device ID parameter in the request. The developer can put %DEVICEID in any field of the form (or the [d<x>.<y>] equivalent for a native application). The Web clipping proxy server then searches the entire POST/GET data for a string of the form [d<x>.<y>], where *x* and *y* are Base 26 numbers, and then it reformats that string to add the validation code. This means that the Palm proxy has no way to inform the destination site whether a substitution was made. A native application can always supply any string as the device ID and claim it to be valid, as long as it includes the "1." prefix and does not use the [d<x>.<y>] format. The proxy would not even know what is happening behind its back.

If the Palm OS had been designed in such a way that it always used a reserved field name (for example, *palm_device_id*), this issue would

Continued

would have been resolved. The proxy can always make sure that any usage of the form element *palm_device_id* passed through the proxy will either be verified or removed. Coupled with the check on source IP address, the destination site can be sure that the request will have a device ID that is guaranteed to be valid, or not have the field at all.

Every site visited by the user from Clipper can potentially know that user's device's identifier. All it needs to do is include %DEVICEID as a hidden field in a form submitted back to their server, where it can be stored in every database along with user identifiable information. Let us assume that a site uses %DEVICEID to maintain sessions for users who are already authenticated by a username and password. If we had a Web site and the customer accessed our service at least once, we would have received the device ID. Now imagine a bank that uses %DEVICEID to maintain its sessions. We now know the identifier that would let us prove we were that user to the bank. You may argue that the bank logon could involve a username and password. However, after the real user goes through the logon once, all subsequent pages are validated only by %DEVICEID. Therefore, if we know when the user logged on to his bank, or if we were willing to run a hacking program continually, we would definitely be able to access his data someday. The user would not even know that the account has been compromised.

However, cookies are generated by the server and are unique to that server. They also will expire after a certain time, and either the user or server can also force a change in the cookies by deleting all cookies stored on the PDA. The browser will only send cookies back to the machine that originally sent them, so knowing a user's cookie ID doesn't give you access to other sites. With device ID, the same ID is given to all sites, and you will have to replace the whole device if you suspect that someone is misusing your device ID.

Hence, the device ID should be used only if cookie support is not available. Even then, you should consider adding a session ID field to every transaction. In short, device ID can be used to "remember" the username, just to print a "Welcome back John Smith" message, but should always require a password or session ID to log on. Device ID may also be used in creating sessions for sites that do not require authentication (news sites, for example), where the session would only keep track of user preferences.

Providing Configuration Aliases

A configuration is a specific set of values for several of the Internet library settings. A configuration can also be just an alias for another configuration. INetLib will accept either the configuration index or its alias. Any configuration whose name starts with a "." is considered built-in and cannot be renamed, created, or deleted.

We have put together an application called ConfigBrowser that will list all available configurations and what they point to. Running ConfigBrowser on your device will enable you to view and test configurations. However, in most cases only three of the default configurations are of any use: *.CTPWireline*, *.CTPWireless*, and *.CTPDefault*, which points to one of the other two. Configuration listings of a real Palm VII and Emulator are shown in Figure 11.22.

Figure 11.22 INetLib Configuration Mapping on a Real Palm VII Device

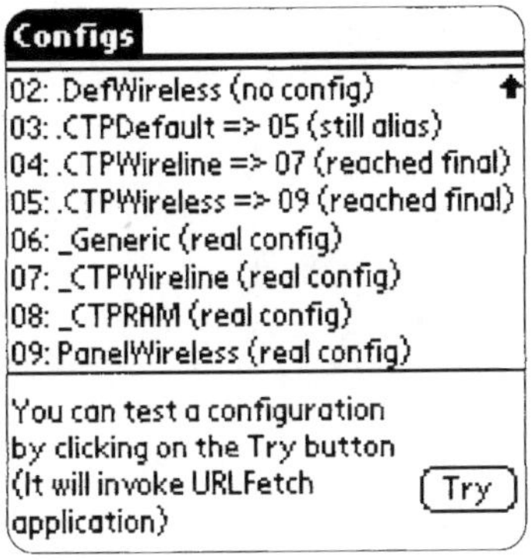

Now we will look at Emulator emulating a Palm VII and see what is different in it (see Figure 11.23). Note that Configuration 4 (configurations start at zero) points to Configuration 7, and Configuration 5 points to Configuration 9, which is the PanelWireless. Even though Emulator also provides *.CTPWireless*, Figures 11.23 and 11.24 show how it is different from a real device. Figure 11.23 is the Emulator emulating a Palm m505 handheld running Palm OS 4.0; Figure 11.24 is the Emulator running Palm OS 3.2 as a Palm VII device. Also notice the difference between the two emulator configurations.

Figure 11.23 INetLib Configuration Mapping on Emulator (Emulating Palm m505)

Figure 11.24 INetLib Configuration Mapping on Emulator (Emulating Palm VII)

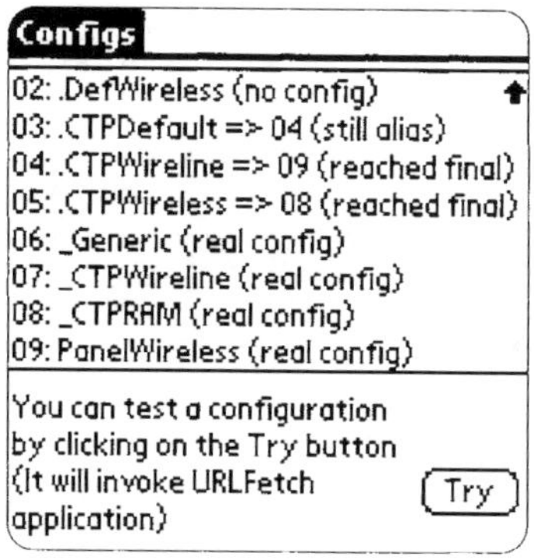

Displaying Signal Strength

Applications running on Palm VII devices can retrieve the coverage information and display a bar similar to the one shown by Clipper—also referred to as the Wireless Signal Strength Indicator (WSSI). Unfortunately, signal strength is not supported on OmniSky devices, even though they are also "wireless" devices. Signal strength is retrieved by calling **NetLibIFSettingGet** with *netIFSettingRssiAsPercent* or *netIFSettingRssi* as the parameter value. Applications should make sure that they are really running on a Palm VII device before calling this function, because these calls fail on devices using OmniSky or the Mobile Internet Kit.

Detecting Palm VII

We have borrowed the code from the INetLow example in the Knowledge Base. The INetLow example assumes that WSSI (wireless signal strength indicator) is always supported if we are using the *.CTPWireless* (*inetCfgNameCTPWireless*) configuration. In the case of OmniSky devices, *inetCfgNameCTPDefault* points to *inetCfgNameCTPWireline*, and hence it would not be same as *inetCfgNameCTPWireless*. In fact, *inetCfgNameCTPWireless* points to an invalid configuration on OmniSky devices. This rule will fail on the Emulator though—Emulator running Palm OS 3.5 or 4.0 does have *inetCfgNameWireless* pointing to a usable configuration. This means that even if the current configuration points to *inetCfgNameCTPWireless*, it still does not guarantee that the device is a Palm VII. However, because POSE (running Palm OS 4.0) handles the call and gracefully returns a zero, we need not worry too much about it. For lack of better code, we stick with the solution that is described in the INetLow example. It is considerably long code, spanning more than 50 lines just to detect whether the application is running on a Palm VII. The two routines that detect it are **GetAliasActualCfgIndex** and **IsSupportedWSSI**. The code is given in the URLFetch example (InetInterface.c).

Displaying WSSI

After we detect that we are running on a compatible device, we can use the following code to display the signal strength indicator. We chose (140,0) as the location of the indicator.

```
g.inet.wssiSupported = IsSupportedWSSI(g.inet.inetRefNum,
     g.inet.cfgIndex);
if (g.inet.wssiSupported)
{
     INetLibWiCmd(g.inet.inetRefNum, wiCmdInit, 0, 0);
     INetLibWiCmd(g.inet.inetRefNum, wiCmdSetLocation, 140, 0);
     INetLibWiCmd(g.inet.inetRefNum, wiCmdSetEnabled, 1, 0);
}
```

Figure 11.25 shows the WSSI displayed on a Palm VII device.

Figure 11.25 URLFetch Displaying WSSI on a Palm VII

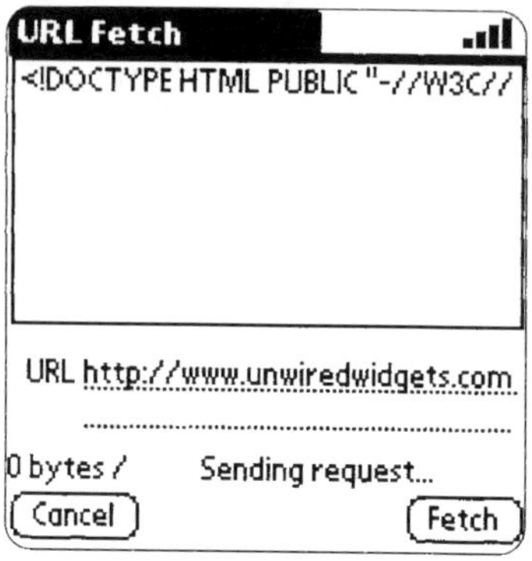

Optimizing Transport

After you have decided what needs to be sent across the connection, you have to decide how to do it—you need a data and transport format that will be easy for the client to recognize and that will save you valuable bandwidth. Although a decision to choose one option will also influence the other, for the sake of discussion, let's split the issue.

Data Format

What should your server-side application generate? HTML? XML? Proprietary format? It mainly depends on what you are willing to do on the client. HTML is not an appropriate format unless you are writing a browser.

Proprietary Format

Most applications would use either this or XML format (explained in the following section). The format is flexible; you send exactly what your client expects. Your data can be 8-bit values. Our example, the Unwired Widgets Mail Reader, uses a proprietary format for its over-the-air protocol.

XML

If you ever had to write a simple C structure to a file, you could simply copy the bytes from memory directly to the file. The version of the structure in the file is a direct image of the memory used by the structure. This fails when storing a linked list of such structures in memory, because a linked list will be spread out everywhere in the memory, and you would not be able to find an easy way to "dump" it to a file. Just directly dumping each structure would not work because the pointers embedded in the structures would be meaningless when restored from the file. In this case, we would have to copy each record to a file and represent the "links" between them using something other than pointers, such as an item index to link them. This is just the beginning of the trouble. If your structure had a 2-byte integer item, and a file was subsequently read on a device that used a different byte order, the data would appear very different. In such a case, we would probably convert the data to printable text and have each side convert it to native format. Now if the data is printed in text, how do we separate the variable-length fields? Do we use commas? What if the data contains commas? How would you represent a linked list of array of structures? Welcome to XML!

Developing & Deploying...

XML Optimized for Wireless

SyncML is one practical implementation of the XML format. SyncML is an initiative started by nine companies, including Palm, Inc. SyncML defines an XML-based protocol for providing synchronization between a mobile client and a server. The SyncML protocol uses an algorithm that is very similar to Palm's HotSync protocol but is implemented using XML over HTTP connections. Their Web site (www.syncml.org) provides a reference implementation of SyncML libraries for Palm OS devices.

The binary XML standard (WBXML) provides a method to optimize the XML document even further by binary encoding XML tags (see http://www.w3.org/TR/wbxml). The binary XML content format is designed to allow for compact transmission with no loss of functionality or semantic information. The binary format encodes the parsed physical form of an XML document—that is, the structure and content of the document entities. Meta-information, including the DTD and conditional sections, is removed when the document is converted to the binary format. WBXML can be used along with SyncML or with your own XML implementation.

XML is well suited for representing structured data. It provides a textual format for data exchange that is the same across different platforms and applications.

Unfortunately, XML's simplicity is also a weakness, because each system that uses it needs to develop its own convention for tags, also known as a Document Type Description (DTD). You would also need to implement an XML parser for the Palm OS. Unless you are developing a large application with a complex collection of data types, the effort to use XML may not be justified.

Transport Format

This section discusses the data formats commonly used between the client and server. If you control both the client and server code, you can use any format you want.

No Compression

So far in this chapter, we have not been compressing data. This is easy to develop and debug, but very inefficient considering the amount of bytes sent over the air. Receiving noncompressed data works on all versions of INetLib and with all versions of the Palm.Net proxy.

Using the Proxy's Built-In LZ77 Compression

You can ask the Palm.Net proxy to compress the data sent to the Palm. If you do this, your client will need to decompress the data using the Lz77.lib decompression library. Your server-side code remains unchanged, because the compression occurs only between the proxy and the device. Your client code needs minimal changes to call to **INetLibSettingsSet** to request the compression and to call the LZ77 Manager library to decompress the received data.

LZ77 Usage

Before we post the request, we set a flag in INetLib to indicate that we would want to use LZ77 compression. The proxy will fetch the requested URL as usual and compress the data using LZ77. After the data is received on the Palm device, our application will decompress the data using LZ77Mgr. The code shown in Figure 11.26 illustrates the use of LZ77Mgr to decompress the received data.

Figure 11.26 Using LZ77Mgr with Elaine LZ77 Compression

```
/* Before you make the http request */
convAlgorithm = ctpConvNoneLZ77;
error = INetLibSettingSet( inetRefNum, inetHan,
          inetSettingConvAlgorithm, (UInt8*)&convAlgorithm,
```

Continued

Figure 11.26 Continued

```
            sizeof(convAlgorithm));

/* After you get the response from server */
if(convAlgorithm == ctpConvNoneLZ77)
    error = DecompressLz77(&responseBufH, &totalBytesRead);

/* DecompressLz77 implementation */
Err DecompressLz77
(
    MemHandle* bufferHP,
    UInt32* bufferLen
)
{
    Char*           bufferPtr = NULL;
    MemHandle       newBufferH = NULL;
    MemHandle       lz77SessionH = NULL;
    UInt32          expandedSize    = 0;
    UInt32          lz77BitOffset  = 0;
    UInt16          lz77RefNum;
    Err             error = 0;

    error = LZ77LibIsPresent(&lz77RefNum);
    if (error) return error;

    Lz77LibMaxBufferSize( lz77RefNum, lz77Expand,
        *bufferLen, &expandedSize );

    newBufferH = MemHandleNew(expandedSize);
    if (newBufferH == NULL)
        return 1; // TODO: make an error class

    error = Lz77LibOpen(lz77RefNum, &lz77SessionH, lz77Expand,
                *bufferLen, &newBufferH, &expandedSize,
```

Continued

Figure 11.26 Continued

```
                    0, NULL, 0, 0);
    if (!error)
    {
        bufferPtr   = (char *)MemHandleLock(*bufferHP);
        lz77BitOffset = 0;
        error = Lz77LibChunk(lz77RefNum, lz77SessionH,
             (UInt8 *) bufferPtr, *bufferLen, &lz77BitOffset);
        MemHandleUnlock(*bufferHP);
    }

    Lz77LibClose(lz77RefNum, lz77SessionH, &expandedSize );
    if (error < lz77ErrFatalFirstErr)
    {
        MemHandleFree( *bufferHP );
        *bufferHP = newBufferH;
        newBufferH   = NULL;
        *bufferLen = expandedSize;
    }

    if (newBufferH)
    {
        MemHandleFree(newBufferH);
        newBufferH = NULL;
    }
    return(error);
}
```

LZ77 Compression and inetSettingMaxRspSize

If you use LZ77 compression, you have to keep in mind that *inetSettingMaxRspSize* now refers to the maximum size of the compressed data. For example, if you set *inetSettingMaxRspSize* as 4K, the final uncompressed size of the data may be as big as 20K, or even bigger. The buffer assigned for

INetLibSockRead need only be 4K. However, the program must be able to handle 20K of uncompressed data everywhere else in the code.

If the server finds that the result does not fit within the limit specified, it will truncate the compressed data and send back whatever it can. When we receive the truncated compressed data, we should be aware of the fact that **Lz77LibChunk** might return an error, due to incomplete compression codes at the end of the received data. If your application is willing to accept truncated data, you should also be willing to ignore nonfatal errors from the LZ77 library. The LZ77 library classifies some errors as fatal and some errors as nonfatal. Refer to LZ77Mgr.h for more information.

One advantage to using LZ77 compression is that it involves less work on our part. The code can be copied as such to any project you need and will not normally require any changes. You can assume that it is part of INetLib.

A disadvantage is that LZ77 compression is not completely transparent to the application programmer. Unlike ECC encryption support, which is also activated by a flag, this requires explicit decoding of the data by the user. It is probably very difficult for Palm OS to provide decompression inside **INetLibSockRead** because the compression and decompression require a minimum chunk size to work with. INetLib's built-in compression works only from proxy to Palm. The data flow from the proxy to your Web server is still raw data. However, considering that the connection between Palm.Net and your site is usually a big pipe, it is not much of a disadvantage.

End-to-End Compressed Data

You can compress the data at your server using LZ77 compression using a publicly available LZ77 compression library. After the data reaches your Palm device, you can decompress using the LZ77 Manager. You may also use the zlib implementation available for Palm OS. It may be harder to find a pure LZ77 library for desktops, so you may want to stick with zlib, which is an LZ77 derivative. Zlib uses the Deflate algorithm which includes applying Huffman coding before the LZ77 algorithm. According to Palm's documentation (in "Web Clipping Guide.pdf"), they do not seem to be using Huffman coding. Therefore, if you use zlib on the server side and LZ77Lib on the Palm, it may not be compatible. You can obtain Zlib for Palm from http://palmzlib.sourceforge.net. The official site of zlib is www.info-zip.org/pub/infozip/zlib.

End-to-End LZ77 Usage

We must first buffer the server output and compress the whole response in one single operation. We will disable INetLib's compression, because we cannot compress the data any further, and when we receive the data, we will decompress the message using the same DecompressLZ77 routine.

The advantage to this method is that it may be used even without the proxy. If you are developing your own replacement for INetLib using NetLib, this is a better option for you. If your server has a bad connection to the Internet, you will notice an improvement in speed, because the number of bytes transferred from your server to the Palm device has decreased.

A disadvantage is that you have much more work to do on the server side. Your application must buffer the data and compress it before you send it to the client. This includes even the error messages. The URL will not be usable from other interfaces.

An Unwired Widgets Mail Reader Example

We will now look at a complete example, the "Unwired Widgets Mail Reader" (UWMail). UWMail uses most of the INetLib features discussed so far and provides you with a real, useful program that uses INetLib. UWMail allows the user to quickly view her e-mail and optionally download the body of messages. In this respect, this example is very similar to iMessenger, except that we do not implement all of the iMessenger features. The example concentrates more on INetLib, data formats, Palm OS UI, and Palm OS databases, rather than specific e-mail features. Moreover, the program does not allow the user to send messages; that has been left out to limit the size of the example (moreover, support for sending e-mail is much easier to implement than that for receiving e-mail). The following section describes the design and implementation of UWMail.

Requirements for UWMail

The first step of any project is to list out the requirements:

- **Basic features** UWMail should fetch the mail from an existing mail server.
- **Optimization** UWMail should use a protocol/format optimized for transmission over a wireless network such as Palm.Net.

- **Complement the desktop** UWMail should complement the desktop mail reader (Outlook, Netscape, and so on.) and not try to replace it. In other words, UWMail should not delete messages from the server when it retrieves them, and the messages should still be available to the user when he gets back to his desk.
- **Preview** UWMail should provide a preview of the mail to the user and download the entire mail only if the user requests to do so. The preview should include at least Sender and Subject information.
- **Management** Nowadays, people receive more spam (unsolicited mail) than regular mail. After having previewed the mail on the client, it would really be nice if the user did not have to do it again on her desktop. When the user deletes a message from her Palm device, we must give her the option to remove the mail from the server as well. In addition, messages read on the client must be "marked" as read on the server too, so that the user can easily recognize previewed mail.

Design of UWMail

We first investigate the existing protocols to access e-mail. The most popular ones are Internet Message Access Protocol version 4 (IMAP4) and Post Office Protocol version 3 (POP3). Neither of these protocols is accessible over HTTP, which seems to be the only one available for us. Hence, we decide to put a proxy in the middle which will talk HTTP to the Palm device and IMAP4/POP3 to the mail servers. The proxy can be written using any standard server-side technology, such as CGI scripts, Servlets, JSP, ASP, or Cold Fusion. We choose Perl-based CGI scripts for the sample implementation in this chapter.

A Brief Discussion on Mail Format, Storage, IMAP4, and POP3

Internet Mail travels around the world using Simple Mail Transfer Protocol (SMTP). All of the mail servers speak SMTP as they transfer mail from system to system. In the early days of Internet, this was the only protocol required, because the mail was always stored at a central mail server for each organization. Users would log on to the server either locally or remotely and read mail using a text terminal interface. The advent of graphical clients and disconnected client PCs led to the development of POP, of which POP3 is the third iteration. POP3 specifies a method for remote user authentication and mail retrieval. Once retrieved, a copy of the mail physically resides on the client machine even when it is disconnected from the server. Unlike SMTP where the sender loses the copy, POP3 allows both the server and client to keep duplicate copies of mail. Unfortunately, initial versions of POP were minimal and did not provide a foolproof solution to many of the problems in mail synchronizing. POP2 did not even allow the client to download headers without downloading the body of the message. However, POP3 provides an adequate set of commands and is still one of the most widely used protocols. IMAP4 is a protocol designed to solve many of the problems with disconnected clients. IMAP4 is based on a *folder-sync* concept rather than the *pull* concept of POP3.

IMAP versus POP3

In order to implement all the requirements given to us, we need IMAP4 support. POP3 provides a one-way download and does not let us change the Read/ Unread status of a message. However, POP3 is much simpler to implement and more widely used than IMAP4. In this case, we made a tradeoff, sacrificing the requirement to show read status on the desktop for ease of implementation.

Mail Message Format

POP3 specifies the mail to be returned in RFC 822 format. This RFC document specifies how mail messages are divided into a header and a body, and how each header item contains a name-value pair separated by a colon. A carriage return and line feed separate each header item from the next, and two such pairs separate the entire header from the body. Messages with attachments follow the same pattern, with the body of the messages represented as a multipart item, where each item recursively obeys the same pattern, with each attachment having its own header and body. RFC822 can be obtained from http://www.ietf.org/rfc/rfc822.txt.

Message Identification

POP3 expects the server to associate every message with a unique ID. The unique ID of a message is an arbitrary server-determined string, consisting of one to seventy characters in the range 0x21 to 0x7E, which uniquely identifies a message within a mailbox and which persists across sessions. The server should never reuse a unique ID in a given mailbox for as long as the entity using the unique ID exists.

The TOP, RETR, and UIDL Commands

Among all the POP3 commands, **TOP**, **RETR**, and **UIDL** are the three commands the server must support for us to implement this solution. **TOP** returns the header of a message, **RETR** (Retrieve) returns the header and body of a message, and **UIDL** (Unique Identification List) returns a list of all messages on the server along with their unique IDs. This command is crucial for us to differentiate old messages from new. As mentioned earlier, we do not intend to delete messages from the server. When we connect to the server the next time, we must have a infallible way to identify "old" messages from "new." To do this, we will compare the current **UIDL** with the list returned in the last session with the difference being the list of new messages.

Mail::POP3Client Perl Module

Fortunately, we have a wide array of modules at our disposal when we use Perl. Net: POP3 is one of the modules that come preinstalled with Perl. However, we will choose Mail::POP3Client, which works at a higher level and provides a better abstraction. Mail::POP3Client was written by Sean Dowd and is available from all Comprehensive Perl Archive Network (CPAN) mirrors. Figure 11.27 shows its usage.

Figure 11.27 Using Mail::POP3Client to Retrieve Mail

```
/* Connection and login */
my $pop = new Mail::POP3Client( USER      => $username,
                                PASSWORD => $password,
                                HOST      => $hostname );


/* retreiving UIDL */
@new_uid_list = $pop->Uidl();
/* retreiving header */
$rawHdr =  $pop->Head($msgNum);
/* retreiving body*/
$rawBody = $pop->Body($msgNum);
/* message deletion */
$pop->Delete($msgNum);
```

Server Architecture

Our server runs as a CGI script written in Perl that accesses a POP3 server via the Mail::POP3Client module. We will accept the hostname, username, and password via POST variables and pass them to Mail::POP3Client module. In order to avoid having a database on the server, we will require the client to explicitly include the hostname, username, and password in every request.

As an enhancement, we may optionally store the user's preferences (hostname, username, and password) on the server itself. This is particularly useful if we intend to provide support for multiple POP3 servers, server-side filters, and so on.

Request Format

We expect the client to send the request using the following POST variables:

- ***hst*** A text string consisting of the complete Internet hostname of the POP3 server. This server and the POP3 port must be accessible from the Internet because we are using Palm.Net proxy.
- ***usr*** Logon username to access the POP3 server.
- ***pwd*** Logon password to access the account.
- ***del*** (Optional) A list of message UIDs for messages that should be deleted from the server. Item separator is line feed (LF character - ASCII 10). Remember that all values are URL-encoded.
- ***dwn*** (Optional) A list of message UIDs for messages that should be downloaded from the server. Item separator is line feed (LF character - ASCII 10). Remember that all values are URL-encoded.
- ***msz*** (Optional) A number represented in printed format that denotes the maximum number of bytes the clients can receive. The server must exclude messages that do not fit within this limit. The server cannot arbitrarily truncate the response and must make sure that each message either fits in completely or is not included at all.
- ***mct*** (Optional) A number represented in printed format that denotes the maximum number of messages the client can receive. This is particularly useful for the first session. Your mail server may have messages that date back to the Ice Age. This option will make sure that we only get the newest 25 or so from the list.

- ***all*** (Optional) A value *y* will make the server ignore the previous UIDL and assume that the user has never downloaded anything before. If the client loses its mail for any reason, it may use this option to download previous mail.

Assume that the proxy resides at the URL http://www.unwiredwidgets.com/bin/ch11/getMail. A request to fetch new mail for user "foobar" at mail.unwiredwidgets.com, delete the message with UID AA3547878, and download messages with UIDs AC7788497 and AC7788498 will appear as follows:

```
POST /bin/getMail

hst=mail%2Eunwiredwidgets%2Ecom&usr=foobar&pwd=secret123&del=AA3547878&d
wn=AC7788497%0AAC7788498
```

UIDL Storage

As discussed earlier, we must store the list of message UIDs returned by the server in order to compare them to the same in the next session. Instead of using a database, we will store them in flat files, one file per user. Perl provides excellent features to manage flat files. In order to avoid username (and hence filename) conflicts, we will create one directory per server (remote POP3 server) and then create one file per username in the server. Two different users will never have the same server name and same username. In addition, we will make sure we will not read or write a UIDL file until after the user has logged in to the POP3 server. This should prevent any accidental corruption of UIDL files if two users have the same username by mistake. The UIDL for the user "foobar" at mail.unwiredwidgets.com will be stored at /tmp/uidl/mail.unwiredwidgets.com/foobar, assuming that "/tmp/uidl" was chosen as a the data storage directory. We will allow the site administrator to change these settings. The Perl functions in Figure 11.28 implement the UIDL storage and retrieval.

Figure 11.28 Perl Functions to Store and Retrieve Mail UIDL

```
sub SaveUIDL # (string $fileName, ref to array $uid_list)
{
    my ($fileName, $uid_list) = @_;
    local *UIDL_FILE;
```

Continued

Figure 11.28 Continued

```
    if (open UIDL_FILE, ">$fileName")
    {
        print UIDL_FILE join("\n", @$uid_list);
        close UIDL_FILE;
    }
    else
    {
        die ("Unable to open UIDL file ->$fileName<- for writing");
    }
}

sub ReadUIDL # (fileName)
{
    my $fileName = shift;
    local *UIDL_FILE;

    my @array = ();
    if (open UIDL_FILE, "<$fileName")
    {
        my $save = $/; undef $/;
        @array = split /\n/, <UIDL_FILE>;
        $/ = $save;
        close UIDL_FILE;
    }
    return @array;
}
```

Response Format

Mail messages are always in plain text—including binary attachments, which are encoded using 7-bit characters. Hence, we will choose a text-based format for our response. The first line of response will indicate the status of the request as well as the number of messages that will follow. Header items include "From:",

"To:", "Cc:", and "Subject:" lines of a message. We will save a few bytes and omit the field tags themselves and consider the first line of data to be "From:", the second line of data to be "Cc:" and so on. If the header item for "To:" or "Cc:" itself occupies multiple lines, we will unfold the header into a single line. New lines (CR+LF) in headers are not important, and RFC822 specifies how to do this unfolding.

We will also have to send message bodies as part of the response. Although a message body will usually have multiple lines, we cannot apply the same unfolding rules here because line breaks are important in a message, and we need to preserve them throughout the transmission. To handle this, we will replace the CR+LF breaks in the message with a single character: CR. Because our client parser looks for the LF character as a line terminator, the entire body would appear to the parser as a single line. After the data reaches the client, we will substitute LF for CR characters, because Palm OS fields use LF to denote a line break. This scheme allows us to use the same parser for headers and message bodies. However, because header fields can be sent separately from message bodies, we need to count them separately and include a separate count field in the status line. A sample output is given in Figure 11.29. Text in italics is not part of the response.

Figure 11.29 UWMail Response Format

```
+OK 000002 000001                               <== status line
AA7828997                                        <== Message UID
Donald <donald@unwiredwidgets.com>             <== From: header
Mickey <mickey@unwiredwidgets.com>             <== To: header
                                                   <== An empty line for Cc:
Howdy?                                            <== Subject
KA5678909                                        <== Next header starts
here
Buzz <buzz@unwiredwidgets.com>
Andy <andy@unwiredwidgets.com>
Rex <rex@unwiredwidgets.com>, Mickey <mickey@unwiredwidgets.com>
Woody is missing!!
GA9068474
Hi mickey,\rI got your card.\rThanks!\r— \rMinnie
```

Client Architecture

UWMail client—the native Palm OS program—will be based on our earlier URLFetch program. In addition to the basic framework set by the URLFetch example, we need client-side code to interpret our protocol for talking with the mail server proxy. Moreover, the database records are now more than one chunk of text; they have six fields (Message UID, From, To, Cc, Subject, and Body). In addition, we also need flags to denote the read/unread status of the message, as well as the future action to be taken on the message. A list was used to display the items in URLFetch, but we will use a table in UWMail. The table provides much better control than a list and is well suited for multiple column listings.

User Interface Details

Compared to the URLFetch example, UWMail requires many additional text fields for the user to enter the hostname, her username, and that username's associated password. Instead of stuffing the main screen with more text fields, we will move these preferences into a separate form, the "Mail Preferences" form which is tagged as 'PrefsForm' in the code (see Figure 11.30). The PrefsForm is accessed via a menu item in the main screen: MailListForm.

Figure 11.30 UWMail Preferences Dialog

A Trick to Hide a Password

A password field acts like a write-only field. You can modify the existing password by writing a new value. However, you cannot view the existing password. Palm OS does not support "password" fields, so the programmer has to implement them with additional code. When we initially load the form, we will fill all of the field values available except the password field. If the password is completely empty, we will display the tag "<Not Set>". This is to warn the user that he has not set a password. If the password really has some data, it will appear empty. The user can always enter text into the password field, and any text entered will replace the existing password. When the user taps on the **Save** button, we check to see if the password field has been modified. If it has, we use the new text as the new password. The code shown in Figure 11.31 from the UWMail source illustrates the trick.

Figure 11.31 Trick to Hide Current Password

```
/* field initialization */
fldPtr = GetObjectPtr(PrefsPassword, frm);
if (!prefs.password[0])
    FldInsert(fldPtr, "<Not Set>", 9);

/* saving password field */
fldPtr = GetObjectPtr(PrefsPassword, frm);
if (FldDirty(fldPtr))
{
    fldValue = FldGetTextPtr(fldPtr);
    if ((fldValue != NULL) && (*fldValue != 0))
        StrNCopy(prefs.password, fldValue, MAX_PASSWORD_LEN);
    else prefs.password[0] = 0;
}
```

Mail List View

UWMail uses a table to display the list of e-mails. Tables have many advantages compared to lists, with the most important being the ability to recognize a tap on one of several columns. For example, in UWMail, we divide the table into four columns (see Figure 11.32). Currently, the last column, a very small one, is unused. The second and third columns are used to display the sender ("From:" field) and subject of the message. The first column functions as a indicator of the requested action to be performed on the item. UWMail can differentiate between a tap on the margin (first column) and a tap anywhere else, which we use to add an extra feature to UWMail. The user can tap on the margin to toggle the download/delete flags on the message. A user can mark a message for download by tapping on the first column of the table. Another tap marks it for deletion, and the next tap returns the message to its default state, which is "do nothing."

Figure 11.32 UWMail Mail List View

The All check box requests the program to ignore previous download history. The LZ checkbox uses LZ77 compression if available. The CType checkbox was mainly used for debugging—it sets the Content-Type of the outgoing request to be "application/x-www-form-urlencoded". The Stop button ends the current INetLib session, if any.

Database Record Format

The database record format is quite different from the URLFetch example. URLFetch had a trivial database where each server response was dumped directly to the database. UWMail needs to save many details of each message in a variety of string and numeric fields. The MailRecordType structure defines a mail record. (Note that we have left out descriptions of the standard mail fields whose details are irrelevant here.)

```
typedef struct {
     UInt8  readFlag;  // one of ReadStatusFlagType
     UInt8  msgComplete;      // one of DownloadStatusFlagType
     UInt8  nextReq;          // one of MsgCommandType
     Char * msgUID;
     Char * from;
```

```
    Char * to;
    Char * cc;
    Char * subject;
    Char * body;
} MailRecordType;
```

When the record is written to a database record, fixed length fields are written first, followed by string fields. String fields are separated from others by a null terminator character that will always be present, even when the field is empty. When we read the record back from the database, we usually will not copy the string fields out from the record. The string fields of the struct are made to point to appropriate places in the locked record. You can refer to MailRecord.c for more information on the packing and unpacking routines.

Parsing Server Response

The first line of the server response starts with "+OK..." or "-ERR..." depending on the status. I have borrowed this convention from POP3 itself, which uses a very similar response style. The "-ERR" string is usually followed by helpful text that can be displayed to the user. The "+OK" response will always be followed with one space and then two 6-digit numbers, again separated by one space. The crux of the proxy implementation lies in three crucial functions: **CheckResponse**, **ParseNSaveHeaders**, and **ParseNSaveBodies**, shown in Figure 11.33.

Figure 11.33 Parsing Server Response

```
Err CheckResponse
(
    Char *response,
    Boolean silent,
    UInt16 *numHdrs,
    UInt16 *numBody
)
{
    if (StrNCompare(response, "+OK", 3) == 0)
    {
        if (numHdrs) *numHdrs = (UInt16)StrAToI(response + 4);
        if (numBody) *numBody = (UInt16)StrAToI(response + 11);
```

Continued

Figure 11.33 Continued

```
            return 0;
        }
        if (StrNCompare(response, "-ERR", 4) == 0)
        {
            if (!silent) FrmCustomAlert(CustomErrorAlert,
                    "Server responded", response + 5, NULL);
            return 1;
        }
        if (!silent) FrmCustomAlert(CustomErrorAlert,
                    "Invalid response from server", NULL, NULL);
        return 2;
}

Char *ParseNSaveHeaders(Char * response, UInt16 *numHeaders)
{
        UInt16 len, recIndex;
        MailRecordType mail;
        Char *buffer;
        Err     err;

        while ((*numHeaders != 0) &&
                (response != NULL))
        {
            MemSet(&mail, sizeof(MailRecordType), 0);
            mail.msgUID = response;
            mail.from = response = GetNextLine(response, '\n');
            if (!response) break;
            mail.to = response = GetNextLine(response, '\n');
            if (!response) break;
            mail.cc = response = GetNextLine(response, '\n');
            if (!response) break;
            mail.subject = response = GetNextLine(response, '\n');
            if (!response) break;
```

Continued

Figure 11.33 Continued

```
            // More forward for the next response.
            response = GetNextLine(response, '\n');

            buffer = PackMailRec(&mail, &len);
            recIndex = 0;
            err = SaveData(g.dbP, &recIndex, buffer, len);
            if(err) ErrAlert(err);
            MemPtrFree(buffer);
            (*numHeaders)—;
        }
        return response;
}

Char *ParseNSaveBodies(Char *response, UInt16 *numBodies)
{
        UInt16 recIndex, len;
        MailRecordType mail;
        Char *buffer, *msgUID, *body;
        Char *recPtr;
        Err err;

        while ((*numBodies != 0) &&
                (response != NULL))
        {
            MemSet(&mail, sizeof(MailRecordType), 0);
            msgUID = response;
            body = response = GetNextLine(response, '\n');
            if (!response) break;

            recIndex = FindRecordByMsgUID(msgUID);
            if (recIndex != dmMaxRecordIndex)
            {
                err = LockRecord(&recPtr, g.dbP, recIndex);
```

Continued

Figure 11.33 Continued

```
                if (err) break; // unlikely
                UnpackMailRec(recPtr, &mail);
            }
            mail.msgUID;
            mail.msgComplete = type_complete;
            mail.nextReq = type_cmd_none; // clear the flag
            mail.body = body;
            SubtCRwithLF(mail.body);
            buffer = PackMailRec(&mail, &len);
            UnlockRecord(g.dbP, recIndex);

            /* delete the old one. But we can only* do that *after*
              'packing' the new one.
             * Don't try to move this line inside the * earlier if() loop
             */
            if (recIndex != dmMaxRecordIndex)
                DmRemoveRecord(g.dbP, recIndex);

             err = SaveData(g.dbP, &recIndex, buffer,len);
             if(err) ErrAlert(err);
             MemPtrFree(buffer);

            // More forward for the next response.
            response = GetNextLine(response, '\n');
            (*numBodies)—;
        }

        return response;
}
```

Browsing Documentation and Source Code

We have commented the source code using the javadoc format. The comments were then extracted out into a HTML format by CCDOC, modified to link the generated pages with LXR-based documentation. To start viewing the documentation, please open Chapter_11\docs.html in the CD that accompanies this book.

Developing & Deploying…

Deploying Your Application

Standalone applications, built as files with the .PRC extension, can be distributed the same way as WCA files (.PQA extension). You can let the user download the file as it is or package the file inside a .ZIP file. However, note the following differences:

- Standalone .PRC files are usually bigger than WCA applications. This does not mean that your application is inefficient—the WCA application had only the startup page.
- Multiple files may be associated with your application. You may choose to divide your application into shared libraries, helper .PDB files, and so on. This means that the user may have to install multiple files.
- Your application may have a conduit, which contains Windows or Macintosh code, and may require special installation steps (for example, registration with the HotSync manager).

Palm OS HotSync software includes a library that provides an "Installation API" to Windows or Macintosh applications. You may use this API from native desktop applications as well as Installation Scripts such as InstallShield. If your application has a conduit, you must use the InstApp API. Your deployment options include the following:

- **Leave the hard work to the user** Include all files in a .ZIP, .SIT, or similar package and have the user install each file one by one. This is the way to go if your application includes just one PRC file; special installation software may be overkill. However, remember to keep the user guide in a separate directory, and don't confuse the user with too many files.

Continued

- **Give the user a break** Use a standard installation software such as InstallShield. Palm provides sample project files along with the Conduit SDK. If you do not have a conduit, you may ignore the references to conduit in the sample project files. The Conduit SDK can be downloaded from www.palmos .com/dev/tech/conduits. You may also use other installation software such as Install VISE from www.mindvision.com or WISE Installer from www.wisesolutions.com. InstApp API is a Windows DLL file, and any installation software that can access Windows DLLs can serve your purpose. You may have to look at the InstallShield example and write equivalent scripts for that package.
- **And save some bandwidth, too** Use an installation software custom-made for Palm OS software distribution. Setup software built with these usually have a smaller footprint than those built-in with InstallShield. The InstApp API will be completely hidden from you, although you may miss some of the scripting features of InstallShield, VISE, or WISE. However, a wizard interface will usually substitute the lack of scripting. Pilot Catapult from www.beiks.com is one such installer.

Enhancing UWMail

Although UWMail serves as a starting point, it lacks many features required for a mail reader. Limitations and solutions regarding *message limits* include the following:

- Right now response size and count limits are hardcoded on each side. This should be passed from the client to the server as request parameters. The server code already includes some of the code for it—the client needs to send those values as parameters.
- If the response size or the count exceeds the limit, the remaining messages are ignored and no error information is passed to the client. The server should inform the client about the messages that were left out. A more advanced solution would fragment the mail retrieval into many requests.
- Based on the current server implementation, if a message that is bigger than the response limit appeared in the mail spool, no messages are returned to the client, even if smaller messages are available. According to

our algorithm, we stop whenever we find that the limit will be exceeded. A more advanced solution must try to accommodate more messages in the remaining space by skipping over the big message.

Limitations and solutions regarding *mail features* include the following:

- The mail reader should provide support for all e-mail headers, including Date and Priority.
- A solution to receiving a message that is too big to download is to download just part of the message. An even more interesting feature would be to provide a "More" button for the user to download the next 1K block of a message.
- Deleting a message automatically removes the message from both the server and the Palm device; it should ideally be a user option.

Securing Data

This section discusses the security issues associated with native applications accessing your Web site. Although in most cases they are similar to WCA applications, you need to handle some special circumstances in native applications.

Obscurity Does Not Constitute Security

When you expose your corporate data over a Web interface, you should make sure that the Web interface is properly secured. Just because you have made a native Palm OS application using SSL to access the content does not mean that your server data is secure. Your server application can be accessed from any device connected to the Internet with a reasonably modern browser. Opening the PRC in a regular hex editor or disassembling the PQA file will easily reveal the URL used and any parameters passed. You also should not rely on Clipper's (or your application's) inability to show raw HTTP data.

Securing Server Access

Securing your transport via SSL along with the use of username and password can ensure security. However, the user must manually enter the username and password. A hard-coded username and password in a program, however encrypted they may be, is just as bad as leaving your server wide open.

Securing HTTP Transactions

Palm VII uses Certicom's ECC encryption from the handheld to the Palm.Net servers and SSL encryption from Palm.Net servers to the Internet. This is sufficient security for most applications. However, you should note that this differs from the security offered by Internet Explorer or Netscape. When a user visits your site using an SSL-enabled browser, your data is secure based on the following four assumptions:

- You trust the browser vendor (Netscape/Microsoft/Palm, Inc.) to have implemented the security layer accurately. Palm, Inc. uses Certicom's encryption technology.
- The user obtained his browser from a trusted source, such as a secure server within your company or a vendor CD. In our case, this would be the preinstalled Clipper or your application.
- Your Web server is secure, both physically and over the network, and the server has not been compromised.
- You trust the certificate authorities (VeriSign, et al) to keep their private keys secure.

Note, for the desktop model, you do not need to trust your ISP or your user's ISP. This is due to the data being encrypted from end-to-end, with no access in clear form by either ISP. Palm.Net encryption differs from this. When a user accesses your site or application from the handheld device, the data is decrypted at the Palm.Net server, then encrypted again to be sent on to your own server. In this case, you have to trust the Palm.Net gateway machine to be secure and assume that Palm.Net does not log the data or its properties in any way. This assumption cannot be made for certain kinds of applications. However, in reality, Palm.Net would never do that and risk losing trust. Therefore, if you are not that paranoid, the existing transport via Palm.Net should be quite enough.

Palm, Inc. had to take this approach for valid reasons. The whole concept of a Web clipping proxy server cannot exist if they provided end-to-end encryption. If Palm Inc.'s proxy cannot look at the data, it will not be able to reformat the data and provide a solution optimized for wireless. Alternate solutions to Palm.Net are offered by third parties that provide this end-to-end encryption support. However, in most cases, the solutions may be the same as Palm.Net's. The fact that the server physically resides in your premises make the same solution end-to-end secure. In short, if you are paranoid about end-to-end security, you may want to license a Web clipping server (or a similar client-server solution) from Palm.Net, Omnisky, or JP Mobile.

Palm, Inc. has put a very nice document in their Knowledge Base regarding this issue. If you are worried about end-to-end security, you should definitely look at it. It is available at http://oasis.palm.com/dev/kb/faq/1994.cfm. (The URL may change in the future.) A relevant section reads as follows: *"...There are restrictions in place to prevent such an insider attack. The Palm programmer, who has access to the source code and compiler, does not have access to the production server farm. Production servers are housed in redundant, secure, co-located data centers, which maintain stringent security at both router and system levels. Likewise, Production Operations personnel have no access to source code or compiler information."*

Testing for Proxy Issues and Known Bugs

This section discusses issues, existing bugs, and problems with INetLib, Palm.Net, and OmniSky proxies. Keep in mind that these issues should be minor, or that they are bugs that may be fixed by the time this book goes to print. Always test to see if this behavior occurs in your device and act accordingly.

OmniSky Servers

OmniSky, Inc. provides Web-clipping service for the Handspring Visor Platinum, Prism, and Edge, and for Palm's V and V*x* devices. Initially, this was the only way to get Web clipping on these devices. However, with Palm OS 3.5 and above, Web clipping services are available directly from Palm.Net as an add-on to any device with a modem. This section discusses problems and differences of OmniSky servers compared to Palm.Net service.

Unwanted Characters in Server Response

If you look at how PQAs get displayed on a Palm device with OmniSky service, you will notice that the same PQA running on an OmniSky browser will have a footer added to all pages. The footer provides links to "Home" and "Legal," and also an "Add Bookmark" command. At first glance, it may seem that the browser is adding this footer while displaying the page, but a closer look reveals that the server itself adds this text to every outgoing response. If you were to write your own browser, it would still look the same. Even when you use INetLib to fetch arbitrary URLs from the Internet, the response will include this blurb.

Testing the Header Addition

Let us modify our Hello_World example (refer back to Figure 11.1) and change the link from hello.txt to hello.html. Rebuild and generate a new PRC via CodeWarrior, Falch.net, or bare PRC-Tools. Install this new PRC into a device with OmniSky service and test it. A sample output from this program is shown in Figure 11.34.

Figure 11.34 Blurb Added by OmniSky Servers

Now, let us modify the URL to point to a CGI script. Name the CGI script "hello.pl" with the following contents:

```
#!/usr/bin/perl -w
print "Content-Type: text/html\r\n\r\n";
print "Hello World!\n"
```

Make sure that you put this script in a directory where scripting is enabled. It may be called cgi-bin or bin in your Web server directory. After modifying the URL appropriately, rebuild and reinstall the PRC into the device. Running the program shows that the client still produces the same result.

Now change the Content-Type to "text/plain" or "application/octet-stream". Rerun the test and you will see that the blurb disappears. However, now the response includes a header line "Content-Length" (see Figure 11.35). It appears that the server is adding a Content-Length field if one is not specified. However, the Content-Length is incorrectly being added as part of the data rather than part of the header. Because we did not request headers, this could be a surprise to our application if we are not careful.

Figure 11.35 Server Response with Mixed Headers

Add the following line to the Perl script and you will get the correct response:

```
print "Content-Length: 13\r\n";
```

Setting the Content-Length field can be a little tricky. Because it is a header line, it must appear before any application data sent to the client. If you have an application (ASP, Perl, CGI, or JSP) spitting contents as arbitrary chunks, you may have to either buffer the output until the complete length is known or find another way to precalculate the response length.

Solving the Header Addition

One solution is to use Content-Type of text/html and find a way to filter out the blurb. Another option is to use Content-Type of text/plain and calculate the Content-Length appropriately.

A final option that may work is setting the Content-Length to a value greater than the real content's length. Use Content-Type of text/plain, set Content-Length to a huge value, and be ready to repent when your app breaks one day!

The Omnisky INetLib Implementation and *ctpWireless*

OmniSky service uses Minstrel Modem from Novatel Wireless. Minstrel is a wireless modem, but it acts like a standard wired mode, so it uses *ctpWireline* to connect to the proxy. *ctpWireless* points to an invalid configuration. You can use the ConfigBrowser to test this. As you might have noticed, ConfigBrowser shows that *ctpWireline* points to AIM, the real configuration used by OmniSky (see Figure 11.36). Trying this selection gives us an "Interface not found" error (see Figure 11.37). Because the OmniSky service does not use *ctpWireless*, the Signal Strength Indicator is also not available for OmniSky devices.

Figure 11.36 Configuration Available on OmniSky Device

Figure 11.37 Testing inetCfgNameCTPWireless on OmniSky Device

Summary

Writing a native application is substantially more difficult than writing WCA applications. Before you decide to rewrite your WCA application in C/C++/Java, you must evaluate and weigh the advantages and disadvantages. If efficiency, speed, bandwidth, and offline access are the key issues, developing a native application is well worth the effort. Instead, if maintenance effort and time to market are your major concerns, you should stick with the WCA interface.

Before you venture into INetLib and over-the-air optimizations, you must first create a good user interface and a code framework that is reliable. If your code is not as reliable and intuitive as Clipper, users may not like it no matter how many bytes you save for them. Most casual users would worry only about how the application "feels" and what it does for them, not how we do it. Creating a user interface similar to that rendered by a browser is not a simple task, but we should still give our best effort on it.

Unlike serving WCA applications, the server code cannot bail out any time with a simple error message. The error message is now being served to a program. The server-side code must always exit gracefully, sending appropriate error codes to the client.

Developing a native application by itself does not give you any advantages over the WCA unless you use the transport better than a WCA interface. You must have access to the server-side code to optimize it for "syncing" rather than viewing. For example, your server-side code should be capable of packing many records together, weeding out unnecessary information and providing the data as a single chunk. It must also be able to accept data similarly. In most cases, you may have to have a proxy that does some translations. You or your company must have enough resources to do so.

Anything that can be done by a Web clipping application can always be done by a native application (because the Clipper itself is one such application). However, the reverse is not true. There may be many applications where reliable offline access of data is crucial. A browser may provide a cache, but that is neither predictable nor accessible in any other format. Offline data provided by the cache cannot be reformatted, analyzed, or even used for anything other than displaying the exact same page. In developing a native Palm OS application, you must leverage as many benefits as you can. For example, the Mail Reader example in this chapter uses Palm database and UI tables to let the user manage his/her mails offline. Downloaded messages can be read at any time without using the network. By giving the user the choice to download or delete messages, we make sure that unwanted messages are not downloaded. The feature of offline reading and deferred deletion should be the envy of your Web clipping applications.

Solutions Fast Track

Introduction to INetLib

- ☑ The most popular language choice is C and the second most popular is C++. Currently, writing advanced applications requires solid knowledge of one of these languages.
- ☑ If you are interested in Java, check out Waba at www.wabasoft.com; IBM Visual Age/J9 at www.embedded.oti.com; and KVM at http://java.sun.com.
- ☑ Wireline support for INetLib was a recent addition to Palm OS, so you cannot use INetLib over a regular modem on a Palm VII. If you upgrade the operating system to Palm OS 3.5 or above, you will be able to use the wireline channel.
- ☑ Design your application to use a request-response model for transactions. This will allow your application to be accessed from a variety of channels. Even if your device supports full TCP/IP, sticking to HTTP would make your application accessible over wireline and wireless channels.

A Hello World Program

- ☑ Although INetLib library has more than 30 API calls, you need only a few of them to get started. The Hello World example in this chapter illustrates the basic sequence of calls.
- ☑ Internet Library is a Palm OS shared library. You must first verify that the library is present on the device before you can use it.
- ☑ Unusual errors are handled by fatal alerts. They are frequently used in Palm OS examples. Use of fatal alerts is a very clean and efficient way to bail out of an unexpected error.

Finding and Initializing Internet Library

- ☑ Not all Palm OS devices come with the Internet Library. You should call **SysLibFind** to locate the library.
- ☑ You must choose an INetLib configuration to use or provide an interface for the user to make the selection. Run the ConfigBrowser example to view existing configurations. *.CTPDefault*, *.CTPWireless*, and *.CTPWireline* are useful configurations.
- ☑ *.CTPWireless* does not always mean Palm VII radio. OmniSky devices use it to mean the Minstrel modem. However, OmniSky's *.CTPWireless* would be an alias to another configuration.

Creating an INetLib Connection

- ☑ Decide on the type of conversion: None, CML, or LZ77. Unless you are writing a browser, None and LZ77 are the only viable options.
- ☑ Verify that the proxy supports LZ77 before you use it.
- ☑ LZ77 is an optional module—it can be downloaded as part of the INetLow example from PalmOS.com.

Moving to an Event-Driven Model

- ☑ Good programs are always event-driven. An event-driven mechanism saves battery power and increases the responsiveness of the application.
- ☑ You must replace **EvtGetEvent** with **INetLibGetEvent** in your event loop.
- ☑ In the sequence of events generated for an INetLib transaction, all except the last one are of type *inetSockStatusChangeEvent*. The last one is *inetSockReadyEvent*. If you are interested only in the data, you can ignore all *inetSockStatusChangeEvents*, except when they show an error.

Accessing a Server-Side Application

- ☑ **INetLibURLOpen** supports only GET requests. If you need POST, you must substitute it with calls to **INetLibSockOpen**, **INetLibSockHTTPReqCreate**, and **INetLibSockHTTPReqSend**.
- ☑ All variables to POST and GET must be URL-encoded. URL encoding converts nonalphanumeric characters to the %HH format, where *HH* is the hexadecimal representation of the ASCII value.
- ☑ Through at least Palm OS 4.0, INetLib looks at the first few characters of the URL to determine the security level. The *schemeEnum* argument to **INetLibSockOpen** is ignored. However, do not rely on it being ignored—it may change at any time.
- ☑ Through at least Palm OS 4.0, INetLib looks at the value of *writeP* argument to **INetLibSockHTTPReqSend** to determine the request type. The *verbP* argument to **INetLibSockHTTPReqCreate** is ignored. However, do not rely on it being ignored—it may change at any time.
- ☑ Both GET and POST are capable of exchanging data. However, each has a role of its own and limits vary.
- ☑ As far as security is concerned, POST does not give you any more security than GET. Contrary to popular belief, POST does not hide business logic/form variable names from users.

Receiving Responses from the Server

- ☑ Remember that you have to catch two INetLib related events: *inetSockStatusChangeEvent* and *inetSockReadyEvent*.
- ☑ Server errors (401, 404, 500, and so on) cannot be caught unless you check the error via **INetLibSockHTTPAttrGet**.
- ☑ Palm OS error returns use 2 bytes; the first byte is used to classify the errors. In Palm OS header files, error classes are listed in hex, and individual values are listed in decimal.
- ☑ Your application will get multiple *inetSockReadyEvents*, and you may have to make multiple calls to **INetLibSockRead** to read the complete data.

Authenticating the User and Device

- ☑ Never rely too much on the device ID. The cookies specification is intended to be much more secure than device ID.
- ☑ Native applications may not require either of these unless you are trying to connect to an existing framework built on cookies.
- ☑ Palm.Net adds the validation codes only if the device ID was printed in Base 26. Also, the validation code cannot be trusted any more than you trust the user.

Providing Configuration Aliases

- ☑ You can run ConfigBrowser on any Palm device or Emulator and find the real mapping of configurations.
- ☑ If your application needs a user interface to select configurations, the example in this section shows you how to use INetLib calls to extract the configuration list and their names and aliases.
- ☑ Use ConfigBrowser along with URLFetch to test a configuration before you use it in an application.

Optimizing Transports

- ☑ A complex data format does not necessarily make the application efficient. Eight-bit formats are harder to debug. A text format combined with Palm.Net's LZ77 should give good results.
- ☑ Use of XML, and SyncML in particular, leads to better and more manageable architecture if you have tools on either side. A reference implementation of SyncML is available from syncml.org.

An Unwired Widgets Mail Reader Example

- ☑ A mail reader makes use of the offline capabilities of Palm OS. Messages can be read and marked for download or deletion. It also shows you how to defer message deletions until it can be synced up with the server.

- ☑ Our transport format was very simple, and it can be debugged using a desktop browser.
- ☑ Although the Mail Reader lacks a conduit and does not handle other launch codes, it servers as a complete example that makes use of databases, user interface (tables), an optimal transport format, and INetLib. Make sure that you browse the source code and documentation.

Securing Data

- ☑ Using SSL ensures that the data cannot be viewed or corrupted by a third party on transit. However, it does not (and is not meant to) protect your server.
- ☑ If you access corporate data from the client and you use a password stored in a database or an application, your server data is only as secure as your handheld. No matter how encrypted the password is, it can be recovered unless the encryption involves a key entered by the user.
- ☑ Palm.Net is not end-to-end secure. However, the reason Palm.Net uses a different encryption is that straight SSL is not suited for wireless. Moreover, it cannot function as a Web clipping proxy unless it can access plain text data. If you are paranoid, licensing a copy of Elaine server or a similar implementation developed by a third party may be a solution.

Testing for Proxy Issues and Known Bugs

- ☑ OmniSky, Inc. provides Web-clipping service for the Handspring Visor Platinum, Prism, and Edge, and for Palm's V and V*x* devices. Initially, this was the only way to get Web clipping on these devices. However, with Palm OS 3.5 and above, Web clipping services are available directly from Palm.Net as an add-on to any device with a modem.
- ☑ OmniSky service uses Minstrel Modem from Novatel Wireless. Minstrel is a wireless modem, but it acts like a standard wired mode, so it uses *ctpWireline* to connect to the proxy. *ctpWireless* points to an invalid configuration. You can use the ConfigBrowser to test this.

Frequently Asked Questions

The following Frequently Asked Questions, answered by the authors of this book, are designed to both measure your understanding of the concepts presented in this chapter and to assist you with real-life implementation of these concepts. To have your questions about this chapter answered by the author, browse to **www.syngress.com/solutions** and click on the **"Ask the Author"** form.

Q: How much data can I send and receive through Palm VII?

A: Per HTTP POST, approximately 7K of upload and around 32K of download. However, you should fragment your downloads into multiple requests for better error handling. You should fragment your data into multiple chunks of approximately 4–10K each. Never stretch the network to its limit—wireless networks have higher error rates than your LAN connection. You may be able to download 1MB at 60K chunks each from your test lab, but it may not work for a user who is on the road.

Q: How do I prevent the device from powering off while I am downloading data?

A: You should cCall **EvtResetAutoOffTimer** frequently while your transaction is in progress. You could make it in your event loop or animation code, as long as this call is made frequently enough to avoid the power timeout. However, you should never try to set the auto-off timer to a very high value trying to avoid multiple calls. If your application crashes before you can restore the value of the auto-off timer, the Palm OS device will run out of battery power within a few hours.

Q: My application cannot reach the server. Why do I get "Error: Incomplete Setup" messages? Why does POSE have problems connecting to the proxy?

A: Three factors are involved for a successful connection. First, that you chose the right INetLib configuration; second, that you have enabled "Redirect NetLib calls to host TCP/IP" checkbox in the emulator; and third, that you have entered the correct proxy hostname or IP address under "Web Clipping" preferences. Please note that reinstalling a new version of POSE may revert settings back to their defaults.

Q: Where do I find the meaning of HTTP error codes?

A: Most usual error codes are 401, 403, 404 (400 series), and 500 series. A 400 series error indicates a problem in the URL, and a 500 series error indicates a problem inside your server application. If the file is absent, or does not have appropriate permissions, you will get a 400 series error. If your script does not print the required headers or if it terminates with an error, the client would get a 500 series error. If you need more details on HTTP protocol, you can find them at www.w3.org/Protocols.

Q: How do I distinguish if my application is running on a real Palm VII or OmniSky device?

A: You can look at the Configuration Alias for *.CTPWireless* and recurse through aliases until you reach the end. If the recursion stops at "PanelWireless," the application is running on a real Palm VII. Refer to the section on "Providing Configuration Aliases" for more help.

Q: Where do I get help?

A: Palm Knowledge Base has articles on INetLib-related issues. Most FAQs are answered there. Then you should look at newsgroup archives. You can search the newsgroup archives from egroups.com, as well as escribe.com. Because INetLib does not really come under WCA, most people post most questions in the palm-dev-forum as well as the comm-dev-forum and pqa-dev-forum. Make sure that you check all these places. If you still have your question unanswered, post a message to one of the newsgroups.

Appendix

Palm OS Web Applications Fast Track

This Appendix will provide you with a quick, yet comprehensive, review of the most important concepts covered in this book.

❖ Chapter 1 Introducing Web Clipping

What Is Web Clipping?

☑ Web clipping is a technology created by Palm, Inc. for delivering Web content on its line of Palm OS devices.

☑ Web clipping is a subset of the HTML specification. The specification keeps elements from standard HTML that translates well to its devices, modifies elements to improve its delivery on its devices, and trims elements that do not translate well to its devices.

☑ Static elements of an application, such as HTML documents and graphics, are combined into a database that is loaded onto the device. This database also contains the programming for contacting servers to build and deliver dynamically created content.

Loading Web Clipping Applications on Your Device

☑ Use the Palm Install Tool to prepare a Web clipping application to be installed onto a device in the same manner that a standard Palm OS application is installed onto a device.

☑ Perform a HotSync operation to install the application.

Loading Web Clipping Applications on the Palm OS Emulator

☑ If you do not own one of the wireless Palm OS devices or simply want to evaluate this technology, an application called the Palm OS Emulator (POSE) simulates the operation of an actual Palm OS device on your desktop computer.

Using Clipper

☑ The Clipper browser is launched when a Web clipping application is selected from the Application Launcher.

☑ The History stores pages dynamically built from a Web server. Static pages are not listed because they are already stored in the Web clipping application on the device.

Chapter 1 Continued

Using Clipper on Palm OS Devices

☑ The Clipper browser is part of the permanent software of the Palm VII and VIIx devices. Clipper can be installed as an add-on to the m100, m105, III, IIIx, IIIxe, IIIc, or V series devices.

☑ The Palm VII and VIIx use the Mobitex wireless network to communicate to the Internet. The OmniSky service provides a wireless modem that uses the CDPD network to communicate to the Internet. The Mobitex network is more widely available than CDPD, but the CDPD network is much faster than the Mobitex network.

Using Clipper to Get Access to Web Information

☑ Numerous Web clipping applications are available for download from Palm.Net and other file databases.

☑ You can use Web clipping applications to communicate with people, access the enterprise, manage finances, follow the news, travel the world, shop online, and refer to information.

❖ Chapter 2 Building a Simple Web Clipping Application

Writing Simple Web Pages

☑ HTML tags indicate document formatting and processing instructions. HTML tags are flanked by less-than (<) and greater-than (>) characters.

☑ The <HTML> tag indicates the beginning of an HTML document. HTML tags inside the <HTML> and </HTML> tags are processed by Web browsers.

☑ Text located between the <BODY> and </BODY> tags is displayed by a Web browser in its main window.

Running the Web Clipping Application Builder

☑ The filename of the utility is WCABuild.exe.

Chapter 2 Continued

- ☑ Select the HTML file that will be the first HTML displayed in the application by selecting the **Open Index...** choice from the **File** menu.
- ☑ After the index file has been determined, build the application by selecting the **Build PQA...** choice from the **File** menu. Type a name for the file, select large and small icons (if desired), and click **Build**.
- ☑ Applications can be built with the WCA Builder from its Windows user interface or by supplying command line options. For the list of command line options, refer to Table 2.1 in this chapter or run the WCA Builder and add ***/h*** to the command line.
- ☑ WCA Builder supports new Web clipping features available in Palm OS 4.0 including color graphics and icons support and HTML and POST file encoding tags.

❖ Chapter 3 Building WCAs Using HTML

Starting HTML Documents with a Header

- ☑ Tags in the header section of an HTML document define properties that apply to the entire document. This includes information such as the title of the page, who made it, and if it is a "Palm-friendly" document. These header tags are not shown directly to the user, although they might affect how the page is displayed.
- ☑ The header is completely enclosed in a <HEAD> tag, starting with <HEAD> and ending with </HEAD>. If you specify the header-specific tags outside of a <HEAD> section, you will have an invalid HTML document, and the browser might ignore their values.
- ☑ You should supply a title in each document and keep the length of this text short.
- ☑ The PalmComputingPlatform META tag tells the Palm.Net proxy that the page was designed specifically for the Clipper browser. The PalmLauncherName, PalmLauncherRevision, PalmLargeIconFilename, and PalmSmallIconFilename META tags can be added to your main page to affect how the Web clipping application appears in the Palm OS Launcher.

Chapter 3 Continued

Providing HTML Content with Block and Text Markup Body Tags

- ☑ Body tags define the content and page presentation of a Web document. The most common body tags available in the HTML 3.2 specification are available in the Web clipping HTML definition. Content with these tags applied may render differently to fit the small Palm OS device's screen.
- ☑ The body of the HTML document should start with a <BODY> tag and close with </BODY>.
- ☑ Block markup tags are used to describe sections of text. A new block of text will be separated from the last block by whitespace. Block markup tags format paragraphs (<P>), small and large headline text (<H1>, <H2>, and so on), horizontal lines (<HR>), sizing and alignment of images (<IMG>), lists (<OL> and <UL>), and tables (<TABLE>).
- ☑ Text markup tags let you change the appearance at the character and word level. These tags are generally used in short stretches of text to provide some sort of special effect, such as making the text boldface or italic. Text markup tags include *physical markup tags* (bold <B>, italic <I>, and so on), font size and color, logical markup tags (strong <STRONG>, emphasized <EM>, and so on), hypertext links (<A>), and line breaks (<BR>).

Linking to Application Pages and Web Sites

- ☑ A Web application can link to documents and images in the same Web clipping application; it can be developed and built with documents and images in the same directory or located in subdirectories. The directory specification is relative to the root and not absolute to the physical location of the document on the local computer.
- ☑ When a Web clipping application is built from a local file set with subdirectories, the Web Clipping Application Builder collapses all the subdirectories into a single directory to build the PQA file.
- ☑ One Web clipping application can link to a different Web clipping application entirely.
- ☑ Hyperlinks can also be created for remote pages and graphics located over the air. Secure links (HTTPS) can also be defined.

❖ Chapter 4 Using Images in Web Clipping Applications

Dealing with Limited Screen Size

☑ The available screen size on a Palm OS device is 153 pixels wide by 144 pixels high.

☑ Web clipping can use both local and remote images.

☑ Use the LocalIcon META tag to include images that are not referenced from local pages.

☑ The WCA Builder flattens the folder hierarchy when compiling, so be sure to use unique file names.

Specifying Nonlinked Images

☑ Use local images compiled into the WCA to save on download times.

☑ Remote pages can refer to local images with the syntax <img src="file:mywca.pqa/image.gif">.

☑ Save on downloaded text by omitting the *height*, *width*, and *alt* attributes of <IMG>.

Using Colors and Grayscale

☑ Palm OS 3.5 Web clipping applications support only four shades of gray.

☑ The WCA Builder in SDK 4.0 allows you to save in several bit depths, including color.

☑ Ensure that color graphics are still readable in 2-bit grayscale.

Optimizing Image Size

☑ Keep image dimensions as small as possible to keep file sizes down.

☑ Some image-editing programs optimize much better than others.

☑ The Palm.Net proxy image conversion can reduce image quality.

Chapter 4 Continued

Using the Palm Image Checker to Validate Your Images

☑ Use PIC to preview images at different bit depths before building your WCA.

☑ Convert graphics to grayscale in an image-editing program to increase image quality.

☑ Bit depth can have a significant effect on the size of your WCA.

❖ Chapter 5 Interacting with Forms

Using Standard HTML Forms

☑ HTML forms enable data to be sent to a server or received from a server.

☑ Three main form tags exist to capture user input: <INPUT>, <SELECT>/<OPTION>, <TEXTAREA>.

☑ Tags are case-insensitive in standard HTML.

☑ HTML form tags typically have a *name* and *value* attribute. Other attributes are tag-specific. *Name* and *value* attributes are lowercase and short.

☑ <INPUT> tags have many various types, including: *text*, *password*, *checkbox*, *radio*, *submit*, *reset*, and *hidden*.

☑ <OPTION> tags do not typically need the *value* attribute within WCAs.

☑ <OPTION> tags should be alphabetized by label, and labels should not contain any special characters and/or spaces. This is so the Palm OS UI can quickly jump to <OPTION> labels as graffiti characters are entered.

Tracking Widget Inventory Example

☑ Many form tags can be incorporated into a single WCA.

☑ Many choices exist in applying form tags to a particular application.

☑ When applying form tags, several rules of thumb exist to optimize server communication.

☑ Using POSE's network redirection coupled with IIS is a reasonable environment in which to develop WCAs. This approach avoids the need for both a

Chapter 5 Continued

Palm OS device and Palm.Net account—including associated charges. Also, this approach allows you to test full server communication, including server-side form data reception and parsing.

Placing a Widget Order Example

- ☑ Using a WCA similar to that in the Inventory Example enhances the user's experience, not to mention providing the developer the benefits of code reuse.
- ☑ Customer Key is one application of a *password*-type <INPUT> tag that can be used to identify existing customers. The net effect is to minimize the interaction necessary to conduct a transaction. This benefits both customer (the UI experience) and WCA (bandwidth conservation).

Enhancing Forms for Clipper

- ☑ *Timepicker* and *datepicker* are Palm-specific types of <INPUT>.
- ☑ *Timepicker* data can be specified in either 12- or 24-hour format. The display format is specified in the Preferences application, with the default being the 12-hour "HH:MM am/pm" format. Server communication is done using the 24-hour "HH:MM" format.
- ☑ *Datepicker* display format is specified in the Preferences application, with the default being the same as that for directly specifying a date: MM/DD/YY. Server communication format is YYYY-MM-DD.
- ☑ Current time and date can be accessed, or a specific time and date can be set via the *value* attribute.

Setting Delivery Dates for Widget Orders Example

- ☑ *Timepicker* and *datepicker* can be used to augment WCAs.
- ☑ *Timepicker* and *datepicker* can be used for several applications, including time stamping activity logs, scheduling, and so on.

❖ Chapter 6 Optimizing WCAs for Palm OS Devices

Making Pages Useful on Both Desktop and Palm Devices

☑ You can write pages that work well on both desktop browsers and Palm OS devices.

☑ Ensure that pages and graphics are no more than 153 pixels wide.

☑ Use the <SMALLSCREENIGNORE> tag to mark off sections of HTML you don't want displayed on the Palm device.

Making Unwired Widgets Pages for Both Desktop and Palm Devices

☑ Some minor modifications to your HTML can make it easier to optimize for Palm devices.

☑ Use alternate text-only navigation links with the special *button* attribute.

☑ Decide on what content is truly crucial and put this in one table, because Palm OS does not support nested tables.

☑ Minimize nesting errors, although some are unavoidable. Modern browsers will ignore these.

Using Tables for Page Layout

☑ Tables must be formatted to be no more than 153 pixels wide.

☑ Nested tables are not supported.

☑ Use *border* and *cellpadding* to create "breathing room" around your content.

☑ Use tables to lay out text and images to create a more pleasing arrangement.

Specifying History Text

☑ Palm OS appends the time automatically if you do not specify it.

☑ The HistoryListText META tag is limited, so keep your labels concise.

Chapter 6 Continued

- ☑ Use *&date* and *&time* variables in the HistoryListText.
- ☑ Specifying *&date* and *&time* allows you to use longer history text.

Using MAILTO Links to Send E-Mail

- ☑ Use MAILTO links to allow visitors to send e-mail from within your Web clipping.
- ☑ Append arguments to the MAILTO to prefill the "To:," "Subj:" and "Body:" fields.
- ☑ iMessenger is the default mailer on Palm VII, but Palm OS 4 will allow other applications to handle this.

❖ Chapter 7 Debugging Web Clipping Applications

Emulating Web Clipping by Using the Palm OS Emulator

- ☑ POSE mimics the operation of a Palm OS device using actual Palm OS software.
- ☑ POSE allows WCAs to be tested without using an actual device, and it requires no batteries, no wireless connection, and no connection charges.
- ☑ POSE operation is not limited to the wireless coverage area.
- ☑ POSE is tightly integrated with the desktop, providing for widely visible presentations and/or demonstrations and easily obtained screen shots.
- ☑ POSE can emulate multiple types of device.

Understanding the Palm.Net Proxy

- ☑ Palm.Net is a server farm that facilitates WCA connections to the Internet.
- ☑ Palm.Net protects data between itself and POSE/device using ECC, and between itself and content servers using SSL.

Chapter 7 Continued

- ☑ Palm.Net responds to requests with Web clippings in the WCA format (a compressed form of HTML 3.2).
- ☑ Web clippings are not cached.
- ☑ Dynamically generated Web clippings can cause problems for Palm.Net relative to Palm.Net's link hashing algorithm.
- ☑ Given the broad scope of Palm.Net's responsibilities, it is susceptible to a variety of problems.

Using Tools to Debug WCAs

- ☑ HTML validators check HTML source code for compliance with the WCA Document Type Definition (DTD).
- ☑ Link checkers verify that no hypertext links are stale.
- ☑ WCA decompilers help verify that what is actually contained within a WCA and/or Web clipping reflects what was specified in the corresponding source code.
- ☑ Palm's InetLow application demonstrates how to use the InetLib API for obtaining and displaying raw data from a URL.

❖ Chapter 8 Identifying Users and Sessions

Using %DEVICEID to Uniquely Identify a Device

- ☑ Many devices that support Web clipping will send unique identifiers when the string %DEVICEID is used in a URL or form.
- ☑ Because the device ID can be spoofed, you should not rely on it to give the users access to sensitive data.

Identifying Sessions Using URL Rewriting

- ☑ By adding a server-generated identifier to all of your page's URLs, you can track a user across pages on a Web site.
- ☑ PHP 4 provides a powerful system for generating content for the Web.

Chapter 8 Continued

- ☑ To use PHP's session rewriting, each page must enable sessions using the **session_start** or **session_register** commands.
- ☑ PHP's sessions allow you to preserve the values of variables across multiple page loads without directly exposing the values of those variables to the user.

My Unwired Widgets Order Example

- ☑ PHP sessions can be used to implement a simple shopping cart system.
- ☑ When implementing a real system, you should pay close attention to user authentication and the security of form submissions.

Identifying Sessions Using Cookies in Palm OS 4.0

- ☑ Cookies let you store data on the device that can be retrieved at a later time.
- ☑ Cookies are supported only in Web clipping on Palm OS 4.0 and later devices.
- ☑ Although cookies can be used to make the user's life much easier, by storing preferences or login information, they can also be used to secretly track which sites a user visits.

Cookie Explorer Example

- ☑ The Cookie Explorer PHP script can be used to set and delete cookies on your Palm OS 4.0 device.
- ☑ The script can be customized to automate your cookie explorations.

❖ Chapter 9 Locating Mobile Users

Finding a User's Position with the Palm VII

- ☑ %ZIPCODE provides an approximate measure of a Palm VII's location.
- ☑ %ZIPCODE is the ZIP Code of the current base station with which a Palm VII is communicating. Its value will be 00000 if the base station's ZIP Code has not been recorded.

Chapter 9 Continued

- ☑ ZIP Codes are not always defined by fully enclosed geometric shapes, and they can cross state, county, and city boundaries.

Address Locator Example

- ☑ A direct comparison of a %ZIPCODE value to a database can be made (with limited success) to locate a close entity.
- ☑ No match is guaranteed when performing a direct comparison of a %ZIPCODE value to a database.
- ☑ Base stations are typically 5 to 10 miles away from the user.

Mapping ZIP Codes to Coordinates

- ☑ Several databases exist for mapping ZIP Codes to latitude/longitude coordinates. A free data source is the U.S. Census Bureau: http://ftp.census.gov/geo/www/gazetteer/places.html. Note the file *zips.txt*.
- ☑ Also from the U.S. Census Bureau—counties.txt, places.txt, and mcds.txt can be used to model operation of the Palm OS 4.0 variable %LOCATION.

Determining the Closest Address

- ☑ Pythagorean-based minimum distance searching is more robust than direct ZIP Code matching for "closest address" determination.
- ☑ More than one ZIP Code match exists if the application-specific address database/file contains more than one entry for a given ZIP Code.
- ☑ A possible %ZIPCODE value of 00000 must be handled by a Closest Address algorithm.

Locating the Closest Widget Outlet Example

- ☑ Latitude/longitude processing can take the earth's curvature, but not surface elevation, into account.
- ☑ Latitude/longitude processing is not necessary if a direct ZIP Code match is found.
- ☑ ZIP Codes of 00000 should be anticipated.

Chapter 9 Continued

Using Enhanced %LOCATION Information in Palm OS 4.0

- ☑ Palm OS 4.0 is required for the %LOCATION variable to be interpreted.
- ☑ %LOCATION can be used to obtain a variety of position qualifiers, including: City Name, GPS Longitude/Latitude, State Name, State Code, County Name, County Code, Raw Location, Hexadecimal Data, Country Name, Country Code, and ZIP Code.
- ☑ The U.S.-specific entities of county and state are used as placeholders for, respectively, the small and large political division of countries other than the U.S.
- ☑ Country entities are based on *Codes for the Representation of Names of Countries, ISO 3166-1993 (E)*. This document is available from the appropriate national standards body. In the U.S., it's the American National Standards Institute; in the United Kingdom, it's the British Standards Institute.

❖ Chapter 10 Integrating Web Clipping with Palm OS Applications

Launching and Sublaunching Applications

- ☑ Two Application Programming Interface (API) calls are used to launch other programs on the Palm OS device: **SysUIAppSwitch** and **SysAppLaunch**.
- ☑ **SysUIAppSwitch** is used when you want to end your current program and start another. Palm OS uses this call to handle switching applications when you hit one of the hard buttons. It looks in the system preferences to find out which application is mapped to that button, and if it isn't the running program, it calls **SysUIAppSwitch** to switch to the mapped program.
- ☑ **SysAppLaunch** leaves your current program suspended while another program is opened temporarily to handle a request. This is called a *sublaunch* by the Palm OS documentation, because the caller uses the program as a subroutine.

Chapter 10 Continued

Calling Clipper from Palm OS Applications

☑ Check for the existence of Clipper before calling it and assign memory that holds the URL string to the system.

☑ Have an orderly shutdown of your program after setting up the Clipper launch.

☑ Use Clipper as an easy way to Web-enable Palm OS applications.

Calling iMessenger from Palm OS Applications

☑ Use iMessenger to add e-mail interactivity to your programs.

☑ Messages are just placed in the iMessenger Outbox, they don't get sent immediately.

☑ Take extra precaution with memory if you are allowing the user to immediately edit the e-mail.

Unwired Widgets Application About Box Example

☑ This example shows how to use Clipper and iMessenger in a realistic program.

☑ Using a dialog box as a testbed is a quick method to try out new code without building a huge application.

Calling Palm OS Applications from Web Clipping Applications

☑ Plug-ins for Clipper allow Web pages to interact with other programs on the device.

☑ Plug-ins are also useful for complex user interfaces and for rendering data in an efficient manner.

Unwired Widgets Sales Chart Example

☑ A plug-in for Clipper is used to draw a bar chart based on textual data.

☑ This code shows one technique for parsing parameters to a Clipper plug-in.

Chapter 10 Continued

Using iKnapsack to Add PIM Data

☑ iKnapsack provides an interface for users to manipulate Clipper and its plug-ins.

☑ The Add Palm Data plug-in allows Web clipping applications to add data to the applications that come standard on the device.

☑ When using this plug-in, be very careful with the parameters, or you could find the Palm's databases corrupted.

Adding PIM Data for Unwired Widgets Example

☑ The Add Data Plug-in for iKnapsack is an effective tool when combined with Clipper to save data about an important event.

☑ The plug-in can also be used to create templates for frequently added data on the device.

❖ Chapter 11 Using the Internet Library in Palm OS Applications

Introduction to INetLib

☑ The most popular language choice is C and the second most popular is C++. Currently, writing advanced applications requires solid knowledge of one of these languages.

☑ If you are interested in Java, check out Waba at www.wabasoft.com; IBM Visual Age/J9 at www.embedded.oti.com; and KVM at http://java.sun.com.

☑ Wireline support for INetLib was a recent addition to Palm OS, so you cannot use INetLib over a regular modem on a Palm VII. If you upgrade the operating system to Palm OS 3.5 or above, you will be able to use the wire-line channel.

☑ Design your application to use a request-response model for transactions. This will allow your application to be accessed from a variety of channels. Even if your device supports full TCP/IP, sticking to HTTP would make your application accessible over wireline and wireless channels.

Chapter 11 Continued

A Hello World Program

☑ Although INetLib library has more than 30 API calls, you need only a few of them to get started. The Hello World example in this chapter illustrates the basic sequence of calls.

☑ Internet Library is a Palm OS shared library. You must first verify that the library is present on the device before you can use it.

☑ Unusual errors are handled by fatal alerts. They are frequently used in Palm OS examples. Use of fatal alerts is a very clean and efficient way to bail out of an unexpected error.

Finding and Initializing Internet Library

☑ Not all Palm OS devices come with the Internet Library. You should call **SysLibFind** to locate the library.

☑ You must choose an INetLib configuration to use or provide an interface for the user to make the selection. Run the ConfigBrowser example to view existing configurations. *.CTPDefault*, *.CTPWireless*, and *.CTPWireline* are useful configurations.

☑ *.CTPWireless* does not always mean Palm VII radio. OmniSky devices use it to mean the Minstrel modem. However, OmniSky's *.CTPWireless* would be an alias to another configuration.

Creating an INetLib Connection

☑ Decide on the type of conversion: None, CML, or LZ77. Unless you are writing a browser, None and LZ77 are the only viable options.

☑ Verify that the proxy supports LZ77 before you use it.

☑ LZ77 is an optional module—it can be downloaded as part of the INetLow example from PalmOS.com.

Moving to an Event-Driven Model

☑ Good programs are always event-driven. An event-driven mechanism saves battery power and increases the responsiveness of the application.

☑ You must replace **EvtGetEvent** with **INetLibGetEvent** in your event loop.

Chapter 11 Continued

- ☑ In the sequence of events generated for an INetLib transaction, all except the last one are of type *inetSockStatusChangeEvent*. The last one is *inetSockReadyEvent*. If you are interested only in the data, you can ignore all *inetSockStatusChangeEvents*, except when they show an error.

Accessing a Server-Side Application

- ☑ **INetLibURLOpen** supports only GET requests. If you need POST, you must substitute it with calls to **INetLibSockOpen**, **INetLibSockHTTPReqCreate**, and **INetLibSockHTTPReqSend**.
- ☑ All variables to POST and GET must be URL-encoded. URL encoding converts nonalphanumeric characters to the %HH format, where *HH* is the hexadecimal representation of the ASCII value.
- ☑ Through at least Palm OS 4.0, INetLib looks at the first few characters of the URL to determine the security level. The *schemeEnum* argument to **INetLibSockOpen** is ignored. However, do not rely on it being ignored—it may change at any time.
- ☑ Through at least Palm OS 4.0, INetLib looks at the value of *writeP* argument to **INetLibSockHTTPReqSend** to determine the request type. The *verbP* argument to **INetLibSockHTTPReqCreate** is ignored. However, do not rely on it being ignored—it may change at any time.
- ☑ Both GET and POST are capable of exchanging data. However, each has a role of its own and limits vary.
- ☑ As far as security is concerned, POST does not give you any more security than GET. Contrary to popular belief, POST does not hide business logic/form variable names from users.

Receiving Responses from the Server

- ☑ Remember that you have to catch two INetLib related events: *inetSockStatusChangeEvent* and *inetSockReadyEvent*.
- ☑ Server errors (401, 404, 500, and so on) cannot be caught unless you check the error via **INetLibSockHTTPAttrGet**.
- ☑ Palm OS error returns use 2 bytes; the first byte is used to classify the errors. In Palm OS header files, error classes are listed in hex, and individual values are listed in decimal.

Chapter 11 Continued

☑ Your application will get multiple *inetSockReadyEvents*, and you may have to make multiple calls to **INetLibSockRead** to read the complete data.

Authenticating the User and Device

☑ Never rely too much on the device ID. The cookies specification is intended to be much more secure than device ID.

☑ Native applications may not require either of these unless you are trying to connect to an existing framework built on cookies.

☑ Palm.Net adds the validation codes only if the device ID was printed in Base 26. Also, the validation code cannot be trusted any more than you trust the user.

Providing Configuration Aliases

☑ You can run ConfigBrowser on any Palm device or Emulator and find the real mapping of configurations.

☑ If your application needs a user interface to select configurations, the example in this section shows you how to use INetLib calls to extract the configuration list and their names and aliases.

☑ Use ConfigBrowser along with URLFetch to test a configuration before you use it in an application.

Optimizing Transports

☑ A complex data format does not necessarily make the application efficient. Eight-bit formats are harder to debug. A text format combined with Palm.Net's LZ77 should give good results.

☑ Use of XML, and SyncML in particular, leads to better and more manageable architecture if you have tools on either side. A reference implementation of SyncML is available from syncml.org.

An Unwired Widgets Mail Reader Example

☑ A mail reader makes use of the offline capabilities of Palm OS. Messages can be read and marked for download or deletion. It also shows you how to defer message deletions until it can be synced up with the server.

Chapter 11 Continued

- ☑ Our transport format was very simple, and it can be debugged using a desktop browser.
- ☑ Although the Mail Reader lacks a conduit and does not handle other launch codes, it servers as a complete example that makes use of databases, user interface (tables), an optimal transport format, and INetLib. Make sure that you browse the source code and documentation.

Securing Data

- ☑ Using SSL ensures that the data cannot be viewed or corrupted by a third party on transit. However, it does not (and is not meant to) protect your server.
- ☑ If you access corporate data from the client and you use a password stored in a database or an application, your server data is only as secure as your handheld. No matter how encrypted the password is, it can be recovered unless the encryption involves a key entered by the user.
- ☑ Palm.Net is not end-to-end secure. However, the reason Palm.Net uses a different encryption is that straight SSL is not suited for wireless. Moreover, it cannot function as a Web clipping proxy unless it can access plain text data. If you are paranoid, licensing a copy of Elaine server or a similar implementation developed by a third party may be a solution.

Testing for Proxy Issues and Known Bugs

- ☑ OmniSky, Inc. provides Web-clipping service for the Handspring Visor Platinum, Prism, and Edge, and for Palm's V and V*x* devices. Initially, this was the only way to get Web clipping on these devices. However, with Palm OS 3.5 and above, Web clipping services are available directly from Palm.Net as an add-on to any device with a modem.
- ☑ OmniSky service uses Minstrel Modem from Novatel Wireless. Minstrel is a wireless modem, but it acts like a standard wired mode, so it uses *ctpWireline* to connect to the proxy. *ctpWireless* points to an invalid configuration. You can use the ConfigBrowser to test this.

Index

A

D

H

J

K

L

Q

R

S

V

W

X

Z

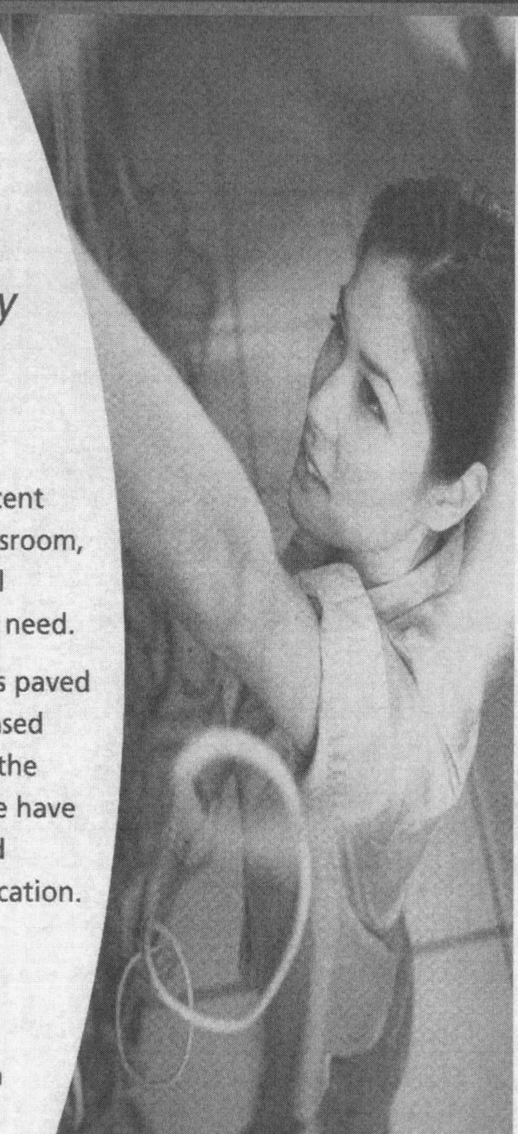

this could be you
Win a 2002
Chrysler PT Cruiser
It's simple to sign up to win. Visit globalknowledge.com. Completely fill out the form and you're entered! See our web site for official rules.
www.globalknowledge.com. Not valid in Florida and Puerto Rico.
Global Knowledge™

Global Knowledge™

9000 Regency Parkway, Suite 500
Cary, NC 27512
1-800-COURSES
www.globalknowledge.com

At Global Knowledge, we strive to support the multiplicity of learning styles required by our students to achieve success as technical professionals. We do this because we know our students need different training approaches to achieve success as technical professionals. That's why Global Knowledge has worked with Syngress Publishing in reviewing and recommending this book as a valuable tool for successful mastery of this subject.

As the world's largest independent corporate IT training company, Global Knowledge is uniquely positioned to recommend these books. The first hand expertise we have gained over the past several years from providing instructor-led training to well over a million students worldwide has been captured in book form to enhance your learning experience. We hope the quality of these books demonstrates our commitment to your lifelong learning success. Whether you choose to learn through the written word, e-Learning, or instructor-led training, Global Knowledge is committed to providing you the choice of when, where and how you want your IT knowledge and skills to be delivered. For those of you who know Global Knowledge, or those of you who have just found us for the first time, our goal is to be your lifelong partner and help you achieve your professional goals.

Thank you for the opportunity to serve you. We look forward to serving your needs again in the future.

Warmest regards,

Duncan M. Anderson
President and Chief Executive Officer, Global Knowledge

P.S. Please visit us at our Web site www.globalknowledge.com.

Enter the Global Knowledge Chrysler PT Cruiser Sweepstakes

This sweepstakes is open only to legal residents of the United States who are Business to Business MIS/IT managers or staff and training decision makers, that are 18 years of age or older at time of entry. Void in Florida & Puerto Rico.

OFFICIAL RULES

No Purchase or Transaction Necessary To Enter or Win, purchasing will not increase your chances of winning.

1. How to Enter: Sweepstakes begins at 12:00:01 AM ET May 1, 2001 and ends 12:59:59 PM ET December 31, 2001 the ("Promotional Period"). There are four ways to enter to win the Global Knowledge PT Cruiser Sweepstakes: Online, at Trade shows, by mail or by purchasing a course or software. Entrants may enter via any of or all methods of entry.

[1] To be automatically entered online, visit our web at www.globalknowledge.com click on the link named Cruiser and complete the registration form in its entirety. All online entries must be received by 12:59:59 PM ET December 31, 2001. Only one online entry per person, per e-mail address. Entrants must be the registered subscriber of the e-mail account by which the entry is made.

[2] At the various trade shows, during the promotional period by scanning your admission badge at our Global Knowledge Booth. All entries must be made no later than the close of the trade shows. Only one admission badge entry per person.

[3] By mail or official entry blank available at participating book stores throughout the promotional period. Complete the official entry blank or hand print your complete name and address and day & evening telephone # on a 3"x5" card, and mail to: Global Knowledge PT Cruiser Sweepstakes, P.O. Box 4012 Grand Rapids, MN 55730-4012. Entries must be postmarked by 12/31/01 and received by 1/07/02. Mechanically reproduced entries will not be accepted. Only one mail in entry per person.

[4] By purchasing a training course or software during the promotional period: online at http://www.globalknowledge.com or by calling 1-800-COURSES, entrants will automatically receive an entry onto the sweepstakes. Only one purchase entry per person.

All entries become the property of the Sponsor and will not be returned. Sponsor is not responsible for stolen, lost, late, misdirected, damaged, incomplete, illegible entries or postage due mail.

2. Drawings: There will be five [5] bonus drawings and one [1] prize will be awarded in each bonus drawing. To be eligible for the bonus drawings, on-line entries, trade show entries and purchase entries must be received as of the dates listed on the entry chart below in order to be eligible for the corresponding bonus drawing. Mail in entries must be postmarked by the last day of the bonus period, except for the month ending 9/30/01 where mail in entries must be postmarked by 10/1/01 and received one day prior to the drawing date indicated on the entry chart below. Only one bonus prize per person or household for the entire promotion period. Entries eligible for one bonus drawing will not be included in subsequent bonus drawings.

Bonus Drawings	Month starting/ending 12:00:01 AM ET/11:59:59 PM ET	Drawing Date on or about
1	5/1/01-7/31/01	8/8/01
2	8/1/01-8/31/01	9/11/01
3	9/1/01-9/30/01	10/10/01
4	10/1/01-10/31/01	11/9/01
5	11/1/01-11/30/01	12/11/01

There will also be a grand prize drawing in this sweepstakes. The grand prize drawing will be conducted on January 8, 2002 from all entries received. Bonus winners are eligible to win the Grand prize.

All random sweepstakes drawings will be conducted by Marden-Kane, Inc. an independent judging organization whose decisions are final. All prizes will be awarded. The estimated odds of winning each bonus drawing are 1:60,000, for the first drawing and 1:20,000 for the second, third, fourth and fifth drawings, and the estimated odds of winning the grand prize drawing is 1:100,000. However the actual odds of winning will depend upon the total number of eligible entries received for each bonus drawing and grand prize drawings.

3. Prizes: Grand Prize: One (1) PT Cruiser 2002 model Approx. Retail Value (ARV) $18,000. Winner may elect to receive the cash equivalent in lieu of the car. Bonus Prizes: Five (5), awarded one (1) per bonus period. Up to $1,400.00 in self paced learning products ARV up to $1,400.00 each.

No substitutions, cash equivalents, except as noted, or transfers of the prize will be permitted except at the sole discretion of the Sponsor, who reserves the right to substitute a prize of equal or greater value in the event an offered prize is unavailable for any reason. Winner is responsible for payment of all taxes on the prize, license, registration, title fees, insurance, and for any other expense not specifically described herein. Winner must have and will be required to furnish proof of a valid driver's license. Manufacturers warranties and guarantees apply.

4. Eligibility: This sweepstakes is open only to legal residents of the United States, except Florida and Puerto Rico residents who are Business to Business MIS/IT managers or staff and training decision makers, that are 18 years of age or older at the time of entry. Employees of Global Knowledge Network, Inc and its subsidiaries, advertising and promotion agencies including Marden-Kane, Inc., and immediate families (spouse, parents, children, siblings and their respective spouses) living in the same household as employees of these organizations are ineligible. Sweepstakes is void in Florida and Puerto Rico and is subject to all applicable federal, state and local laws and regulations. By participating, entrants agree to be bound by the official rules and accept decisions of judges as final in all matters relating to this sweepstakes.

5. Notification: Winners will be notified by certified mail, return receipt requested, and may be required to complete and sign an Affidavit of Eligibility/Liability Release and, where legal, a Publicity Release, which must be returned, properly executed, within fourteen (14) days of issuance of prize notification. If these documents are not returned properly executed or are returned from the post office as undeliverable, the prize will be forfeited and awarded to an alternate winner. Entrants agree to the use of their name, voice and photograph/likeness for advertising and promotional purposes for this and similar promotions without additional compensation, except where prohibited by law.

6. Limitation of Liability: By participating in the Sweepstakes, entrants agree to indemnify and hold harmless the Sponsor, Marden-Kane, Inc. their affiliates, subsidiaries and their respective agents, representatives, officers, directors, shareholders and employees (collectively, "Releasees") from any injuries, losses, damages, claims and actions of any kind resulting from or arising from participation in the Sweepstakes or acceptance, possession, use, misuse or nonuse of any prize that may be awarded. Releasees are not responsible for printing or typographical errors in any instant win game related materials; for stolen, lost, late, misdirected, damaged, incomplete, illegible entries; or for transactions, or admissions badge scans that are lost, misdirected, fail to enter into the processing system, or are processed, reported, or transmitted late or incorrectly or are lost for any reason including computer, telephone, paper transfer, human, error; or for electronic, computer, scanning equipment or telephonic malfunction or error, including inability to access the Site. If in the Sponsor's opinion, there is any suspected or actual evidence of electronic or non-electronic tampering with any portion of the game, or if computer virus, bugs, unauthorized intervention, fraud, actions of entrants or technical difficulties or failures compromise or corrupt or affect the administration, integrity, security, fairness, or proper conduct of the sweepstakes the judges reserve the right at their sole discretion to disqualify any individual who tampers with the entry process and void any entries submitted fraudulently, to modify or suspend the Sweepstakes, or to terminate the Sweepstakes and conduct a random drawing to award the prizes using all non-suspect entries received as of the termination date. Should the game be terminated or modified prior to the stated expiration date, notice will be posted on http://www.globalknowledge.com. Any attempt by an entrant or any other individual to deliberately damage any web site or undermine the legitimate operation of the promotion is a violation of criminal and civil laws and should such an attempt be made, the sponsor reserves the right to seek damages and other remedies from any such person to the fullest extent permitted by law. Any attempts by an individual to access the web site via a bot script or other brute force attack or any other unauthorized means will result in the IP address becoming ineligible. Use of automated entry devices or programs is prohibited.

7. Winners List: For the name of the winner visit our web site www.globalknowledge.com on January 31, 2002.

8. Sponsor: Global Knowledge Network, Inc., 9000 Regency Parkway, Cary, NC 27512. Administrator: Marden-Kane, Inc. 36 Maple Place, Manhasset, NY 11030.

Metrowerks Software License Agreement

THIS METROWERKS SOFTWARE LICENSE AGREEMENT ("LICENSE") IS AN AGREEMENT BETWEEN YOU AND METROWERKS CORPORATION ("METROWERKS"). METROWERKS IS WILLING TO LICENSE THE ENCLOSED SOFTWARE TO YOU ONLY UPON THE CONDITION THAT YOU ACCEPT ALL OF THE TERMS CONTAINED IN THIS LICENSE. PLEASE READ THIS LICENSE CAREFULLY BEFORE USING THE SOFTWARE, AS BY USING THE SOFTWARE YOU INDICATE THAT YOU AGREE TO BE BOUND BY THE TERMS OF THIS LICENSE. IF YOU DO NOT AGREE TO THE TERMS OF THIS LICENSE, METROWERKS IS UNWILLING TO LICENSE THE SOFTWARE TO YOU, AND YOU SHOULD PROMPTLY RETURN THE UNUSED SOFTWARE TO THE PLACE WHERE YOU OBTAINED IT AND YOUR MONEY WILL BE REFUNDED.

1. Grant of License. The application, demonstration, system and all other software accompanying this License, whether on CD-ROM or any other media (the "Software") and the related documentation are licensed to you by Metrowerks according to the terms of this License. If you purchased or otherwise received this Software packaged with any other host-platform versions of the same software (e.g., a Macintosh(R)-hosted version with a Windows(R)-hosted version), all such host-platform versions together shall constitute the "Software" for purposes of this License. This License allows you to use each host-platform version of the Software on a single computer corresponding to that host-platform version, provided that you are the only individual using the Software. You may also use a copy of the Software on a home or portable computer for each host-platform, as long as that extra copy is never running at the same time the Software is running on the primary computer for each host-platform on which you use the Software. You may make one additional copy of the Software in the form in which it is provided to you, only for backup purposes. You must reproduce on all copies you make of the Software the Metrowerks copyright notice and any other proprietary legends that are on the original copy of the Software. You may also transfer to another party all your license rights in the Software and related documentation by transferring to that party both the original media on which the Software and related documentation were provided and a copy of this License, provided that the other party reads and agrees to accept the terms and conditions of this License. Immediately upon transfer, you have no further rights to use or own copies of the Software or related documentation and must destroy all copies in your possession or control. If this Software includes more than one host-platform version, then any such transfer must include all host-platform versions together. You may not transfer one host-platform version alone without the other host-platform versions. If this Software is an upgrade to a prior version, then you must be licensed to use the prior version of the Software in order to exercise the license rights granted hereunder, and any transfer of the Software must include all prior versions of the Software. If you are a corporation or other organization, you must designate one individual to have the rights provided herein.

2. Restrictions. The Software contains copyrighted material, trade secrets, and other proprietary material of Metrowerks and its licensors. You agree that in order to protect those proprietary

materials, except as expressly permitted by applicable legislation, you will not decompile, reverse engineer, disassemble or otherwise reduce all or any part of the Software to human-readable form unless Metrowerks provided it to you in human-readable form. You may not modify, rent, lease, loan, distribute or create derivative works based upon the Software in whole or in part, except as expressly permitted in Section 3. If the Software is labeled as an academic version or is otherwise licensed to you for academic use, you may not use the Software for commercial product development, but you may use the Software to develop freeware or shareware. If the Software licensed to you is part of the Discover Programming series or is labeled as a Learning Edition, Demo Version, Evaluation Edition or Lite version, you may not use the Software to develop any product for distribution, whether commercial, freeware, or shareware. No press releases or any other public announcements regarding this Software shall be made without the written consent of Metrowerks.

3. Software Modification and Redistribution. Appendix A to this License lists the specific portions of the Software which you may distribute according to the terms of this License ("Distributable Code"). If Metrowerks has provided Distributable Code to you in human-readable form, you may modify the Distributable Code and the resulting modifications will also be considered Distributable Code. In order to protect Metrowerks' and Metrowerks' licensors' intellectual property rights in the Software, you may modify and distribute Distributable Code only according to the following terms:You may distribute Distributable Code only in executable object code form and only as incorporated into application programs you create using the Software and which have substantial value in addition to the Distributable Code. You may distribute Distributable Code incorporated in such applications to end users directly or indirectly through dealers, distributors,VARs, OEMs and other relicensors, but all distribution, whether to end users or relicensors, must be made pursuant to a valid written agreement that is at least as protective of Metrowerks' and Metrowerks' licensors' rights as this License. In no event shall you expand or attempt to expand Metrowerks' warranty or other obligations for any portion of the Software beyond those obligations set forth in this License nor extend those obligations to end users or relicensors of your applications. Last, you must reproduce on each copy of such applications a copyright notice that clearly states: "Copyright (c) by [Licensee Name] and its Licensors." Under no circumstances are you permitted to distribute any portions of the Software not listed on Appendix A, nor to distribute any portions of the Software (including those listed on Appendix A) in human-readable form, unless (i) specific license terms that may accompany such portions of the Software on the media containing the Software expressly authorize you to distribute such portions of the Software, in object code or human-readable form as the case may be, or (ii) you have express written authorization from an authorized officer of the company which owns that portion of the Software. In the event you distribute such portions of the Software based upon express authorization by one of the two means stated, you must adhere strictly to the specific terms of such authorization in addition to the terms of this license.You agree to indemnify and hold Metrowerks harmless from any damages, costs, or expenses Metrowerks may suffer as a result of your distribution, under either of the forms of permission described in the previous sentence, of any portion of the Software owned by a third party.

4. Ownership. The Software and documentation are licensed, not sold, to you for use only under the terms of this License, and Metrowerks reserves all rights not expressly granted to you in this License. You own the media on which the Software and documentation are recorded but Metrowerks and/or Metrowerks' licensors retain title to the Software and related documentation, and all intellectual property rights therein.

5. Termination. This License is effective until terminated. You may terminate this License at any time by destroying all copies of the Software and related documentation in your possession or control. This License will terminate immediately without notice from Metrowerks if you fail to comply with any provision of this License. Upon termination you must destroy all copies of the Software and related documentation in your possession or control.

6. Export Law Assurances. You agree and certify that neither the Software nor any other technical data received from Metrowerks, nor the direct product thereof, will be exported outside the United States except as authorized and as permitted by the laws and regulations of the United States. If the Software has been rightfully obtained by you outside of the United States, you agree that you will not re-export the Software nor any other technical data received from Metrowerks, nor the direct product thereof, except as permitted by the laws and regulations of the United States and the laws and regulations of the jurisdiction in which you obtained the Software.

7. Government End Users. If you are acquiring the Software and fonts on behalf of any unit or agency of the United States Government, the following provisions apply. The Software constitutes a "commercial item", as that term is defined at 48 C.F.R. 2.101, consisting of "commercial computer software" and "commercial computer software documentation", as such terms are used in 48 C.F.R. 12.212, and is provided to the U.S. Government only as a commercial end item. Consistent with 48 C.F.R. 12.212 and 48 C.F.R. 227.7202-1 through 227.7202-4, all U.S. Government End Users acquire the Software with only those rights set forth herein.

8. Limited Warranty on Media. Metrowerks warrants the media on which the Software is recorded to be free from defects in materials and workmanship under normal use for a period of ninety (90) days from the date of purchase as evidenced by a copy of the receipt. Metrowerks' entire liability and your exclusive remedy will be replacement of the media not meeting Metrowerks limited warranty returned to Metrowerks with a copy of the receipt. Metrowerks will have no responsibility to replace any media damaged by accident, abuse or misapplication. ANY IMPLIED WARRANTIES ON THE MEDIA, INCLUDING THE IMPLIED WARRANTIES OF MERCHANTABILITY AND FITNESS FOR A PARTICULAR PURPOSE, ARE LIMITED IN DURATION TO NINETY (90) DAYS FROM THE DATE OF DELIVERY. THIS WARRANTY GIVES YOU SPECIFIC LEGAL RIGHTS, AND YOU MAY ALSO HAVE OTHER RIGHTS WHICH VARY BY JURISDICTION.

9. Disclaimer of Warranty. THE SOFTWARE, RELATED DOCUMENTATION, ANY APPLICATIONS CREATED WITH THE SOFTWARE ARE PROVIDED "AS IS" AND WITHOUT WARRANTY OF ANY KIND. YOU EXPRESSLY ACKNOWLEDGE AND

AGREE THAT USE OF THE SOFTWARE AND RELATED DOCUMENTATION IS AT YOUR SOLE RISK. SHOULD THE SOFTWARE OR RELATED DOCUMENTATION PROVE DEFECTIVE, YOU (AND NOT METROWERKS OR ANY METROWERKS REPRESENTATIVE) ASSUME THE ENTIRE COST OF ALL NECESSARY SERVICING, REPAIR OR CORRECTION. METROWERKS AND METROWERKS ' LICENSORS (FOR THE PURPOSES OF THIS SECTION 9, METROWERKS AND METROWERKS' LICENSORS SHALL BE COLLECTIVELY REFERRED TO AS "METROWERKS") EXPRESSLY DISCLAIM ALL OTHER WARRANTIES WITH RESPECT TO THE SOFTWARE AND RELATED DOCUMENTATION, WHETHER SUCH WARRANTIES ARE EXPRESS OR IMPLIED, INCLUDING, BUT NOT LIMITED TO, THE IMPLIED WARRANTIES OF MERCHANTABILITY, FITNESS FOR A PARTICULAR PURPOSE AND NONINFRINGEMENT. WITHOUT LIMITING THE GENERALITY OF THE FOREGOING, METROWERKS MAKES NO WARRANTY OR REPRESENTATION THAT THE FUNCTIONS CONTAINED IN THE SOFTWARE WILL MEET YOUR REQUIREMENTS, THAT THE OPERATION OF THE SOFTWARE WILL BE UNINTERRUPTED OR ERROR-FREE, THAT DEFECTS IN THE SOFTWARE WILL BE CORRECTED, NOR WITH RESPECT TO THE CORRECTNESS, ACCURACY, OR RELIABILITY OF THE SOFTWARE AND RELATED DOCUMENTATION. METROWERKS DISCLAIMS ANY AND ALL EXPRESS OR IMPLIED WARRANTIES OF ANY KIND, AND YOU EXPRESSLY ASSUME ALL LIABILITIES AND RISKS, FOR ANYONE' S USE OR OPERATION OF ANY APPLICATION PROGRAMS YOU MAY CREATE WITH THE SOFTWARE. YOU ACKNOWLEDGE AND AGREE THAT THE SOFTWARE HAS NOT BEEN DESIGNED, TESTED, OR MANUFACTURED FOR USE IN DEVELOPING APPLICATIONS WHERE THE FAILURE, MALFUNCTION, OR ANY INACCURACY OF THE APPLICATION CARRIES A RISK OF DEATH, SERIOUS BODILY INJURY, OR DAMAGE TO TANGIBLE PROPERTY, INCLUDING, BUT NOT LIMITED TO, USE IN FACTORY CONTROL SYSTEMS, MEDICAL DEVICES OR FACILITIES, NUCLEAR FACILITIES, AIRCRAFT OR AUTOMOBILE NAVIGATION OR COMMUNICATION, EMERGENCY SYSTEMS, OR OTHER APPLICATIONS WITH A SIMILAR DEGREE OF POTENTIAL HAZARD. NO ORAL OR WRITTEN INFORMATION OR ADVICE GIVEN BY METROWERKS OR ANY OF ITS EMPLOYEES, REPRESENTATIVES, OR RESELLERS SHALL CREATE ANY WARRANTY IN ADDITION TO THOSE GIVEN HEREIN. SOME JURISDICTIONS DO NOT ALLOW THE EXCLUSION OF IMPLIED WARRANTIES, SO THE ABOVE EXCLUSION MAY NOT APPLY TO YOU.

10. Limitation of Liability. UNDER NO CIRCUMSTANCES SHALL METROWERKS BE LIABLE FOR ANY INCIDENTAL, SPECIAL OR CONSEQUENTIAL DAMAGES THAT RESULT FROM THE USE OR INABILITY TO USE THE SOFTWARE OR RELATED DOCUMENTATION UNDER ANY THEORY, INCLUDING CONTRACT, TORT, OR NEGLIGENCE, EVEN IF METROWERKS HAS BEEN ADVISED OF THE POSSIBILITY OF SUCH DAMAGES. SOME JURISDICTIONS DO NOT ALLOW THE LIMITATION OR EXCLUSION OF LIABILITY FOR INCIDENTAL OR CONSEQUENTIAL

DAMAGES SO THE ABOVE LIMITATION OR EXCLUSION MAY NOT APPLY TO YOU.

IN NO EVENT SHALL METROWERKS' TOTAL LIABILITY TO YOU FOR ALL DAMAGES, LOSSES, AND CAUSES OF ACTION (WHETHER IN CONTRACT, TORT (INCLUDING NEGLIGENCE) OR OTHERWISE) EXCEED THE AMOUNT PAID BY YOU FOR THE SPECIFIC LICENSE OF THE SOFTWARE AND RELATED DOCUMENTATION TO WHICH THE LIABILITY IS RELATED.

11. Controlling Law and Severability. THIS LICENSE SHALL BE GOVERNED BY AND CONSTRUED IN ACCORDANCE WITH THE LAWS OF THE UNITED STATES AND THE STATE OF CALIFORNIA, EXCEPT FOR ITS CONFLICT OF LAWS PRINCIPLES. If for any reason a court of competent jurisdiction finds any provision of this License, or portion thereof, to be unenforceable, that provision of the License shall be enforced to the maximum extent permissible so as to effect the intent of the parties, and the remainder of this License shall continue in full force and effect.

12. Complete Agreement. This License constitutes the entire agreement between the parties with respect to the use of the Software and related documentation and supersedes all prior or contemporaneous understandings or agreements, written or oral, regarding such subject matter. No amendment to or modification of this License will be binding unless in writing and signed by an authorized officer of Metrowerks.

Should you have any questions or comments concerning this License, please do not hesitate to contact Metrowerks Corporation at 9801 Metric Boulevard, Austin, TX, 78758, USA. attn: Warranty Information or by email: info@metrowerks.com

SYNGRESS PUBLISHING LICENSE AGREEMENT

Printed in Dunstable, United Kingdom

91343467R10315